LIVING DANGEROUSLY

VILLARD

NEW YORK

LIVING DANGEROUSLY

THE ADVENTURES OF
MERIAN C. COOPER

CREATOR OF
KING KONG

MARK COTTA VAZ

Published in the United States by Villard Books,
an imprint of The Random House Publishing Group,
a division of Random House, Inc., New York.

VILLARD and "V" CIRCLED Design are registered
trademarks of Random House, Inc.

Grateful acknowledgment is made to the following for permission to
reprint previously published material:
AMERICAN CINEMATOGRAPHER MAGAZINE: Excerpts from articles entitled
"Grass" (February 1983) and "Creation" (March 1987). Reprinted by
permission of *American Cinematographer* magazine.

Frontispiece image credit: Cooper Papers, BYU

LIBRARY OF CONGRESS CATALOGING-IN-PUBLICATION DATA

Vaz, Mark Cotta.
Living dangerously: the adventures of Merian C. Cooper,
creator of King Kong/by Mark Cotta Vaz.
p. cm.
Includes bibliographical references and index.
ISBN 1-4000-6276-4
1. Cooper, Merian C. 2. Motion picture producers and
directors—United States—Biography. I. Title.
PN1998.3.C6697V38 2005   791.4302'3'092—dc22
2004061184
[B]

Printed in the United States of America on acid-free paper

www.villard.com

987654321

FIRST EDITION

Book design by Barbara M. Bachman

To James V. D'Arc, whose preservation of the

legacy of Merian Cooper made this book possible,

and to Bob Wyatt, friend and font of inspiration, who's always

on the lookout for the next cruise ship to Skull Island.

MERIAN COOPER, FLANKED BY WARRIORS IN SUDAN.

Cooper Papers, BYU

"Keep it distant, difficult, and dangerous."

—MOTTO OF MERIAN C. COOPER
AND HIS PARTNER ERNEST SCHOEDSACK

CONTENTS

COOPER TAKES THE DIRECTOR'S CHAIR
ON THE SET OF *MIGHTY JOE YOUNG,*
A 1949 RKO RELEASE. *Cooper Papers, BYU*

INTRODUCTION

ARLY IN THIS ENTHRALLING BOOK, MARK COTTA VAZ REFERS TO A DEFINING
moment of Merian C. Cooper's early life. A "moment of becoming" is the
way he describes it. I know exactly what that means, because I experienced
my own moment of becoming at the age of nine: I saw a movie Merian
Cooper made called *King Kong*. That film was made twenty-eight years before I was born, yet its power and magic had an instant and profound effect
on my young imagination. From that day on I wanted to do nothing else
with my life other than make movies—movies like *King Kong*. Watching that
film propelled me into a love of making movies and learning how to do visual effects, the very stuff of movie magic.

Another thirty-four years passed, and today I find myself putting finishing touches on my own remake of *King Kong*. It has been a case of third
time lucky. I tried to remake it several years ago, after finishing *The Fright-
eners,* but it was canned, and we went on to *The Lord of the Rings* instead. But
an even earlier failed attempt happened at the age of twelve, when I made a
small stop-motion Kong puppet (using my mother's fur stole), a cardboard
model of the Empire State Building, and a New York skyline painted on an
old bedsheet. I still have them—sentimental relics of a lifelong journey I've
taken, inspired by a man I never met—Merian C. Cooper. I also got inspired
by *Planet of the Apes* (apes again!) and sculpted and molded a latex ape mask
that I once wore while sitting in the backseat of the school bus on my way
to school. I was making faces at this car following the bus and didn't realize the driver was one of the schoolteachers. As the bus pulled into the
school yard, she parked and stormed to the bus as we were getting out and
demanded my ape mask, confiscating it right there. I guess some people
are impervious to the allure of movie magic.

But that's what movies can do to you—they open up your mind, make you dream. And in that dreaming you see nothing but blue sky, endless possibility.

I think *Living Dangerously* is a wonderful addition to the literature of movies and popular culture but, on a personal level, it allowed me to understand the man who made the movie that had such a powerful effect on me. I was vaguely familiar with the life of Merian C. Cooper, but there was so little written about him and then only fragments of a life story. I'd read sketchy accounts of his being a war hero, an aviator twice shot down, once in flames, the stories went. I vaguely knew he was an explorer and adventurer. But you never really knew what to believe. There was only the shadow of a legend. Now finally, thankfully, Mark has written the first biography of Cooper, and the legend comes out of the shadows.

I was fascinated to learn how much of his personal experience Cooper brought to crafting the story, characters, places, and plotlines of *King Kong*. I suppose the big clue was always there, staring us in the face—it's a *movie expedition* that sails to Skull Island in search of the mythical Kong, not a ship full of naturalists, explorers, or even big-game hunters. Cooper and his partner, Ernest Schoedsack, gloried in their movie expeditions. Filmmaking really was their passport to adventure. We forget what a revelation the moving-picture medium was to people in the early twentieth century. Cooper and other early filmmakers were simply compelled to head off with their cameras to document the wondrous peoples and places on the planet, then bring back what they had filmed so audiences could vicariously share in their adventures. They blazed a trail, pioneering the very art of making documentary and adventure films and leaving for present and future generations irreplaceable documents of a truly lost world.

Making my version of *King Kong* has given me a deeper understanding of the times in which Cooper and his talented production team made their film. I made a conscious decision to set my production in the time period of the original, back in the Depression days of the 1930s. Although it was a decade of economic trouble, it was also an amazing era, with technology emerging that would change the world, from cracking the secrets of the atom to the development of television and the building of skyscrapers that began transforming city skylines and urban life. But there was also mystery over the horizon, places still unknown and waiting to be discovered or explored; there were tribal cultures untouched by modern civilization. Cooper had experienced those remote places and peoples, and he brought that truth to *King Kong*. He knew what it was like to be on a seafaring expedition, to explore primordial jungles, to witness exotic rituals and live among "savage" peoples (which he seems to have preferred to the civilized variety), and he had even visited a remote island where he saw giant lizard creatures that recalled a "lost" world! Cooper also knew New York; he moved among the movers and shakers in Manhattan as an executive in the fledgling aviation industry. He really *was* Carl Denham, the moviemaker who bridges the wilds and the concrete jungle with the bombastic showman's flourish of putting on display the "Eighth Wonder of the World." Even Kong's end had a personal Cooper touch. He was a bomber and fighter pilot in World War I and in Poland's war against Russia, and that's Cooper in the pilot's seat, with Ernest Schoedsack in the rear cockpit, of the fighter plane that mortally wounds Kong in the film. (Of course, as we all know, it wasn't the bullets fired from the planes, but beauty that killed the beast.)

The world today has metaphorically shrunk; vast distances that took Cooper months to traverse can today be made within hours. We have communication systems that in the blink of an eye connect people on opposite sides of the planet. We have orbiting space stations and robotic probes exploring other worlds by remote control or flying to the ends of our solar system—we're living the stuff of the science fiction of Cooper's day.

It's easy to become jaded by these modern miracles, lulled into losing our sense of adventure. But it's *still* a wide, mysterious world. Movies can still make one look at the world anew—maybe even inspire one to go out and explore it! Movies provide fabulous entertainment but the best ones, by the end credits, leave you a different person than you were before you began watching. The best movies fire your imagination.

Which brings me back to the power of movie magic. I was touched as a kid by *King Kong*—as were the great Ray Harryhausen and so many other filmmakers. That movie changed my life. I didn't fight in a war or hunt man-eating tigers in the jungle like Cooper did before he made *Kong*. But I understand Cooper and feel very much at home in the world he created. It's a wide, wild world and it's big enough to have allowed me to mount my own movie expedition, to scout out, explore, and bring back visions of a fantastic place that time forgot. I went exploring with the enthusiasm of that boy beguiled by *Kong* and the experience of the grown-up filmmaker who gets to conjure worlds for a living. Ultimately, that's what the world of *King Kong* represents to me—it's the mystical, mysterious realm of imagination itself.

Peter Jackson
Wellington, New Zealand, May 2005

DREAMS OF ADVENTURE

MERIAN COOPER DREAMS UP
THE WORLD OF KING KONG IN
THIS RKO PUBLICITY SHOT.

Cooper Papers, BYU

CHAPTER ONE

THE MAN WHO CHEATED DEATH

When a man knows how to live dangerously,
he is not afraid to die.
When he is not afraid to die,
he is, strangely, free to live.

—William O. Douglas, OF MEN AND MOUNTAINS[1]

THE SCENE IS THE EARLY 1930S, THE PLACE A NOCTURNAL HARBOR IN HOBOKEN, across the Hudson River from Manhattan, where a docked ship christened the *Venture* is ready to sail at dawn. Out of the darkness a tall, impeccably dressed man appears and asks a grizzled night watchman, "Say, is this the moving-picture ship?"

"Pictures, yeah." The watchman nods. "You going on this crazy voyage?"

The destination of the *Venture* is cloaked in mystery as deep as the darkness shrouding the city. All that's known is that Carl Denham, famed and fearless filmmaker, is at the helm of his latest movie expedition and eager to set sail for a top secret production at a far-flung and undisclosed location.

"They say he ain't scared of nuthin'," the watchman declares. "If he wants a picture of a lion, he goes up to him and tells him to look pleasant!"

And that's what's troubling the impeccably dressed man, theatrical agent Charles Weston, who's come aboard the ship to personally break some bad news to Denham: He can't provide a young actress for so secretive and potentially dangerous a production. True, there's only one Carl Denham, and whenever he embarks on a moviemaking expedition he always brings back a picture. But that's not the problem.

"Everyone knows you're square," Weston tells Denham, gentleman to gentleman, "but you have a reputation for recklessness."

Carl Denham, stocky, energetic, and exuding confidence, doesn't need to hear this. The moviegoing public, bless them, *must* have a pretty face—and Denham won't be denied a leading lady. He's poised on the brink of the ultimate moviemaking expedition and dreaming dreams no picture-maker has ever dared to dream before.

"I'm going out to make the greatest picture in the world, something that nobody's ever seen or heard of," Denham exults to a skeptical Weston. "They'll have to think up a lot of new adjectives when I come back."

Thus opened *King Kong,* the 1933 RKO Radio Pictures production unveiled at the nadir of the Great Depression. The picture included a glimpse of the nation's economic troubles as Denham took a taxi into the heart of Manhattan and witnessed a line of women waiting for soup at a rescue mission. Then he encountered a young woman who was trying to steal food from a corner stand, a virginal beauty named Ann Darrow who was nearly faint from hunger.

When the bombastic showman bought a meal in a diner for Darrow and shared his dangerous dream, Denham's crazy, cockeyed, all-American optimism beguiled his new leading lady. And it gripped movie audiences as well. Like Ann, audiences could leave their troubles behind and vicariously join the *Venture,* sailing for the mystery that waited just beyond the horizon. Moviegoers, like the loyal crew, were spared details of their destination until Denham finally shared a strange tale—of a meeting in Singapore with a Norwegian skipper who had once picked up a canoe of dying natives blown by the winds into the open ocean. The skipper had sketched a map based on the natives' account showing an uncharted island west of Sumatra. A map of a dream that in turn became the film producer's quest.

The allure for Denham was the story that went with the map, the weird rumors of an ancient wall built by a forgotten civilization and the legend of Kong, the gigantic ape of Skull Island, a prehistoric isle that time had forgotten. . . .

KING KONG HAD been one of the great gambles in movie history, but when it finally emerged into public view, after a long creative gestation, it was a roaring box-office success. *Kong* beguiled an entire generation, and its financial returns marked the turning point for an entire film industry that had recently bottomed out but was back on an economic upswing. Kong's triumphant creator would be crowned in glory, thus raising Merian Cold-well Cooper to the pinnacle of Hollywood power and influence.

"Coop," as he was known to many, took it all in stride. In many ways he was the unlikeliest of moviemakers. Before coming to RKO in the autumn of 1931 as the trusted right-hand man for production head David O. Selznick, he had produced only three other films. What Cooper lacked in film credits, though, he made up for in creative instinct and passion.

Although studio ballyhoo for *King Kong* hailed Cooper as a renowned adventurer, what was left unsaid was that Carl Denham *was* in fact Merian Cooper. Cooper, like Denham, had himself sailed to a lost island and discovered seemingly prehistoric creatures. Cooper had witnessed the massing of tribal warriors on the windswept plains of a kingdom in Africa, had hunted man-eating tigers in the steaming jungles. The Cooper-inspired touches for Denham ranged from allusions to celebrated movie expeditions to Weston's declaration to Denham, "You have a reputation for recklessness." Even Denham's pipe smoking was a noted Cooper affectation, and there was a distinct physical resemblance between Cooper and Robert Armstrong, the veteran actor who played *Kong*'s intrepid filmmaker.

As with his cinematic alter ego, moviemaking became Cooper's passport to adventure. During the 1920s, he created moving pictures that served audiences as a window onto the world, in an era when radio was in its infancy and television and satellite communications remained in the realm of science fiction. This was a time when oceans could be crossed only by boat, and maps had vast regions stamped "unknown." Those early movie expeditions, which Cooper further celebrated in books, articles, and public presentations, influenced an entire generation and forged a paradigm for adventure that still resonates into the present day.

In Cooper's time, one could still strike out into a wide, wild world, sometimes guided only by legends, or seduced by the mystery of unknown places whose secrets, waiting like buried treasure, fired the imagination. Yet only a hardy few had the mettle to mount such death-defying expeditions—Cooper's hunger for adventure was unusual for any age. During his life he would make his home in places like New York and Los Angeles, but Cooper was always contemptuous of the conceits and conveniences of the modern world. To him "civilization" was a pejorative for all that was soft and weak. He sought out danger and wilderness without regard for personal safety; the rougher it was, the better he liked it. Often it took weeks of boat travel to span the oceans and days or weeks more to reach the places where the roads came to an end. From there one had to carry on by foot or camel or horse, with each step moving farther from the remotest outpost of civilization and deeper into territories often ruled by violent peoples, places governed by magic and spirit worship, where deadly diseases and wild animals regularly thinned the local population.

Merian Cooper lived for such things. He seemed to view himself as an artist, and life itself was his art, each amazing adventure woven into an unfolding tapestry of dramatic experiences. Other men, with similarly passionate ambition, might seek to forge financial empires, and, indeed, Cooper had a taste along those lines himself. But in the final analysis, he found big business boring. Adventure, manifesting in all its forms and possibilities, was his desire. Cooper would know the terror of slipping into the brush with his rifle to face a wounded and cornered wild animal; his memories would echo with the drums and war shouts of warriors and the exotic clamor of ancient rituals. Through his heart's desire he molded his very existence like a potter at the wheel, dreamed his great dreams of adventure and made them come true. In a way, natural-born showman that he was, his own life story was his greatest production, and he burnished his own legend to a shining luster with each dramatic exploit.

For Coop, living dangerously was particularly sweet when he could share experiences with similarly brave souls. One of his earliest adventures was a sea voyage that nearly ended in disaster as his ship ran aground on the Red Sea. Cooper later recalled that brush with death in a diary account that revealed much of what drew him to danger: "You risk your skin, and in the moment when life balances with death, no matter how afraid you may be, you get a touch of the animal value of existence. . . . Wind and rain beat on your face as you brace yourself to swing the wheel, as a giant wave comes crashing towards your little sailing ship. Some man trusts you above all other men and you realize what friendship means.

"These are the seconds which give the zest and fire to existence. . . . These are the moments when conscience and memory alike are drowned in the fine physical or spiritual beauty of life."[2]

Cooper wrote that diary entry in April 1924, while camped in the mountains of Persia, where he had joined a tribal migration, an adventure he was sharing with two other Americans, his young friend Ernest Schoedsack and the mysterious Marguerite Harrison, an heiress and reputed professional spy who had once saved his life. He was sitting in a tent overlooking the moonlit valley where the massing clans of the nomadic Bakhtiari tribe had pitched their black tents. The grass that sustained their flocks was dying, and a seasonal imperative and an ancient rite of survival forced their mass migration to a distant plateau, the promised land of verdant fields.

To Cooper this was the ultimate adventure—he had finally merged with the epic struggle for survival that took him to the heart of "the animal value of existence." He and his two partners would not only be the first foreigners to make the dangerous migration but would do so with an exotic piece of equipment: a moving-picture camera.

Grass, the result of this movie expedition, Cooper's first, was released in 1925 and marked the official beginning of the Cooper-Schoedsack filmmaking partnership. The two men would sum up the spiritual imperative of their movie expeditions with the phrase "Keep it distant, difficult, and dangerous." It was that guiding spirit of adventure that would take them deeper into the wild, unconquerable realm of imagination, a creative journey that led to their shared directorial work on *King Kong.*

Even before the *Grass* expedition, Cooper had taken to heart the advice given him by Vilhjalmur Stefansson, an Arctic explorer who had traveled the frozen wilderness and had lived among the Eskimos. "Stefansson said, 'If you think hazardously, as I have done, then you'll think of at least ninety-five percent of the things that could possibly happen to you, [and] you'll be prepared,'" Coop once recalled. "Men get killed easily when they don't live dangerously."[3]

FROM HIS YOUTH, Merian Cooper was schooled in the perilous art of living dangerously. He was one of that first generation to take to the skies in airplanes—clattering contraptions that often became flying death traps—and he would be among the first men in history to fly into battle during wartime.

Cooper eagerly embarked on the path to war: He wanted combat and got it. He had promises to keep, spiritual debts he owed himself, his family, and his heritage, and he'd be damned if he didn't answer the call. In the early days of World War I he wrote home that if his own life was lost it would be a small thing, and his premonition of danger proved prophetic in the skies above Dun-sur-Meuse, France, on September 26, 1918; he was among seven American DH-4 Liberty planes returning from a successful bombing mission when they were attacked by a "hunting pack" of German Fokkers. In the ensuing aerial dogfight Cooper's plane was riddled with bullets and his cockpit burst into flames—not for nothing were these Liberty planes known as "flaming coffins." He began to fall from the sky. Like many fliers going down in flames, his only thought was *Escape,* and since

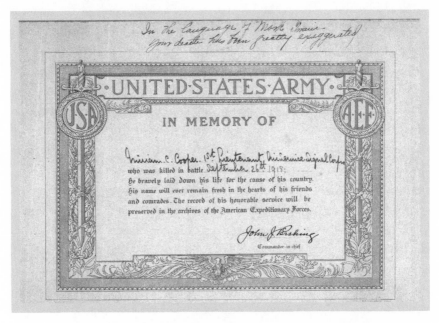

**MERIAN COOPER'S WORLD WAR I DEATH CERTIFICATE, SIGNED BY
GENERAL PERSHING, WITH "MARK TWAIN" ALLUSION WRITTEN IN LATER.**
Cooper Papers, BYU

Cooper, like other American airmen, had gone up without a parachute— part of the gallant code of some of these early air warriors—he frantically pulled his plane up, fighting the centrifugal force of the screaming tailspin to teeter on the edge of the flaming cockpit for his leap into the abyss. . . .

In the heroic style of the most outlandish movie cliffhangers, Coop went down in flames—but survived. In later years, he'd point with an ironic pride to the official United States Army death certificate made out "in memory of Merian C. Cooper" and signed by General John "Black Jack" Pershing himself. He would recall that the day he was shot down and survived became a second birthday, all his days thereafter a "bonus period."

Cooper had entered World War I in the bloom of youth, when death and destruction were abstract notions. He came away with a firsthand awareness of the price of war, having watched comrades and friends die before his eyes, and having tended to their foreign graves. Nevertheless, with the fires of the Great War still smoldering, Cooper resolved to remain in Europe. For a time he performed humanitarian duty, bringing food to the starving populations of ravaged cities held under siege, and soon he was fighting again, leading an all-American squadron of airmen to help Poland battle the invading Bolsheviks. In that conflict, Coop suffered his own deprivations as a prisoner of war in squalid camps where madness and death were always near. The nightmarish pain and torture stretched into months and marked him forever.

But he would have no regrets.

It was a code of honor that had put Cooper on the path to war and kept him in war-torn Europe. That code, mixed with a lust for adventure and risk, was a combustible combination that would be characterized, like Carl Denham's own legend, as recklessness.

Merian Cooper was a mass of contradictions. He was usually described as stocky, but his physique actually tended toward lean and muscular, particularly in his younger days, and he moved with a boxer's grace and agility. He possessed a devil of a temper that regularly got the best of him—once, in Siam, an impulsive slap he gave a tribal chief almost cost him his life. But in a life-or-death situation he could be counted on to be cool and clearheaded.

He was a showman but also self-deprecating and humble, particularly when it came to his own exploits in war. He became a public figure but gloried in pulling the levers of power from behind the scenes. He seemed a practical man, but at heart he was a dreamer—indeed, *King Kong* publicity photographs show him exhaling smoke from his ever-present pipe, the floating cloud revealing images of the gigantic ape and Skull Island as if conjured from his imagination.

Cooper's idealistic spirit was his shield and armor; his soul was buttressed by a code of honor and devotion to duty. He had learned those values in a cultured, comfortable home that fed his imagination and nurtured his dreams. During the dreaming time from boyhood to youth, he was steeped in entrancing tales of war and adventure that inspired him, and that set the course of his life journey.

CHAPTER TWO

TALES OF EXPLORATION AND ADVENTURE

*They believe, in all this country, that there is a kind of gorilla—
known to the initiated by certain mysterious signs, but chiefly by
being of extraordinary size—which is the residence of certain
spirits of departed natives. Such gorillas, the natives believe,
can never be caught or killed.*

—Paul Du Chaillu, EXPLORATIONS AND
ADVENTURES IN EQUATORIAL AFRICA[1]

MERIAN C. COOPER WAS BORN IN JACKSONVILLE, FLORIDA, ON OCTOBER 24, 1893, the youngest child of John and Mary Cooper, after older brother, John Cobb Jr., and his sister, Nancy. Merian's father was a prominent lawyer who had grown up in Jacksonville and whose powerful friends included Florida's Senator Duncan U. Fletcher. The Cooper lineage had a venerable pedigree: The first of the Coopers arrived in South Carolina in the 1600s, and some of Merian's forebears were among the earliest settlers of Florida. Merian was the latest in the line who'd first established cotton plantations north of Jacksonville, near the St. Marys River, which forms a natural stretch of Florida's border with Georgia.[2]

Merian's boyhood was immersed in comfort and tradition. But in the very year he was born, dramatic developments in the realms of science and technology were under way that would change the world forever.

The emerging future took metaphoric form that year at the Columbian Exposition in Chicago, a world's fair laid out on waterways and canals, boasting white neoclassical structures adorned with fountains and statuary and vaulting steel arches. There were elaborate exhibition sites like Machinery Hall, which stood as a monument to the steam machines of the industrial age. The "White City," as the fairgrounds became known, was erected on the brink of revolution.

A snapshot of America in 1893 would have revealed a rural expanse, with farmers leaning against horse and plow. But the gaslight era was already ending as cities became illuminated with electric lights, and the archetypal metropolis would be defined by massive towers reaching to the heavens.[3] The Columbian Exposition promised a future of miracles, including two emerging phenomena that would beguile Cooper.

One was manned flight, with the International Conference on Aerial Navigation holding its annual meeting at the exposition, in the spirit of a similar gathering at the French Exposition of 1889. Flight was moving beyond the realm of inventors tinkering with flying machines—what an opening address by one O. Chanute called eccentrics and "cranks"—into the practical realm of scientists and engineers. Topics at the sessions, attended by a hundred air enthusiasts, ranged from navigable ballooning to sending convicted murderers up in flying machines as test pilots. After all, if they crashed it'd be justice. If the flight was successful, science would advance, and "the culprit will come down presumably frightened enough to choose a life of virtue thereafter," as Professor Todd of Amherst College proposed.[4]

The 1893 Chicago Exposition also boasted the "Zoopraxigraphical Hall," wherein photographer Eadweard Muybridge offered for sale paper discs of his celebrated high-speed photography, which broke physical movement into increments of still pictures revealing every frozen moment, from the gait of a trotting horse to the stride of an athlete. After Muybridge, the next generation of "motion studies" would become the phenomenon of moving pictures.

Cooper's involvement in moving pictures was decades away, but the lure of manned flight locked him in its grip from the start, as he would dream of becoming a soldier. For service in war, with its call to duty and honor—the notion that one's manhood was best forged in the crucible of battle—was a long-standing Cooper family tradition.

ONE OF THE most storied of his fighting ancestors was Merian's great-great-grandfather and his father's namesake, Colonel John Cooper of Savannah, whose family had received grants of land in southeastern Georgia. John Cooper, a young man at the start of the Revolutionary War, personally raised a cavalry and joined the fight as a leader of the Georgians who fought the British until their region was overrun. His own son, James G. Cooper, would leave Georgia for Florida Territory, where he would settle in Nassau County, become a member of the territorial council, and serve as a major of territorial troops in the first Seminole Indian wars.[5]

The most celebrated story of Colonel John Cooper, handed down through the family generations, involved his role as senior officer to Kazimierz Pułaski, a dashing cavalry commander from Poland who fought against Russia, Prussia, and Austria until his forces were crushed and he himself was forced into exile. The freedom-loving Pułaski never accepted defeat and found another cause to fight for in 1776 when, in Paris, he met Benjamin Franklin, who was there on a recruitment mission on behalf of General George Washington's Continental army. The next year, the Continental Congress, suitably impressed with the young officer's love of liberty and fighting renown, charged Pułaski with organizing, equipping, and commanding America's first cavalry unit.

Cooper family annals hold that John Cooper and Pułaski became the closest of friends and that Pułaski, one of the world's expert swordsmen, trained Cooper to become similarly skillful with the blade. Pułaski reportedly stood out against the gray of Washington's embattled army, wearing his plumed helmet and hussar's uniform woven with gold braid. But Pułaski was more than a strutting peacock; he was an expert guerrilla fighter and organizer who transformed ordinary horsemen into "the Pułaski Legion," a crack cavalry unit that bedeviled the British.[6]

Cooper was riding alongside his friend at the Battle of Savannah when a British bullet struck down Pułaski. Cooper family lore holds that Colonel Cooper personally spirited his fallen commander from the battlefield to the Savannah River estuary, where the American warship *Wasp* was anchored. Two days later, with the *Wasp* headed for Charleston, Pułaski died in Cooper's arms, and the freedom-loving cavalry officer was given a burial at sea.[7]

To Merian, this was more than an oral tradition, brought out for show like some prized heirloom. Merian was so inspired by visions of Polish patriots fighting for America's freedom that in the future he'd return the favor, leading the all-American Kościuszko Squadron to help Poland fight the invading Russian Bolsheviks. The squadron itself was named for Tadeusz Kościuszko, another freedom-loving Pole who'd helped the American colonies.

Many of the tales Merian's father shared with him must have made war seem pure adventure. Another favorite was John Cooper's own boyhood memory of the day an old Confederate colonel returned to the sleepy town of Jacksonville after years of wandering. Following the Civil War, the colonel had drifted to the frontier to fight in the Indian Wars, then crossed into Mexico and kept going, roaming the planet as a soldier of fortune. He'd ended up in Egypt, along with comrades from the lost Confederacy, where they helped train an army of conquest organized by the khedive of Egypt. And when that army was ready with a force fifteen thousand strong, they rode south, ready to conquer Abyssinia—or so they'd dreamed. The Abyssinians almost wiped out the khedive's army.

"I've fought against Apaches and Mexicans and Yankees, damn 'em, but for sheer pluck and fighting ability, young man, the Abyssinian is the best soldier in the whole round world," the old soldier had growled. Many years later, Merian would find himself in Abyssinia, seeing with his own eyes those legendary black warriors as they assembled across a sunbaked plain in his honor, called there by the will of the all-powerful heir to the throne of King Solomon.[8]

MERIAN'S IMPRESSIONABLE SPIRIT and burning idealism drew him to noble causes and legends of knighthood and chivalry. One seminal influence was Miguel de Cervantes Saavedra's novel *Don Quixote*, which Cooper recalled as the first book he read after having "tolerably mastered my letters." Cooper began the saga of the hapless knight one bright spring morning, having left home for a nearby garden where he could sit on a moss-covered stone bench by a waterfall and trees where songbirds nested. As he read, Merian's esteem for the brave, if flummoxed, hero grew. But the knight's quixotic quests opened the boy's eyes to mortality, and in that garden he felt he had lost his innocence.

"I was a child," Cooper wrote, "and knew nothing of the irony God had interwoven into the world, and which the great poet had imitated in his miniature world; and I wept most bitterly, when for all his chivalry and generosity the noble knight gained only ingratitude and cudgels."

By the time he finished the book it was a cloudy autumn day. The song-birds were gone, and the world itself seemed bent in sorrow. "From every side the transitoriness stared at me—and my heart was ready to break up as I read how the noble knight lay on the ground, stunned and bruised, and through his closed visor said, in tones faint and feeble, as if he were speaking from the grave, 'Dulcina [*sic*] is the fairest lady in the world, and I the unhappiest knight on earth, but it is not meet that my weakness should disown this truth—strike with your lance, sir knight!'

"Ah me! That brilliant knight of the silver moon, who vanquished the bravest and noblest man in the world, was a disguised barber!"

But for Cooper, even the tragedy of Quixote couldn't dampen his spirit for long. With triumph, he wrote of the idealism that had emerged from the experience like the mythic phoenix: "In my breast, however, still blooms that flaming love, which soared so ardently above the earth, to revel adventurously in the broad yawning spaces of heaven, and which, pushed back by the cold stars, and sinking again to the little earth, was forced to confess, with sighing and triumph, that there is in all creation nothing fairer or better than the heart of man. This love is the inspiration that fills me, always divine, whether it does foolish or wise deeds—and so the tears the little boy shed over the sorrows of the silly knight were in no wise spent in vain. . . ."[9]

IF IT'S POSSIBLE to zero in on the defining moment of a life—the moment of *becoming*—that moment for Merian Cooper was when he decided to become an explorer, and it came when he was six years old.

The inspiration arrived courtesy of his namesake and great-uncle, Merian R. Cooper, who'd joined the Confederacy at sixteen as a private in the 2nd Florida Infantry and by age twenty had been twice wounded and commissioned as a captain in the Confederate army.[10] His uncle's military renown must have been impressive to young Merian, but it was the gift of a book that had the lasting impact on the young boy: *Explorations and Adventures in Equatorial Africa*, a first-person account of explorer Paul Du Chaillu's journey into a mysterious region of Africa.

"I made up my mind right then that I wanted to be an explorer," Cooper later revealed to film historian Rudy Behlmer.[11] *Explorations and Adventures*, published in 1861, featured the explorer's account of his hunt for wild gorillas. It planted a seed in the young boy's fertile imagination that would burst into full bloom decades later, taking the form of that gigantic gorilla King Kong.

Du Chaillu had set off on his expedition to kill a wild gorilla, accompanied by a trio of local youths, including two sons of the king of the Mbondemo people, and a half dozen "stout women" to haul supplies and provisions. The beginning of the expedition resembled a crossing over into

"THE GORILLA," FRONTISPIECE ILLUSTRATION FROM THE 1861 EDITION OF *EXPLORATIONS AND ADVENTURES IN EQUATORIAL AFRICA*, ONE OF THE INFLUENTIAL BOOKS THAT SHAPED THE OUTLOOK AND CAREER PATH OF YOUNG MERIAN COOPER.
Cooper Papers, BYU

a lost world, as they ascended the forested heights of the Sierra del Crystal mountain range and passed mountain rapids that coursed down like sea waves, the boulders in the river giving the explorer the mythic impression that "the Titans had been playing at skittles in this country." Above the rapids the white explorer rested under a tree and dreamed of when the ancient forests around him would give way to plantations and "the light of Christian civilization."

Du Chaillu's meditations were suddenly interrupted when he chanced to gaze above—and found a black serpent coiled on an overhanging branch.

He jumped away, picked up his rifle, and shot the serpent dead. The creature, which boasted venomous fangs and measured more than thirteen feet in length, seemed a guardian of the gates to the unknown jungle ahead. Before moving on, the natives cut off its head and roasted and ate the serpent on the spot, as if fortifying themselves for the hunt with the atavistic energy of the jungle itself.

Soon the hunters came to their first gorilla tracks. To white men, the great apes were mysterious creatures; to the natives, they were figures of supernatural awe. Du Chaillu felt his heart beating wildly with anxiety, knowing that at any moment they might encounter "the king of the African forest." The women were particularly terrified, and it was decided to leave them at some abandoned trading huts while the men followed the tracks.

Their first sighting came while crossing a fallen log bridge over a stream. On the other side were four young gorillas, which, at the first rifle shot, bounded off into the jungle with howling cries that thrilled Du Chaillu with their strangely human discordance.

That night around their campfire, the excited natives shared gorilla stories, including one that told of two Mbondemo women who had been borne off by an "immense gorilla." One of the women quickly escaped, but the other returned to the village later, with news that the gorilla "had misused her." One native mused that this had probably been "a gorilla inhabited by a spirit"—and so could never be caught or killed.

In the days that followed, the gorilla hunters moved on into the densest part of the jungle and the territory of a tribe of cannibals. While following a trail one day, the hunters were startled by the sound of breaking branches and a tremendous roar, as a male gorilla burst through the brush on all fours. "When he saw our party he erected himself and looked us boldly in the face . . . with immense body, huge chest, and great muscular arms, with fiercely-glaring large deep gray eyes, and a hellish expression of face, which seemed to me like some nightmare vision: thus stood before us this king of the African forest.

"He was not afraid of us. He stood there, and beat his breast with his huge fists till it resounded like an immense bass-drum, which is their mode of offering defiance; meantime giving vent to roar after roar.

"His eyes began to flash fiercer fire as we stood motionless on the defensive . . . his powerful fangs were shown as he again sent forth a thunderous roar. And now he truly reminded me of nothing but some hellish dream creature—a being of that hideous order, half-man, half-beast, which we find pictured by old artists in some representations of the infernal regions. He advanced a few steps—then stopped to utter that hideous roar again—advanced again, and finally stopped when at a distance of about six yards from us. And here, just as he began another of his roars, beating his breast in rage, we fired, and killed him."

The creature fell forward with a death groan "which had something terribly human in it," the explorer wrote. The hunters pitched their camp by the fallen ape. By dinnertime the white hunter had shot and was eating a deer, while the natives feasted on the vanquished jungle king, even carving out the brain, which was a charm, the explorer learned, for "a strong hand for the hunt . . . and success with women."[12]

Reading the account, young Merian conjured up a mental image of that "hellish dream creature"—those would be close to the words he'd use, decades later, to describe the giant gorilla god spawned by his own fevered imagination.

IN 1893, MERIAN Cooper's birth year, Thomas Edison erected a milestone, constructing what history records as the first film studio. The seminal "studio," not far from Edison's lab in West Orange, New Jersey, was a ramshackle, black tar-papered structure dubbed the Black Maria, after the slang term for a police lockup van. The taking of moving pictures needed plenty of natural light, so the Black Maria's roof was made to open to the sky, while the structure itself was set on railroad tracks that allowed it to be rotated to follow the sun.

"With its great flapping sail-like roof and ebon complexion, it has a weird and semi-nautical appearance," W. K. L. Dickson and Antonia Dickson wrote in 1895, "like the unwieldy hulk of a medieval pirate-craft or the air-ship of some swart Afrite."[13]

The Dicksons were inspired to heights of mystical rhapsody in their prophecies for the "kinetographic" medium, which they called "the crown of nineteenth-century magic, the crystallization of Eons of groping enchantments . . . possibilities undreamt of by the occult lore of the east."[14] Among the coming wonders, the Dicksons predicted the recording of "thrilling dramas of jungle and forest." From a comfortable chair even the most patrician viewer would be able to "contemplate the awful rush of maddened brutes, the tawny flesh of the savage eyes, the lightning play of the vigorous muscles . . . at the wave of a nineteenth-century wand."[15]

That prophetic vision would be fulfilled by a generation of adventuring movie pioneers, Merian Cooper among them. Strangely, the Dicksons added that "monkeys have contributed liberally to the kinetographic collection. . . . Monkeydom has an inexhaustible fund of varied emotions, underlying the unfathomable antiquity, the measureless sadness of its exterior."[16]

Still, it would be years before Cooper gravitated into the orbit of the emerging motion-picture industry. In 1903, when he was ten, the Edison company released *The Great Train Robbery,* one of the earliest narrative films, but Merian was far more excited by news from a place called Kitty Hawk in North Carolina. It was on December 17, around noon, when a man named Orville Wright sat at the controls of a prototype flying machine that coasted down a wooden rail as his brother Wilbur ran alongside and held on to the wing, steadying the craft—which then lifted into the air, traveling 120 feet and defying gravity for twelve seconds. It was the first liftoff and sustained flight, and the idealistic dreams of ten-year-old Cooper lifted with it, sparking his lifelong passion for aviation.[17]

Only a few short years after Kitty Hawk, pioneering aviators were entertaining crowds in dazzling air shows where prizes were awarded for distance, speed, and time aloft. But the miracle of flight, with its inherent poetry, was also turning to more destructive ends, as military planners and engineers seized on the obvious strategic possibilities. Within a decade factories would be mass-producing fighter planes, and warfare would take to the sky. Merian Cooper would follow, becoming one of those pioneering warriors of the air.

CHAPTER THREE

THE ROAD TO WAR

*By the time [Merian Cooper] reached adolescence, he was like
a gun loaded and ready to fire. He wanted to not only defend
America against all enemies, foreign and domestic, but also—
somehow, somewhere, sometime—to repay what he saw as
America's 150-year-old debt to Poland.*

—Lynne Olson and Stanley Cloud, A QUESTION OF HONOR[1]

*Pray for me. I have often blasphemed my God. I failed the
service of my country in time of peace. Now I only ask humbly
that I may prove worthy in the test of steel and blood.*

—Merian Cooper, letter to his father[2]

WHEN MERIAN COOPER FINALLY EMBARKED ON A FILMMAKING CAREER, HIS
third production would be based on a favorite book, A. E. W. Mason's
novel *The Four Feathers,* the story of the scion of an English family who
turns coward when called to duty and thereafter seeks redemption in battle. For much of his life the book held special meaning for Cooper, and it
would provide solace during a trial by fire in which his sanity—his very
life—hung in the balance.

The theme of redemption in *The Four Feathers* also had a personal meaning for Cooper. In 1911, after graduating from the Lawrenceville School
(near Princeton), Merian won a prestigious appointment to the United
States Naval Academy through the intercession of his father's influential
friend Senator Duncan Fletcher. But he didn't make it through his senior
year; he was kicked out of Annapolis. Ashamed that he had disgraced his
family, and convinced that only combat could purge his guilt, he would
seek out war like a condemned man seeking salvation.

"DESTROY THIS MAD BRUTE"—WORLD WAR I
PROPAGANDA POSTER PICTURES APE-LIKE
FIGURE CARRYING OFF A WOMAN,
AN INCARNATION OF THE GERMAN ENEMY.

Image courtesy of the author

Cooper later claimed that his failure at the academy had *not* been dishonorable, that he'd washed out largely because of his dawning belief that "air power," not naval might, was the key to winning wars. "Besides, I had been interested in aviation ever since the Wright Brothers' flight at Kitty Hawk, and I wanted to get into World War I and fly, and realized I couldn't get into flying in the Navy," he once told Rudy Behlmer. But despite his protestations, Cooper added an enigmatic note about his Naval Academy troubles: "I was high-spirited, loved excitement, took chances, and got caught too many times."[3]

Indeed, Christmas of 1914, during his fateful senior year, found him in the midshipmen's prison, an old wooden Spanish ship docked at Annapolis and called the *Reina Mercedes*. He'd write a few years later that he was "the black sheep of my class" and had been stripped of honors and privilege.

But that Christmas he happily hit the deck, because all the incarcerated were allowed the freedom of a day on the academy grounds in honor of the holiday. The weather was crisp and cold and a girlfriend joined him. "We laughed at the world together," he later recalled. Yet that night, walking back to the prison ship, Cooper contemplated the world beyond the horizon, imagined all the exotic cities, wilderness, and adventures he was missing. "Dear God," he prayed, "let me play some little part in this great world of adventure. Break me, hurt me, kill me, God, but let me taste of life."[4]

Leaving Annapolis under a cloud in his senior year—so near to graduating—dented Cooper's considerable pride, bruised his inherent sense of honor. He shipped out as a seaman on a transatlantic ship in the desperate hope of joining the air service in Britain or France, but was thwarted by passport difficulties.[5]

Cooper then embarked on a personal journey of self-discovery during a footloose year when he was damned and determined to go it alone. He roamed like a penitent suffering for his sins, scrounging around in nameless towns for a roof over his head, counting out his remaining pennies for cheap bakery buns to fill his gnawing hunger. He kept in touch with his family but refused all aid, a painful ritual that would continue for years. Two years after the prison ship at Annapolis, Cooper wrote his father a Christmas letter recalling a promise that he'd live morally and be a good and loyal son. "I would stop drinking, and play the game straight as I saw it. . . . I have lived up to my code," Merian declared. His go-it-alone code included mailing back or giving away his family's Christmas gifts of candy and oranges—anything that seemed a "luxury" item. It wasn't a diminishing of affections, he would note in a follow-up letter; "It is just that I must stick to the game and see my life through alone as far as help from my family is concerned."[6]

His dismal wanderings came to an end when he landed a job as a reporter for the *Minneapolis Daily News*. Within the next couple of years he moved on to positions at the *Des Moines Register-Leader* and the *St. Louis Post-Dispatch*. It was a fitting station for a restless young man, because in those days journalism was the nearest thing to being where the action was, outside of war. This is when he seems to have begun smoking a pipe, as a substitute for the alcohol that had often fueled his reckless ways.

"My chief pal nowadays is my corncob pipe," he wrote his father during his newspaper stint in Des Moines. "I stick to that boy, and I reckon he will stick to me. He soothes many, many a hatred and many a regret, and whenever I have wanted a good stiff drink the old corncob has always stuck by me, and taken the place of John Barleycorn."[7]

The life of a newspaper reporter occupied his energies and provided thrilling glimpses of the dark underbelly of human behavior. While working for the *Minneapolis Daily News* he covered the sensational murder case of a man named Price, who was charged with throwing his wife off a cliff for her money and so that he could marry another woman. Cooper went to the murder scene to cover the jury inspection and watched as the accused man called out to the prosecuting attorney, who was leaning over the brink of the cliff, "Don't slip, George, we have work for you to do."

"His nerve is wonderful to behold," Cooper wrote his father. "I rode home in the car with Price, and we talked and chatted together. He is a mighty pleasant and courageous chap, but I think he is guilty as Hell."[8]

Although Cooper stayed at the Minneapolis paper for only six months, he was promoted four times by managing editor W. C. Robertson. In a 1916 "To Whom It May Concern" letter recommending Cooper for military service, Robertson hailed the young reporter's "intense energy and devotion to his work" and urged him to apply for the Marine Corps.[9]

Probably the first recorded inkling of Cooper's desire to become an airman came in a "Dear Dad" letter he sent off on *Minneapolis Daily News* stationery, applauding a speech President Woodrow Wilson had given before Congress on military preparedness. "His suggestion of forming an aviation corps, ten officers to be appointed every year, and to be allowed to train two years, interested me greatly. I certainly would like a chance to get into that corps. If I had the money I would go to an aviation school now and start training for it. Next to going in the British army or the French army I do not know anything I would rather do."[10]

But Cooper first joined the Georgia National Guard and shipped off from Macon, Georgia, bound for the Mexican border and General George Pershing's hunt for the notorious Pancho Villa, a man the Americans considered an agitator and bandit but who was a revolutionary Robin Hood figure to many of his Mexican countrymen. It was a ten-day trip to the border of Mexico, and as they got closer, reports of Villa's activities increased, stirring the blood of the young men longing for combat.

"If you wish me well pray God I may have the opportunity to distinguish myself, and when the chance comes, that I may play the man," Cooper wrote his father after arriving at their destination of El Paso, Texas.[11] That letter also revealed the eye for detail that characterized a good newspaperman. Merian wrote of blazing hot days and bitterly cold nights in a town whose population had doubled, virtually overnight, to some one hundred thousand souls, its streets crowded with Mexican women in shawls and long black skirts, thousands of marching soldiers, Yankees and cattlemen, and streams of refugees from Mexico.

Cooper also saw death up close for the first time on Christmas Eve 1916. A few of his Georgia regiment had headed into the Mexican section of El Paso to attend midnight Mass at a Catholic church. But as they crossed some railroad tracks, they heard two gunshots and a scream. Two men came running down the tracks and Cooper and his comrades gave chase, catching two Mexicans who had shot a black railroad porter in a fight over some blankets. After tying them up for the authorities, Cooper found the victim, his shirt crimson with blood, his fear mixed with a kind of childlike innocence as he asked, "Has I got to die on Chrismus, mister?" And then he did. Cooper heard the church bells tolling midnight, heralding another Christmas Day, and he made a mental note of the drama of life and death.[12]

Nevertheless, Cooper wouldn't see the combat he longed for, at least not yet. He served outpost duty and night patrol on the lookout for smugglers, without incident. The closest he got to Pancho Villa was an intelligence mission when he had dinner at the ranch of a man known to the

Secret Service as Villa's chief agent in the United States, and where he talked in his halting Spanish to a Mexican woman he later learned was probably Villa's sister.[13]

Pershing himself never caught up with the elusive Villa. In 1999, Thomas Franklin Brice, a 103-year-old veteran of the expedition, recalled their long and fruitless patrols. "I do remember [Pershing] addressing the troops one morning. He was on his horse, looking out over all of us, and said, 'You aren't soldiers; you're an organized mob.' I guess he didn't like the way we looked. We were a bit of a ragtag group of boys at that time. As for Pancho Villa, we stayed on our side of the river and he stayed on his side."[14]

IN MARCH 1917, when the troops were called home, Cooper obtained a thirty-day leave of absence in order to act as city editor at the *El Paso Herald*.[15] He reported on the festival atmosphere as ten thousand locals cheered El Paso's own—"the boys of Company K, Fourth Texas Infantry"— when they returned from eleven months of border duty. The train bearing the sixty-two soldiers home was two hours late, increasing the anticipation, and its arrival was greeted with a collective roar. The men in uniform who appeared on the platform had left as young recruits but returned as "soldiers, bronzed with long field service," Cooper reported. Despite the celebration, the ensuing festivities were tempered with anxiety over the European war that had begun in 1914, and the fear that El Paso's young men might soon be called back to duty to fight Germany.[16]

A few days later, when Cooper attended the Company K homecoming dinner dance at the Hotel Paso del Norte, the ecstatic, flag-waving happiness that had greeted the returning infantry was further overshadowed by the ominous realization that this welcome-home celebration was probably a farewell party, as well. Cooper saw and recorded the personal side of war, the cracks in the brave front: worried mothers whispering out of earshot of their sons, sweet young girls who bit their lips "to make the smile steady" for the next soldier who'd ask for a dance, stoic fathers extending firm handshakes to the soldier boys. And then Cooper witnessed one young girl who seemed to tell the whole story: "Over at the dark, far corner of the roof garden stood alone a slim figure of a girl in white, apparently looking down on the lights of El Paso. Her shoulders were shaking, the reporter noticed, and he thought she was laughing at some funny sight among the tiny figures in the El Paso street, far below. But she was not laughing. The Teutonic menace had already pierced her heart."[17]

WHILE CONTINUING IN service with the Georgia National Guard, Cooper wrote his father that he'd become an assistant instructor at officers' training camp, and all that awaited his commission as first lieutenant was his signature on the dotted line. But, he added, "My only objection to it is that I want to do duty immediately in the [combat] line."[18] Sure enough, Merian turned down the commission—and what seemed a certain appointment as a captain in the reserve corps—to go to the Military Aeronautics School in Atlanta to learn how to fly. He hoped that within six months he would be sent to France to complete his training and join the fighting.[19]

Finally, in one of his stream of letters to his father, he proclaimed: "I am flying at last." He took pride in the year he had worked to get his wings. "And it is great sport—not that I know anything about it really, as I've only made four flights—about three hours in the air—but I am getting so I am beginning to feel at home in the air, and can take off, turn, and land a 'bird.'" He was proudest that on August 11 he'd taken his examinations and had not only been awarded a certificate of graduation from the Military Aeronautics School but had graduated first in his class of 150. The commandant of the school had even sent a telegram to Washington recommending Cooper for service abroad, adding, "He is the best man in every respect who has yet entered this school."[20]

Another ringing endorsement came from General Walter Harris, commander of the 2nd Georgia Brigade. "I wanted to keep Merian with me more than I have wanted anything else since I have been in the military service," General Harris wrote Merian's father, "but his heart was set on flying and I am glad that he has at last got what he wanted."[21]

Cooper was so eager for combat that he described a family friend who'd already gone to the front as "the lucky dog." He was also dazzled by one Lieutenant Fred Blount of Pensacola, Florida, a decorated soldier who had been three years in the trenches, had experienced battle from France to Egypt, and whose uniform glittered with medals that included the

Medaille Militaire and the Croix de Guerre. "Every time I look at him," Cooper wrote breathlessly, "my eyes almost pop out of my head with envy."[22]

AS AMERICA ENTERED World War I in 1917, air power advocates argued that aerial bombing would demoralize Germany and usher in a swift victory. That summer saw a relentless battle for air supremacy that lasted until the winter rains forced a lull, allowing the buildup of the American air program in anticipation of the return to combat in the spring of 1918. In addition to a massive $640 million aviation bill, aviation schools were established across the nation. "Hundreds of pilots, full of dash, are being trained, and they are going about their work with the same zeal which they formerly displayed on the football field at college," Major Joseph Tulasne exulted in a January 1918 article for *National Geographic Magazine.*[23]

In truth, aerial warfare was dangerous business, *not* a spirited football match. Cooper went to France as an adjutant of the 201st Squadron in October 1917 and attended the flying school at Issoudun, where Colonel Walter G. Kilner permitted him to fly. Cooper sheepishly admitted in a letter to his father that during "a joyride" with his buddy "Doc" Taylor of Tennessee, their plane plunged two hundred feet. Taylor was cut around the face and Coop was knocked out, but they survived.

"I landed on my head, and as that is solid ivory it didn't do much harm," Cooper wrote with self-deprecating humor. "A long period of depression and nervousness followed which the surgeon says was the natural result of the sock, but I am absolutely all right now, except I am having to learn a lot of flying all over again." It would be six weeks before Cooper returned to the air. The joyride hinted at the recklessness that had cost him his appointment at Annapolis, but his letter home was contrite, and he resolved not to repeat past mistakes. "We got [the accident] by taking an unnecessary chance. But I'm the most careful pilot on the field now so you need not worry about me at all."[24]

Cooper was convinced that aerial bombardment, which was hazardous and less glamorous than other aspects of air service, would put maximum hurt on the enemy and be the decisive weapon in the entire war, and would attract fewer volunteers. He requested that Colonel Kilner send him to Clermont-Ferrand for training as a bomber pilot, and Kilner agreed.[25]

Thus motivated, Coop did well. He graduated as a bomber pilot and was ordered to England to take command of a newly formed squadron, complete with immediate promotion—which he refused. The training period for the new squadron would have meant a delay in getting to the front, so Cooper asked that his orders be changed and that he be sent on, without promotion, to an active combat unit. Colonel Kilner granted his request, and Merian Cooper was made a pilot in the 20th Aero Squadron, which would soon become part of the historic 1st Day Bombardment Group.

Merian would also be proud to note that his brother, John, had signed up with the navy. For Merian, his dreams were coming true: He would be-

COOPER, FORMAL PORTRAIT AS A MEMBER OF
THE U.S. ARMY AIR SERVICE IN WORLD WAR I.
Cooper Papers, BYU

come a pilot and was ready to embark on the adventure of war. What would happen in the weeks ahead might, for anyone else, confirm the adage of being careful about what one wished for. But even if Merian could have glimpsed his future, he no doubt would still have happily headed to the war zone. For there in the ravaged trenches and embattled skies lay his redemption.

FORTUNATE
SOLDIER

CHAPTER FOUR

THE TEST OF STEEL AND BLOOD

"As I fell straight down towards the earth in a spinning nose dive it looked to me as if the whole world was on fire. I had never been able to understand before why men jumped from a burning plane to a certain death below but I knew then death did not seem to matter at all. The only thing in the world that I wanted to do was to get out of that pain, so I jerked off my belt and started to hop out when it flashed through my mind that I was leaving Eddie to burn up while I died easy; so I thought I would take one crack at it."

—Merian Cooper, letter to his father[1]

EAGER FOR "THE TEST OF STEEL AND BLOOD," MERIAN COOPER FLEW INTO battle on the wings of America's Liberty plane, a British De Havilland 4 aircraft outfitted with a Liberty motor and two Marlin machine guns, including a front gun synchronized to fire through the propeller and a British Wimperis bombsight outside the fuselage, which allowed rear observers to fire while standing.[2] The famous flying ace Captain Eddie Rickenbacker was contemptuous of the plane and once described its usual fate in battle: "From every side Fokkers were diving on the clumsy Liberty machines which, with their criminally constructed fuel systems, offered so easy a target to the incendiary bullets of the enemy that their unfortunate pilots called this boasted achievement of our Aviation Department 'Flaming Coffins.' "[3]

At the time, there was a tremendous scandal over the controversial Liberty planes. James V. Martin, an aircraft inventor and a confidant of airpower advocate General William "Billy" Mitchell, described the monopoly of American "automobile manufacturers and smart politicians" that had refused to make good planes. "They'd grabbed an old English plane design

COOPER AND HIS COMRADES IN ISSOUDUN,
FRANCE, DECEMBER 1917. LEFT TO RIGHT: BILL
CONANT, MERIAN COOPER, ESTES ARMSTRONG,
LUCIAN, UNIDENTIFIED, JIM OSGOOD, GEORGE
CRAWFORD, AND UNIDENTIFIED OLDER MAN.

Cooper Papers, BYU

known as the DeHaviland 4, with the tank right in back of the pilot. They could make them cheap. Our men were killed on the training fields by the dozens every week. In France all the Germans had to do was to shoot into the gas tank and our pilots were burned alive before the machines crashed. . . .

"But Mitchell had to take those 'flaming coffins' and order his men up in them. He flew them himself."[4]

Merian wrote his father about his first flight in a Liberty, describing how when he opened her up the aircraft "jumped like a stricken deer," and how she shot up like an elevator when he aimed her nose to the sky. "I am delighted with my machine, motor, pilot (that's *me*) and observer are all-

THE "DAY BOMBING TEAM" OF PILOT MERIAN COOPER AND EDMUND LEONARD, HIS REAR MACHINE GUNNER AND BOMBARDIER.
Cooper Papers, BYU

American . . . if I happen to get mine don't worry or grieve a bit, for thousands of better Americans than I have died gladly over here, and I am where your son should be—at the front."[5]

He wasn't alone. Edmund Leonard was Coop's pal and observer in the back seat of their two-man DH-4 Liberty, and he was Cooper's physical opposite. In a photograph of the period the duo stand in their flying overalls as the very image of cocky airmen ready for action: Coop, a great grin on his face, and the tall and dashing Leonard with a slight mustache, a piercing gaze, an inscrutable smile, and his cap and goggles on his head, the strap dangling loosely.[6]

Another young airman Cooper became pals with during the war, one he met at Issoudun in October 1917, would become one of the closest friends of his life, a leader and dreamer who was born for the air.[7] Just as Ernest Schoedsack would become his partner in moviemaking expeditions, so would Cooper join John Hambleton in shaping the postwar potential of commercial aviation.

Lean and handsome and the son of wealth and privilege, Hambleton shared Cooper's vision of martial valor. A future cofounder of Pan American Airways, he was a fearless pilot who would fight at the battles of Château-Thierry, St.-Mihiel, and Meuse-Argonne, and his decorations would include the Distinguished Service Cross. General Billy Mitchell, for whom Cooper would fly a top secret mission at the battle of St.-Mihiel, first took notice of Hambleton at the airdrome of Toul in April 1918, in the aftermath of a five-plane patrol Hambleton had led. They'd been attacked by a superior force and lost two planes, but in the battle Hambleton had shot down three of the enemy before bringing the rest of the patrol back to base. As their bullet-riddled planes taxied to position, Mitchell saw that the right strut of Hambleton's plane had been shot away.

"A further glance showed me that small fragments of spent bullets had lodged in his head and shoulders," Mitchell recalled. "In spite of the intensity of the combat . . . this young officer made one of the best reports of the patrol that I ever heard."[8] Pan Am historian Horace Brock adds the kicker to the story: "After reporting to General Mitchell, [Hambleton] saluted and, when the general returned the salute in dismissal, he did a smart about face and fell flat on the floor unconscious. He had been badly shot in the shoulder and blood was now pouring out one trouser leg."[9]

By August 20, 1918, while Hambleton was already in the thick of things, Cooper and Leonard were stationed at Orly, on the Seine River outside Paris, still awaiting orders. The war seemed as tantalizingly close as the distant puffs of smoke from the antiaircraft fire they could see in the sky above Paris. Leonard was of the same mind as Cooper, eager to get into the fight against the hated Hun, the "Boche." Like Coop, Leonard was envious of comrades he had trained with and who had already seen action, now veteran air fighters who returned from their baptisms of fire flushed with the glory of having fought and survived.

Nevertheless, Leonard was shocked when he realized how close he had always been to the specter of death. That realization had come the morning when he breakfasted with two pilots who were preparing to ferry a plane to England. "They were having a great discussion as to which one should pilot the machine," Leonard wrote in his diary. "Just as we went to lunch at noon, they crashed in taking off, one of them receiving a fractured skull which resulted in his death during the afternoon. The other pilot was not scratched. This certainly is some game; at breakfast you talk to a man who is as healthy as yourself and at noon he is gone."[10]

There was a phrase for war dead, Leonard noted: "gone West." A combat flier had to steel himself to follow the setting sun if necessary, but most still felt it was better to die fighting than perish in an accident.

BY AUGUST 29, Cooper and Leonard were among the forty officers reporting for duty at the new airfield at Deleuze. They were part of the 20th Aero Squadron, and the news was that they would be getting in the offensive as either observers or bombers—or both. Days later, just before the St.-Mihiel offensive, the 1st Day Bombardment Group was formed out of the 11th, 20th, and 96th squadrons. Cooper would keep the headquarters document that listed those who had reported in Paris and ordered them to proceed to Deleuze. After the Armistice he noted the fate of each man, writing it in ink beside his name.

As of September 4, the action was at hand. "Something is about due to happen for troop trains have been going by here all night long," Leonard wrote. "The wagon roads are full of truck trains and doughboys. Last night we could see lots of gun flashes and rockets in the sky. . . .

"The 96th came back from a raid today with three observers and one pilot wounded. The wounded pilot flew his plane with a machine gun bullet in his stomach and waited until the other three wounded had been given first aid, before he let anyone know he had been hit. The ambulance started to drive away without him when he yelled and asked if they had any more room. He has all the sand in the world. He came very close to 'going West' after getting to the hospital, but is all right now."[11]

The goal of the 1st Day Bombardment Group was to smash German supply lines and hit enemy ground troops, sending them into disarray. Cooper and Leonard, who by then were stationed at Amanty airfield, had to suffer through hazardous flying weather, from southwest winds that disrupted flying formations to heavy rains that muddied the Amanty airdrome and caused an estimated half of the airplane propellers to break during takeoffs. Despite the hazards, the group was reportedly eager for the dangerous missions that lay ahead.[12]

Among the eager pilots were Cooper, Leonard, and their friend Lieutenant George "Buck" Crawford. The three were called to report to their commanding officer and received exciting news: They were being briefly detached from the 20th Aero Squadron to fly to Maulan for top secret special duty under direct command of First Army headquarters. They arrived on the winds of more stormy weather, whereupon General Mitchell put

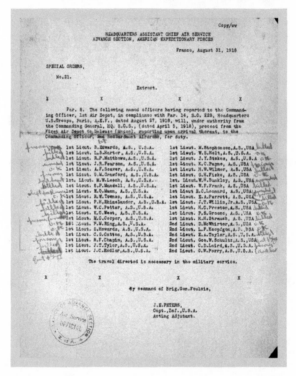

COOPER ALWAYS KEPT HIS COPY OF THE ORDER FROM THE AMERICAN EXPEDITIONARY FORCES IN EUROPE THAT DIRECTED HIM AND FELLOW OFFICERS TO DUTY. IN THE MARGINS, COOPER WROTE THE FATE OF HIS COMRADES-IN-ARMS.

Cooper Papers, BYU

Cooper in command of a temporary headquarters observation unit for the battle of St.-Mihiel, a detachment of seven DH-4 airplanes from the 20th and 11th squadrons. Cooper would lead his pilots across the front lines on special information-gathering missions to observe the progress of the offensive and personally report back to Mitchell.[13]

"Almost as soon as we landed, orders came to fly over Dampvitoux and Rembercourt, points on the old Hindenburg line, to see whether the Germans were bringing up reinforcements," Leonard wrote.[14]

In a letter to his father dated September 14, 1918, Cooper revealed that he was in charge of missions operating in the worst flying weather he'd ever seen. "I sent my best friend in the air service out on a dangerous mission two days ago in a driving rain and fog, and he has never returned, so he is either killed or a prisoner in Germany," Cooper lamented. "I followed him about a half an hour later, and was forced down by lack of gasoline and managed to land our side of the lines near Verdun, but smashed up. Both I and my observer were uninjured."[15] The missing pilot was Buck. On the sheet of names of fellow officers who'd reported for duty, Cooper would later write: "prisoner."[16]

On one of their last nights in Maulan, the sky cleared and Leonard noticed a propitious omen: rings around the moon that seemed to glisten red, white, and blue. The offensive had been a success: "Got the new front line from Headquarters this evening and it sure looks good," Leonard noted in his diary. ". . . St. Mihiel is cut off in a pocket with from nine to fourteen thousand prisoners."

By September 20, Cooper and Leonard were back with their squadron, but the muddy airfield at Amanty was under a dark cloud, and it was more than the continuing bad weather. "Pretty gloomy around here and no wonder," Leonard confessed to his diary. "The 11th sent over a flight of six machines and five were shot down, three in flames. The 96th sent a flight of four over and none came back, and another time two out of three were shot down in flames. Altogether thirty-seven men from the three squadrons are missing as a result of the week's action. Some of them will surely turn up in German prison camps, but it will be weeks before we know who they are."[17]

On the morning of September 26, 1918, Cooper and Leonard were in one of the seven planes waiting to lift off for a bombing mission over Dun-sur-Meuse to mark the beginning of the Meuse-Argonne offensive. As at St.-Mihiel, the 1st Day Bombardment Group was charged with hitting troop concentrations and vital targets, notably railroads. The orders were to lift off from the field at Maulan by 8:00, and on the appointed hour they had loaded four bombs into each plane, then checked the guns and motors. The runway was shrouded in thick fog and the airmen were ready in their flying clothes and goggles, grabbing a few smokes and waiting in hopes that the fog would lift. But after a half hour they could hear the distant artillery fire of the Argonne offensive, which had just gotten under way, and though the fog was still heavy, they began boarding their Liberty planes.[18]

Cooper and Leonard waited their turn in *Celeste II,* as Cooper had dubbed his plane. The fog was so thick that they could hear only the motors of the other planes firing up for takeoff. A low-flying machine would burst through the obscuring clouds, climb higher, and disappear again into the obscuring fog. When it was Cooper's turn to be airborne, there was the danger of collision in the disorienting, enveloping mist; "It was like another world," Leonard recalled. But as they lifted off the runway they saw a smudge of sun bleeding through the fog, which became brighter until they flew through the mist and into the brilliant blue.

Ahead flew their comrades and below they could see the fog, blanketing the valley like snow. The seven planes settled into a protective V-formation. "I was flying in number five position, which is the third plane on the right," Cooper later recalled. They climbed to optimum cruising altitude, the ascension made difficult because each plane's bomb load weighed more than four hundred pounds.[19]

They were almost three miles in the air and flying for an hour when they could see, fifteen miles in the distance, trench lines slashing the earth and the drifting smoke from artillery and shell fire. Few of the fliers realized that most of them would soon be "going West." Only two planes would return home, and one of those would carry a dead observer slumped in his cockpit. Among the missing would be Cooper's plane, and before long he and Leonard would be counted among the dead.

OVER THE NOISE of the plane's motor, Leonard heard the first antiaircraft shell break—he recalled it sounded like linen ripping—while Cooper saw a shell burst in the middle of their formation, miraculously missing the planes. Cooper flew through, maintaining his position. Leonard looked over to a brother observer, and they gestured to each other with clasped hands, anticipating the bombs they were about to drop. The flight leader fired a rocket as a signal to prepare to bomb.

But then things began to go wrong, Cooper recalled, when the observer in the plane ahead of him misunderstood the "ready" signal and prematurely dropped his payload. Suddenly freed of four hundred pounds of explosives, the plane shot forward and ahead of the flight leader, casting the formation into disarray.

The lead plane then dropped its bombs and tried to get back into position but was forced under the formation. Cooper had begun maneuvering his plane to allow the pilot, his friend Phil Rhinelander, to climb back into place when yellow and black specks appeared on the horizon: Five German Fokkers were firing at them.

One of the Fokkers got on the tail of the *Celeste II,* blasting a stream of bullets. When the enemy was some seventy-five yards away, Cooper swung wide to shake the fighter and allow Leonard a clear shot. Each time Cooper swung wide, Leonard opened up with his guns, and finally a stream of tracer bullets hit the German's cockpit, sending the Fokker crashing to earth. The remaining German planes flew away, but Cooper was concerned because the Americans' lead plane was straying deeper into enemy territory, and they were all forced to follow.

Suddenly, more yellow and black specks appeared, stretched over the horizon line—a dozen Fokkers now heading for them. Their own formation was still out of sync, with Cooper struggling to allow Rhinelander, who was flying unprotected, to slip back into the formation. Cooper's Liberty motor now began acting up, holding him back. While he was trying to help Rhinelander, Cooper's plane drifted fifty yards below the rest of the formation.

And then the Fokkers were upon them, firing and swooping through the formation. Leonard swung his machine gun, shooting at the Germans who were buzzing above and below. All the guns of the diving planes blazed until the crisscrossing tracers seemed to slice up the air with smoke and fire. Cooper maneuvered to protect a plane that lay below the formation, but this left his own aircraft exposed, although it allowed Leonard to fire at the enemy.[20]

And then Cooper saw the plane of Dick Matthews, one of his best friends, burst into a fireball that almost struck his own craft—Coop glimpsed Matthews's observer as he was trying to jump out of the consuming fire. A German plane was also falling, and then the *Celeste II* shot down another enemy plane. But then two more of their own went down.

Suddenly, a bullet sliced through Leonard's neck, knocking him down into his seat. The Fokker from which the bullet had come dived in for the kill from their now vulnerable rear. Leonard somehow opened his eyes and struggled to his guns. He was bleeding badly and the enemy plane was within fifty yards when he opened up and watched the bullets hit the cockpit. The enemy stopped firing; the plane fell out of view. Cooper would later say they'd shot it down in flames, but by the time the enemy plane was falling out of the sky, Leonard had lost consciousness and was slumped back into his seat.

Cooper still hadn't given up hope that they would return home and was making a long turn back to their line when his motor began sputtering. He pulled the plane's nose up, sending it spinning, trying to present a harder target for the hungry Fokkers that were riddling the *Celeste II* with bullets. Then the left side of his motor burst into flames, the fire spreading into Cooper's cockpit.

He dropped his plane into a flaming tailspin. Leonard's eyes fluttered open as he felt the dizzying force of the tail-first plunge. The thought drifted across his strangely calm mind that Coop must have been shot and everything would soon be over—and then his eyes closed again.

Cooper had his goggles and face mask on, which helped protect his face, but his hands were burning up. It was so painful that Cooper threw off his safety belt and stood up to leap out of the burning plane. One step over the edge and . . .

Cooper jerked his head around and looked to the rear cockpit.

Leonard opened his eyes and saw Coop standing up with one foot over the side of a cockpit that was a mass of flames.

In the instant their eyes met, Cooper knew he couldn't leave his partner; it would mean certain death. So he sat back into the flames and turned his attention to the controls.

Cooper pulled out of the spin and into a vertical dive, opening the throttle wide in an effort to burn out the gas in the motor and snuff out the fire. But with his belt unbuckled, he was now struggling not to fall out of the plane. They were plummeting so fast that Coop thought the wings might break off from the stress, while Leonard wondered when the flames would ignite the gas tank.

Suddenly, Cooper's maneuver worked—the flames were sucked out. He began piloting the plane into a glide and tried to point it back toward their line, until he realized he couldn't make it. He was in horrible pain, his hands so badly burned the stick was slipping from his charred flesh. The sputtering engine itself sounded, Leonard would remember, "like a couple of tin cans rattling together."

Coop and Leonard shot each other brave, "What the hell" grins.

Cooper turned back to landing the plane, working the stick with his elbows and knees, aiming for the open field that was rushing up to meet them. He glided toward the ground and hit with force enough to jack the plane up on its nose, snapping off the wings—but pilot and observer weren't thrown.

They didn't have time to contemplate their ordeal. One of the Fokkers had followed them down and was flying some fifty feet above, circling and signaling for them to get out of their plane. Leonard looked over their downed Liberty and estimated that it had been hit with more than sixty bullets; only divine providence, he thought, could have kept the bullets away from vital parts. Cooper was in agony, praying to himself that someone would come and chop off his burned hands.

The Fokker landed and the German strode over, the very image of the flying ace: handsome and clean-cut, with medals pinned to his uniform, including the Iron Cross First Class. To the surprise of the two Americans, the enemy airman saluted them.[21] They had landed near an enemy infantry reserve camp, and German soldiers who had watched the aerial battle and miraculous landing rushed over to join them, bringing aid and comfort. In short order, the men were bandaging Leonard with an emergency field dressing and Cooper was taken to a doctor for immediate work on his damaged hands.

Although Coop and Leonard had miraculously survived, it would officially be presumed that the two missing airmen were dead. Merian Cooper's plane was still missing in early October, although there was a glimmer of hope among Cooper's comrades. It was the consensus of the squadron that Merian and Leonard were alive, that a bullet had disabled his motor and forced an emergency landing, not a fatal crash.[22] On November 2–3, 1918, a flurry of Western Union telegrams was touched off by a request from John Cooper Jr. that the War Department investigate the casualty lists to solve the mystery of Merian's whereabouts. In response, Senator Fletcher had the Red Cross investigate, and on November 3, a telegram from the International Red Cross reached the Cooper home in Jacksonville with happy news: "LIEUT MERIAN COOPER PRISONER RESERVE HOSPITAL 4 TREVES SLIGHTLY WOUNDED."[23]

Cooper and Leonard waited out the war in different hospitals and prison camps until the Armistice on November 11, 1918. Both had been lucky. The quick work of the German doctor saved Cooper's hands, while Leonard's bullet had entered the right side of his neck at the collarbone and miraculously passed out his back between his spine and shoulder blades. "A quarter of an inch variation would have meant death," Leonard later recalled.[24]

Leonard wrote Merian's father from Base Hospital 26 in Allerey, France, to recount their ordeal and confess how amazed he was that devotion to a comrade had been stronger than the fire that had been so painful and that Cooper, despite his horrible burns, had somehow safely landed their battered plane.[25]

Decades later, a letter from a Mrs. Charles M. Garrison to Hollywood columnist Hedda Hopper noted her World War I service with the American Red Cross Missing and Prisoner Bureau in Paris. Garrison had been in charge of files A to C, so Cooper had been among her concerns. "I was in the Paris headquarters at the time of the Armistice," Garrison wrote Hopper, "and shortly thereafter, Merian C. Cooper came into the office and reported in person that he was no longer missing or a prisoner of war. I can so well remember the yell of joy that went up from all of us when he told us who he was."[26]

R. G. Hutchins Jr. was also at the Paris office that day and had been dictating a cablegram on the Cooper case when a young fellow dressed in a corduroy coat, buttoned to the neck with an old sweater sticking out of the collar, sauntered into his office and announced that he was Merian Cooper. "Cooper did not know we were looking him up at all," Hutchins wrote when he returned to his cablegram, relating the breaking news. "He landed in Paris this morning and came to Red Cross Headquarters to seek information as to his observer, who was with him when their plane was shot down behind the German lines. As the people knew that I was interested in the Cooper case they brought him into my office immediately. This boy evidently has had a most thrilling experience and his story was as simple as the story of a child telling of an adventure in an afternoon's play."[27]

Cooper reported the particulars of his adventure to his father on January 23, 1919, with an apology: Because his badly burnt hands were still healing, instead of a handwritten letter he'd had to dictate to a stenographer.

It was after his release from the hospital—after the Armistice—that Merian learned he had been promoted to captain in the Air Services, a rank set from August 1, 1918.[28] He was recuperating from his war wounds in Silesia, a little town near Breslau, Poland, when a number of fellow prisoners, including Russians who spoke English or French, told Cooper of the ambitions of bolshevism to conquer the world. Cooper was convinced that communism and America were on a collision course, and he later marked the end of 1919 and early 1920 as the beginning of his lifelong crusade against the Communists.

ON THE FIRST Christmas Eve of the Armistice, Cooper and Buck Crawford had a joyful reunion in Paris. They headed to Montmartre, and the raucous hours till dawn were a blur of cafés, cabarets, and dancing girls as they spent all the months of back pay that had accumulated while they'd languished as prisoners of war. But when Buck headed back to his hotel, Cooper set off for the train station. He had been directed by General Headquarters to assist in determining the fate of those squadron comrades who had been lost in the bombing mission over Dun-sur-Meuse. Only two of the seven planes had made it home, one bearing pilot Clarkson Potter and his observer, Shultz; the other, pilot Sidney Howard and his dead observer, Lieutenant Ed Parrott. Howard would go on to a storied writing career, including writing the screenplay for *Gone With the Wind*.[29]

Cooper was met at the station by Thomas Rhinelander and Mrs. Clarkson Potter, who'd come to find their lost sons. In one of the tragic vagaries of war, young Potter had survived the September 26 air battle only to be reported killed during a mission on October 10. In the gray light of that Christmas morning the parents looked "worn by sorrow," Cooper recalled. He knew that what awaited them in the wasteland once known as the front was not the promise of life, but the twisted steel of downed planes, the shallow graves of dead pilots—the young men who were his friends and comrades.[30]

Thomas Rhinelander had already found his son's grave on the second day of his trip to Europe, in the village cemetery of the little town of Murville, ten miles northwest of Briey, where villagers told of watching the aerial battle and how the plane piloted by young Phil Rhinelander and his observer, Harvey C. Preston, valiantly fought five of the Fokkers before being downed. But by late January, Mrs. Clarkson Potter still hadn't found her son's final resting place.[31]

Cooper accepted his assignment with grim determination, even reporting on dead or missing aviators from other squadrons. He questioned

French villagers to learn what had happened to the bodies of pilots, made arrangements through the families of the dead to have their sons' foreign graves tended and blessed with flowers, found plane wrecks and utilized scraps of information, such as a downed plane's serial number, to solve the mystery of each crew's fate.[32]

"I have been in the country we were operating over, hunting for the graves of thirteen of the fellows in our squadron who were killed over enemy lines . . . ," Cooper wrote home. "The French peasants in most of the cases had given the boys funerals and had made crosses for their graves which they had strewn with flowers. In one instance the French girls had made a funny little American flag which they had placed on the grave of one man. They said in making it they had wept . . . it wasn't much like an American flag. The stripes were wrong, and it only had four stars, but to see it resting on this single grave in a lonely field it almost made me cry too. Many of my best friends were killed. I found the graves of the six American officers who were killed in the fight in which I was shot down. I sure wish the war wasn't over so I could go back and have another crack at the Boche."[33]

In a February 17, 1919, letter dictated to his father, Merian enclosed a copy of a German newspaper he had saved from prison camp that told of the kaiser's abdication, and Cooper's own recommendation for the Distinguished Service Cross—which he had refused. "It is my earnest request that you do not show this recommendation for the D.S.C. outside of the family, or make any talk about it," Merian cautioned, adding in a postscript: "This recommendation for the D.S.C. overestimates my work—Chief reason for my refusal."[34]

In an official letter to the "Chief Decorations Section," Cooper stated: "I consider it sufficient honor to have served with the squadron . . . and I would feel in receiving any honor or decoration that I would be dishonoring my dead and living friends."[35]

There was one government certificate from the war that Coop happily treasured and that seemed to sum up his personal redemption: the official United States Army death certificate "in memory of Merian C. Cooper," signed by General John J. Pershing, commander in chief. Above the death notice, handwritten in ink at some unknown point in time, someone would add: "In the language of Mark Twain your death has been greatly exaggerated."[36]

CHAPTER FIVE

THE KOŚCIUSZKO SQUADRON

> *Your son and I have been fighting literally shoulder to shoulder*
> *against one of the hardest propositions that I have ever seen.*
> *Aviation in open warfare means hard, exciting dangerous work*
> *and plenty of it. . . . Flying and fighting, it seemed the entire day,*
> *he [seems] to be absolutely tireless and fearless. The hotter it was*
> *the better he liked it. He is already the hero of this city [Lwów],*
> *because of his previous [humanitarian] work here, and if he keeps*
> *on at the rate he is going he will surely become one of Poland's*
> *National Heroes.*
>
> —Colonel Cedric Fauntleroy, commander of
> the Kościuszko Squadron, to John Cooper[1]

THE MAN WHO WOULD BECOME MERIAN COOPER'S GREAT PARTNER IN ADVEN-
ture, Ernest B. Schoedsack, was born in Council Bluffs, Iowa, in 1893, the
son of Gustav and Ruth Schoedsack. A restless youth, he began running
away from home when he was twelve, an urge he later ascribed to such influences as Robert Louis Stevenson's *Treasure Island.*[2] When Ernest turned seventeen and graduated from high school, he headed west and arrived,
penniless, in San Diego. Park benches became his bed, the California sky the
roof over his head. He knocked about the state, worked as a deckhand on a
boat to San Francisco, and joined engineering road gangs as a surveyor.[3]

Schoedsack also had a stint in Hollywood as a cameraman, filming the
likes of Wallace Beery and Mabel Normand on the old Mack Sennett lot. As
photogenic a presence as the subjects for whom he cranked his cameras,
Schoedsack stood six foot six, with long, wavy black hair and a physique
that combined the lean and muscular frame of Gary Cooper with the boyish demeanor of Jimmy Stewart.

Schoedsack had found his calling. When World War I began, he joined the U.S. Signal Corps to film the war, and headed to Château-Thierry. But things were so badly organized he couldn't get a light Debrie camera and was saddled with a bulky Bell & Howell.

"They didn't even issue me a helmet, nor a gas mask," he recalled for film historian Kevin Brownlow. ". . . So we came to the combat zone and they wouldn't even let me through because I didn't have a helmet or a gas mask! But there were some graves along the road and I got a helmet that hung on one of the graves. The helmet was bashed in on one side and that was the one I wore. The name 'Kelly' was on the inside. I got his gas mask, too. That's all I had."[4]

In the war's aftermath, Schoedsack found himself in Vienna, helping desperate refugees flee the Russians. One day, at the Franz Josef Railroad Station, Schoedsack saw a short, husky young fellow—his physical opposite and a curious sight to behold.

"Down a platform came this Yank," Schoedsack recalled, "wearing one French boot and one German one, and he was wearing a U.S. Navy sword. It was Coop. He was just out of a German prison and he wanted to get to Warsaw. He had once been kicked out of the Naval Academy and had sold his sword. Now he found the guy who had it and he'd bought it back."[5]

Because the war had torn up transportation systems throughout Europe, it had been a circuitous journey through Italy and Vienna for Cooper, who was headed to Poland. Before meeting Schoedsack he'd stopped in Venice for three days and had gone to an American destroyer for an appointment with a fellow stationed at the ship. Howard Chapman was the Annapolis man from whom Cooper would buy back the Naval Academy graduation sword he had sold when he washed out.[6]

Though brief, Cooper's chance encounter with Schoedsack changed both their lives. Separately, each would get their fill of adventure in Poland, which, in the confluence of postwar upheavals, was the site of one of the biggest of the unfolding dramas.

Russia and Prussia had brutally occupied and oppressed the Polish people for generations, but with a push from Polish statesman Ignacy Paderewski and U.S. president Woodrow Wilson, the Allies who had just won the Great War certified Poland as an independent state. Poland celebrated its newly won independence on May 3, 1919. However, the Treaty of Versailles had not resolved many of Poland's territorial concerns in the eastern borderlands of Lithuania, Byelorussia, Eastern Galicia, and the Ukraine. Lithuania and Eastern Galicia, with its major cities of Wilno and Lwów, respectively, were of particular importance to Poland as centers of Polish history and culture. Soviet Russia had its own territorial designs and did not feel bound by the terms of the Armistice—indeed, the Allies did not even have diplomatic representatives in Moscow.

The Poles were already wary of the revolutionary Bolsheviks who had come to power under Vladimir Lenin. In late April 1920, Poland launched a preemptive strike at Ukraine and captured the city of Kiev. In response, Lenin unleashed his Red Army, which quickly drove the Poles out of Ukraine. Against the advice of Joseph Stalin, Lenin ordered the Red forces to follow the routed Poles into their homeland. "It would be the Soviet Union's first penetration into Europe proper," historians Lynne Olson and Stanley Cloud note, "the first attempt to export the Bolshevik Revolution by force. Less than two years after regaining its independence, Poland was in mortal danger of losing it again."[7]

SCHOEDSACK WOULD RECALL the Polish-Russian campaign as "a great time." He did everything from driving ambulances to leading Polish refugees to safety. Most of all, though, Schoedsack was there to capture history on film.

For Cooper, an intensely personal promise was keeping him in Europe— he was still on the road to redemption. "I surely would like to see Jacksonville," he wrote his father. "It is the place of all my dreams, and I think about it like a good Catholic does of heaven, but you know I have to carry out my vow first, so I will have to stick to the high roads . . . you know I must do what is right, and I must carry on like I said I would. I will come home in a manner to make you proud of me, or I will not come home at all."[8]

World War I had been fought and won, but Cooper felt that the threat to global peace wasn't over—not with Russian bolshevism on the march. He had written to the General Staff in France offering to go to Russia as an American officer or resign to join the White Russian forces battling the Bolsheviks (the Reds would ultimately win the Russian civil war). When there was no movement on his request, the restless Cooper asked to be sent to Poland with the humanitarian food mission being spearheaded by future American president Herbert Hoover. "Here I learned more about Bolshevism, and finally determined to get in the fight against it," Cooper explained in a 1920 letter from Poland to Senator Duncan Fletcher.[9]

One of Cooper's major assignments was in Eastern Galicia, in the besieged town of Lwów (also known as Lemberg) where his responsibilities included seeing that some twenty thousand children were fed. Coop was contentious when dealing with the various political factions in the coun-

ALTHOUGH COOPER HAD TO REMAIN NEUTRAL DURING HIS HUMANITARIAN WORK IN POLAND, THAT DIDN'T PREVENT HIM FROM GOING UNARMED TO THE TRENCHES. HE WRITES ON THE BACK OF THIS PHOTOGRAPH: "A POLISH LT. AND I IN FRONT OF POLISH BARRICADE. THIS SPOT IS SWEPT BY UKRANIAN [*SIC*] MACHINE GUN FIRE BUT WE WERE UNDER THE WHITE FLAG OF TRUCE TO LET AN ITALIAN CAPTAIN THROUGH TO SEE ABOUT FORMER ITALIAN PRISON- ERS IN AUSTRIA. TAKEN BY THE ITALIAN LT. WITH MY CAMERA. ON RETURNING THE ITALIAN LT. AND I WERE FIRED ON BY ANOTHER DETACHMENT OF UKRANIANS [*SIC*], AND HAD A CLOSE CALL OF IT."

Cooper Papers, BYU

try—he wrote his father despairing at his short fuse of a temper—but he became a legend for his tireless efforts to bring food to the starving population. Although he was still a member of the U.S. Army, as a humanitarian agent Cooper had to remain a neutral and was forbidden to carry arms. Still, he made regular visits to the trenches and firing lines, earning the undying respect of the embattled Poles.

By now, Merian's war burns had healed, without scarring (although his scrawl of a handwriting would ever after attest to some loss of sensitivity in his fingers). During his time in Poland, he also pursued romantic interests, and in a letter to his father he alluded to a serious relationship: "I thought for a while I might marry a Polish girl over here, but I guess she is a lot too good for me, so I have given it up. I have decided to be the bachelor of the family. No women for me. I know I could never get along with one over a week at the longest and besides I am too bad an egg to ask a nice girl to tie herself to me for life. I've done too many bad things in my day to ask that of anyone."[10]

Cooper saw other women in Poland, including an American he later recalled dancing with at a hotel in Warsaw: Marguerite Harrison, who soon thereafter played a pivotal role in his life.

In his old age, when outlining the autobiography he never wrote, Cooper drafted a list of high points from this time. Below "City with roof of gold" and "Kiev" he wrote the words "Beautiful Polish girl." Elsewhere on that typewritten page he'd captured a shining fragment of memory: "The day I flew down a street in Kiev, with a wing almost shot off, so I could wave to my beautiful luscious blonde—and have her blow a kiss at me and if that wasn't worth risking your life for, I don't know what is—particularly as I had a date with her that night (if I didn't get assinated [*sic*] on the way to her flat—and that almost happened too)."[11]

But other than the occasional dalliance, Merian took hold of his humanitarian work in Lwów with a firm hand. In addition to coordinating food deliveries and preparing in-depth reports on conditions in the region, he showed an instinct for propaganda and psychological warfare. He contacted newspapers in Lwów, lobbied for prominent display of all information related to distribution of food supplies, and urged a "pitiless... relentless war" against black market profiteers. He asked that the papers not write in the abstract or generalize the problem, but hire detectives to ferret out the "vile extortioners" and publish their names and addresses in bold headlines, along with complete details as to their black market transactions. "They should be branded as thieves and murders [*sic*] of children and the poor," Cooper declared.[12]

The relief effort proved as dangerous as his combat duty in France. Merian provided his father with a firsthand account of the siege of Lwów, where a ragtag army of Poles that included women and boys was holding out against desperate odds. Only three weeks before, he reported, Ukrainian forces had managed to take some fourteen kilometers of railway, and that effectively cut the Poles off from the world. Merian had arrived with the army that reopened the lines of communication, and the people were praying the railroad could be repaired. "The first provisions will come in tonight by automobile trucks," he wrote. "Tomorrow we hope that the trains will come through. . . .

"Here a patriotism is exhibited which baffles all description. It is hard enough to be brave in a long defensive battle at any time, but to fight on an empty stomach, with the body weakened by weeks of near starvation, with one's wife and children in the extremities of hunger—to fight on, and to [ask] 'no surrender' is a thing for the Gods to praise and envy. Every day I wish that I was in the trenches too, or flying here if there was any air service (there are 3 or 4 broken down old planes), but I am a neutral and we are supposed to be friends with both sides. However, I am glad to do what work I can, and to think that if anything saves this city, American food will save it. Thank God for that."[13]

One damp, cold day Cooper visited the muddy trenches where the fighting women were holding the line. Many weren't expert at firearms; some closed their eyes and fired over the heads of their targets. But their dedication and ferocity kept the enemy at bay. Among them was a young American from Chicago who had her rifle and a bandolier of cartridges slung over her shoulder and a combat decoration pinned to her blouse. Cooper stood, shivering in his overcoat, as the woman explained to him that she'd come to Poland in 1914 to visit her grandparents and was caught when the Great War broke out. "But here there is still war," she said, proudly throwing her head back. "And I fight for the new freedom of Poland. It is good to fight for that."

As Cooper watched her turn and slog back to her position in the muddy trench, her words echoed in his head: *It is good to fight for that!*[14]

Cooper burned to fight for Poland. In another undated, handwritten letter to his father—a correspondence that formed an emotional lifeline to home and a more peaceful world—he recalled the childhood stories that had led him to this war-torn place.

"It grieves me every day that I am doing so little for the cause of Polish liberty, when Pulaski did so much for us, and I always remember the stories you have told me of how he died in my ancestor's arms. . . . If I can return that debt to Poland at any time I stand ready to do so. But, don't worry at all, because my work is very peaceable indeed—too D——d peaceable."[15]

There was even a hint that he went beyond the restraints imposed by his status as a humanitarian agent. A 1920 Polish newspaper article noted that, during the defense of Lwów, Cooper "organized an action bringing up at his expense and that of his comrades, thirty orphan defenders."[16]

Cooper finally requested a transfer out of his humanitarian duties, and William R. Grove, chief of mission to Herbert Hoover, the "U.S. Food Administrator" in Paris, recommended Cooper's request. "Captain Cooper has handled a very difficult relief situation in the City of Lemberg during the siege," Grove wrote, "and has the universal respect of all the parties and factions in that town." The request was approved "By Authority of Herbert Hoover," on June 2, 1919.[17]

Cooper personally lobbied Poland's head of state, Marshal Józef Piłsudski, asking to become a pilot in the Polish air force, evoking the selfless spirit of Pułaski and Kościuszko. With Piłsudski's blessing, Coop went to Paris to recruit an all-American squadron to fight alongside the Polish airmen. His first recruit was a tall, lean pilot from Mississippi, someone he had met at a sidewalk café and who went by the flowery name of Cedric Errol Fauntleroy, thanks to a mother who had been infatuated with the story of Little Lord Fauntleroy.

The saving grace was that "Faunt," like Merian, had also grown up with tales of the great Polish patriots of the Revolutionary War, notably Tadeusz Kościuszko. The resulting unit would be named for Kościuszko, and although the squadron had been Cooper's idea, because of Colonel Fauntleroy's higher rank he was given command, with Captain Merian Cooper second in succession.

No matter. Coop's fellow southerner was an experienced, battle-tested pilot who'd flown with Eddie Rickenbacker's squadron and was a tough guy; with a name like Fauntleroy, he'd grown up learning how to fight.[18]

In addition to Coop and Faunt, the charter members of the Kościuszko Squadron included Captain A. H. Kelly of Richmond, Virginia; Captain Edward Corsi of Brooklyn; Lieutenants Edwin Noble and E. P. Graves of Boston; Lieutenant Carl Clark of Tulsa, Oklahoma; Lieutenant Kenneth O. Shrewsbury of Charleston, West Virginia; Lieutenant Elliott W. Chess of El Paso, Texas; and Cooper's old friend from the 20th Aero Squadron, Lieutenant George W. "Buck" Crawford of Wilmington, Delaware.[19]

The squadron, hailed as the "Flying Yankees," also established itself as a far-flung post of the American Legion after a chance meeting between Cooper and George Palmer Putnam, who'd come to Europe after attending a Legion organizing caucus in St. Louis. They'd sat in one of Europe's oldest wine shops and discussed the Legion over a powerful honey liqueur. The next day the squadron joined the Legion. Putnam would write that the first reason the Americans enlisted in the Polish cause was to fight bolshevism; the second was "the lure of adventure."[20]

"[POLISH STATESMAN IGNACY] PADEREWSKI RECEIVING THE KOSCIUSZKO SQUADRON IN PARIS GIVING ME THE GLAD PAW," SQUADRON LEADER COOPER WROTE ON THE BACK OF THIS PHOTOGRAPH.

Cooper Papers, BYU

MERIAN COOPER WOULD estimate his time in active combat in Poland from January 1920 to a fateful July 13, during which he flew more than seventy combat missions. The squadron's main aircraft were the single-seater Austrian Albatross D-3 Chasse aeroplanes, equipped with 220 H. P. Daimler motors, for which Cooper and Fauntleroy developed a method of low-level bombardment by fastening crude bombs to their planes.[21] The Flying Yankees became the scourge of the feared Cossack cavalry commanded by General Semyon Budenny, striking the enemy as they attempted to sweep through eastern Poland for Warsaw, buying time by delaying the Bolsheviks' advance with their lethal anti-infantry bombing tactics, which recalled St.-Mihiel and Argonne. In a one-two punch, the bombers would glide over the Cossack columns at six hundred feet and drop their bombs by hand, then dive down to strafe the scattered cavalry with machine-gun fire, pulling up only a few dozen feet from the ground. They'd then pursue and pick off the fleeing Cossacks.[22]

The Kościuszko Squadron's renown and success had its price: The Yanks knew that downed pilots captured by the enemy were in danger of torture and death. Cooper, as co-leader with Fauntleroy, had the additional burden of a price on his head, so he flew each mission with a vial of poison. "I was very afraid of torture," Cooper later admitted. "I was determined to kill myself rather than die more slowly at the hands of the Cossacks. They had an unpleasant trick of nailing an officer's stars to his shoulders and, as I had three stars on each shoulder, the idea was rather an objectionable one to me."[23]

The fighting was furious and relentless. In one two-month stretch, the squadron moved six times and Cooper participated in sixteen raids. At one point, with Fauntleroy off on a mission to Warsaw, Cooper took command of the squadron. He would later proudly report that upon Faunt's return, he'd suffered only one dead, one wounded, and two lost planes.[24]

By June 1920, luck seemed to have run out for both Cooper and Buck Crawford. The two made an emergency landing in an open field in heavily forested country, where they were discovered by some of General Budenny's fearsome Cossack cavalry. The two Americans manned their machine guns and fired at the Cossacks. They were hopelessly outnumbered, but Coop and Crawford set fire to their plane and, under cover of the flames, plunged into the woods and miraculously escaped.[25]

Later that month, while enjoying rest and reorganization, the squadron was honored by a grateful Polish government.[26] Merian, reflecting on the medals and honors, wrote a letter that was equal parts optimism and foreboding: "We succeeded in checking the Cossack cavalry long enough to help the Polish infantry get out of the trap in their retreat from Kiev. We are all feeling pretty set up just now, as the squadron [received] a citation in the orders of the whole Polish army. Our big job . . . is attacking ground troops at low altitude, and I'm afraid we're pretty sure to lose more men in the next show."

Within a month, one of those lost men would be Cooper himself, while south of Lutsk. While leading an air attack on General Budenny's Cossack cavalry, Colonel Fauntleroy would be wounded in his right arm and leg by rifle fire.[27]

The *American Legion Weekly* summed up the saga of the Flying Yankees in vivid, dramatic terms:

> Hovering over the field of battle before the gates of Warsaw . . . was a group of planes that bore the white eagle of Poland. In these planes, their fingers to the triggers of machine guns, were men of the American Legion—the swift flying, chance-taking adventurers of the Kosciusko Squadron Post, every man of whom had known what it was in the old days to tackle the Hun avion above the blazing fronts of France. . . .
>
> They have done heroic work, have these American fliers, since last autumn they entered the service of Poland and almost at the same time formed their Post of the Legion. But all the charter members are not present today. . . . The last word of Captain Merian C. Cooper, of Jacksonville, Fla., listed him among the missing, and there are others who also vanished in the smoke of battle. . . .
>
> On a distant front under another eagle than that of their native land, the Legionnaires of Kosciusko Post have been making history. The membership of their post is dwindling slowly; shrapnel and machine gun bullets are taking a toll of men that can not be replaced.[28]

Once again Cooper had "vanished in the smoke of battle." Once again he was given up for dead, as a Polish newspaper article noted: "Captain Pilot Merian Cooper, the American, who met with such a tragic end and on the field of glory . . . loved Poland from his earliest years . . . and when an opportunity arose decided to serve her with his life. . . .

"Honor to his memory."[29]

WHAT PROVED ONE of the grimmest ordeals of Merian Cooper's life and the ultimate test of survival began on July 13, 1920, when he set out on a strafing mission with a group of fliers. Cooper was piloting a new, single-seater Italian Bellia airplane on another low-flying mission. Since he wasn't going into the cold of higher elevations, he'd decided to leave behind his heavy coat with its officer insignia and put on the secondhand BVDs he'd gotten a few weeks before, long underwear stenciled across the chest with the name "F. M. Mosher." Both decisions were among the intangibles of fate that saved his life.[30]

On July 12, the day before Cooper's fateful combat mission, his new friend Ernest Schoedsack was in Ukraine as the Polish lines, which had been occupying Kiev and bravely holding out, were ordered into full retreat. In spite of the chaotic exodus, Schoedsack coolly recorded all that he could with his movie camera. "The high point of the Polish adventure was, for me, at Kiev, when the great retreat began," Schoedsack once explained. "I was the last to get across the great Dnieper Bridge and the excited Poles blew it up on my heels, but I did get a chance to turn around and get the thing coming down—with a motion picture camera."[31]

About the time Schoedsack was making it across the Russian lines to Warsaw, his friend Cooper was falling out of the sky into enemy territory near Eastern Galicia. Cooper had been separated from the rest of the mission as the planes split up to attack the Cossacks. During the battle his fellow pilots, busy with their own maneuvers, didn't notice the absence of Cooper's plane or that enemy bullets had hit his low-flying Italian Bellia, knocking out a gas tank. Cooper had switched to his reserve tank, but it hadn't taken, and his plane was going down. . . .

As he descended, Cooper saw Cossacks on horseback moving through the forest below, riding hard in pursuit of his falling aircraft. Cooper aimed for a clearing beyond the woods, the ground rushing up at him. He landed at high speed, his wheel hit a ditch, and the impact launched him out of the plane.

He staggered upright, disoriented, and for a moment thought he was walking away from the joyride crash he'd shared with Doc Taylor during pilot training in France.

Cooper stopped; something was holding him back. Then he realized his automatic parachute had pulled loose and opened when he'd been thrown from the plane. He was dragging it behind him.

Even though his enemies were closing in, Cooper blacked out.

PRISONER OF WAR

*It is a very ticklish matter for me to do what I am doing for him
under the circumstances, as you might recognize. . . .
Consequently, I must ask you, for my sake, not to tell any one
unless you subsequently get the information from other sources,
that you have heard from him or know of his whereabouts. The
result for me would be very serious. I shall try to send you news
about him from time to time.*

—Marguerite Harrison, message smuggled
to Merian Cooper's family[1]

COOPER'S EYES OPENED AT THE KICK OF A HEAVY BOOT. HE INSTINCTIVELY FELT
in his pocket for the poison, but the suicide vial was gone, probably lost
when he'd hit the ground. Cooper faced the Cossacks encircling him. He
later recalled the fellow prisoner who perfectly described the hungry look
of the brutal Cossacks as they took a prisoner: "They looked like wild dogs
jumping after a piece of raw meat."

This wild bunch had the solid builds, swarthy complexions, and droop-
ing mustaches of the mountaineers of the Caucasus, but each was dressed
in a different outfit, some reminding Cooper of what Morgan's buccaneers
might have looked like on horseback or the scouts of the American frontier if they had carried sabers. He noticed that they all had whips and
swords, some adorned with jewels and thrust into silver scabbards that
were doubtless trophies of war taken from fallen Russian officers.

The Cossacks roughly pulled off Cooper's oil-stained clothes, stripping
him to his BVDs. As he was being manhandled, he saw a strange sight: a
boy on horseback yelping in triumph while draped in a beautiful green silk

like a fancy Roman toga. The boy, Cooper realized, was wearing his parachute.[2]

Cooper was whipped as the Cossacks began shouting in Russian, a language he didn't understand. Forced to march behind the horses and a wagon bearing some of the Cossacks' own wounded, he collapsed so often he was finally thrown into the cart. The procession came to a Bolshevik regiment that had earlier been under fire from Cooper's own squadron. The regiment stopped the wagon and gestured to him, then brought him to a tree and made him stand up on a farm cart. When one of the Cossacks brought out a rope, Cooper realized they were going to have a lynching party, and he was guest of honor.

They dropped the noose around his neck, threw the rope over the overhanging branch, and tied it off.

Then several Cossacks on horseback brandished their swords and one galloped toward him, charging hard, sword raised—slashing within a few inches of Cooper's face. Another horseman rode forward and brought his sword down with equally deadly skill, coming close to clipping off the prisoner's nose. Cooper struggled to keep from screaming for them to get it over with, trying not to show weakness in the face of his impending death.

And then, suddenly, the grim sport ended. A personage who seemed to be a regimental commander appeared and angrily began ordering that Cooper be taken down. Even Cooper's oil-stained trousers were returned to him—"worthless as loot even to Cossacks," he later commented wryly.

It was a two-day march to the brigade headquarters in a Russian village, and Cooper spent the entire time calculating his odds of survival. He reasoned that he had been spared because he was a foreigner, and a potentially valuable prisoner. He was thankful he had flown without his officer's coat and that his hands, still rough from war burns, gave him the appearance of a laborer and simple soldier. But he would certainly be tortured and killed if it was discovered that he was Merian C. Cooper, leader of the Kościuszko Squadron.

Cooper then realized that his BVDs, stenciled with the name "F. M. Mosher," might provide his salvation. It was a long shot, but he decided to become Frank Mosher, a working-class stiff eager for the salvation of the Bolshevik gospel.

It was night when they arrived at brigade headquarters, a humble two-story peasant house with earthen floors. He was led to an inner chamber where two candles glowed over a map spread out on a wooden table. A young Cossack sat behind the table; he wore no official insignia but radiated martial authority. Cooper slumped against the wall opposite his interrogator and an interpreter, his mind seeming to float over the scene, surveying it all with a cinematic eye.

"We must have made a strange picture . . . there against the wall I stood, barefooted, dirty, my clothes torn, and my face scratched and bruised, making every effort to put on a bold, defiant front. . . . With his elbow resting on the table facing me, his face set like granite, and his eyes never shifting from mine, was this young Cossack commander." The tenuous discipline of the march had begun dissipating among the Cossack cutthroats crowding into the room: "Just within the circle of the candle light, their shadows dancing back and forth as they growled at each other, the silver and jewels of their sabers dimly glistening, was this group of wild cavalarists."

Cooper realized that if he was to survive, this was the moment to take the initiative. He stepped forward, extended his rough hands to the commander, and proclaimed, "Work man, work man." He opened his shirt and pointed to the stamped name, repeating he was "Mosher, Frank Mosher."

The ruse worked. That night Frank Mosher dined in Cossack fashion, dipping into a dish of meat and potatoes with six cavalry men. Afterward, Cooper was taken to a peasant house where he spent the night with eleven other prisoners. He was feeling cocksure from the meal and the success of his ruse, but a conversation with a Polish Jew who spoke a little English shocked him out of his smugness with one simple comment: "We go to Rovno tomorrow."

On an earlier mission, Cooper had been at the Rovno railroad station ahead of pursuing Bolsheviks, and had gotten a transport train moving by angrily seeing to the temporary arrest and rough treatment of several Russian railworkers who had tried to obstruct their retreat. They had made it out of the station, the Bolsheviks practically breathing down their necks, but those railroad workers knew his face and name.

The next morning Cooper was again on the move, but so weak he could barely walk. He was put in a horse-drawn wagon with two other wounded Polish prisoners and followed by three mounted guards. Cooper would recall that it was a strangely beautiful day. He even saw a plane passing overhead and later learned it had been one of his squadron, searching for him.

It was almost midnight, the third day of Cooper's captivity, when their procession left the wooded countryside for the great broad road that led into Rovno. The night became wild with a thunderstorm, torrential rain drenching them as lightning flashes illuminated scenes of dead men and horses and overturned wagons, the wreckage left in the wake of the Polish retreat that had occurred the day of Cooper's fateful mission. At the sight of dead horses, the tamer horses pulling the wagon began shying, while the Cossack steeds reared and snorted. The fury of the beasts "seemed to stir all the wild blood in our guards," Cooper recalled. The riders rose up in their stirrups with each lightning flash and crash of thunder. The storm's fury and their relentless march to Rovno only reminded Cooper that the mask of Frank Mosher wouldn't save him if they reached the train station.

But fate again spared Cooper.

The news came that the railroad station at Rovno wasn't operating; they'd be continuing on foot another 125 miles to the town of Zytomir. Before leaving, Cooper was herded into a room holding some fifty Polish prisoners. He was praying to be lost in some prison camp among the Poles, his identity as an American forgotten, when one of his captors called out: "*Mosher!*" He came forward and was taken several hundred yards to a private home. This wasn't the rough peasant home where he had first been interrogated but a spacious, comfortable place. Cooper realized he was in General Budenny's own headquarters! And then he was escorted into the presence of the man himself.

Merian Cooper would spend his entire life opposing the Communists, but something about his soldier's code of honor allowed him to be impressed with anyone—friend or foe—whose actions commanded respect, and he respected this fellow warrior. Budenny, a man of some forty years, possessed a stern face and piercing eyes; despite an ill-fitting coat and Russian leather cap, Cooper's instant impression was that here "was a soldier . . . there was something about his entire aspect that told of the open sky and windswept fields of long nights and wild marches." Cooper knew that Budenny had risen from the rank of noncommissioned officer to command of a formidable cavalry, that he was said to have killed almost two dozen Poles with his own saber.[3]

Budenny first asked, through an interpreter, what Frank Mosher thought of being a prisoner. Cooper replied he'd rather have shot himself through the head. The conversation then settled into a more intimate conversation, man to man. "As such, I will always have a great respect for him," Cooper later wrote.

It was clear to Budenny that his prisoner was one of the volunteer fliers, and he asked, *Why* would an American fight for the Poles? Cooper replied that Poland had been a divided country for too long, oppressed by other nations, of which Russia had been the most brutal. Budenny then asked Mosher about the leadership of the American squadron, particularly Colonel Fauntleroy and Captain Cooper. "I gave them both a splendid reputation—especially Captain Cooper," Coop recalled wryly. Budenny must have bought Cooper's deception, for he even attempted to persuade the pilot to join the Bolshevik cause as an aviation instructor, an offer Cooper refused.[4]

During a break in the interrogation, Cooper was dismissed to another room, where he saw a Russian woman in a blue gingham dress who reminded him of a simple farmer's wife. It was Budenny's wife, a woman said to have several times dressed as a man to ride on raids alongside her husband and his Cossack horsemen. The woman left the room and returned with lavish gifts of white bread, cherries, and packs of cigarettes for Frank Mosher.

After his ordeal, Cooper learned why Budenny and his wife had treated one of the Kościuszko fliers with such respect. In the past, the squadron had had the chance to bomb Budenny's private train, but knowing the general's wife was aboard, they'd allowed it to pass. Cooper would later feel that some "divine force" had guided his comrades in this exhibition of martial honor, a compassion that was returned when Coop's life was in the balance and he was accorded the kindness of the wife of his enemy, who treated him more like a son than a prisoner. Cooper even felt like "a dog ... a fake and a fraud" for the falsehoods of fake identity and phony testimony made to this "splendid woman."

When Cooper returned to his fellow prisoners, he shared the cherries and cigarettes, keeping only a pair of shoes Mrs. Budenny gave him.

That night, Cooper was separated from his fellow prisoners and taken to a large truck, with two guards accompanying him. They drove some fifty miles before he and the guards continued on foot. They marched through familiar territory, passing the very house where, only a month before, Colonel Fauntleroy had maintained an office. In front of the house, Cooper saw the same little girl he'd often greeted with a smile and a chocolate bar, but he passed her unrecognized; as Mosher he was a worn and bedraggled prisoner, not the proud officer and flying ace that the little girl had known.

As they walked along country roads through Jewish villages, Cooper felt the palpable fear engendered by the Russians. But despite their fears, the Jewish farmers and villagers took pity on him and provided comfort during the march, as he later wrote in gratitude: "They seemed to look upon me as a dead man already. . . . But when I was tired and hungry and heartsick they fed me and gave me drink and I washed my face and hands in their house."

Three weeks after his capture, which included a desperate escape attempt that failed, Cooper arrived in Moscow with the shoes Mrs. Budenny had given him slung over his shoulder, his guards marching alongside. He saw an entire population starving, a civilization on the brink of collapse.

"Moscow is dying," he thought.[5]

"THE BOLSHEVIKI MAY have written 'thirty' after the name of big-hearted Captain Marion [*sic*] Cooper to mark the end of his career," read a newspaper report from the Polish front, dated July 20, 1920. The grim mention of "thirty"—old-time newspaper slang for the ending of a story—noted that Cooper's comrades had flown into enemy territory in a fruitless effort to find him. The article also, however, included a hopeful note: "The American flyers, most of whom knew Cooper when he was a pilot in the Twentieth American squadron on the western front, swear by him as a man who 'will pull himself out of any hole if it is humanly possible.' "[6]

In Jacksonville, the Cooper family once again suffered the anxiety of wondering if Merian was dead or alive. Meanwhile, Senator Duncan Fletcher used every available diplomatic and political channel to learn his fate. Fauntleroy wrote Merian's father in early August, promising that if a proposed armistice with the Bolsheviks came off he'd immediately set out with a motorcar in search of his comrade.[7]

But in mid-August a telegram came to Senator Fletcher from the American chargé d'affaires in Warsaw reporting that the Kościuszko Squadron had abandoned hope that their missing comrade would be found alive. "For your confidential information," the report grimly added, ". . . Captain Cooper carried on his person prussic acid with a view to escaping the possibility of capture by the Reds."[8]

MERIAN WAS ALIVE, if not well, and being shuttled from prison camp to prison camp around Moscow.[9] But his captors couldn't imprison Cooper's restless mind, and his thoughts drifted to his old life, particularly the hard time when he was bumming around after Annapolis. He remembered, like a vivid dream, the city where he'd pawned his suitcase for $1.50 and found a boardinghouse where for a dollar a week he flopped in the attic, portioning out the remaining fifty cents for bakery buns that cost a nickel for a half dozen. Back then, haggard and hungry, he had dreamed of beef and potatoes and paused at diner windows to watch fry cooks at their griddles turning pancakes and waffles. But he had also paused at bookstore windows and lingered over the leather-bound treasures behind the glass. "Book hunger," he called it, and book hunger won out over food, leading him to a public library where he could properly gorge himself on words.

Now, in the Russian prison camps, he relived those wandering months. He was again starving, subsisting on a basic daily prison ration of a half pound of bread. But that old book hunger was also gnawing at him.

He satisfied himself at the second camp to which he was relocated, one that was an exception in its humane treatment of its prisoners, with decent food, a more educated class of prisoner—and hundreds of books. But then he got the news that he was being transferred again, to a camp that was typically Spartan and tough. He would be allowed to bring along no more than four books, and he picked them with care: *Sesame and Lilies* by John Ruskin, *Mightier Than the Sword* by Alphonse Courlander, *The New Machiavelli* by H. G. Wells, and *The Four Feathers* by A. E. W. Mason. He stuck the precious volumes in a bag he called the Enchanted Sack, and from there he would draw respite from the physical and mental punishments he later bitterly described as the earliest Communist psychological-warfare techniques.

Winter weather had arrived when he was assigned to work with a railroad gang. He would leave his wooden bunk in the long room he shared with eighty other prisoners and suffer the sting of sleet and wind as he swung his ax to crack apart the ice that had gathered along the tracks. He felt himself skittering along the razor's edge of madness—he laughed at memories of the soft ways of women and the civilian life, so alien to him now. He would scratch the beginnings of his scraggly beard, look at his tattered clothes, and mutter to himself.

But at night, as his fellow prisoners restlessly tossed in what passed for sleep, Cooper would pull a book from the Enchanted Sack, read by a fire, and set his imagination free. The book that most inspired him when his courage and strength flagged was the novel *The Four Feathers*. Because of his getting washed out of Annapolis, Cooper identified with Harry Faversham, the soldier presented with the four white feathers symbolizing cowardice by three fellow soldiers and his own fiancée. But Harry—like Cooper—won back his honor in bloody battle in Africa and returned those feathers.

"I read how Harry suffered real hardships and real torture," Cooper later wrote. "I see him bareheaded under a burning sun, in a dirty little Soudan town, with parching lips and bleeding body; I see him . . . fighting to stay on his feet amid a mob of howling blacks night after night.

"When these visions had passed, then I thought of my own slight discomforts, and knew them to be nothing."[10]

FOR JOHN COOPER in Jacksonville, the big break came in the form of a typed letter dated "Moscow, September 20" from one "M. E. Harrison," a female reporter from the *Baltimore Sun* and Associated Press who had discovered Merian in the Koschukovski camp.

"I discovered his whereabouts by accident, in pretty poor physical condition, but have been able to send him everything he needs," Marguerite Harrison assured the family. "He has not been wounded, [and] is living under pretty trying conditions, but he is keeping his nerve, which is the main thing. There is no chance for him to get out until peace is signed, but as I am detained here with other Americans, I will see that he is well provided for as long as he is here."[11]

Harrison enclosed a smuggled strip of torn paper one and a half inches wide and five inches long. In the upper-left-hand corner the number 1020 was printed in black, and the paper, possibly torn from an accounting ledger, had a faintly penciled message almost entirely without punctuation: "Dear Dad: My address: Corporal Frank Mosher prisoner 4608 I am well and carrying on I owe my life to Mrs. Harrison of the Baltimore Sun who found me sick from starvation and cold and who has given me every aid."[12]

Marguerite Harrison had come to Cooper's aid by an accident of fate. She had been doing good works in Moscow, obtaining through the Czechoslovak Red Cross supplies of sugar, coffee, chocolate, condensed milk, and other goods to distribute to the prisoners. One day she was called into the French Red Cross office, where she met a gaunt Yugoslav prisoner who had been allowed the rare privilege of leaving his camp, which held mostly Polish and Hungarian prisoners—without an escort. He had a note for Harrison from an American prisoner named Frank Mosher, who wrote that he had volunteered for service with the Kościuszko Squadron after the Armistice, was in bad condition, and hoped the French Red Cross could help him. Harrison hadn't heard of this man Mosher, but she remembered once meeting a member of the Kościuszko Squadron: Merian Cooper. In any case, it was clear that a fellow American was in desperate condition and had to be helped at all costs.[13]

Harrison arranged for the Yugoslav prisoner to act as their go-between. They would meet at the home of a man who was the agent in Moscow for the American Kodak company, and at their next rendezvous the Yugoslav brought a note in which Mosher listed his need for blankets, food, and toilet articles. "And if you can," the note added, "for God's sake send me some tobacco." The note also asked the name of the American lady he was told was his benefactor. Harrison was afraid to write a note, so she told the Yugoslav to simply speak her name to the grateful prisoner.

"One day I received a note from Mosher, finely written, on cigarette paper, and twisted into a little spill," Harrison recalled.

"My name is not Mosher," the note read. "I am Merian C. Cooper of Jacksonville, Florida, and I met you in Poland. Don't you remember dancing with me in the Hotel Bristol in Warsaw?"[14] (There would be suspicions, among those familiar with Cooper's life story, that he and Marguerite had maintained a brief love affair in Warsaw.) The note begged Harrison to get word of his predicament to his family.

Merian would later learn another side of the benefactress who risked everything to help him. "She was supposedly a correspondent for the *Baltimore Sun,* but she was hired by the U.S. Army as a professional spy, the only one I ever knew," Cooper would one day recall. "She saved my bloody life in prison, no question about it."[15]

MARGUERITE HARRISON, BORN in 1878, was the daughter of Bernard N. Baker, the founder of the Atlantic Transport Company and a trustee at Johns Hopkins University. In 1901, she married Thomas B. Harrison of Baltimore, a wealthy stockbroker. In 1902 they had a son, but Marguerite's domestic life ended with her husband's death in 1915.

"She discovered he really didn't have any money, and she had to get a job," noted Patrick Montgomery, a filmmaker who became intrigued with Harrison's life story. "She had been a society woman, that was the world she knew, and she got a job as a society columnist on the Baltimore paper. At that time, it was unusual for people of her class to work, but she wanted to be a writer, and parlayed this society column into muckraking reporting, investigating the slums of Baltimore and things like that. She aspired to bigger things and talked the paper into paying her way to go to Europe to cover the war even before America got involved. Her son, Tommy, was more or less abandoned by Marguerite, who left him with relatives in Baltimore when she went off to Europe."[16]

It was said that Harrison was among the first English-speaking correspondents to reach Berlin after the Armistice. In September 1919, she returned to the United States, but by the end of October was bound for Poland as a special correspondent for the *New York Evening Post*, with Russia as her ultimate destination. She would later write, "I entered Russia through the Polish Front, without documents or papers on February 8, 1920."[17] During her travels she used her journalist's badge as cover; in fact, she was a spy for the U.S. government.

Her life of intrigue had begun two years earlier, when she'd contacted a family friend in the Department of the Navy, proposing herself as a government agent. On September 15, 1918, Harrison filled out a questionnaire for the Office of Naval Intelligence and followed up with letters noting a preference for working under the army's jurisdiction.[18] On September 28, an agent from the War Department met Harrison at the Emerson Hotel in Baltimore at exactly 3:00 P.M. The resulting report, completed the following day, noted that she was a "cultured lady, a widow . . . of very attractive personality and of high intelligence. . . . She is an accomplished linguist."

Harrison herself proposed that going abroad as a correspondent for the Baltimore paper, writing "harmless feature stories," would provide her with the perfect cover. "She remarked she is fearless, fond of adventure and has an intense desire to do something for her country," the report continued. "I can readily believe her. She also said she is 'callous' as to love affairs and that with her years, she has passed the foolish stage. She could easily be considered ten years younger.

"... I discussed with Mrs. Harrison the necessity for discretion and told her if she did go abroad for us she would have nothing to do with contra espionage. I believe she would be discreet; she impressed me most favorably."[19]

"She went to Moscow from Warsaw, basically on foot," Montgomery recalled. "She was really risking her life, but I think she thought that being a woman and a journalist, she was untouchable. Moscow was basically a police state, and there weren't many Americans and they were probably being watched all the time. She stood out and it was known she was a journalist. And what's the difference between a journalist and a spy? Both are collecting information. They were probably unhappy she was writing about conditions there because they were trying to seal the borders."[20]

On April 14, 1920, a telegram from London reached the War Department, Office of the Chief of Staff, Military Intelligence Division, with bad news: "Mrs. Harrison was arrested by the Bolsheviki because she asked too many questions. This explanation given by the British."[21]

Harrison was placed in solitary confinement, and her arrest made for a dramatic headline in the Baltimore paper: MRS. HARRISON IN DIRE STRAITS IN MOSCOW CELL. The article noted that besides having to endure bad food, she was "denied permission to read or sew." She was soon released, but it was clear that she continued to be under suspicion or, worse, that her cover had been blown altogether. H. N. Brailsford, a journalist and friend who'd visited Marguerite in Moscow, noted "she is very clever in adapting herself ... she has many friends and has endeared herself to many of the foreign colony who were in difficulties." But, he added, she was basically "a hostage under surveillance ... and was finally told she would be allowed to leave Russia only in exchange for someone of real importance; e.g. in return for the release of Eugene Debs," a Socialist Party leader in the United States.[22]

Still in Russia, Harrison remained under a cloud of suspicion when, a few months later, she learned of Cooper's incarceration. She was staying at a hotel for foreigners but was virtually a hostage and under surveillance, as her friend Brailsford would note. Not only was it risky bringing aid to "Frank Mosher"; she also had the burden of knowing his true identity. Harrison took extra precautions, but still managed to get packages to Cooper every week or so, even money and books. This kept up for a month, until Frank Mosher was transferred to another camp.[23]

Harrison also found herself under arrest again, in October 1920, within a month of receiving the note from Merian—the one she'd managed to smuggle out to Jacksonville. The charges against her were full of intrigue: She was accused of being not only an agent for the American government but a counterspy for the Soviets who had double-crossed the Bolsheviks! One of her prime accusers was Louise Bryant, the widow of famed radical journalist John Reed. On January 4, 1921, with the permission of the Soviet government, Bryant sent a wireless telegram to Carl von Wiegand, a correspondent in Berlin, explaining that Harrison had been working as an agent for U.S. Military Intelligence and had visited England, Switzerland, Belgium, Germany, and Lithuania before arriving in Russian territory.

Bryant claimed that Harrison had pretended to be sympathetic to the Russian Revolution and had already gathered so much information on the Russian military that it was with supreme confidence that she had headed to Moscow. When she was finally arrested by the suspicious Soviets, she had confessed all, Bryant declared in her telegram. "She offered information and future services to the Soviet government. . . . As agent of the Soviets, she is responsible for the arrest of many of her compatriots. In some cases she gave correct information, in others absolutely false. As a logical conclusion, her double existence led to her own arrest."[24]

The press back home followed Harrison's ordeal and painted the portrait of a woman of mystery. Was she a spy for America or a "Red agent"? Was she a double agent who double-crossed her Soviet masters or a humanitarian who fearlessly provided aid to suffering prisoners?

Harrison would later admit to acting as a double agent, but claimed that she had, indeed, pulled a double cross. She wrote that after she'd been paroled in April, "pressure" had been brought upon her to work for the Soviet government. "For certain imperative reasons I did not reject the offer but temporized with the Soviet authorities, always refusing to come to a definite agreement, and furnishing them with worthless information, thus affording ample justification for my subsequent arrest in October 1920, and for trial and condemnation to the death penalty had the Soviet government seen fit to impose it."[25]

Despite having the odds stacked against her, Harrison had influential supporters working behind the scenes to secure her release.

While imprisoned, she kept up her morale by applying makeup with her last grains of face powder and using bits of rags or paper to style her hair.[26] Harrison would express relief that during her ordeal she managed to keep Merian Cooper's identity a secret. "When I was arrested later," Harrison recalled, "and cross-examined . . . as to my relations with American and British prisoners, my chief dread was that questions might be asked about Mosher, but his name was never mentioned. I heard nothing more about him for over a year."[27]

IRONICALLY, WHILE COOPER was imprisoned, a Polish counteroffensive led by President Józef Piłsudski turned back the Red tide, sending Russian soldiers retreating into Lithuania and East Prussia and allowing Poland to reclaim most of the territory it had lost in 1919.

On October 12, an armistice was signed in Riga, Latvia, a fact of which "Frank Mosher" would be unaware during his entire imprisonment.[28] The news would have provided little comfort, though, since Cooper had come to know the hell of the execution area, where the sound of rifles boomed before dawn. His psychological torture included being notified three times that his own execution was to take place at dawn—but after each appointed sunrise he lived on, with no explanation for the reprieve.[29]

Years later, Richard Cooper—Merian's son—would recall the time in the prison camps as "the formative part" of his father's life. Richard, born in 1936, would grow up around military commanders and combat veterans and, of course, be regaled with stories of his father's wartime exploits. Of those calls to execution, he would recall his father telling him that at least one time he was actually lined up to be shot, facing down the gun barrel as the trigger was pulled—and clicked, the rifle empty of bullets.

"I remember my dad talking about one hut he was in that had one hundred prisoners and he'd see people kill each other for a piece of bread," Richard said. "By the time he got out of that particular place, he was one of the few survivors—practically the entire one hundred people had rotated out [through killing, disease, and starvation]. He said that from his experience in the camps he resolved never to complain again about a bite of food, and he never did. It marked him, but he never lost his code of honor."[30]

Finally, after ten months of imprisonment, Merian Cooper was convinced that the next time he stood on the firing line there would be real bullets. He and two Polish prisoners, Lieutenant Stanisław Sokolowski and Lieutenant Stanisław Salewski, made a pact for a do-or-die run for the freedom of the Latvian border, hundreds of miles to the west.[31]

Cooper would later describe his final prison as "a forest prison camp" outside Moscow, where each dawn the prisoners would be sent into the surrounding forests and forced to cut wood. They were so emaciated that few guards accompanied them; their captors reasoned that it would be a death sentence for any prisoner who headed off into the wilderness. But on the cold dawn of April 12, the three prisoners—armed only with an old pocketknife between them—took that chance and slipped away.[32]

For the first five days of their escape the three fugitives traveled by jumping freight trains, what Cooper called "American hobo methods." Sometimes they hiked forest trails paralleling the rail lines to the frontier. They usually traveled by night, catching a little sleep during the day. On the rare occasion when they needed assistance, they risked knocking on the doors of peasant homes, which usually opened as the residents received them.[33] "Had many narrow escapes, obliged to remain one night in water to avoid being detected by sentries," Cooper would later relate in a telegram.[34]

Their luck finally seemed to run out the day they took an unfortunate turn on a forest trail—and walked right into the gun barrel of a lone Red soldier. They were placed under arrest and found themselves being marched at gunpoint. Cooper knew that Red guards never traveled alone, and that they would soon be delivered into the custody of the soldier's patrol.

Cooper walked meekly ahead, then suddenly stopped and bent down to tie the string that served as a shoelace. It was a signal they had arranged in case of capture.

"From that stooping position I whirled and tackled the surprised Red guard," Cooper later wrote. "Almost before he hit the ground my Polish comrades, like a pack of wild wolves were atop him each holding one arm pinned while I let go of the guard's leg, yanked out our old single bladed pocket knife, grasped his hair pulled his head back and cut his throat—I knew if we were brought back into a town . . . we were dead men. It was his life or the lives of the three of us."[35]

THE CLOSER THE trio moved to the frontier, the more guards they saw, particularly at railways and bridges. The last days of their escape they stayed off the main roads entirely, moving through the sheltering tangle of heavily wooded countryside. They were tantalizingly close to freedom, but the closer they came to the Latvian border, the thicker the enemy patrols became. It seemed impossible to slip through. Still, there was one place the Red patrols never went, a no-man's-land that was both the fugitives' one sure path to freedom and a deadly obstacle: a thick, fetid, seemingly impenetrable swamp where the slightest misstep would suck the unsuspecting traveler down to a suffocating death in the quicksand-like muck.

One of the Poles found a smuggler who claimed he knew the path through the deadly swamp, and they arranged for him to lead them through. In a region suffering war and starvation, the price was high: an overcoat and a pair of shoes. Sokolowski gave up his overcoat and Cooper sacrificed his shoes, cutting out strips from his tattered shirt to bind and protect his bare feet.[36]

They were almost through the swamp when the smuggler demanded more clothing and money or he'd turn them over to the Bolsheviks. Though he had no shoes to tie, Cooper bent down to signal the two Poles. They quickly pinned the smuggler and covered his mouth to hide his screams as Cooper pulled out the pocketknife. He told his comrades to tell the smuggler they would kill him unless he led them to the frontier as promised. The smuggler violently nodded his head: *Yes!*

It was a moonlit night when the treacherous smuggler finally paused at a clearing in the swamp, pointed to the Latvian border, then disappeared back into the woods.[37] Ahead of them, ghostly in the moonlight, was a cordon of barbed wire, layers upon layers.

It was in agony that the fugitives made their way through the barbed-wire jungle as their clothes were ripped to shreds, their flesh left cut and bleeding.[38] In a letter written many years later to his friend and fellow adventurer Lowell Thomas, Cooper summed up the odyssey: "[We] slept in the snow, slush and ice . . . robbing and begging food from the peasants, until at last, one moonlight night, we braved the Cossack patrols and climbed that 10 foot high, 6 feet broad barbed wire border between Russia and Latvia."[39]

Having won their freedom, the men contacted the American Red Cross, and learned that the fighting between the Poles and the Bolsheviks had already ended. After visiting a delousing station and enjoying a blissful bath, the trio were provided clothing, and the very next day they were on a train to Riga.[40] In a cable Merian sent from Riga, he described the moment they "set foot on Latvian soil two o'clock morning April twenty-third. We came to Amcross in rags and without shoes, hungry and completely fa-

COOPER POSES WITH HIS
FELLOW FUGITIVES AT THE
END OF THEIR RUN FOR
FREEDOM; PHOTOGRAPHED
AT THE LATVIAN BORDER,
MAY 1920.
Cooper Papers, BYU

tigued. Could not have received greater kindness aid and civilization in our home."[41]

At one point, Cooper was taken off the Warsaw-bound train for some medical treatment.[42] But when he finally arrived in Warsaw he was lean and sunburned but in miraculously good health. One of his first acts of freedom was celebrated in an American newspaper article datelined "Warsaw, May 9." "MERIAN C. COOPER ENJOYED SHAVE MORE THAN ANYTHING ELSE AFTER ESCAPE FROM RUSSIAN PRISON CAMP—Jacksonville Aviator Didn't Know War Was Over Until He Made Getaway. Being Feted in Warsaw." The article immortalized the shave and placed Cooper's Poland exploits in the larger, mythic context of his adventures in World War I: "All Warsaw is at the feet of the American ace who was twice shot down from the clouds, twice endured the squalor of prison camps, twice was reported dead."[43]

Cooper was in Warsaw when he received the happy news that his benefactor, Marguerite Harrison, had herself been released from the Red prisons. Cooper met Harrison in the lobby of a Berlin hotel room and his reaction made the papers, from Associated Press wire reports to his hometown paper, all hailing Harrison's role in Cooper's survival and the drama of Merian's messages that she had smuggled out to Cooper's family in Florida.

"I would have gone around the world to see you," Cooper exclaimed, "and tell you I should never have lived to escape if it had not been for the supplies you sent me. The news of your recent release gave me the greatest thrill of my life."[44]

There were honors and the recognition of a grateful government still to come. On May 10, 1921, at the presidential residence, Polish President Piłsudski attended the demobilization of the Kościuszko Squadron. During the ceremony Cooper, Fauntleroy, George Crawford, Edward Corsi, and Elliott Chess were awarded Poland's highest honor, the Virtuti Militari—"the Cross of the Brave."[45]

Cooper wasn't planning on resting on his laurels, though; Americans still languished in the Russian prison camps. On June 7, 1921, he wrote about their plight to his former superior in the American relief effort, Herbert Hoover, who was now secretary of commerce. Hoover's reply assured him the American Friends Service Committee was delivering foodstuffs to American prisoners in Russia.[46]

Cooper also offered to personally lead a strike force to liberate the prisoners. A subsequent letter to Cooper in care of the American Legation in Warsaw, from Charles E. Hughes at the Secretary of State's office, observed that Cooper's "patriotic and self-sacrificing attitude" was understood, but the U.S. State Department couldn't authorize a mission that might result in Cooper's own death and set off grave "international complications." Hughes reported that a "careful handling" of the matter had indeed resulted in freedom for the American prisoners.[47] But Merian's daring proposal won plaudits in the Department of State, with the ambassador to Poland writing Cooper that "even such an impersonal institution . . . was pretty well warmed up by the feeling that we still have the sort of people who would do what you were ready to do for real conviction."[48]

While he was being toasted in Warsaw, Cooper had a liaison with a woman named Marjorie Crosby-Słomczyńska, known as Daisy. After his many months of war and imprisonment, he probably had a need for female companionship that surpassed even his vaunted book hunger. But Marjorie was particularly irresistible to the heroic airman. She was ten years older, beautiful, and worldly. She had been raised in London, in the house

MARJORIE "DAISY" CROSBY-SŁOMCZYŃSKA, LATE 1920S. IN WARSAW, AFTER HIS TRIALS AND TRIBULATIONS AS A PRISONER OF WAR, MERIAN HAD A LOVE AFFAIR WITH DAISY AND A BOY WAS EVENTUALLY BORN OUT OF WEDLOCK.

Collection of Malgorzata Słomczyńska Pierzchalska

of a successful lawyer, and as a teenager had moved with her family to Russia and a glamorous life among the fellow expatriates of the English aristocracy. The Russian Revolution had spurred her move to Poland and the social whirl of the English-speaking community. It was a small group, and it was natural that they would fete the celebrated American and that Marjorie—who had an eye for attractive and charismatic men—would meet him.

Their affair would have a lasting impact: Cooper would return to America but leave behind a son, Maciej Słomczyński.[49]

Through the years, Merian would write and send money to support his former lover and their out-of-wedlock child. But he would never fully embrace Maciej, shunting the boy's existence to the shadows. It was a part of himself that Merian Cooper would keep private, all the way to the grave.

When Cooper finally headed back to America, he stopped to visit his new friend Ernest Schoedsack, who was, by his own admittance, "starving in London on a non-paying newsreel job." There they discussed for the first time the dream of making an epic motion picture that would bring to audiences visions of some mysterious part of the world.[50]

Although Cooper had expressed longing for his Florida roots, he wasn't heading home to Jacksonville. When his boat finally arrived in America, Coop would be seeking his fortune in New York. Many years later, he would recall this period in a letter to Margaret J. Corcoran, the seventeen-year-old daughter of President Franklin Delano Roosevelt's powerful "fixer," Thomas Corcoran. Ostensibly advising her about the craft of writing, the eighteen-page typed letter recalled Cooper's Polish war experiences and his refusal of a sizable land grant and money offered by the grateful Polish government: "I didn't want to profiteer by killing my fellow man—and I had killed a lot of them. So I refused it all.

"I got a nominal job as a purser coming back on a freight line, landed in New York on a cold blowing winter day, with a dollar in my pocket and exactly one dollar—and a Polish overcoat, which was quite warm. My first act was to give the overcoat to the first beggar I saw, and the dollar to the next beggar. And I set out to take New York by storm—absolutely penniless."[51]

It would be a relatively brief respite from adventure. Cooper would begin to fulfill his childhood dream of becoming an explorer on a ship called the *Wisdom II*, which would set sail from Singapore to explore mysterious corners of the world.

SEA GYPSIES

CHAPTER SEVEN

MYSTERIOUS ISLANDS

> *I know of no good reason why she should have been called the* Wisdom *unless it was because the men on her were wise enough not to stay in cities when there was the open sea before them and all the world to roam. . . . for if ever there was a ship in search of all the romance and adventure to be found in the queer corners of the earth this was one. She followed no regular travelled route nor any schedule of time, but sailed where and when she pleased.*

> —Edward A. Salisbury and Merian C. Cooper, THE SEA GYPSY[1]

IN AN UNPUBLISHED MANUSCRIPT WRITTEN WHEN COOPER WAS RESIDING ON Sullivan Street in New York's SoHo district, he recalled the thrill that night when the tramp steamer bearing him from Europe glided into New York Harbor. He'd been away for nearly four long years of war and triumph and suffering.

"The shore breeze beating across my face was a wind from the Land of Lost Desire," he wrote. "The beach line in the distance was the rim which circles Paradise."[2] He had gone to the bridge, where the ship's captain had newspapers that were full of the latest dope on the Roscoe "Fatty" Arbuckle scandal, the screen star whose wild party in a suite at the St. Francis hotel in San Francisco had ended in a woman's death and a manslaughter charge against Arbuckle. But Cooper's attention was on the glittering city spread out before him.

Cooper had missed all the parades that had honored the victorious soldiers of World War I throughout the spring and summer of 1919, marching along Fifth Avenue to the cheers of more than three million people.[3] This first night home, he walked alone up Broadway, but happily, as if in a

THE *WISDOM* DOCKED IN THE SOUTH SEAS.

Cooper Papers, BYU

dream. In his eyes, the America of legend, the oasis of plenty, truly existed! He marveled at the bright lights, clean pavements crowded with people dressed in silks and fine suits and wearing good leather shoes, the streets full of mighty automobiles.

Cooper walked those streets until dawn. It was at the end of that long night that he paused within the shadow of the American dream. He stood in front of the great stone lions flanking the steps of the New York Public Library, which seemed like a temple against ignorance. The great library had been a backdrop for the victory marches and crowds of cheering spectators, but all was now silent and dark. He walked around to Bryant Park, behind the library, where he found huddled masses of gaunt, unshaven men on park benches, stirring from the cramped and troubled slumbers of the long, cold night. Cooper himself wasn't far off from those homeless men, yet, somehow, to a stubborn, ambitious young man who had already endured so much, that made the odds of taking on the big city about right.

It was probably during this New York period that Cooper wrote his essay recalling his childhood tears over the futile adventures of Don Quixote. His writing plunged into a nightmare reverie that seemed to bleed out on paper the hell of prison camps, the terrors of a fugitive, the fear of death. Identifying with Quixote in his own "madness" and suffering "for the honor of my lady," Cooper ended with a nightmare vision: "I must strike through unspeakable opposition, and fight battles every one of which costs me my heart's blood. Day and night I am in straits, for those enemies are so artful that many I struck to death still give themselves the appearance of being alive, changing themselves into all forms, and spoiling day and night for me. . . . Everywhere, and when I should least suspect it, I discovered on the ground the traces of their silvery slime . . . they poured hell into my heart, so that I wept poison and sighed fire; they crouched near me even in my dreams; and I see horrible specters, noble lackey faces with gnashing faces and threatening noses, and deadly eyes glaring from cowls, and white ruffled hands with gleaming knives.

"And even the old woman who lives near me in the next room considers me to be mad, and says that I talk the maddest nonsense in my sleep; and the other night she plainly heard me calling out—'Dulcina [*sic*] is the fairest woman in the world, and I the unhappiest knight on earth; but it is not meet that my weakness should disown this truth. Strike with your own lance, Sir Knight!' "[4]

———

COOPER SETTLED INTO life as a Manhattan émigré by reviving his old newspaper career. This time he would be hired at *The New York Times,* where his work included a series of autobiographical pieces written under the apt byline "A Fortunate Soldier." These would be collected in the book *Things Men Die For,* published by Putnam in 1927 under the alias of "C."[5] His comrade Buck Crawford also joined him in the city, and they took an apartment together.

Christmas 1921 would be another strange, memorable holiday for Cooper. He planned a special party with Buck because the previous Christmas they had been separated, with Buck forced to command the crippled Kościuszko Squadron while Merian suffered in a prison camp. Two days before the holiday, Cooper was home when the phone rang, and he took the call that ended his glorious plans. It was his city editor with a blunt message: "Murder down in Jersey. Twenty minutes to catch the train at the Pennsylvania station. Hurry."

On the train he grabbed a late-edition newspaper to catch up on what had already been reported on the murder case he was being sent to cover. A monster in the guise of a man had lured a four-year-old girl to her death by saying he was Santa Claus. Cooper spent the next couple of days touring the "bits of dingy horror" that he shrugged off as the stock of the news trade: the dirty flat above the bootleg bar where the poor child's body was laid before the half-mad young mother, who muttered profanely in Polish and broken English; the cheap, bare lodging-house room where the killer was said to have lived; the woods a few miles away where he was said to have fled.

The police caught the killer in those woods, and the clock was nearing midnight on Christmas Eve when Cooper found himself in a prison cell with the chief of police and a hard-faced detective, the three of them facing the sullen and defiant prisoner. Cooper would remember how strange it was, how this man had been free only two hours before, yet his existence had suddenly narrowed to a prison cell.

The chief's voice was calm and even, but the hard-faced detective hectored the man to admit the murder. "Yer can all go to Hell," was the angry answer.

The exasperated detective stormed out of the room and returned with a bundle that he tossed over the murderer's knee—the white dress of the little girl, stained with drops of blood and one large stain that reminded Cooper of a rose.

The cell was in complete silence when they clearly heard, from outside the prison walls, a chorus of passing carolers singing: "God rest you merry, gentlemen, / Let nothing you dismay; / Remember Christ our Savior / Was born on Christmas day."

"Far away a clock struck twelve, and the mellow sweet play of chimes told that already it was Christmas," Cooper wrote. "The sound of the carol grew fainter, then died away.

"Silence.

"Then rasping and biting, the voice of the detective: 'You dog! Come clean. Confess.' "

The murderer looked up from the bloody dress and growled, "Yer can all go to Hell." But his defiance would do him no good. A month later he was executed in the electric chair that sat at the end of a narrow hall, a short walk away.[6]

COOPER HAD OTHER goals than to live out his life as an eyewitness and scribe to the "dingy horror" of the news trade. He had twice done his honorable duty as a soldier and was now determined to embark on his other great childhood dream of becoming an explorer. The dream included plans to be the first man to fly over the vast expanse of Arabia known as "Rub al-Khali"—the Empty Quarter.

He took his ambitions so seriously that in addition to working the night shift at *The New York Times,* he devoted his daylight hours to researching potential adventures for his first great expedition. He did this within the halls of the American Geographical Society, where he pored over maps and became interested in the migratory tribes that ranged between the Persian Gulf and the Black Sea.[7]

The American Geographical Society had been established in New York on September 19, 1851, with a notice placed by one Jon Disturnell in a new newspaper, *The New York Times,* inviting "citizens and strangers" to visit his Geographical Rooms and Statistical Library at 179 Broadway, then a hub of travel agencies. Three weeks after that notice, the *Times* reported on the formation of a "Geographical and Statistical Society" for which Disturnell was named to serve as a "Domestic Corresponding Secretary and Agent."[8] During those early days, Disturnell marketed such cartographic material as a "New Map of the United States and Canada Showing All the Canals, Railroads, Telegraph Lines and Principal Stage Routes." When the World War I peace conference assembled in Versailles, the society provided the maps used by various of the delegations. When Isaiah Bowman, who had been named the society's first director in 1915, returned from the peace conference, he and the society embarked on the "Millionth Map project," which mapped South and Central America at the scale of 1:1,000,000.[9] Bowman personally introduced Cooper to the wonders of maps and exploration, and became a friend and supporter who always encouraged Coop to dream his great dreams.

Merian Cooper, a born and bred southerner, embarked on his world travels instilled with a personal sense of Manifest Destiny. "The lust of power is in us, we white men," he wrote. "We'll sacrifice anything for the chance to rule. And I believe that it is right that black, brown and yellow men should be dominated by the white."[10]

His note of racial superiority was typical of a southern white man who grew up in times when the American cultural memory still recalled the practice of slavery. And racism was endemic throughout white America, from farmers and shopkeepers to captains of industry and the nation's presidents. To his credit, Cooper would journey far beyond the safe precincts of white society, bound not for conquest but for exploration. Ultimately, to Merian Cooper the gravest sin was to be boring, and his fascination with native peoples overcame some of the ingrained prejudices of his time.

Strangely enough, the personal highlight of Cooper's first expedition would be his unforgettable encounter with an all-powerful black ruler in Africa who traced his lineage to mighty King Solomon, a man whose kingdom Cooper entered during a sea voyage on the *Wisdom II*, a ship commanded by a colorful explorer over fifty years old, Captain Edward A. Salisbury.[11]

ALTHOUGH COOPER WOULD one day return to his interest in the migratory tribes, he jumped at the Salisbury expedition, which was specifically designed to be documented through films and articles. Having just spent six months polishing his reportorial skills at the *Times,* Cooper was hired on as chief scribe and first officer at $25 a month. He arranged to produce a series of articles for *Asia* magazine, a commission publisher Louis D. Froelick awarded Captain Salisbury and Cooper on August 30, 1922.[12] The adventures of the *Wisdom* became a book, *The Sea Gypsy,* published by G. P. Putnam's Sons in 1924, which listed Edward A. Salisbury and Merian C. Cooper as coauthors. (Cooper later maintained that he wrote the entire book, which is presented in the first-person voice of Captain Salisbury.)

When Cooper joined the *Wisdom,* the ship had already been three years out to sea, having first left port in Los Angeles "to wander up and down the strange waters of the world," as was recorded in *The Sea Gypsy.* The original crew had been white, the book noted, except for the cook and a messboy. But with the *Wisdom II* docked and waiting in Singapore, the crew assembled for the next leg of the voyage presented "a strange appearance, as strange . . . as ever was collected on one ship." There was Little Johnny, a "wharf waif" from Tahiti whom the ship had picked up the previous year; a

THE CREW TOILS AT THE CAPSTAN OF THE *WISDOM.*

Cooper Papers, BYU

Singhalese messboy named Shamrock; the powerfully built Andy, a "New Caledonian half-caste"; Big Johnny, son of a Fijian princess and a Scotch trader; old Joe, an emaciated Malay; Jean, a pearl diver from the Paumotu Islands; Jack, a Fijian bushman; Red from Seattle; Chu and Chin and Chow, from Singapore; Taylor, the navigator, a California engineer and an expert seaman; McNeil, the first officer, who had been an athlete at Yale; El Burghard, a hardy young ex-Columbia man; "Cooper, from Florida, who had been an airman in France and Poland"; Dresser the Dane, fresh from three years in the Malayan jungle; and Zeller from Los Angeles. Of this number, only Taylor, McNeil, and Red had started the voyage with Salisbury.[13]

This time the voyage began in San Francisco, where Salisbury's company was ensconced at the elegant Palace Hotel in preparation to take a steamer, the *President Taft,* to meet their waiting ship in Singapore. On September 11, 1922, the very day the party was set to depart, an article featuring an interview with Salisbury appeared in the *San Francisco Chronicle.* The *Wisdom II* was described as an eighty-eight-ton, 120-foot-long vessel constructed of teak by the Nicholson Company of England, makers of a famous racing yacht, and outfitted with "elaborate laboratories" including "several dark rooms for the development of photographic films."[14]

Salisbury, a man of adventure but a shameless self-promoter, tantalized the local press with visions of lost worlds, leading the *San Francisco Chronicle* to the title and subhead of its article: "SCIENTIST TO SEEK 'MISSING LINK' IN MALAY ARCHIPELAGO; Captain Edward A. Salisbury, scientist and explorer who sails today for the far east [*sic*] to search for a tribe of primitive men with tails." Salisbury told of native game hunters he had met on his last trip through the Solomon and New Hebrides Islands, who had told him of apelike men with short tails. He had heard tell of such creatures in other corners of the world, and hoped to finally find this lost tribe.

The *Wisdom* set sail from Singapore for the Bay of Bengal and on to the Indian Ocean and the Red Sea. Theirs would be a rambling, swashbuckling search for exotic ports of call, where they would drink deep from the cup of adventure before sailing ever onward in the quest for more adventure.

ULTIMATELY, THE CLOSEST the expedition would come to the celebrated missing link was an encounter with the primitive "beast men" of Malekula, largest of the New Hebrides Islands and a place the *Wisdom* crew called "the

Island of Fiends." They also met headhunters in the Solomon Islands who practiced human sacrifice to appease angry spirits. In the Andaman Islands there was a stop at the place called "Murderers' Island," where the British maintained a colony of some ten thousand convicted murderers and whose thick jungle was populated by a mysterious, feared tribe of black pygmies that hunted with bow and arrow, Stone Age style.

But the most mysterious island came after they left Murderers' Island. At the first sighting of this isle Jack, the Fijian bushman, pointed out a spot he said had plenty of turtle eggs they could gather. Salisbury was

A BOWMAN OF THE ANDAMAN ISLANDS.
Cooper Papers,
BYU

agreeable to the egg-hunting expedition, so he brought the ship in a hundred yards from shore. A dory was lowered with Cooper, Jack, Dresser the Dane, Andy, and Big Johnny aboard. They took along a shotgun and rowed through the rolling breakers close enough to wade out and pull the little boat through the surf to the white, sandy beach. Seeing that they had landed safely, Salisbury spent the next several hours sailing around the other lonely islands.

After the dory had been secured, the party trudged up the white sands to the jungle to search for turtle eggs. Jack had gone ahead some fifty yards when he suddenly stopped and ran back, shouting in his heavy accent, "Run, run. Dis island full of debils!" The Dane, Andy, Big Johnny, and Cooper gathered to calm the excited Fijian, who exclaimed that by the jungle's edge he'd seen a strange creature, bigger than a canoe, crawling in the bushes. It had shot out a tongue colored like blood that seemed four feet long.

While Dresser the Dane took hold of the shotgun, the rest picked up sticks and branches, and they cautiously moved toward the area.

All of them at once saw a dozen black, scaly creatures resembling gigantic alligators—some as big as "young horses," the Dane later related. The strange lizard creatures froze at the sight of the intruders. The men advanced, and one of them picked up a shell and threw it at the nearest creature, who spat out a long red tongue in response. Dresser fired his shotgun into the monster's open maw, and as the creature rolled over, the rest of the men pounded its head with sticks while the other beasts scuttled back into the jungle.

After Cooper measured the dead creature, which he would later claim stretched out to a full fourteen feet, they raced back to the beach to await the return of the *Wisdom*. They stayed away from the jungle, which seemed to be teeming with the alligator creatures—seemingly hundreds, some bigger than the one they had killed, they later claimed. The group realized the monsters had eaten all of the turtle eggs, so instead they caught giant crabs and stuffed them into the great bag they had brought, while one of them stood guard with the shotgun, nervously facing the jungle.

When the *Wisdom* picked up the landing party, they told their strange story. One of the crewmen suggested that they trap one of the creatures, but Jack would have none of that, and the *Wisdom* sailed on without a specimen. But the mysterious island stayed in Cooper's mind.[15] (Decades later, Cooper recalled that when he wrote about the fourteen-foot "giant lizard" in *The Sea Gypsy,* he was off to Persia and didn't have the chance to correct the proofs when a skeptical copyreader changed the fourteen-foot creature to a "four-foot dragon lizard.")[16]

BY SPRINGTIME THEY'D sailed to the green coast of Sumatra, where Cooper, Salisbury, Burghard, and the expedition's movie cameraman journeyed to the plateau and mountain lake of the demon-worshipping Batak, their trek, as detailed in *The Sea Gypsy,* reading as if it had been torn from the pages of Sir Arthur Conan Doyle's *The Lost World:* "We rode all day up through jungle-covered mountains until we came at last up on a plateau, cool and high, cut off from the world by a ring of smoking volcanoes."[17]

It was in the Bay of Bengal that a storm buffeted the *Wisdom* and so frightened the expedition's movie-camera operator that he jumped ship when they docked in Colombo, Ceylon. Cooper would forget the camera-man's name—he recalled only a "little red-haired man"—but he knew that Ernest Schoedsack was in Paris, and suggested that they get in touch with him.[18] The ship was preparing to enter the remote African kingdom of Abyssinia when the towering cameraman nicknamed "Shorty" got the call.

Schoedsack had been involved in relief efforts during the Greco-Turkish War of 1921–22 and had been present as the Greeks were driven out of the seaport of Smyrna on the Aegean Sea, during which more than three-fifths of the four hundred thousand inhabitants were massacred. Schoedsack had done more than crank his camera during such atrocities, risking his life to save others.[19]

Schoedsack caught up with the expedition at Djibouti, French Soma-liland, in February 1923, in time for the journey into Abyssinia. He wasn't particularly impressed with Salisbury who, being over fifty, was positively an-cient to the mostly young crew and conducted himself in an imperial fashion. The self-effacing Shorty was uncomfortable when he saw Salisbury in his gold-braided uniform holding court with local authorities and their wives over cocktails, regaling them all with vivid accounts of his adventures.[20]

Schoedsack's verdict on Salisbury would be sealed by subsequent events in Abyssinia, also known as Ethiopia. While Cooper, Schoedsack, and the steely navigator Taylor spent an eventful week in the kingdom, Captain Sal-isbury took sick and languished aboard his docked ketch. But a subsequent Salisbury-produced movie travelogue, featuring footage shot by Schoed-sack, was presented as if Salisbury had personally been on hand to record the events, and was to be feted by Abyssinia's monarch.

Cooper himself was too distracted by their visit to the capital city of Addis Ababa to anticipate such troubles. It would be the opening act in the Cooper-Schoedsack partnership: "Cooper's first awareness of the poten-tialities of movies came from these experiences with Schoedsack in Ethiopia," historian Rudy Behlmer notes.[21]

The adventure in Abyssinia would inspire a three-part series Cooper penned for *Asia* magazine. And it was in an official letter to Louis Froelick, editor of *Asia*, dated February 3, 1923, that His Imperial Highness Ras Tafari, heir to the throne of Ethiopia—the ruler the world would come to know as Haile Selassie—announced he would welcome the Salisbury expedition and receive with honor Captain Salisbury and Colonel Cooper.[22]

NATIVES OF NEW HEBRIDES IN POSED GAG SHOT ABOARD THE *WISDOM*.

Cooper Papers, BYU

CHAPTER EIGHT

THE GOLDEN PRINCE

> " 'It isn't real,' I said to myself, 'It's a dream—
> of living in an age long, long dead.' . . . A dream—
> a vision—a memory of the Age of Kings!"
>
> —Merian Cooper, ASIA report, October 1923[1]

THE LEGEND OF KING SOLOMON HELD THAT THE GREAT RULER, THE SON OF KING David and guardian of the sacred Ark of the Covenant, sexually communed with the virgin Sheba. After their night together, Solomon gave Sheba a ring engraved with the seal of the Lion of Judah, which she was to bestow upon her first male child. She was on the long journey home to Ethiopia when a son was born of their union. Sheba named him Ebna Hakim, "son of the wise man."[2]

Millennia later, the man who would be crowned in 1930 as the two hundred and twenty-fifth emperor of the Solomonic dynasty, the Elect of God, Lord of Lords, King of Kings, and Conquering Lion of the Tribe of Judah would be described as "a thin, seemingly fragile man who stood but five feet four inches tall and had rarely been heard to raise his voice."[3] Throughout his life, Cooper would meet kings and generals, captains of industry, movie stars and celebrities. But few, if any, would maintain about them the golden aura and renown of Ras Tafari ("ras" meaning prince). His birth had been preceded by signs and portents divined by the astrologers of his father, Governor Ras Makonnen, who governed the city of Harar. It was said that as a boy Tafari could speak with animals, that he knew sorcery and occult traditions, and that he filled the nation's royal priests with wonder and fear. The child was believed to be the direct descendant of King Solomon and Queen Sheba, and he would marry the

AN ABYSSINIAN CHIEFTAIN.

Cooper Papers, BYU

daughter of the ruler of the land, Menelik II. But Menelik, who was ailing and would suffer an incapacitating stroke, had named his grandson to succeed him. Tafari would bide his time.[4]

Ras Tafari had been the de facto monarch long before his official coronation. The Empress Zaoditou had been the acknowledged ruler, but ultimate power had been invested in Tafari, and he wielded it in a manner that exceeded his frail physique and gentle demeanor. He installed his own confidants in positions of power in the capital of Addis Ababa and opened diplomatic channels to the West, ushering Ethiopia into the League of Nations by 1923. He became the personification of his exotic country, a land of mystery seldom visited by Westerners, and reportedly traveled with a retinue that included zebras and lions.[5]

The aura of the biblical and mystical enhanced Cooper's amazement when he viewed Addis Ababa from atop a mountain. As his horse chewed grass near a deserted monastery where hyenas lurked, he breathed air as heady as wine and gazed at "the fantastic dream-city below," every detail illuminated in sunlit relief.[6] Stretched across the valley were the rooftops of what seemed a hundred small villages amid a forest of eucalyptus trees. The encircling mountain peaks rose out of the forest, topped with Christian churches and sprawling estates.

In the "Forest City," as Cooper called Addis Ababa, were dusty roads where peasants moved on foot or by mule, and nobles rode on horseback with entourages made conspicuous as sunlight glistened off the metal and steel of their rifles and swords. Cooper could see the opening in the forest, and the market square where peasants from the countryside came to buy food and grain, spears or ammunition, wood, leopard and zebra skins, whips made of rhino hide, sheep and goats and ostrich feathers. In the market stood a great tree whose spreading limbs served as a gallows on Saturdays and, nearby, a stretch of green where habitual thieves had their hands and feet hacked off. But Cooper and his fellow visitors saw no hanging bodies or mutilations; in honor of their expedition there would be no judgments executed during their stay.

Cooper experienced the whole tableau, its pomp and poverty, as a revelation proclaiming the truth of the romantic legends of Arthur and his Knights of the Round Table, how outside their mighty castle walls dirty serfs had trudged, scavenger dogs roamed. Forest City was how the world had truly looked back in the "Age of Kings," of that he was certain.

At the edge of the city stood houses for state officials, and a complex of stone buildings covering many acres—the *gibbi*, or "palace" of Ras Tafari, "Golden Prince of Abyssinia." It was through the beneficence of the prince regent that Cooper, Schoedsack, and Taylor were staying within the great complex, behind the stone walls of a three-story palace. Cooper and company traveled in and out of the royal estate on horseback along a gravel path through the ruins of an outer wall and across the grounds, which included inner courtyards, stone walls, and a garden whose green lawn spread in front of the palace, its gates guarded by caged lions.

The palace history intrigued Cooper, for this had been the sanctum of Lyg Yasu, the power-mad former emperor, and his advisers and sycophants. The ruler who had been placed on the throne by Menelik, along with his inner circle, had been deposed by the sword of Ras Tafari, but the palace still had many of the trappings from when it was a citadel of power. Trapdoors led to now empty dungeons; the dining room walls were still hung with portraits of Yasu's cabinet members dressed in their golden robes—a royal circle now shattered and scattered to prison or exile.

Cooper was haunted by the tale of young Emperor Yasu. On moonlit nights he gazed from the palace balcony at the slumbering silhouette of Forest City and breathed the intoxicating smells of earth and vegetation. He looked down at the courtyard, imagining the virile young Yasu and his vassals riding in, and he could almost hear their lusty shouts and the thundering hoofbeats of their horses. In the very rooms of this palace, Lyg Yasu had feasted, made love, and dreamed of power.

Cooper learned that when Emperor Menelik had died, in 1913, he hadn't left the scepter of power to his daughter, the Empress Zaoditou, but to his seventeen-year-old grandson. It had seemed a wise choice. The handsome Lyg Yasu was a brave horseman, a skilled shot and great hunter, a martial artist with sword and spear. "He seemed the ideal leader of a warrior race," Cooper recalled. "Nor did his people love him less because of his savage blood-lusts and mad gallantry with women. That was the way of a true king, they said."

But Yasu's great dream was to convert the Christian kingdom of Abyssinia into an Islamic nation and then, as all-mighty warrior king, to lead a great army in a conquest of the entire African continent. And so Yasu began massing his forces to march on Addis Ababa in 1916, when the Western world was at war.

The Christian rulers of Abyssinia assembled in the capital to discuss the emergency. At the solemn gathering Prince Tafari, then in his mid-twenties, urged his countrymen to brand Yasu a false emperor and excommunicate him, choose a new ruler, and meet the traitor and his army with the sword. All eyes turned to Tafari and proclaimed *him* ruler. But the wise young prince proposed that they rally the people in the name of the late Emperor Menelik and proclaim his daughter empress. Tafari added that if it was the will of the assembly, he would rule in her name as regent and assume the throne upon her death. But Zaoditou, Menelik's childless, middle-aged daughter, would be only a figurehead; it was Ras Tafari who held the true power.[7]

And then came the reckoning. "Twice in bloody battles fought in Zaoditou's name, [Tafari] beat the Mahommedans to the earth, driving Lyg Yasu into the desert with a handful of followers," Cooper recorded. "For four years Yasu wandered there. At last, broken by thirst and hunger and hardship, he rode back into captivity. Now he sits in a palace miles from Addis Ababa, living in royal luxury with his slaves and women, but imprisoned for all that and fastened, it is said, by silver chains to a close kinsman of the Golden Prince. He has grown fat and ugly, men say, and eats and drinks night and day, ever striving to forget how he would have united all Africa with his iron fist in the faith of the prophet."[8]

During his moonlit reveries Cooper would gaze out from the deposed emperor's palace balcony to the palace walls of Ras Tafari. Cooper thought of how Lyg Yasu had gambled for power and lost, and he felt that a wiser, better ruler now slept in the royal palace of Forest City. With that thought, Cooper would turn away from the balcony and go to bed.

THE ROARING OF the caged lions greeted each dawn. Back to the balcony Cooper would go, to look upon the waking wonders of this world. In the courtyard a child princess and her female slaves would be softly singing while sewing and weaving baskets. Trains of donkeys and camels would pass the palace gates, along with knights and their vassals and slaves heading to the royal palace. All of Forest City glowed as the sun rose above hills crowned with churches and fortresses. The sky was clear, the air was cool, the forest green. "It seemed Paradise," Cooper recalled.[9]

Cooper first met the all-powerful ruler—"King Solomon come to life," he'd later describe him—in the royal palace. Cooper was ushered into a long room at the end of which, across a floor of Oriental rugs, was a sofa where the prince sat in regal splendor. Sunlight streamed in from two great windows, illuminating the slightly built and bearded man dressed in a long black coat, who arose with a smile. Up close, Cooper saw the sun shine upon the broad forehead of a scholar, the deep black eyes of a dreamer, the firm mouth of a born soldier—"dignity, power, command" all shone in that

RAS TAFARI (SEATED) HOLDS COURT.

Cooper Papers, BYU

face, Cooper noted. The prince's hands were small and delicate, but Cooper knew they had raised a sword in the battle that had won him a kingdom.

It thrilled Cooper when Ras Tafari, through an English interpreter, confessed that he dreamed of "progress" and admitted to Cooper that Abyssinia had to learn the ways of modern civilization. Ras Tafari also explained to him that the empress was the supreme ruler of the land, that he merely exercised power in her name. But what power—*supreme* control of the army, the economy, the legal system.[10]

Cooper had come to Abyssinia armed with childhood memories of the land's legendary warriors, and being a former soldier, he was curious and eager to see them for himself. One day, Cooper rode his horse to the palace for another audience with Ras Tafari, and he posed an audacious question: Would it be possible to see the army of Abyssinia assemble for maneuvers?

"Would early tomorrow morning please you?" the prince replied, to Cooper's astonishment.[11]

"Here was a chance for a wonderful picture," Cooper thought. Although befuddled as to how an entire army could assemble overnight, that very day Cooper and Schoedsack went to the appointed assembly place near the royal palace, a wide plain surrounded by hills. There, with the aid of some servants, they constructed a thirty-foot-high platform on which Schoedsack would set up his movie camera.

The next day, Cooper and company rose with the dawn and roar of the caged lions. That morning an old man came by their palace to reassure them that the promised army would appear. Before the rule of the late emperor Menelik, the old man explained, the country had been like Europe in the Middle Ages, where feudal armies had aligned with great nobles who often warred against one another. But Menelik had centralized and strengthened the power of the throne by making it a requirement that a certain number of lords always be in residence at the capital, no matter how distant their province, and that they always bring their full contingent of knights and foot soldiers.

Ras Tafari continued the tradition and had at his command tens of thousands of ready warriors.

Cooper and Schoedsack quickly breakfasted, saddled up, and rode out of their palace gates to the plain, where they began marking off an area with flags, through which they hoped the warriors would charge. They had just finished staking out the flags when Schoedsack shouted: "Look, look, *there they come!*"

Armed riders and foot soldiers began pouring out of the mountain passes, sunshine glittering off thousands of shields and spears. A procession of black warriors in battle regalia was still massing a half hour later when an exuberant Cooper could restrain himself no longer and swung up onto his horse and rode out to meet them.

WARRIORS GATHERING IN ABYSSINIA.
Cooper Papers, BYU

"As I approached within fifty yards of the nearest mass," Cooper recorded, "there broke forth from it a score of mounted men, galloping straight at me. Like flames sweeping across a burning prairie they rode, and like flames they sparkled with light and color as the sun beat down on their accouterments. At their head, riding with as much abandon as the youngest of his warriors, sped a fierce old *detzmarch,* or general. Directly in front of me he jerked back on its haunches his fiery little horse, caparisoned from head to knees in vermilion silk. Then as he brandished in greeting two long spears he carried in his right hand, he swung to the ground. As one man his followers dismounted behind him."

Cooper also dismounted and approached to shake the hand of the general, trying to repress an amazed stare at the leader's headdress of lions' manes, his flowing robe of purple silk and cloak of leopard skins, the round leather shield rimmed with gemstones, the curved scimitar by his side, and his horse fitted with an ornamental saddle.

Meanwhile, the warriors kept pouring into the plain. And then, from the distant gates of Prince Tafari's palace, came the herald of trumpets and war drums as the palace gates opened and a procession of warriors, all shaking their spears, began streaming out to meet the massing army. Cooper hungrily drank in every detail, made a mental note of the war horses, which seemed "mad with the lust of battle"; the drummers smeared a dark red who sat on horseback and pounded drums of animal hide; the *detzmarch* leading columns of men, "their dark faces savage as they listened to the sound of the war-drums ahead."

The warriors answered the approaching palace drums with a war chant:

Brothers, are you hungry, are you thirsty?
Are you not birds of prey?
Forward!
Behold the flesh of your enemy!
And I will be a carver at your feast.
Forward!
If you lack wine, I will give you blood to drink!

Then Cooper and Schoedsack, who was still operating his movie camera atop the high platform, heard another flurry of distant trumpets. In the distance appeared "a moving spot of golden light," Cooper observed.

The golden light took the form of the Golden Prince, adorned with an ebony velvet cloak threaded with gold. He was riding a black steed and atop his head was a golden crown, his belt a golden band of precious stones, the gold sparkling in the sun as the ruler of Abyssinia passed in review of his troops. As he rode by, the thousands of warriors began shouting and jousting across the plain.

"I'll bet the Connecticut Yankee in King Arthur's court never threw his peepers on anything half so wonderful as the show we've seen today," Schoedsack said to Cooper with a smile as they rode back to their palace.

———

ONE MORNING SOON thereafter, Cooper was standing at the palace balcony when he was hailed by Monsieur Abraham, keeper of the prince's private purse, who had ridden into the courtyard on a mule with an offer from the prince. He asked Cooper to join him at a feast of warriors.[12]

"In ten minutes we were on horseback," Cooper recalled happily. Taylor joined him, and they rode with Abraham. "Never have I felt more gloriously alive. The air was nectar; the road a picture out of a romance." To Cooper it seemed a scene from the Middle Ages: nobles followed by their knights, creditors with their debtors chained to them, ladies riding mules, wandering musicians playing flutes.

The visitors came to the outer court of Ras Tafari's palace, where thousands of fierce, barefoot warriors stood in flowing white robes strung with wide cartridge belts. Cooper and his company dismounted and were led past as Monsieur Abraham explained that the warriors were waiting to take their turns to feast in the banquet hall. Through an inner court, they came to a one-story building painted dark red. A chamberlain opened a door, and they entered a vast, empty hall with a high ceiling, a place out of the mead halls of *Beowulf.* The floor was flattened earth, crowded with rows of tables so long that each could seat five hundred warriors, by Cooper's estimate. The chamberlain led them to the far end, where a raised platform was hidden by a white curtain that hung from the roof.

The chamberlain parted the curtain to reveal what Cooper, with his naturally cinematic eye, described as "a gorgeous stage-setting." Nobles and those of the ruling class sat cross-legged on a floor covered with multicolored carpets, and in the center of the room was a throne upon which sat the prince regent. "He was staring straight ahead," Cooper recounted, "a far-away look in his eyes, as if dreaming dreams of empire."

At the sight of Cooper and company, the Golden Prince seemed to come back to the real world, greeting them with a smile. Speaking in French, he invited his guests to dine with him. In an instant slaves brought over a table and chairs to make a place of honor at the foot of the throne. Exotic foods began appearing, and Cooper and Taylor ate like nobles, dipping into the dishes with their fingers and washing down the spicy taste with a clear white liquid that tasted like vodka. It was only ten o'clock in the morning, but the slaves began bringing in bottles of French champagne, the noble drink of hospitality. No matter the hour, a gladsome welcome wasn't complete without champagne, Cooper was told.

Cooper had his fill of food, but still the champagne kept coming. The curtain behind them was parted, opening onto the vast and empty hall. And then the head chamberlain raised a wand, and at a signal the doors opened and the first mass of feasting warriors poured in. As they took their seats at the rows of tables, slaves entered with the carcasses of slaughtered bullocks swinging from the poles hoisted upon their shoulders. To his astonishment, Cooper realized the meat was bloody red and raw. As the slaves stood in the aisles between the tables, the warriors turned and bit into the hanging flesh and cut off hunks with deft slices of their blades and a tear of their teeth. The keeper of the prince's purse explained to Cooper that the meat had been freshly slaughtered, not more than a half hour before.

"Raw flesh makes strong hearts for war, they say," chuckled Abraham, who noted that 150 bullocks had been killed for the feast.

Cooper then looked up at the Golden Prince and saw him still sitting on his throne, motionless as a statue. But his eyes were open—"looking into the visions of his open-eyed dreams."

The champagne kept flowing as the meat went around, and a parade of minstrels entered and played as the musicians served strong spirits from bullock horns. The five thousand warriors tore into their smoking meat, drinking the potent liquors and shouting orders to the slaves. Cooper watched and listened as minstrels sang to the music of flutes and the boom of war drums.

Cooper again looked back at the Golden Prince, still motionless on his throne. Ras Tafari seemed to awaken from his inner dream only when Cooper and Taylor, tipsy from the champagne, paused at the throne to say good-bye. The Golden Prince bestowed his farewell blessing.

While Cooper galloped back to his castle home, his thoughts were not of the strange, magnificent banquet but, as he later wrote, of "the lonely Prince, sitting there on his purple throne in the midst of his shouting warriors and dreaming his great dreams."

By the end of the decade, Tafari's army would crush any opposition and the Empress Zaoditou would be dead, the reasons for her demise shrouded in mystery. Tafari's dreams would take the form of a glittering coronation ceremony, with bales of lion skins made into garments by tailors in London. A million dollars' worth of gold and jewels would adorn the crown stamped with Solomon's seal and the crest of the Lion of Judah that would be placed upon the head of the slightly built man with the piercing black eyes, who would be acclaimed as Haile Selassie, emperor of Ethiopia.[13]

CHAPTER NINE

THE LAST LANDFALL

I clung to the railway . . . for the Wisdom *was almost on her side,
and she shook and quivered like a mad thing. I knew it could only
be one of two things—reef or rocks; . . . the little sea gypsy could
not stand buffeting long; it would tear the bottom out of any craft
that ever floated.*

—Captain Edward Salisbury, THE SEA GYPSY[1]

THE *WISDOM II* LEFT THE KINGDOM OF ABYSSINIA IN FEBRUARY 1923 FROM THE
main port of Djibouti, French Somaliland, and sailed into the worst
weather of the voyage. It wasn't just the rough waters of the Red Sea but
the fearsome wind blowing down from the north that forced them to take
"long, zig-zagging tacks," Schoedsack recalled. The ship had to stay close
to the rocky coast of Yemen, where pirates lurked. Captain Salisbury had
been warned, by sailors who worked the Arabian coast, that he'd be
damned if he went aground in those parts—there were cutthroat Bedouins
who'd kill them without a second thought for what they could loot from
their ship.[2]

The *Wisdom* was moving toward the coastal ghost town of Mokha, a
once-thriving coffee center now long abandoned. What remained, they'd
been told, was its famous lighthouse, which they trusted would help them
steer clear of the coastline's treacherous reefs at nightfall. The Mokha
lighthouse was said to be visible for eighteen miles, and the crew searched
for that guiding light—in vain.

The record of *The Sea Gypsy* describes the very moment of the night the
wandering ship struck something with such force it almost tossed Captain
Salisbury from his bunk. He scrambled up the companionway stairs, and

when he emerged he saw that the ship was almost on her side and knew they were caught on reef or rocks. The ship was shaking, and he realized that even as stout a vessel as this would have its bottom torn away if the thunderous buffeting continued.[3]

At the very moment Salisbury made it to the deck, a wave broke over the ship and would have swept him out into the darkness if he hadn't grabbed onto a lifeline. The captain gazed at the tilted deck, soaked in water and moonlight, and saw that the crew had also sprung from their bunks. Cooper was bare to the waist, with a Malay sarong tied around his waist, the towering Schoedsack was dressed in purple pajamas soaked to the skin, and Taylor, the navigator, and big Mac and Fiji Jack and all the hands were on deck, even Shamrock, the messboy. Salisbury could see, beyond the crashing of the waves, the moonlit shoal and the mainland, a few hundred yards away. He prayed they were only stuck on a sandbar and could slide off; they were doomed if it was rocks upon which they'd run aground.

Taylor shouted to bring down the mainsail, which had nearly dipped into the water. The crew lined up along the mainsheet, which controlled the angle of the mainsail, struggling to stand firm on the slippery and tilted deck as wave after wave buffeted the ship and broke over them. "Lay on her, boys, lay on her!" went the shout as they began to pull in the full sail. "Pull for life."

"And how they lay on her!" *The Sea Gypsy* recorded. "Mac's New England twang sounds slow and undisturbed, in regular cadence: 'Heave—heave—heave.' And somehow, with the word, they grip that sliding slippery deck with their bare feet and heave away. Someone starts the old chanty, sung on the *Wisdom* at a hundred up anchors.

" 'I'd a Bible in my hand, when I sailed, when I sailed . . .'

"And to the beat and swing of it they heave. Through the dark, above the crash and roar of the sea, sounds the last harsh rhythm of the chanty:

'I'd a Bible in my hand
By my father's great command,
But I sunk it in the sand . . .
When I sailed.' " [4]

"The ship was stuck fast, broadside to the wind," Schoedsack later recalled, "and it took all our manpower, clinging to the wave-swept deck, to haul down her sails before her masts broke or her hull split."[5]

They were hauling down the sail when the *Wisdom* lurched, sliding off the sandbar they had been stuck upon. There was a ripping of the mizzen; then the boat rose on a swelling wave and crashed as the stern scraped bottom. They were now trapped in the lagoon. The crew anchored to keep from hitting the shore, but every swell lifted and dropped the boat, causing a shuddering sensation as it scraped bottom. Their only chance was to wait for dawn and low tide to find a way out.

But then they beheld a fearsome sight: *lights* flickering along the shoreline. Around campfires, pirates sat like spiders, watching their trapped prey flail in the web. As the *Wisdom* crew later learned, the pirates had wrecked the lighthouse and had been patiently waiting for an unsuspecting ship to run aground in the darkness.[6] Salisbury ordered Cooper and Dresser the Dane to get the guns ready, and Schoedsack to secure the motion-picture film. The impact had knocked out the ship's electrical lighting, so the men sprang to the task by the weirdly flickering light of two candles. When Salisbury went below to see how things were progressing he found Cooper preparing for a bloody siege, lining up four sawed-off shotguns, two rifles, and a collection of revolvers and automatics, along with open boxes of buckshot shells. Shorty and the Dane were busy with the cans of film while Taylor was working the pumps to drain the water they'd taken on, trying to keep their ship afloat.[7]

The tide began coming in with the dawn, and the sun rose round and red over the mountains, the tip of a mosque minaret on the coastline glistening white. The crew could see the pirates running back and forth on shore, even as their numbers were increasing; through his glasses Salisbury spotted a line of Arabs squatting on the sand, patiently waiting—like vultures.[8]

But as the sun rose, so too did the morning tide, and an opening in the sandbar revealed a beckoning bit of blue water beyond the breakers. With the sails down, it was up to the auxiliary gas motor to power the *Wisdom* as they hoisted anchor. The bow of the *Wisdom* was soon touching blue water—and then was clear, out into open sea.

The ship had been wounded, the lead keel caught in the banks and ripped loose, leaving holes through which water had poured into the bilge, necessitating the pumps and a makeshift blocking of the holes. The ship limped on into the Red Sea under motor power and shortened sail, resolutely heading north for Suez, where they planned to dock and make repairs. But they were again sailing into their nemesis, that furious wind blowing down from the north.

Rather than fight it, the *Wisdom* sought temporary haven in Jidda, the port city near the holy city of Mecca—the fabled "Port to Paradise." They soaked up the sights, from caravans of camels led by desert Bedouins to makeshift settlements outside the city walls where stranded pilgrims scratched out a desperate existence.

During their stay, Cooper and Schoedsack met two Russians, including a former colonel who had been riding as a jockey in Cairo until he had put on too much weight and lost his job. The "little Colonel," as Cooper called

THE *WISDOM* IN THE HARBOR OF SAVONA, ITALY,
BEFORE THE MYSTERIOUS FIRE THAT DESTROYED THE SHIP.
Cooper Papers, BYU

him, had drifted to Jidda, where he was flying planes in the service of the king of the Hejaz. The little Colonel would invite Shorty for a flight over Jidda, enabling Schoedsack to take the only aerial pictures of Jidda, *The Sea Gypsy* recorded.[9] Cooper would recall that pilot years later when he and John Hambleton began sharing dreams of commercial aviation.

On their eleventh day in Jidda, the stranded sea gypsies finally decided to brave the elements. But the northern wind was unrelenting as the crippled craft slowly made its way to Suez, where they hoped to effect repairs. The *Wisdom* was only a few miles from Suez when the fickle wind shifted around and blew from the south, and the men could only curse the wind and sea that seemed to toy with them. But, worse yet, at Suez they discovered that they couldn't get the ship properly repaired, and then several crew members sickened with a fever.[10]

They were stuck in Suez for two weeks before Salisbury took a chance and sailed for Italy. Good fortune finally smiled upon them, and the *Wisdom* limped into Savona. The battered boat was left in dry dock, and the crew settled into a nearby villa. It was spring, and the land offered welcome respite to weary sailors. They'd see that their ship was made seaworthy and then sail for America. They settled in at their rented villa and left one of the Greek hands they had picked up in Suez as a night watchman.

But the next morning they were awakened with the local ship chandler shouting the worst possible news: "Your ship, she burn!"

They were rushed by automobile to the waterfront only to see their graceful, stout ship already reduced to a broken mass of smoke and flames.

"The sea gypsy had made her last landfall," Salisbury and Cooper recorded.[11]

THE MYSTERIOUS FIRE that consumed the *Wisdom* has been variously attributed to a gas explosion or a careless worker with a kerosene lamp. Some accounts claimed that Schoedsack's undeveloped negatives were consumed in the flames. Kevin Brownlow has mused that Merian Cooper essentially disowned the spectacular footage—which *does* exist and records everything from the marketplace of Addis Ababa to the massing of the warriors—because Salisbury had rights to the film and later fashioned it into a pedestrian travelogue.

Cooper later recalled that because he had become friends with the absolute ruler of Abyssinia, it was a missed chance for an amazing film. "Abyssinia [would have been] turned over to my hand to make a picture I would call *The Golden Prince*," Cooper once explained to Brownlow. "This was really an unknown kingdom, an unphotographed kingdom.... Oh, this *Golden Prince* would have made a great picture—probably the greatest [Schoedsack] and I would have ever made. [That's how Schoedsack] and I really would have started making pictures together.... But it was not to be."[12]

Cooper also became involved in diplomatic and entrepreneurial intrigues regarding Abyssinia. On March 21, 1923, he wrote the president and State Department from Port Said, explaining the prince regent's hopes of securing an American diplomatic representative in Abyssinia and offering information on the political and commercial situation. That letter was answered, in care of the Cooper family address in Jacksonville, in a June 1923 letter from the State Department noting "with interest" the offer of diplomatic relations and asking to see the "detailed report."

Cooper's resulting ten-page "Outline of Plan for the Development of Concessions in Abyssinia" detailed everything from the labor supply to natural resources. In proposing a "Concessions Corporation" that would secure "blanket concessions from the Abyssinian Government" for licensing development deals, Cooper proposed *himself* as liaison between the Abyssinian government and the Concessions Corporation. The deal seems to have gone awry when J. G. White & Co., which was to lend Cooper the money to establish the organization, apparently double-crossed him on an Abyssinian dam project he had proposed.[13]

Despite the failed development scheme and the lost cinematic dream of *The Golden Prince,* out of the voyage of the *Wisdom* emerged a partnership strengthened through death-defying adventure. Cooper and Schoedsack would soon begin plotting their own filmmaking expedition.

The first of Cooper's three-part series of articles on Abyssinia was published in the October 1923 issue of *Asia,* and his accounts of the descendants of King Solomon put him in the company of the renowned and celebrated adventurers of his day. An *Asia* editorial commentary that accompanied the second installment noted that Cooper and Salisbury had established a "favorable position" for Americans in Abyssinia.[14] The magazine further welcomed Cooper into the ranks of explorers, proclaiming, "Merian C. Cooper has in him the spirit of the explorer, and adventurer of the age of chivalry. . . . Only just returned from his trip around the world with the Salisbury expedition, he is off again on another exploration with Mrs. Marguerite E. Harrison and a motion-picture photographer. They have gone to Arabia for a year's work and study among the Arabs, writing and picturing."[15]

NATURAL DRAMA

CHAPTER TEN

JOURNEY TO THE LAND OF GRASS AND LIFE

*And the grass dried up. And without grass their flocks
and herds must die. And upon these animals depended
both the shelter and food of the race—life itself.*

—Merian Cooper, GRASS[1]

LONG AFTER THE MOVIE EXPEDITION THAT RESULTED IN *GRASS*, MARGUERITE Harrison would admit that she was a curious sight, standing between the towering Schoedsack and the short, husky Cooper. But she recalled with affection her partners in adventure in her 1935 autobiography, *There's Always Tomorrow: The Story of a Checkered Life.*

Schoedsack was a grinning, wisecracking fellow with a boyish mop of curly hair, a "truly American" character, Harrison wrote, who had a hard-boiled exterior but also the heart and sensitivity of a true artist. "I have never seen anyone who was more responsive to beauty in all its forms," Harrison concluded.[2]

Cooper was Shorty's physical opposite: short, muscular and stocky, with thinning hair and a sharp pointed nose. "He was disdainful of all the refinements of life which were 'soft' in his opinion," Harrison wrote. He was stubborn, moody, and quick-tempered but was also generous and loyal—"to the point of fanaticism."[3]

Cooper's dream of becoming a great explorer included entering the unmapped gorges of the Brahmaputra River. Harrison, writing when her partner had already become a famous filmmaker, saw in Cooper the soul of an artist and a boundless imagination that matched Schoedsack's: "Merian's turn of mind was essentially dramatic. He was forever striving for

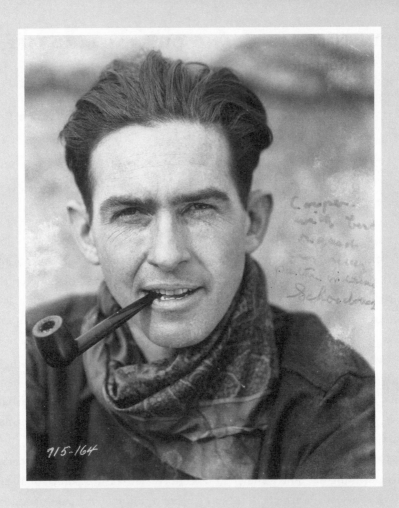

PORTRAIT OF ERNEST "SHORTY" SCHOEDSACK,
TAKEN DURING THE TIME OF *GRASS*. PHOTO IS
INSCRIBED: "COOPER—WITH BEST REGARDS FROM
YOUR PARTNER IN CRIME. SCHOEDSACK."

Cooper Papers, BYU

startling climaxes and sharp contrasts. . . . He already possessed [by the time of the *Grass* expedition] the flair for the bizarre and unusual."[4]

The *Grass* expedition would be bankrolled with $10,000, half of it a loan from Merian's father and brother. Marguerite Harrison put up the other $5,000, with one big string attached: that she be permitted to join the expedition. Cooper agreed, to the dismay of Schoedsack, who had been off in the Middle East while Cooper was raising the capital. Schoedsack was awaiting Coop in Paris when he got the news their expedition was to be a threesome. Although Schoedsack would meet his future wife on such an expedition, years later he would still insist that Harrison, or "Maggie" as she was called, simply didn't belong on such a trip. Indeed, this was a time when women were considered domestic creatures, and it wasn't becoming for a lady to head into the wilds, particularly a single woman journeying alone in the company of two men. Schoedsack probably had his fears confirmed at the first sight of his new partner.

Harrison had arrived as if she was on a cruise to Europe. She had packed riding clothes and an evening dress, toilet articles, a rubber bathtub, and had even had her hair done.[5] Shorty would grumble ever after because Harrison, who appeared in the final film, maintained a sporty look for the camera that was out of place amid the deserts and mountains and nomadic tribes.

Writing of their expedition years later, Harrison seemed to head off any untoward thoughts as regards Cooper. She was too independent a woman for a man of Cooper's southern breeding. "Although I had never considered myself a feminist, I suppose I was instinctively one, as are most women who have had to make their own way in the world," Harrison wrote. ". . . To [Cooper] I was simply a boon companion, a business associate, and the person to whom he claimed he owed an eternal debt of gratitude for saving his life in Russia."[6]

And that latter point is what earned Coop's loyalty and resigned Shorty to having a woman along for the journey to Persia.

AFTER THE VOYAGE of the *Wisdom,* Cooper had returned to his earlier researches at the American Geographical Society and considered anew the nomadic tribes roaming between the Persian Gulf and the Black Sea.

"It was indeed such things as the virgin Rub al Khali—the Empty Quarter of Arabia, and the Turn of the Brahmaputra in Asia, and some other truly unknowns, which interested Dr. Isaiah Bowman and me in the early '20s . . . ," Cooper recalled, decades later, noting that he and Bowman felt there was more mystery in those places than at other destinations, particularly the North and South Poles. "Indeed, Dr. Bowman helped me to pick out what he and I both considered the most formidable migration in the world of which we knew—the Spring migration of the Baba Ahamadi [Baba Ahmedi] Tribe of the [Bakhtiari] of Persia (Iran)."[7]

The truth was more complicated. Doubtless, the long hours with Bowman, poring over maps and discussing migratory patterns, had inculcated a knowledge of Persia and its nomadic tribes in Cooper's mind. But it would be quite by accident that they would meet up with the Baba Ahmedi tribe. In fact, the three partners set off without any prearranged appointment with any tribe, only an interest in the Kurds, whose colorful culture and mountainous home of Kurdistan seemed the most photographically promising. The expedition's preproduction period included no actual script or plan, except the notion of a narrative motif featuring Harrison as a heroine of sorts searching Asia for a mysterious lost race.

In fact, other than Schoedsack's early camera cranking in Hollywood and subsequent newsreel work, they were rank amateurs when it came to making a full-fledged movie. Coop himself had seen only three or four pictures in his life up to that point, and was interested in movies only as a medium for popularizing exploration and documenting wild places and mysterious peoples of the world.[8] But they were moving forward on the momentum of their "super-colossal youthful enthusiasm," as Schoedsack described it.[9]

Their most precious commodity was twenty thousand feet of thirty-five-millimeter film, which would have to last the duration of the expedition. Schoedsack's "contribution to the capital stock," as he put it, included his light, hand-cranked French-made Debrie camera—the camera he had desired when he was recording the fighting in France—which could load and run four hundred feet of film at a time and would be mounted on a heavy tripod.[10]

In January 1924 the partners left Paris for Turkey en route to crossing into Kurdistan from Anatolia. But the Turks had driven their French and

German occupiers out of Anatolia and Constantinople, and were in no mood to accommodate strange visitors from the West, so they kept the trio waiting in Angora.[11] Days of delay dragged into weeks, the Turks presumably hoping that the frustrated foreigners would take the hint and head back home. Cooper and Schoedsack pushed on, always watching out for the secret police and shooting a little of what Schoedsack called "travelogue footage."

The adventure almost ended for Merian Cooper at the start. He was felled by an ailment in Angora, Harrison later wrote, although she never revealed the malady other than to note that it required a simple operation. (Cooper makes no mention of the incident in his book *Grass*.) Both Harrison and Schoedsack suggested that they head to Constantinople and the well-maintained American hospital there, rather than trust in the rundown Turkish military hospital on the outskirts of Angora. But Cooper insisted that he go to the nearby facility.

"I have never seen any other man who so reveled in personal discomfort or who got such a grim satisfaction from physical suffering," an exasperated Harrison later wrote.

Cooper had his fill of suffering to reward his stubbornness. Harrison recalled that after his operation Cooper suffered for four days, as there was no morphine or other narcotic in the hospital dispensary. The doctor did not have sufficient surgical dressings to dress the wound, the food was poor, and the stifling heat caused a plague of flies and mosquitoes to swarm in his sickroom. For several days, Maggie and Shorty worried that their friend wouldn't make it.[12] Even when the indomitable Cooper was ready to go, Harrison worried that he was so weakened that he wouldn't last the next formidable leg of the journey, a crossing of the Salt Desert of Anatolia on a caravan trail almost as old as history. The resilient Cooper not only made it but would later claim that the entire adventure left him as fit as he had been since his physical peak at the naval academy.

Their main transport through the Salt Desert was a horse-driven *araba* painted green and decorated with wildflowers; it had a rounded canvas top that reminded Harrison of an American prairie schooner. Their driver, a lean Turk named Saladin, was captured by Schoedsack's camera as the guide taking Harrison deeper in her journey for "the Forgotten People." With an interpreter named Fettah along, they left Angora with a pack of

ANGORA OCT 1923

THE *GRASS* MOVIE EXPEDITION TEAM GETS INTO A PERSIAN MOOD
IN THIS SHOT TAKEN IN ANGORA, BEFORE THE PARTNERS JOINED THE
BAKHTIARI TRIBE. LEFT TO RIGHT: COOPER, MARGUERITE HARRISON,
ERNEST B. SCHOEDSACK. *Courtesy of Milestone Film & Video; image from Cooper Papers, BYU*

COOPER IN THE
TRADITIONAL
HOODED "BASHLIK"
HE WORE ON THE
ROAD WITH THE
BAKHTIARI TRIBE.

*Courtesy of Milestone
Film & Video; image from
Cooper Papers, BYU*

mongrel dogs snapping at the wheels and a crack from Saladin's whip urging the horses forward, into the arid, barren expanse, scattering a herd of goats and donkeys bound for market.

At night Harrison would spread her sleeping bag inside the *araba,* while the rest of the expedition slept underneath. One night, they stopped at an old caravansary whose walls of stone enclosed an open square and a complex of buildings that were falling into ruin. The caravansary seemed like a mirage in the flat, endless desert, a structure constructed from stones that had long ago been brought across the sands. It appears in the film, Schoedsack's camera documenting Harrison as she joins a circle of merchants and caravan drivers around a camel-dung fire.

"The firelight cast weird reflections on their swarthy faces as they squatted in a circle around the blaze," Harrison recalled. "Beyond, all was dark and still except for the snuffling of the camels and the occasional tinkle of a bell. I felt transported into another age and world."[13]

Harrison would also be shown riding from the caravansary and sitting on the buckboard next to Saladin as they struggled through a sudden sandstorm—a bit of motion-picture illusion. Harrison would write that they had shot the scene on Christmas Eve, a time when even the little seasonal rains the plains received had dampened the sandy ground. They needed a sandstorm and Shorty told them that in Hollywood, the propellers of airplanes were often used to stir up a dust storm on cue. They had no plane, but instead purchased several dozen sacks of bran, hired stalwart hamals (Muslim servants or porters), and waited for the wind. As Shorty cranked his camera, the hamals, stationed out of view to the windward side, opened their sacks of bran as Saladin drove on. The effect was perfectly realistic, but Harrison recalled not only practically choking to death during the filming but spending days after combing bran out of her hair.[14]

That night in Konia, "the City of the Whirling Dervishes," as Cooper called it, they celebrated Christmas with enthusiasm and ingenuity. Coop and Shorty pulled out crumpled dinner jackets from their packs and Marguerite made herself resplendent in a low-necked dress, with a Spanish comb in her coiffured hair. She fashioned a Christmas tree out of a foot-and-a-half-tall lemon tree decorated with blue beads, and Schoedsack brought out a portable phonograph they'd packed as a present for some nomad chieftain they might encounter. They played jazz records and formed a procession, Cooper leading the way like a drum major, spinning a three-foot-long cigarette holder like a baton. They were joined by Saladin, Fettah, and others, and they feasted in a room brilliantly lit with four oil lamps, a blaze to eyes that had become accustomed to candles and lantern light.[15]

That Christmas night they would bed down in an inn so humble that a single wooden board was all that separated them from an adjacent stable. Harrison could hear the whinny of the horse and the movements of the cows, see their dark silhouettes, and smell the pungent straw and manure. There was a hole in the roof, through which she saw a single star. This was the manger in Bethlehem, she thought in wonder, and she was reliving the first Christmas.[16]

IT WAS JANUARY when the adventurers, in their meandering search for a subject for their film, set off in search of the Uruks, a "lost" nomadic tribe rumored to dwell in the Taurus Mountains. They never found the Uruks, but they did find mortal danger when Cooper and Schoedsack embarked with a guide and packhorse on a scouting mission. They were trudging through snow when a sudden blizzard hit. Schoedsack remembered it as "a heavy, wet snowfall" that quickly swamped his six-foot-six frame up to his waist and came even higher on Cooper. The guide lost his nerve, shouting for Allah to save them, as Schoedsack took the lead, using his size to kick and trudge a furrow in the snow, which he widened by "dragging the guide and the pack horse."

It was hard work, but they knew that to stop meant frozen death. Schoedsack led them onward, aiming for any distant object, such as a tree, then the next landmark, and the next—always moving. By dusk, they had made it to an icy but shallow stream full of blocks of ice, and they followed it to a caravansary and safety.[17]

Still searching for the tribe of their dreams, they headed to Syria, where they rented an automobile and drove to Baghdad. Schoedsack journeyed to Mosul and learned that the Kurdish tribes they had hoped to film were busy battling British and Turkish troops. Meanwhile, in Baghdad, Cooper met Sir Arnold Wilson, a British official, and Gertrude Bell, the British woman who was adviser to King Faisal, who told them of the Bakhtiari tribe of southern Persia, and their seasonal migration, which included crossing the Karun River and climbing the glacial cliffs of the Zardeh Kuh mountain peak. Cooper was thrilled with the prospect of filming such a spectacular event, and Wilson made arrangements for the filmmakers to meet the ruling khans of the tribe in Shushtar, the capital of Arabistan.[18]

They had the extraordinary good luck to arrive at Shushtar just prior to the seasonal migration of the tribe—some fifty thousand people and a half million animals, Cooper had been told. By March 30, 1924, Cooper's diary entry would read: "Camp of the Khans, Shushtar." All they knew about the Bakhtiari was the legend of their savage wars and bloody feuds and that they were camped on the tribe's winter grazing ground. Soon the Bakhtiari would strike their tents and head for the distant mountains and the promised land of the far plateau of Iran.[19]

While the rulers of the tribes were considering the foreigners' request to document the migration, the group enjoyed the hospitality of Rahim Khan, who'd been educated at the American college at Beirut. As a prince of the Bakhtiari, the man was rich in tribal land and income from the Anglo-Persian Oil Company, whose fields lay within Bakhtiari tribal territory. Their host led them on horseback through the alleys and bazaars of Shushtar to the green fields of his own domain and the camp where the three foreigners would have an audience with the Il Khani, the all-powerful khan of the tribes, and the Il Begi, the master of the tribes.

The three foreigners waited in a reception tent until the two tribal masters appeared with the greeting of *Salam alikum,* "Peace be with you." The Il Khani had a white mustache that stood out on a dark face weathered from a lifetime spent under the open sky, and was dressed in the traditional black coat, white sash, and black trousers. The Il Begi, also known as Amir Jang, seemed to Cooper "more the city Persian than the chief of wild nomads"; a short, stout, moon-faced man with a black mustache, he wore gold-rimmed glasses, a diamond ring, and a gold watch.

Cooper and company explained that they wanted to follow the tribes and travel in the manner of the people—and they wanted to traverse the most difficult route, the one no foreigners had ever taken. Amir Jang laughed but agreed, promising they could accompany the toughest of the tribes on the toughest road to the promised land.

The next day it was barely sunrise at the camp of the khans when

Cooper and Schoedsack watched the great Il Khani begin a long day of holding court. The Il Khani sat on a rug spread over the ground and received a procession of tribal chiefs arguing land claims, thieves brought for punishment, tribal officials bearing tributes of bags of silver, and sheep-herders with their flocks who'd come for an audience. Cooper and Schoedsack toured the camp with Rahim, who felt he was a tribal prince caught between two worlds: his tribal culture, with its ancient traditions, and the materialistic West, with its notions of democracy and equality.

Rahim even made a proposal to Cooper—they could trade places. Rahim could live under the bright lights of Broadway, and Cooper could become a boss of the Bakhtiari.[20] It was an impossible proposition, but the notion fascinated Cooper and would remain in his imagination as a comforting dream: If civilization ever went *too* soft he could strike out for Persia and rejoin the tribes.

Later, Cooper hiked alone into a mountain gorge and dived into the icy river that flowed past the camp. By the time he hauled himself ashore, he felt every sense tingling, and a kinship with the wild people whose life seemed preferable to the flabby conceit of civilization, who could "touch paradise" by virtue of the elemental world they lived in.[21]

The next sunrise, when the camp was still asleep and a few campfires that had lasted the night were burning low in the morning chill, the restless Cooper was already up. He got the horse Rahim had lent him and gazed at the mountains they hoped to cross with the migrating tribe. "We'll be among you soon," Cooper called out as he set his horse to a full charge, spurring it on with the Arab cry of *lu-lu-lu.*

A FEW DAYS later, on April 2, while still awaiting final permission to join the impending migration, the visitors accepted an invitation from Amir Jang to accompany him on a river journey to Shushtar. The trip was taken in a barge constructed of a large, light raft fastened to a hundred inflated goatskins. They set off with the royal party, some twenty including the three filmmakers, all lounging at the rear under the shade of a tasseled canopy, where thick rugs had been spread with piles of silken cushions.

"You join me?" Amir Jang smiled to his guests as he ritualistically laid a pellet of opium in the bowl of an opium pipe. He picked up a pair of silver tongs and pulled a red-hot piece of coal from a brazier and held it over the pellet, which sizzled as it melted. When it was ready, Harrison recalled, Amir Jang first handed the pipe to her. She drew in the sweet smoke and exhaled. Amir Jang then prepared a pipe for Cooper, Schoedsack, and each of his guests, saving his own pipe for last. And so they leaned back on the cushions as the pipe was prepared and passed around, gazing at the scenery as they glided along.

Harrison fell under the spell of the enchanting song of the boatman. There was the drowsy heat of midday but a cooling breeze off the water, and the sight of strange rock formations on the passing shoreline. It seemed the most natural thing in the world, drifting on this river on inflated goatskins. She dreamed of reincarnation, wondering if that explained her natural facility with languages. Perhaps her ancestors had fought with Darius and Xerxes, she mused as they drifted. Others, perhaps, had swept across Asia with the Golden Horde and ruled over the people of conquered Russia. "I suddenly felt . . . old because of all I remembered, young because of all I had forgotten!" she wrote.[22]

A white gull flew overhead and Jang lifted up a gun and hit it with a single shot, earning applause from the attendants as the bird plummeted into the water. Cooper watched the dead bird floating along beside them until a whirlpool sucked the carcass out of sight.

As they neared the banks of Shushtar they came to a whirlpool that three days before had broken a raft and drowned seven men. But the boatmen worked their paddles and the Il Begi serenely smiled as they shot past the roiling waters and made it safely to shore.

That evening, Cooper and company were suddenly called to a mysterious appointment, led by lantern light down the dirty city streets. They came to a doorway that opened onto a long, shadowy alleyway, which ended in an open courtyard, a romantic Oriental vision of vaulting arches, candles flickering in the warm breeze, and a pool reflecting the glittering stars. At the pool, surrounded by courtiers, sat Amir Jang. Jang introduced them to a man named Baran, brother of Haidar Khan, chief of the Baba Ahmedi tribe. Baran would take the three adventurers to meet Haidar's tribe, the group with which they would be traveling.

"Good," Cooper thought. It was settled. And he knew that somewhere, beyond the beckoning mountain range, were the black tents of the tribesmen. The grass was dying, and soon the migration would have to begin.

So it was that by April 12, the moviemakers, with an interpreter along, were camped at the place from which their journey would begin. Half of their precious film remained to document the migration. The Baba Ahmedi tribe was scattered within its own family units for twenty miles down the valley, Cooper estimated. The tribesmen would split up and travel in different directions to the promised land, with Cooper, Schoedsack, and Harrison following Haidar's tribe along the toughest route. He surveyed the camp and watched the setting sun suffuse the valley and snow-covered peaks with crimson and golden light. Twilight arrived with ethereal clouds shrouding the now purplish peaks, and a pale moon was revealed, shining through a silvery, misty haze. Cooper would enter his open tent and begin writing, noting that he would have come around the world just to spend that twilight hour.

"The candle flame, by which I am writing stands as straight as an arrow; there is not a breath of wind; yet here in our open tent it is cool with the coolness of spring in [the] mountain air."[23] Cooper would gaze out at the moonlit sky; he'd see the shadowy figures moving about the fires burning in the valley camp. "Lord! But this is good! We are away from the stench and bickerings of the city, and with the tribes at last."[24]

By April 15 the grass was brown, and two days later the tribe was finally on the move. Cooper realized the epic scope of the migration. "This is not an affair of Haidar and his tribe." he wrote in his diary. "It is the movement of an entire people. It is a battle of man against nature, staged on a gigantic scale."[25]

THE BAKHTIARI HAD a reputation as fierce fighters who prided themselves on being impervious to the elements. Twice a year the tribe made this migration, spurred on by the seasonal life-and-death cycle of the waving grass upon which their animals fed and the people were, in turn, sustained. There was no easy way to make the journey, and whether young or old, sick or healthy, all had to do or die. Death always claimed a few victims along the road.

The foreigners owned a rifle and pistol between them, but had left the weapons behind. Cooper reasoned that carrying weapons among the notoriously wild tribesmen might have been an "invitation to be killed." They had done the traditional breaking of bread and salt with the princes of the Bakhtiari and that, along with the blessings of the tribal leaders, would provide greater protection than being armed, he hoped.[26]

Rahim Khan, before giving his good-byes, introduced the visitors to the tribal chief and their protector, Haidar Khan. Haidar obeyed, without question, the order of the Il Begi to take along the foreigners and be responsible for them. He even welcomed them by killing a sheep in their honor and serving it with boiled rice and curds and milk. At their first meeting, Cooper was impressed by the physical presence of the tribal leader. Haidar had a brutal look, reminding Cooper of a gorilla with his powerful arms, his great chest, and stocky build that seemed ready to burst the fabric of his long coat.[27] But Haidar's fierceness seemed to soften around his son Lufta, a nine-year-old boy who had already taken on the responsibilities of a man.

Haidar explained to Cooper that the migration itself was divided into five separate groups, each taking a different route over the mountains.

COOP AND SHORTY SHARE A LAUGH AND THE *KALYAN* PIPE
WITH HAIDAR KHAN AND HIS SON LUFTA.
Courtesy of Milestone Film & Video; image from Cooper Papers, BYU

Their own group, numbering five thousand people, would converge with the rest of the tribe in a great valley. The rest of the journey would be a mass migration for their protection, because they would be traveling through the territory of enemy tribes.

During the first leg—from the foothills to a treeless, barren range of mountains—they passed a village that shocked Harrison with its maladies, including malaria, sore eyes, and dysentery. She had brought along a stock of medical supplies and provided the villagers with some cathartic pills, quinine tablets, and other remedies. Haidar's second wife had also come asking her for some remedy that would allow her to bear a child, and soon the flap of Marguerite's tent was being pulled back by people wanting to see the *hakim khamn,* the "lady doctor."

Harrison was dismayed—she had no medical experience—but she accepted the responsibility of doctoring the tribe, and specific "office hours" were arranged. Something about her indomitable spirit inspired confidence in her patients, and she found herself adept at addressing a wide range of ills. For malaria she had the quinine tablets, for venereal disease she bathed sores with a permanganate solution, for stomach problems she offered castor oil and cathartic pills. One time a worried mother brought in a son who was practically a living skeleton from having swallowed a leech, but a solution of lukewarm saltwater helped him vomit it up, and the boy was soon back to good health. On another occasion, a tribesman slashed by knives during a duel over a horse was brought to her by the man's three wives, who cried hysterically and tore their hair while Harrison tended the blood-soaked body, dressing the man's wounds and even using a pair of scissors to clip off a finger that was hanging by a shred of skin. She had drawn the line at dentistry, but had iodine at the ready if someone came to her with a toothache.[28]

At the last village in their territory, the tribes left their tents behind so they would be less encumbered for the mountains and river ahead. Everyone slept out in the open, and Cooper was impressed with the uncomplaining Bakhtiari women who carried their babies in wooden cradles slung over their backs as they traveled on the open trail and in every kind of weather.

Along the route, Cooper rode a horse while Shorty and Maggie rode mules.[29] Like the tribe, Cooper and Schoedsack bedded down in the open. The only exception was a small tent they brought along for Marguerite, who slept with the fragile film negatives and the dwindling cache of money under her bed. The foreigners drank the same sugary tea and joined in the usual noonday meal of bread and sour milk and the evening supper of bread and rice and mutton. Sometimes, at Haidar's camp, they'd smoke the *kalyan* pipe filled with tobacco, not the opium the nobles favored.[30]

The journey was so rugged that the tribe was lucky to cover ten miles in twelve hours, with Cooper and Schoedsack usually going ahead of the migration to pick out the best spots from which to film the nomads as they passed. There could be no rehearsals and retakes but, as Harrison later noted, between Shorty's instinct and judgment and Merian's raw energy and enthusiasm, they never missed an important scene. Sometimes her partners would be ahead of the tribe for days at a time, leaving her in charge of moving their camp and guarding their precious film.[31]

When she was to appear in a scene, Harrison applied makeup before they left camp. The makeup would usually start melting in the hundred-degree heat, so she always had her makeup box ready on the pommel of her mule's saddle for when she needed a touch-up.

The tribe usually broke camp after midnight to avoid the heat of the day, which brought suffering to their flocks. Schoedsack would later recall the suffering it caused the filmmakers, trying to shoot against the blinding sun of early morning or missing altogether the dramas playing out in complete darkness, such as hauling animals up over cliffs by sheer manpower. Schoedsack and Cooper would ride ahead of the tribe with their guide and patiently wait as the sun rose to get one shot, some ten or fifteen feet of film, which was often all they could manage in a day.[32]

The first truly great obstacle faced by the five thousand of Haidar's people was the Karun River, a half-mile-wide expanse of snowmelt that ran from the mountain gorges full of dangerous rapids, crosscurrents, and whirlpools. Schoedsack would recall that previously, Western explorers had reached this river but had gone no farther; the Karun was the great boundary to the unknown, across which no foreigner had trespassed.[33] They camped several miles from the Karun, along a stream that was a trickle of the mighty river that awaited them, and Schoedsack departed alone to scout potential camera positions for the river crossing. Cooper had not yet seen the river when a messenger arrived with a note from Shorty: "Coop! I hate to say it before we start shooting, but this is what we have been traveling months to see. Better be here before sunrise tomorrow. This is it!"[34]

IT WOULD BE almost a week after the start of the Karun River crossing before Cooper would return to his diary again. It took almost that long for the five thousand tribesmen and their many thousands of animals to get to the far shore.

"It can't be done" was Cooper's first reaction when he joined Schoedsack and surveyed the thunderous river and the distance to the far shore. There wasn't a bridge in sight, yet the tribesmen had been making this very crossing, twice a year, for centuries.

The crossing used the same materials as Amir Jang's floating barge: inflated goatskins. Each of the tribesmen carried a ration of goatskins in their saddlebags, which they now inflated and fastened to rows of long sticks to make rafts upon which to float the women and children and some of the baby animals. Still, it seemed as if the undercurrents and whirlpools would smash those makeshift rafts to bits. But a wise khan in olden times had found a way, a passage the tribes had passed down from generation to generation.[35]

The way across was an S-shaped bend in the river that swept to the far shore, so that all one had to do was push off into the slingshot current. While the women and children traveled on rafts, the tens of thousands of animals were swum across by the men, each with a pair of inflated skins fastened together, upon which they threw themselves and rode the river with their animals.

"It was a show, all right," Cooper wrote in an April 24 diary entry. "For five days Schoedsack and I, rushing about . . . watched the greatest piece of continuous action I have ever seen. Long before dawn it started. Sometimes it lasted until late in the night; once it went on all night. Shouting women, squalling children, calves, colts, goats, lambs, saddle-bags, cradles, babies—all piled helter-skelter on the rafts. Out in the stream and off! Shouts! Howls! Beaten in, go a score of cows—with them, after them, among them, a half dozen men on goatskins. Out into the river. There! The current has them! Then down-stream, down, down, like birds blown in a hurricane, down they go. More rafts, horses, more rafts, sheep, donkeys, rafts, cows, sheep—in they go. Out into the current and speeding, speeding, speeding down the stream."[36]

Haidar was in the thick of it all, Cooper noted, stripped to a loincloth and straddling his goatskin float while pulling the halter of a horse being swept with him on the current. He would cross over, then cross back to lead more men and animals. Cooper counted eight times in a single day that Haidar braved the river: "Here in danger, a *man*, by Glory!" Cooper declared.[37]

Finally, Cooper, Schoedsack, and Harrison crossed on their own goatskin rafts. Schoedsack, the fearless cameraman, continued cranking his Debrie on the way, capturing the stunning sight of the floating goatskins and people and animals. Just past his own raft he filmed whirlpools pulling several animals down.

Harrison went with three women, five goats, saddlebags, and other belongings. "We shot out into the current," she recalled, "whirled round and round dizzily until I had to shut my eyes to keep from falling off into the water, and at last reached the opposite bank." Once across, it was a several-mile climb over a rocky hill to a grassy plateau where the animals were sorted out and the nomads rested.[38]

They had made it across, but there had been losses. Dozens of animals, mostly the sheep, had drowned. And the night Cooper returned to his diary he could hear women wailing in the tent of a mother whose young son had been carried away by the cruel rapids.[39]

BY THE END of April, Haidar's five thousand had been marching for weeks and the Americans had settled into a comfort zone of familiarity and shared burdens. The women goaded their sheep along with sticks and the call of "*Yo, Ali, Ali!*" and in good humor, Schoedsack would call back with the same inflection of voice, "Knock 'em for a goal!" The tribeswomen laughed and repeated the foreign slang, to the surprise of the filmmakers. And that's what started the collective singing of the American song and catchphrase "Yes, we have no bananas." After a few days, the infectious ditty echoed along the trail. Cooper would recall, with delight, the bizarre touch of Persian mountain passes echoing with the lyrics, sung by one of the wildest nomadic tribes in Persia.[40]

They called out the silly song as they neared the summit, and down into the Shimbar Valley, where the other tribes of the Bakhtiari were converging. In the gathering place the campfires of the tribes seemed as plentiful as the stars. Here was a place for resting the animals before the next mountain range, a time for the khans to dispense judgments and young men to practice acts of manhood by stealing horses and guns.

During the day, the young men took to the river, and Cooper himself was challenged to swim a race. He had won several and was emerging from the waters after his last victory swim when he saw Haidar striding forward, stripped to his loincloth and coming to uphold the honor of his tribe. The two men plunged into the water and raced neck and neck until the older man left his opponent in his wake. Cooper emerged gasping for breath and cursing the cigars, stifling rooms, and gasoline-laden air of civilization.[41]

The migration pushed on, and the trail narrowed as it ascended the mountain peaks. Cooper and Schoedsack suddenly found themselves behind the tribes, not in front, where they had their usual camera position. Suddenly, their camera donkey slipped and began falling, rolling among the stones. The two men halted the animal's slide and unpacked the undamaged camera. Schoedsack hauled it up himself, and Cooper followed with the tripod braced on his shoulder. Clinging to handholds, they pulled themselves up the trail until they seemed to reach the very clouds; behind them stretched the specks of the tribesmen zigzagging up the mountain. Cooper noticed how smooth the rocks were, worn by centuries of migrations.

Cooper and Schoedsack reached the peak and witnessed a sight that stopped them in their tracks. About forty miles away, across more rugged country, was a towering, snowcapped range that filled the horizon. It was the final barrier to the land of grass—Zardeh Kuh.[42]

The assault on Zardeh Kuh did not begin auspiciously. Harrison was suffering from malaria and had given away all her medicines caring for the tribe. But her healing efforts were returned in kind as Haidar halted the migration. The khans visited her and managed to bring her some of the quinine pills she had distributed that hadn't been used.

Harrison was soon on the mend, but the tribe was stalled again as word went out that the rival Bawardi tribe might attack them. This was because the Bakhtiari were protecting the Beidarwand, a tribe that had raided the

Bawardi on the last migration, and had killed men and stolen horses, tents, and other treasures.

The only consolation was that they were in high forest country and could graze on the sweet grasses of Raki land—the "thief tribe," as Cooper found they were called. A tribal council had been called between the gray-bearded Raki leader and the khans, and the Raki had demanded tribute from the tribes crossing their land. But Haidar was among those who simply laughed and tapped his rifle—*this* was their answer to such demands.

The vast migration pushed on, aiming straight for the sheer mountain barrier that lay ahead, and Cooper found himself daydreaming of life among this wild people. They camped at dusk, and he hiked alone into some woods, marveling at the snowy peaks around them. "Buy horses, a few flocks of sheep, ally with one of the powerful tribes, get a couple of good Persian doctors—oh, there would be no limit to what might be done," Cooper mused to his diary. "Health and freedom and what a chance for power if a man was willing to play the game and run the risks. These people had over-run Persia before. They could put five to fifteen thousand fairly good light cavalry in the field and then..." And then Cooper laughed at himself and his grand notion, still laughing as he got up and headed back to camp in the dark.[43]

ZARDEH KUH LOOMED almost fifteen thousand feet above sea level, most of it a vertical rise that was impossible to climb. This was no-man's-land—even the grass for the animals had to be brought from Raki land, because nothing grew upon the cold mountain wall.

Like the bend in the Karun, which had allowed a seemingly impossible crossing, there was one snowy slope that allowed passage over the summit. The thousands of tribesmen waited as Haidar and a chosen few went ahead to forge a path. He and his men took off their cotton slippers and stepped up with picks and shovels. Then, barefoot in the freezing snow and clad only in thin cotton clothes as protection against the freezing wind, they began hacking a path. They worked for hours, breaking open the path and pushing up snow walls that formed the only barrier between the nomads and a fatal fall off the sheer cliff face.

During the first day's assault, Cooper and Schoedsack took Maggie over the summit to the camp below the snows, then returned to position themselves to film the ascent of the tribe. Evening came and they decided to stay the night, to film the tribesmen who would be continuing in the morning. They settled in with their animals, including their camera don-key, and a helper named Davut, who brought some grains for the ani-mals.[44] The piercing wind was blowing in their faces, they were cold and hungry—and deliriously happy, literally at "the peak of happiness," Cooper

OVER THE BARRIER OF ZARDEH KUH TO THE
LAND OF GRASS—GRASS AND LIFE!

Courtesy of Milestone Film & Video; image from Cooper Papers, BYU

wrote in his diary. "We've done it. There's no doubt about it. We've seen as great a struggle for existence as there is. And we have it for the screen!"[45]

By the next day's passage, the snow was as smooth as glass. At one point, Schoedsack had to step outside the trail to set up his camera. He thrust the ends of the tripod into the snow—and began slipping into the abyss and certain death. But the weight of the secured camera gave Schoedsack the necessary second to regain his balance and hold on.[46]

Other than that heart-stopping moment, the duo found themselves too enthralled with the unfolding drama to worry about personal danger. Cooper would recall the awe-inspiring sight of the mass of people moving higher and higher, through the snow and in the face of the icy wind, the lusty shouts of those driving their weary, faltering animals ever upward. He would recall close-ups of the action, like vivid paintings: an old, bearded man with a child on his shoulders, both crying from the cold as the man moved forward, leaning on two big sticks; a sick boy fastened to the back of a donkey; a little girl carrying on her back a calf that was almost as big as she; the sight of Maggie being escorted by Haidar and his son.

"At last, snow and mountain ended; we broke out of a gorge into the open," Cooper wrote. "Here, out to the horizon stretched green valleys through which, in the golden sunshine, rippled silver streams feeding the luxuriant young grass. Here was the prize of the gallant fight. Here was the land of plenty. Grass. Grass and Life!"[47]

Throughout his life, Cooper would fondly recall this great time of youth and the dream of endless possibilities, even the dream of fleeing civilization, with its soft ways and poisoned air, to join the tribes and share their life in the great, age-old struggle against nature—to perhaps even command a tribal army of conquest!

But he and his partners would soon leave with the shadow of Zardeh Kuh at their backs, heading to Isfahan and Teheran and the well-traveled road to Baghdad, and from there to Europe and across the ocean to the United States. This was the world of the nomads, and the hardships of the migration were already being forgotten as they began scattering across the green land, settling in black tents brought to the valley.

"So we rode away out of the [Bakhtiari] country," Cooper wrote in the final paragraphs of his book on the movie expedition, "and left the tribes in The Land of Grass—there to dwell easily and happily for four or five months, when, the grass being killed, once more they would have to pack their all and go—go back over that glorious mountain country into the foothills of Arabistan.

"Thus once, perhaps, our fathers' fathers lived. Year in and year out, twice a year, spring and fall, through the centuries, fighting nature for the prizes of Grass and Life."[48]

CHAPTER ELEVEN

THE JUNGLE STORY

> *Cooper is like a knight of old in his chivalry, honor and courage. . . .*
> *Schoedsack . . . might have been a pioneer with Lewis and Clark or*
> *others of our explorers of America. . . . Asia readers will join in*
> *wishing them the fulfillment of the dream that sends them on their*
> *new expedition.*
>
> —"Along the Trail with the Editor,"
> ASIA magazine, September 1925[1]

THE AMERICANS SPENT THREE NIGHTS IN THE VALLEY OF GRASS, MARGUERITE Harrison recalled. Ahead of them lay a three-day ride to the nearest town, where they could telegraph to Isfahan for an automobile that would take them on to Teheran and then Baghdad. They had been on the road for nearly a year and Shorty had exposed virtually all the film, with only eighty feet to spare. By the time they left Baghdad they were in a rush to cross the Syrian desert, mindful that the scorching heat could damage their fragile film. As her partners got a head start for Europe, Harrison decided to linger for a week and visit Jerusalem and Palestine.

At Beirut, Cooper and Schoedsack took the first steamer for Marseilles, their funds so low they had to travel in steerage. They hired a boatman to ferry them to the steamer and the boatman tried to double the price, while their film cases attracted the attention of unsavory characters who assumed they were treasure chests. Schoedsack slugged one and Cooper joined in the fight, even as another man tried to throw their precious cases overboard. But a bystander who was a Black and Tan and one of the torturers in Jerusalem with the British—"this little fellow, hard-bitten as heck," Coop recalled—jumped into the fight alongside Cooper and Schoedsack.

After settling accounts with their fists, the filmmakers managed to get their cargo aboard.[2]

Back in Paris they found themselves a cheap room in the Moroccan quarter. Although they didn't know how to develop film, they rented equipment and hired two "film girls," as Cooper recalled, to help them. They had to buy a book and read up on the process, but, astonishingly, they lost no film.[3]

The next stage of the production was back home in New York, where the two partners edited the entire picture themselves.

For Marguerite, the week she spent alone was a chance to decompress and consider the adventure. The migration, which had thrilled Merian with its raw struggle for survival, had troubled her. To her, there was nothing romantic or exotic about the tribal life. The chiefs had the wealth, and the mass of people were poor and lived on a meager diet. Neither she nor Shorty had any regret about their leave-taking.

"Merian was the only one of our party who developed a liking for the Bakhtiari," Harrison would write. ". . . Their two outstanding qualities were an arrogant pride of race and a contempt for physical weakness."[4]

Despite her reservations, Harrison's heart would always be warm with memories of Persia. She traveled by automobile to Baghdad, following Alexander the Great's route of conquest to India. "My last night in Persia was spent at Karind where I slept out under the stars on the flat-topped roof of a caravanserai on the edge of the mountains overlooking the plain of Iraq that stretched away to Baghdad," she wrote.

"The workaday world was before me. Behind me was another world of dim ancestral memories." Both worlds called her—she dreamed of following the ghost of Marco Polo into Central Asia, but would answer the call to Beirut, Paris, and New York.[5]

DECADES AFTER THE great migration, Schoedsack would shock film historian Kevin Brownlow by admitting that when he and Merian returned to the United States from Europe they *threw away* some of their footage—they couldn't afford the duty on all of it. "Now, I'd know the difference between a bad shot and a good shot, wouldn't I?" a smiling Schoedsack drawled in his defense.[6]

Cooper and Schoedsack brought a creative instinct to their work on the epic film, which would emerge as one of the great pioneering adventure documentaries in movie history; somehow they turned blissful ignorance into a positive. Cooper would even reflect that since he'd seen so few films, he was "unspoiled" by the artifice of Hollywood.[7] He later admitted that while he had generally concentrated on which shots to take, Schoedsack had been in charge of the filming and the credit for *Grass* should go to his long, lanky partner.[8]

Schoedsack himself explained that he and Coop had collaborated on the important issues of a production but "we divided our duties according to our likes, dislikes, and abilities." There was one department that Schoedsack always ceded to Cooper: "The business of public relations and publicity . . . which I dislike heartily (being the 'strong, silent type') I always left to Cooper who, fortunately for both of us, was very good at it. Cooper also had the ability to sell ideas to people who were in a position to finance them."[9]

Cooper and Marguerite Harrison were on the 1924–25 list of "celebrated lecturers" at the Pond Bureau of New York. The resulting income was vital, given that back in New York their funds had run so low they all had to scratch for a living as they finished the film. Cooper and Schoedsack went to work with an eye to sustaining their future partnership, and Schoedsack began by selling stills of the migration to earn enough money to rent the room in New York where they could edit the movie. Cooper won another book contract with G. P. Putnam's Sons, the publisher that had released *The Sea Gypsy* earlier in 1924.

Cooper also returned to the States feeling as if he had come into his own as an explorer, and in December 1924 he applied for membership in the celebrated Explorers Club of New York. His application included a supporting letter from James B. Pond, head of the speakers bureau, with seconding letters that included one from explorer William Beebe. "The information he gives about himself on the proposal form is typical of the man," Pond wrote. "He gives only the merest details and in no way tries to attract attention to his unusual exploits. His recent trip through an unknown part of Persia with the Bakhtiari tribe is as unusual a piece of field work as comes within the experience of most explorers." Cooper was elected a member on December 16, 1924, and his election formally noted by the club's secretary on January 17, 1925.[10]

One of Cooper's earliest and most prestigious lectures was given at the

Explorers Club annual dinner, held at the Hotel McAlpin on January 24, 1925. Presentations ranged from a talk on China to a Dr. Willis T. Lee's motion picture of the Carlsbad Caverns of the Southwest. The concluding presentation would be *Grass,* which, the program noted, was being shown for the first time.[11]

The *Explorers Journal* reported on the success of Cooper's presentation: "It is Mr. Cooper's happy achievement to have portrayed poignantly and comprehensively the drama of a people in their primitive struggle with the inexorable forces of nature.... The pictures were a fitting climax to an evening of thrilling entertainment."[12]

Grass became more than a lecture film when it was acquired by Paramount Pictures, the Hollywood studio that was formed out of Famous Players–Lasky. Marguerite Harrison would claim that they had taken their film to a "motion picture broker" who had made the arrangements for its release through the Paramount Corporation.[13] Whether a broker had been part of the process, Cooper later explained that studio executive Jesse Lasky had seen a print of *Grass* at a dinner party. "[Lasky] got hold of me and said he'd like to release it theatrically," Cooper noted.[14]

Meanwhile, Schoedsack had decided to "support the firm of Cooper and Schoedsack," as Kevin Brownlow called the partnership, by serving as cameraman for a New York Zoological Society expedition led by William Beebe and bound for the Sargasso Sea and the Galápagos Islands.[15] It was on the expedition that Shorty met a young, pretty naturalist named Ruth Rose. The two fell in love and became engaged on that voyage. One of the big changes upon their return was that instead of "Shorty," Ruth insisted that Schoedsack's nickname be "Monte"—"Shorty" simply didn't suit him, Ruth said. Cooper, however, would often use both nicknames in the years to come. To confuse matters even more, Schoedsack's new nickname would be spelled both "Monty" and "Monte."[16]

"We had a wonderful partnership, we never had any contract between us," Cooper once wrote, explaining that he and Schoedsack even shared a bank account. There was a tidy $1,000 in the bank when Shorty left on the Galápagos expedition, but upon his return there was only $7 left—and Schoedsack still had to buy an engagement ring for Ruth. "Who had spent the dough? Me—Cooper, the Gambler!!! I gambled everything on trying to put 'Grass' across, and got us another picture to make. Did Monty reproach me? Not a word! And he got Ruth her ring, in spite of my gambling!!! He put the bite on George Putnam, our publisher, to guarantee the cost of the ring."[17]

The studio felt that the two budding renaissance picturemakers—who'd conceived, produced, directed, filmed, and edited the final picture and had even developed the negatives—had to be seen by audiences. Thus, the theatrical release of *Grass* would open with shots of Cooper puffing on his pipe and talking with Shorty, an interlude shot behind Paramount's Astoria Studios in New York before Schoedsack left on the Galápagos expedition.

ALTHOUGH MARGUERITE HARRISON shared in the proceeds of *Grass* and all the benefits of the partnership, she essentially withdrew from any further filmmaking adventures with Cooper and Schoedsack. The old bugaboo of "creative differences" emerged in a disagreement over the intertitles, the interposition of frames of text in silent films. Harrison felt they'd made an authentic record of a "natural drama" and the titles should be natural and realistic. But she was overruled by Coop and Shorty. "Their titles were melodramatic, artificial and of the theater," Harrison wrote. "They put impossible speeches into the mouths of the Bakhtiari tribesmen, whose language was as primitive as their lives. . . .

"I knew that Merian and Shorty understood the mentality of the movie going public far better than I, and that they were quite right from the point of view of the theater, but I simply could not collaborate with them."[18]

Harrison would pursue other adventures, other interests. In 1925, over tea in the New York apartment of fellow explorer Blair Niles, the two women conceived the idea of an organization dedicated to female explorers. Harrison and Niles called Gertrudy Shelby and Gertrude Emerson, and on a snowy, stormy afternoon, the Society of Women Geographers was born—an organization that continues to this day. "We had all been not a little annoyed," Marguerite recalled, "at being interviewed by reporters who seemed convinced that the public would be interested chiefly in whether I had used lipstick in the Gobi Desert, or whether Blair had lost her heart to a descendent of the Incas. . . . So we held an indignation meeting and then and there decided that we would form an organization of our own."[19]

Marguerite Harrison's path diverged from Cooper and Schoedsack's trail, but she watched the success of her former partners from afar. *Grass* made its debut in the Criterion Theater in New York on March 30, 1925.

"It was a hit!" Cooper summed up.[20]

The picture did fine box office by Hollywood standards, particularly given what had been a shoestring budget. Exhibitors characterized *Grass* as an "artistic picture" because it didn't have the popular ingredients of fights and love scenes. A reviewer for *The Detroit News* put the film in a class with Robert Flaherty's seminal 1922 documentary of life among the Eskimos, *Nanook of the North,* and argued that such artistic pictures be given "special exploitation in regular movie theaters."[21]

Most gratifying was the praise that came from Cooper's colleagues in the world of exploration. *Asia* editor Louis Froelick proclaimed that *Grass* exemplified "one of the greatest natural dramas in the struggle for existence, told by dramatists of reality." Isaiah Bowman declared to the head of the Explorers Club in New York that *Grass* was "the best thing I have ever seen," while Gilbert Grosvenor, president of the National Geographical Society, applauded the picture's "geographical knowledge" and entertainment value. Explorer William Beebe weighed in with the pronouncement that "this certainly will be remembered as one of the greatest pictures ever produced."[22]

Grass had its critics. Some claimed it had to be a fake. Among the naysayers was a southern California preacher who announced that the "Persian" mountains were really the local San Bernardino Mountains, though how the novice filmmakers had assembled a cast of thousands of Persians and herds of animals wasn't addressed.[23] To others, the presence of Harrison seemed incongruous—she looked too fashionable to have been on such a perilous migration.

"They little knew how hard I had worked to look presentable!" Marguerite scoffed.[24]

But the harshest critics would be Cooper and Schoedsack themselves. Most annoying for the fiercely independent duo was their first encounter with studio politics, the studio requesting that they restore some one thousand feet of footage they'd cut out toward the end of the picture. Cooper, who already had an instinctive feel for editing and pace, grudgingly agreed, although he always felt it made the last part too long.[25] The box office, which gladdened the studio, earned the three partners only several thousand dollars in participation profit, and an older and wiser Cooper sighed that they had received one of the worst distribution deals in history.[26]

And, in the final analysis, the filmmakers considered their first effort a creative failure. "I never considered *Grass* a good picture," Cooper once confessed.[27]

"I have always considered *Grass* to be a lost opportunity, and a great missed chance," Schoedsack agreed.[28]

The filmmakers had felt that to properly dramatize the migration and allow audiences to relate to the nomads, they needed to focus on the personal experiences of a single Bakhtiari family.[29] Although Haidar and his son had been highlighted to some degree, that hadn't been enough for them. Cooper and Schoedsack had wanted to return to Persia to film a single family during another of the biannual treks, but their dwindling finances dashed those plans. They would ever after call *Grass* the "damned half picture."[30]

Grass might have been a missed opportunity to the picturemakers themselves, but the spectacle of the final film—the crossing of the Karun, the indomitable tribe zigzagging up the glacial face of Zardeh Kuh—awed audiences. Jesse Lasky was eager for a new adventure picture from the team of Cooper and Schoedsack. Contemplating their next expedition, Cooper reasoned that since *Grass* had crossed open, almost barren terrain, they'd find a different kind of drama in the jungle, where the wilderness would close in on them.[31]

Thus, the second Cooper-Schoedsack production was launched with the backing of a major studio and Jesse Lasky, the man they called their "patron saint." The $10,000 the filmmakers had scraped together for *Grass* was eclipsed by a $75,000 budget from Paramount for their expedition to the jungles of Siam, the land known today as Thailand.

Years later, Cooper would hail the resulting 1927 release of *Chang* as the best movie he and Schoedsack ever produced—even when stacked up against mighty *King Kong*. Perhaps one of the reasons was that, in addition to the "distant, difficult, and dangerous" nature of the production, they'd finally have the family they'd missed in *Grass*. "We had a theme in 'Chang' that the jungle was eternal, that man always fought against it and that the struggle would go on forever," Cooper told Lowell Thomas years later. "We decided not to shoot Angkhor [*sic*] Vat, but to stick to the simplicity of a single village and outside of that, a single family and dramatize the whole picture around it."[32]

Schoedsack was still on the Galápagos expedition when Cooper discussed the new production with Jesse Lasky. Cooper's proposal included ideas for scenes of showstopping, crowd-pleasing spectacle he later likened to the chariot race of *Ben-Hur.* The centerpiece that sold Lasky on the proposed production was a dream of hundreds of wild elephants stampeding and destroying a village. The elephants had been a building block of the story, but reports of man-eating tigers would also figure into the emerging story line. However, the camerawork wouldn't begin, Cooper explained, until he and Schoedsack had spent an extensive period on location studying and becoming completely familiar with the native culture and animal life.[33]

Grass had been a pure documentary—with the exception of the bran sandstorm effect, Harrison noted—but *Chang* would be neither a pedestrian travelogue nor a proper documentary. It would stand alone as another stage in the evolving narrative structure of Cooper-Schoedsack productions, following a philosophy of "natural drama," which Cooper once summed up as "drama produced with natural actors in their own environment, living the story of their lives and their struggle for existence."[34]

CONSIDERING, IN RETROSPECT, the film's importance to Cooper, it was ironic that he sailed for Siam in the distracting grip of another competing dream he imagined for himself and his partner. Cooper even confessed his longing to do "the Arabian trip" in a letter to Isaiah Bowman at the American Geographical Society, while bound for Siam on the S.S. *Insuline.* Except for a cursory rundown of the jungle expedition and a final paragraph requesting letters of introduction from the American Geographical Society to present the king and other officials in Siam, Cooper's mind was clearly focused on the Empty Quarter.

Dear Bowman:

I am sending you a line to be mailed at Port Said to let you know that both Schoedsack and I are keener on the Arabian trip than ever.

We are going to feel like the Devil sailing by that coast, and not stopping. Anything that you can do to press it along we will both appreciate immensely. Our offhand plans are to go to Bangkok in Siam, and thence to live with the hill tribes in North Siam. These plans will be subject to change depending upon the kind of country and people we will actually find there. But I only look on this trip as a necessary but inconvenient obstacle to be finished with before we can get on with the Arabian show.[35]

In a September 17 reply sent in care of the American consul's office at Bangkok, Bowman said he hoped backing for the Arabian trip might be secured and brought Cooper's attention back to his current adventure. "Mighty glad to have your note from the S.S. Insuline, and I hope that it will be the precursor of many more. I shall follow your work in Siam with the greatest interest."[36]

JUNGLE CLEARING IN SIAM, SETTING FOR KRU'S JUNGLE HOME IN *CHANG*.

Courtesy of Milestone Film & Video; image from Cooper Papers, BYU

CHAPTER TWELVE

MR. CROOKED AND THE CHANG

> *I have the hunch that motion pictures are going to be one of the great means of transmitting knowledge. . . . But somebody has to begin. Somebody has to say to himself that the so called travel picture of unrelated scenes tells nothing, teaches nothing. Somebody has to discover some way of making a picture which will set down once and for all time the effect of Nature on the lives of different peoples. There is nothing in human geography, history, anthropology etc. which cannot . . . be aided in its understanding by motion pictures. But the trouble is we don't know how to do it. We are only at the beginning of the beginning.*
>
> —Merian Cooper, writing to Isaiah Bowman from Siam[1]

IN APRIL 1924, MERIAN COOPER CAMPED WITH THE BABA AHMEDI TRIBE AND wrote a diary entry by candlelight anticipating the migratory adventure ahead. Now, some two years removed from the mountains of Persia, Cooper found himself in the mountains of northern Siam, where his "jungle diary" chronicled his efforts to catch a man-eating tiger.

One particular night, Cooper was alone in the Buddhist temple of an isolated village, seated under a scarlet-and-gold canopy and writing by the yellowish light of a lantern precariously balanced on a basket. He occasionally paused to gaze up at the gilded statue of Buddha towering above him. In the wooden rafters pennants fluttered in the nocturnal jungle breeze, trying to drag back from the nether regions the lost souls of dead villagers. It was the unwritten law of the jungle that a passing stranger could use a village temple as a guesthouse.

With the coming of night the "jungle closed in around the village like a mighty black wall." And while man slept, the jungle came awake with animals on the prowl. "We are off the track of all travel," Cooper noted in his diary. The village was on the side of a mountain thick with jungle, a stop on a learning curve to study animal life, particularly tigers and how to trap them.[2]

He and Monty always divided up responsibilities, so Cooper had gone ahead to enlist native help for the trapping of wild tigers and leopards to use in their movie. They'd been drawn to the town and district of Nan because it was plentiful with tigers—man-eating tigers. As the night wind blew through the temple and whipped the spirit-catching pennants, Cooper wrote his memories of earlier in the evening, when the deserted temple had been crowded with the village chief and elders sitting cross-legged around him. They'd listened while Muang, a twenty-eight-year-old fisherman and hunter, had served as his translator and read aloud a letter from the governor formally requesting the villagers' help in catching tigers for Cooper.

Muang had then translated the village chief's response. Man-eating tigers, he'd explained, were a great problem in Nan. They were supernatural creatures, called "spirit horses" because demonic entities rode upon their backs. Such was the tiger they called "Mr. Green," a man-eating beast ridden by a green spirit. The chief pointed to a young man sitting in the outer circle; his father had been killed and dragged into the jungle by Mr. Green only a week before. If they dared kill such spirit-possessed tigers, the wrath of the now horseless spirit would kill and transform *them* into a damned tiger to ride.[3]

Cooper, through his translator, assured the chief and the elders that while man-eaters deserved to die, he'd only be taking them into captivity. Cooper then stood and pantomimed an invisible entity riding his back and exclaimed, "And if the spirit does not like this treatment of his horse, he will bring no harm to you; for the spirit will see that you have caught Mr. Green only by my orders, and will come to ride on my shoulders, not yours. On my shoulders, I say, then, let him ride."

Cooper and Muang argued with the village council, there at the feet of the Buddha, until the chief and elders succumbed to "persuasion, threat and bribe." The bravest and strongest youths were picked to help build the tiger traps, the elders declaring that no less than a dozen men would work as protection on trails where man-eaters prowled and men had been killed.[4]

This council meeting in the Buddhist temple was part of the preparatory study period during which Cooper and Schoedsack observed native life and learned the ways of jungle animals, like the elephant—the great *chang* of the movie's title. Cooper's analytical mind was particularly focused on understanding the wild tiger, and at night, when the jungle darkness closed in around him, he found himself listening for the nocturnal call of the huge cats on the prowl. He came to know tiger ways and lore: Scratches on the ground were markings of strength and bravery, tigers hated the crows whose caws alerted the jungle to their presence, the animal's death embrace used its hundreds of pounds of muscle as leverage to break a victim's neck as its sharp fangs sank into the head or chest.

One of the major causes of the region's tiger problems, Cooper and Schoedsack learned, was that man's hunting and the sprawling rice fields had reduced the tiger's natural habitat and the numbers of its normal prey of deer, wild pigs, and other game. Tigers were forced to feed on grazing cattle, which the villagers shrugged off as tribute, a reasonable exchange in the natural scheme of things.

But a tiger hungry for human flesh wasn't considered natural. The main theory was that man-killers were injured tigers unable to bring down even domesticated cattle, and forced to settle for humans. Injury alone, however, couldn't account for the number of tigers who had become man-killers in the district of Nan—several hundred villagers had been killed and eaten in recent years, Cooper learned from government officials and the few white missionaries in the region. He concluded that many man-eaters were actually healthy cubs *taught* to stalk and kill humans by their injured mothers.[5]

Whatever the reason, the result had been a horrific reign of terror. Cooper saw the supernatural effect the stories of Mr. Green had on the natives' minds, and he himself came to half-believe that tigers *were* the vaunted "God-Devil" of native superstition.

One of the deadliest man-killers, Cooper learned, was a particular tiger who left a telltale sign by the bloody remains of its victims, a deformed pawprint indicating a crooked right foreleg. "Mr. Crooked," as the tiger was known, was striking everywhere, catching its human victims on riverbanks, in rice fields, and even in their homes, gorging on human flesh before vanishing back into the jungle.

MERIAN SENT A letter to his father through the American consul in Bangkok when he and Schoedsack first reached Nan, after a five-day journey through the mountains from the railroad that penetrated northern Siam. Their base was an abandoned missionary house in Nan, but they were usually away from it. Cooper reported that he had a servant to do the cooking, a native hunter who spoke some English, carriers for supplies, and that he had trained them into a "crack crew" that moved swiftly and efficiently through the jungle.[6]

Cooper and Schoedsack traveled from village to village, sometimes splitting up, sometimes working together as they tracked and organized tiger traps up and down the Nan River. One of the traps was a classic deadfall, arranged so a heavy weight would be triggered to drop and kill or incapacitate the animal. But the basic trap, which Cooper described as a "glorified enormous rat-trap," was a wood structure with an inner partition of logs protecting the bait, usually a dog. When a hungry tiger entered the open gate and tripped a bamboo treadle, the trap would release a log holding the door and drop it down, trapping the beast.

Time went by, and more tiger traps were built—without success. Cooper chalked up the failures to the tigers' natural cunning and the natives' fear. "Their dread of the tiger is easily understood," Cooper later wrote in an article for *National Geographic Magazine*. "It was one thing for me to go trekking through the bush, armed with a modern rifle, followed by five or six carriers, making a party so large that it would be a brave or hungry killer indeed who would attack unprovoked; it was another thing for a native to live in the heart of the jungle, in a frail bamboo hut, where, half-naked, sometimes alone, armed with only his knife of soft iron, he must one day meet the catlike spring of an enormous beast, terrible in its strength, quickness, and destructive power."[7]

Cooper became frustrated at the lack of success in bagging a tiger, and his irritation finally erupted, his fiery temper nearly costing him his life. One day, he and two native assistants came to a village where a tiger had reportedly been trapped, only to discover that the creature had somehow escaped. Cooper sought out the village chief—and slapped him across the face. "And then I was foolish enough to have dinner with him," Cooper ruefully chuckled years later to Kevin Brownlow. "His wife did a nice chicken stew and it was delicious—only it was full of all these little bamboo cuts. I damn near died. A missionary doctor, Doc Collier, saved my life. . . . I was awfully sick. [Collier] fed me nothing but soft bananas and eventually those things come out of you. It was pretty rough, very painful. You either live or die. I lived."[8]

At long last, Cooper and Schoedsack received the long-awaited news that a tiger had been trapped, alive, along the river in the village of Kamuk. Night was settling in as Schoedsack arranged to take boats upriver with a cage for the trapped tiger. Cooper, Muang, and Dr. Douglas Collier set off for the village on ponies through a stretch of jungle infamous as a stalking ground for man-eaters. They took no chances: Collier was armed with a Colt .45 and a double-barreled .450, Cooper rode with a Springfield rifle, and Muang had borrowed Cooper's Mannlicher. But their weapons offered meager comfort as the darkness worked on their minds.

Cooper would note the eerie feeling as the black wall of night closed in on them, the mystical dread that only a jungle night could produce. The moon would appear through breaks in the clouds, casting silvery light through the trees and onto their path. Then another cloud would roll across the moon and the black wall would again silently close behind them.[9]

It was almost midnight when they arrived at Kamuk. The normal nighttime routine had been shattered in the excitement, and the entire village was wide awake. Cooper and his party enlisted eight villagers to accompany them to check out the trap on the riverbank. Four of the villagers led, and four followed with flaming torches held aloft, surrounding the riders in an orange ball of light, which opened up a path in the darkness. Down toward the river they were greeted by women and children shouting and pointing to where the tiger was trapped.

And then the riders came to a sight Cooper would long remember.

A dozen fires were burning above the riverbank where groups of half-naked, tattooed men lay or sat upon the ground, their bodies and spears and swords gleaming in the crackling flames. In the center was a huge tree and a black shape that seemed to move, animated by the flickering strobe of the fires. Cooper and his company approached, and the amorphous shape revealed itself as the log trap. They slowly approached the pile of logs and bent down to peer through the cracks.

Suddenly, a roar erupted from within and the trap shook as the tiger rammed its wooden prison. The jungle men answered with howls and a waving of spears. The tiger roared back as Cooper and Collier retreated to spread their blankets by a fire.

Muang smiled excitedly as he exclaimed, *"It is Mr. Crooked!"*

THE NEXT AFTERNOON the boats arrived, docking at a landing a half mile away. From there a special tiger cage, strengthened with logs, was raised upon bamboo poles and brought to the trap. The sun was setting when

SCHOEDSACK'S CAMERA CATCHES A STALKING TIGER. ON THE
BACK OF THIS PHOTO IS THE INSCRIPTION "KITTY! KITTY!"

Courtesy of Milestone Film & Video; image from Cooper Papers, BYU

Cooper, Collier, Muang, and a muscular young man named Than were ready to transfer the tiger from trap to cage. From the safety of surrounding tree branches nervous villagers watched as Muang stood atop the cage and lifted the door. Than stood above the log trap, while Cooper and Doc Collier positioned themselves in the narrow space between the trap and the cage.

Than pulled open the trap door.

From within the darkness of the open trap, Mr. Crooked growled.

Cooper grabbed a stick and poked it in. Enraged, the tiger bit the end of the stick off.

At a signal from Cooper, Than secured the open trap door, jumped down, and got a flaming torch. He handed it to Cooper, who thrust it into the trap. Suddenly, three hundred pounds of tiger leapt through the opening and into the cage, and Muang quickly dropped the cage door.

It took a team of villagers to lift the bamboo poles and carry the trap, and by the time they reached the river it was night, resulting in a torchlit procession. The waiting boats looked more like canoes than proper boats to Cooper, and when their tiger boat shoved off into the moonlit waters it was crowded, loaded as it was with the caged animal, Cooper, Collier, Muang, four boatmen, extra wood, bamboo, and ties for the trap. The missionary had also brought along a big bottle of chloroform, thus earning some good-natured teasing from Cooper.

Almost imperceptibly, dark clouds began filling the sky, until they blotted out the moon. Then Cooper felt something wet hit his cheek. The raindrops became a downpour. The darkened sky was slashed by lightning and answering thunder, and a wind stirred, lashing sheets of rain. As if to answer the elemental fury, Mr. Crooked roared and gnawed at the wood so vigorously that Cooper thought he'd better check the cage.

He took a flashlight from Collier and swung out onto the boat's outrigger. He brought the light up, leaned forward with his eyes close to the cage—and jerked his head back. Through a sheet of rain two green eyes were staring at him, and he saw a flash of red jaws and white teeth. One log had been gnawed through and knocked out, and another log was halfway dislodged.[10]

Cooper shouted for help, and the crew quickly moved to reinforce the cage using the extra wood and bamboo. He and Collier fastened a log into the gap, only to have Mr. Crooked immediately rip it out. Meanwhile, the torrential downpour and thunder and darkness made it hard for the men to hear one another.

Collier brought out the bottle of chloroform to anesthetize the tiger. Cooper, who had teased him about it earlier, was now grateful for the missionary's foresight. With daring and desperation, the men forced a tube of bamboo through the cage and into the tiger's jaws, then poured dose after dose of chloroform into the maw of Mr. Crooked to weaken the beast and buy time to repair the damaged cage.

And so it went the whole long night, with the men perched on the outrigger as they were drenched by the downpour and the river ran over their ankles and they fed bamboo tubes of chloroform to Mr. Crooked, the angry man-eater growling and tearing the bamboo sticks to pieces.

"Those last hours before the dawn seem to me now a fantasy, something unreal as a dream," Cooper wrote.[11]

By dawn the rain had stopped, the mighty tiger was sedated, and the bamboo huts and palm trees of the little town of Nan mercifully appeared.

COOPER LEADS NATIVE HELPERS CARRYING THE CAGED MR. CROOKED,
THE MAN-EATING TIGER WHO'D BEEN TERRORIZING THE REGION,
DOWN TO THE RIVER FOR THE BOAT RIDE BACK TO NAN TOWN.

Courtesy of Milestone Film & Video; image from Cooper Papers, BYU

———

AS THE MONTHS went by, an approach for the "natural drama" took form. In a handwritten letter to Isaiah Bowman, composed by the light of a kerosene lamp (Cooper apologizes for the kerosene splattering his precious sheets of paper), he explained that his new picture would be "far more artificial" than *Grass*. "Roughly our method is this—I spend some time finding out some way the people meet a certain difficulty caused by climate, environment, wild animals, etc. Then we, with the group of natives who we have in our 'cast,' try to reproduce this scene. Under the instructions of our head office we are 'working in' a slight dramatic theme. The result will unquestionably be quite artificial; yet, in its way, it will tell—even if caractitured [*sic*]—the very real struggle of the jungle man."[12]

The story line itself would be as basic as the struggle for survival. A pioneering villager in northeastern Siam strikes out from the communal safety of his village, entering the wild jungle to make a home for his wife and two children. Despite their precautions, including building a grass hut home on stilts and erecting a high-walled pen to protect their farm animals from wild creatures, the frontier family is continually threatened by the terrors of the surrounding jungle. The cast members were all local people: Kru, a local carpenter, was "The Pioneer," Chantui, the wife of one of the carriers, played the Pioneer's wife, and a boy named Nah and a girl named Ladah played their children. Show-stealing comic relief was provided by Bimbo, a white gibbon ape and "beloved pet" of the frontier family.

One of Cooper's early tests of the natural-drama method had the two children fleeing in fear from a wild leopard that was chasing them—at least, that was how it was supposed to look in the final edit. In reality, a caged leopard would be released after the kids had a long, safe running start. However, the test almost ended in disaster.

Cooper was practicing with the children when the native in control of the leopard cage released the animal too soon. As the leopard bolted after the children, Cooper took aim and fired; but in a rare miss, he only wounded the leopard. The animal disappeared into the brush, and Cooper had to follow and finish the job. He crawled into the brush on his belly, squinting in the darkness. Then he saw the eyes of the leopard—which leapt at him. Cooper fired as the leopard sprung into midair. The creature landed, dead, its paws on either side of Cooper's head.[13]

ON LOCATION IN SIAM, CLOCKWISE FROM LEFT: COOPER, D. IRENE TAYLOR
(WIFE OF A LOCAL MISSIONARY), LADAH, SCHOEDSACK, AND KRU.

Courtesy of Milestone Film & Video; image from Cooper Papers, BYU

THIS GAG SHOT OF SCHOEDSACK AND THE TIGER
WAS SENT TO PARAMOUNT TO SHOW THERE WAS
NO DANGER IN THE JUNGLE. AN INSCRIPTION ON
THE BACK OF THE PHOTO READS "CATNAP."

Courtesy of Milestone Film & Video; image from Cooper Papers, BYU

Although they'd vowed not to kill animals unnecessarily, there were times when Cooper's expert aim had to bring down a beast to save Schoedsack or a native assistant. He stood watch as Schoedsack worked his Debrie camera, usually filming from behind camouflage, patiently waiting, sometimes for hours, for a wild animal to appear through the brush. Although telephoto lenses existed at the time, the image wasn't as sharp as Cooper and Schoedsack would have liked, so they'd decided from the start that there would be no safe, long-distance lensing of jungle action; the filmmakers wanted audiences to vicariously feel part of the action, so they had to get close to the action themselves.

As cameraman, Schoedsack was on the front line of danger and seemed to glory in it. Once, he was shooting from a camera platform surrounded by barbed wire when a tiger rushed him. It had its head through the wire and its paws on the platform when Schoedsack yelled at Coop, "Don't shoot . . . it's our only tiger!" Mercifully, the big cat ran away.[14]

In one of the most celebrated incidents during the making of the film, Schoedsack was filming a tiger from a camera platform thirteen feet up in a tree. The filmmakers' book research had explained that tigers couldn't leap higher than eleven feet, but the tiger circling at the root of Schoedsack's camera tree leapt so high it nudged the lens, its angry eyes and snarling jaws filling the frame even as Schoedsack kept the tiger in focus.[15] Lowell Thomas later wrote, "But that leap was its last, for Cooper put a bullet through its brain."[16]

There were times when the cocky filmmakers made great sport of the danger. Years later, Schoedsack recalled one such incident from *Chang* while sitting in the comfort of his office at Paramount's studios in Hollywood during a rare interview with a studio publicist. The publicist saw a photograph of a tiger appearing out of the bush, fangs bared, apparently poised to leap at the cameraman. The publicist asked about the picture, and Schoedsack said he'd taken it himself.

"The tiger looks ready to spring," the publicist noted.

"It did," Schoedsack coolly replied.

"What happened?"

"I grabbed a gun and shot it."

"That's quick work."

"Oh, it's not so much." Schoedsack shrugged. "He was so close I couldn't miss. And you know what we did? I got a couple of the natives to get some white cloth, stuffed it to look like a pillow, and put it under the tiger's head. Then I laid down beside it, like we were sleeping together. And we sent the print back to Paramount's home office to prove there wasn't any danger in the jungle."[17]

COOPER WROTE OF the jungle, "We are off the track of all travel." To him, this was a world of magic and supernatural wonder. So it was perfectly natural that the filmmakers were guided in their work by lunar influences, as Cooper later wrote: "Both Monty and I in Siam were deep students of the Moon. The Moon taught us what weather to predict. *All our shooting schedule depended on Moon Phases!!!* We could almost completely accurately predict the behavior of our native cast and elephants, gibbons, tigers, leopards, snakes, bears . . . by the Moon."[18]

His interest in aviation, which included his fascination with the earliest experiments in rocketry—including those of Robert Goddard, the first man to build a working liquid-propellant rocket—had already set his gaze toward the stars. In Siam he met some visiting professors who were studying lunar phenomena, and discussed his belief in the future colonization of outer space. His interest in the moon hailed from the voyage of the *Wisdom,* during which he'd noticed that sailors from the islands never slept on deck under the tropical full moon—"lunatic fever" was said to be the fate for those who did.

Cooper claimed that the white sailors who disregarded the native caution as superstitious nonsense were stricken with the horrifying effects of lunatic fever. By the time he was in Siam, Cooper could distinguish differences in the moon's effects from the north to the south of the country. And late in life, Cooper would write that the old-age health problems his friend suffered actually stemmed from those months in the tropics, "when he scorned Moon 'Lunatic Fever.' Poor Monty!!!"[19]

What was indisputable was that Schoedsack's great struggle in the jungle boiled down to an attack of malaria, combined with the hundred-degree temperatures and steaming humidity. Cooper would later say sunstroke was the prime culprit in the illness that plagued his partner in Siam. The heat also posed a grave problem for the camera equipment and fragile celluloid. Schoedsack had brought his film in four-hundred-foot spools kept in cans that were taped shut with adhesive, then further secured in cans that were soldered shut and could be opened only with a can opener. But during the filming, when Schoedsack ordered new film, he was shocked to find that these four-hundred-foot cans had not been taped but *welded* shut, requiring them to be opened with the can opener in the changing bag. In the messy process, precious film was lost.

"The [changing] bag never got dry between the perspiration and blood from my hands off the jagged edges of the can," Schoedsack remembered. "You were lucky if you got 300 feet out of a 400-foot roll. Pull it out, and it stuck in the jagged tin."[20]

By late April, the specter of disease hung like a fetid fog over the production. Schoedsack's health worsened; at one point he was gripped by a delirium so fearful that Cooper had to spend two nights watching at his bedside. Cooper was finally relieved when he delivered Schoedsack into the more competent hands of a missionary doctor. In a letter to Isaiah Bowman, he described the exhausting vigil, and how he expected to be hit with illness himself before they got out of the jungle. There was also a smallpox epidemic sweeping the area, so he had to watch carefully for signs of sickness in the natives who were assisting them. Perhaps it was the stress of the long, sleepless nights spent with his deliriously sick friend, but Cooper's letter betrayed doubts about the outcome of the movie expedition.

"Our present picture from a geographical standpoint will not be half so good as GRASS. The problem here is a far different one, on account of the photography. There is no light in the jungle. And, as you know, every ten yards that you go into thick jungle, is an entrance into an unknown world. Things of immense interest and value may be happening a half a mile away; but you will never hear of them, never see them, could not photograph them if you were on the spot. Therefore you can appreciate that we have to work like sin for every picture we get. Indeed there is scarcely a thing in our picture that is *real*, if reality means photographing it at the time of its actual happening, as we were able to do in *Grass*.

"To meet this condition we have been working out a method. We have stuck to our main idea of a *Natural Drama*. But we have made a Book of Fiction, a Novel, if you will, instead of a Book of Fact . . . when all is said and done, it is a children's show." Nevertheless, they were creating something that went far beyond a simple travelogue, Cooper maintained, and despite the trials, the possibilities for filmmaking continued to percolate in his mind.[21]

———

BY AUGUST, THE monsoons had arrived. Cooper had recovered from a bout of dysentery, but Schoedsack was still struggling with malaria and the effects of sunstroke. Still, he kept working, even when his temperature reached 104 degrees and he was on the edge of delirium by noontime. Because of his condition, and as a practicality given the withering heat, the prime working hours were set from 6:00 to 10:00 A.M.[22] And it was in the depths of his enervating illness that Schoedsack filmed the spectacular elephant stampede that helped make the film famous.

In the sequence, a mother elephant would wreck Kru's frontier settlement while a stampeding herd of elephants demolishes the main village. It was a dangerous proposition that occupied much of their time and took them to the south, where the wild elephant herds roamed. Because of the royal protection enjoyed by elephants, Cooper and Schoedsack were forced to go through their diplomatic contacts in order to obtain permission to arrange an elephant drive they might film.

Prince Yugala, brother of the king of Siam and the viceroy of southern Siam, also arranged for Cooper to meet an old elephant hunter. It took Cooper a long boat ride and torchlit trek into the nocturnal jungle, where he met the old elephant catcher, a man of wealth who owned some twenty-four elephants of his own, Cooper noted. His brown skin was wrinkled, but he moved with youthful grace. Even now, the elephant catcher explained as he sat cross-legged before Cooper, his men had been out in the field for a week and were driving a small herd of eighteen wild elephants to his kraal.

Thus, several nights later, Cooper and Schoedsack crouched in a clearing, perched on covered platforms high above the elephant catcher's kraal, waiting for the herd. They patiently kept vigil, yet they could barely contain their excitement when they finally heard the cries of the distant drivers, who were firing guns, blasting fireworks, and waving blazing torches to stampede the wild elephants toward the enclosure. The gigantic animals were crashing through the jungle, drawing ever nearer, when, suddenly, the two filmmakers saw waving lights and heard low singing coming from another nearby platform. They feared that the lights and sounds would scare away the herd, and indeed, after a final, earthshaking cacophony of trumpeting and crashing, the roars of the elephants began to fade away into the distance.

The old elephant driver rushed over and revealed that the elephants had turned and broken through the line of the drivers, nearly killing one man, and were miles gone by now.

Coop and Schoedsack were angry at the mystery person who'd been singing and waving the distracting light. To their shock, though, they were informed that the singer was a witch doctor working to overcome evil spirits and allow the elephants to enter the kraal. It was the camera platform that had angered the spirits and driven the elephants away!

Ultimately, Prince Yugala and the royal family would help the filmmakers secure the elephants they needed.[23] The epic elephant sequences, from the trampling of the village to the driving of the herd, all had to be seamlessly constructed from weeks of shooting. Years later, Cooper recalled that when the time finally came for the stampede, they'd gone through their budget and he'd had to request an additional $10,000.

"I got it from Paramount by special cable—Lasky sent it to me," he once explained to Kevin Brownlow. "Monty didn't want to go over [budget]. We thought we were committing a heinous crime, least I did. And Monty didn't want us to have so many elephants if it was going to put us over [budget]. But I didn't give a damn if I went into debt for the rest of my life, I wanted that elephant scene with every goddamn elephant I could get my hands on. I think we got 240-odd elephants."[24]

The stampede itself included amazing ground-level footage, as Schoedsack shot from a pit that "looked like a grave"—and almost became one. The pit had been dug deep in the sand, covered with logs, and then camouflaged with brush, allowing the cameraman to shoot out from the pit through a little hole. The elephants were to be herded around the camouflaged area, but instead they stampeded directly overhead, shaking the logs and threatening to crash through. Schoedsack was already struggling with his nagging malaria and the claustrophobic heat of the pit as he breathed in the stench of hundreds of elephants trampling overhead like "a war dance." Nevertheless, he kept cranking his camera while "swimming in my own sweat and smelling three hundred elephants at close range."[25]

The filmmakers ultimately herded their elephants into a kraal of their own making. Cooper had obtained the dimensions when he'd visited the elephant catcher's own corral, having spent a day studying it carefully and making notes on its construction. He'd noted the heavy logs of jungle wood raised and bound by crosspiece logs to form an oval-shaped corral, with a heavy gate at the entranceway and a V-shaped palisade of wood designed to funnel a herd inside. The Cooper-Schoedsack kraal, built by native labor, was designed to be slightly bigger than the one Cooper had studied. Theirs was out in the open, with a camera platform built into a tree high above the pen, from which a woozy Schoedsack gamely filmed the corralling of the wild elephant herd. There were no witch doctors in sight.

In a case of life imitating art, the filmmakers had their Siamese extras drive the elephants through the high grass while carrying bushes as camouflage—a motif straight out of the climax in *Macbeth,* where the English soldiers, advancing on Macbeth's castle, reach Birnam Wood and cut boughs to conceal their approach. The locals were so enchanted with the idea that they adopted it as a new tradition.

MORE THAN A year after they'd left New York, the work of the *Chang* expedition was nearly completed. Although Shorty was still weak from illness, Cooper himself was in reasonably good health and had even come through the cholera epidemic, which had claimed six of their workmen. The two partners had also had time to blow off steam. Many, many years later, in a letter to a friend, Cooper would note, "Schoedsack and I painted Bangkok a bright crimson in early 1926 when we were making *Chang* and we didn't do such a bad job by Singapore, either."[26]

In a letter to his father, he expressed supreme confidence: "I have played the boldest hand I've ever tried. When we had already spent over half of our money it seemed evident that a lot of our work was on the wrong tact. I advocated, and Shorty concurred, in throwing it all away, practically making the major part of the picture over again, using our own money to do it. . . .

"We could have turned in the picture in a much shabbier form at a cost of $65,000 to $70,000 and, no doubt, gotten by with it. But I am in favor of playing in futures, and know if this picture is successful it is a stepping stone to far bigger work. A mediocre picture would have made us good money now, and dropped our reputation.

". . . My conscience is now clear. We have done everything possible to make a good picture; and I believe we have. If we are not successful I haven't a regret. So just do a little hoping for us that our film gets to New York all right, in good condition and all there."[27]

That wish almost came back to haunt him. The filmmakers had been sending their undeveloped film back to the United States by boat the entire time, but they were so anxious to make sure that the crucial stampede had been caught on film that Schoedsack gave that negative to a man in Bangkok to develop—and one of the most amazing sequences in cinema history was nearly lost.

When they went to retrieve the footage, the man gave him an envelope with samples that Schoedsack held up to the sun—only to discover they were coal black. "I couldn't see through them!" Schoedsack recalled. "I'm afraid he'd run out of ice [while he was working] and went out to have a drink and the stuff boiled. It'd developed a copperish sheen on one side [of the negative]; you couldn't see through one side."[28] Later, at the Paramount lab, Schoedsack would end up having to step-print the negative, giving long exposures to each frame. Although the film, to practiced eyes, appears grainy, by this method Schoedsack saved the sequence.[29]

In the course of their work, they also brought some peace to Nan. An affidavit, written in Nan and dated October 26, 1926, from Dr. Collier, the missionary doctor, reported that the filmmakers had been "over a year in Siam making a motion picture of the jungle life.... Most of the animals seen in the picture were wild ones of the Nan district. One of the tigers was a known man-eater. Since their work in the Nan district the number of people killed by tiger has been reduced from 40 last year to six or seven this year."[30]

COOPER AND SCHOEDSACK returned to New York on separate boats. Ruth Rose met her fiancé at the dock and was shocked at Monty's haggard appearance. "It was so pitiful," she recalled. "There's such a lot of him to be sick when he's sick.... He'd gotten what he considered a warm overcoat but it was a flimsy thing. He arrives with that bitter wind coming off the Hudson, shivering and shaking.... I felt so sorry for him I *had* to marry him!"[31]

Meanwhile, Cooper's boat also arrived, and he began settling back into New York. In a letter to his father he noted, "I have a nice little flat up on 74th street which I sublet for four months but which I expect to be put out of at any day now following a visit of a reunion of the Kosciuszko Squadron [sic] who were rather musically inclined in the early hours of the morning."[32]

Other than making a little noise with his old war comrades, however, Merian was kept busy editing the film at a Long Island facility. Each day began at 8:30 with Cooper dictating to a stenographer for an hour before heading to the studio, where he supervised double shifts of cutting girls and projection men, who had to break eighty thousand feet of film down to a manageable four to five thousand feet.

Although Cooper would always feel that *Chang* lacked the epic sweep of *Grass*, he felt it had a better "theater angle" and would be a hit with kids.[33] The elephant stampede was dramatically magnified by the new widescreen Magnascope projection format. While most of *Chang* was projected on the theater's conventional, smaller screen, for the elephant stampede the screen was enlarged to fit the stage's entire proscenium. Then a special projector in the projection booth capable of a high light output and outfitted with a special wide-angle lens projected the sequence, splashing the dramatic images over the expanded screen surface. The entire drama was augmented with a live score by Dr. Hugo Riesenfeld, who had created the "musical setting" for *Grass*, and the film was unveiled at a gala Criterion Theater screening attended by Cooper, Schoedsack, and the Paramount brass.

"It was a terrific score," Schoedsack recalled, "and a great orchestra, with lots of brass—and six-foot thunderdrums back of the screen. They went into action as the screen opened up on the elephant stampede. You never heard a sound track like it. Coop and I were waiting in the lobby as the big boys came out. Lasky was smiling from ear to ear. Walter Wanger and Adolph Zukor were smiling, too. Zukor said to Lasky: 'How much did the boys get?' Lasky said, 'Forty percent.' Zukor's smile disappeared."[34]

Chang became a sensation, a major box-office hit, and won recognition in the historic first Academy Awards ceremony, where it was nominated in the category of "Unique and Artistic Picture" along with *The Crowd* and *Sunrise* (which ultimately won). In a 1931 *New Yorker* magazine profile on Cooper, writer Gilbert Seldes hailed "the immortal *Chang*" and the influential work of Cooper and Schoedsack. "It is fair to say that wherever the authentic and the simple and the exciting are blended the influence of *Chang* can be felt."[35] Seldes also recalled the thrill of experiencing the elephant stampede in Magnascope as the curtains parted on the widened screen and the audible gasps from audiences at the thundering elephant rampage marked that rare moment in movies: "an authentic achievement."[36]

The New Yorker likened Cooper to the swashbuckling British hero who led an Arab army against the Turks, hailing him as "the T. E. Lawrence of the movies." The success of *Chang*, the *New Yorker* item noted, "is expected to give an impetus to the making of similar pictures."[37]

"We have never heard Cooper or Schoedsack mention art, beauty, the meaning of existence, or utter any similar high-sounding phrase," *Asia* magazine noted in an "Along the Trail with the Editor" column. "Life is too good in the living, beauty too enthralling in its realization, truth too natural a thing in the lives of both, to be talked about. These men would spend their time in expressing these things in mountains and jungles, far from drawing-room discussion.

"So, they move on with their dream. They steadfastly gaze on life as men live it, and they find it absorbing, dramatic and picturable."[38]

PARAMOUNT CONTRACT PLAYER JEAN ARTHUR IS CAUGHT IN
THE MIDDLE AS SWASHBUCKLING ADVENTURERS SCHOEDSACK
AND COOPER SQUARE OFF WITH "FUZZY-WUZZY" SWORDS
AND SHIELDS IN THIS PUBLICITY SHOT FOR *THE FOUR
FEATHERS*. IN THE MAY 1927 "ALONG THE TRAIL WITH THE
EDITOR" COLUMN OF *ASIA*, COOPER AND SCHOEDSACK WERE
HAILED AS "OSTENSIBLY ARTISTS PIONEERING IN THE
FASCINATING UNKNOWN REALM OF PICTURING NATURE'S
POWERS AND MAN'S WILL TO WIN."

Cooper Papers, BYU

CHAPTER THIRTEEN

WANDERING SOULS

> *[The Four Feathers] was the first picture in history where people had gone into the wilderness of Africa to shoot scenes to intercut with Hollywood scenes. It was a really bold, new idea in the year 1928 and if Schoedsack and I had not already had the success of* Grass *and* Chang *behind us and Jesse Lasky had not been a daring man himself, I am sure no studio-head would have agreed to it.*
>
> —Merian Cooper[1]

HISTORIAN KEVIN BROWNLOW ASKED MERIAN COOPER, LATE IN HIS LIFE, IF HE truly identified with young Lieutenant Harry Faversham, who, having earned four feathers symbolizing his cowardice, wipes away his disgrace in battle.

"Your comparison of me to Harry and *The Four Feathers* may be a correct one—I'm not a psychologist," Cooper replied. "And what man looks at himself, truly? Sure not me." Yet Coop went on to recall "the portrait of me in pain"—the disheveled prisoner in Russia who'd clung to the Enchanted Sack and that precious A. E. W. Mason novel.[2]

The Four Feathers would be the final chapter in the seminal Cooper-Schoedsack "distant, difficult, and dangerous" adventure trilogy. Cooper later told Brownlow that after *Chang*, he and Schoedsack were eager to create an adventure fiction, and arranged for Paramount to purchase the rights to *The Four Feathers* on their behalf.

But even that project wasn't the only thing on Cooper's agenda when he and Schoedsack were polishing *Chang* for theatrical release. For starters, there was the mysterious Empty Quarter. In fact, that had been Cooper's main objective after *Chang*, as he and his friend Isaiah Bowman began stirring up interest in the formation of an advisory committee to raise funds for the expedition. "There is no one else whom I have ever met who seems to me to be Cooper's equal in courage and skill," Bowman proclaimed in one fund-raising letter on Cooper's behalf. "He has another quality of equal importance: he is a man of integrity. . . . I believe that if anyone can do the Empty Quarter by airplane it is Cooper."[3]

Even deep in the jungle, Cooper's mind hadn't strayed from that unexplored expanse of Arabian desert; it remained his and Schoedsack's "main aim."[4] Bowman suggested that Cooper prepare an expedition proposal, approach John D. Rockefeller Jr., and secure the backing of a newspaper and the American Geographical Society. "Of course you have to take support wherever you can find it, perhaps, but I am interested in your development and I should hate to see you swallowed by an institution," Bowman wrote his friend. "You are the kind of wandering soul that does best when left out in the free air."[5]

Cooper's correspondence with Bowman, conducted from Siam, noted that the Empty Quarter was ideal for aerial exploration—unlike the Arctic, which had attracted the interest of other explorers, but which, Cooper felt, had a short flying season and other obstacles to establishing a base camp. A year-round base could be established in Rub al-Khali from which its half million acres might be explored.[6] It was during this post-*Chang* period that Cooper and John Hambleton, his friend from the Great War, began talking seriously about the possibilities of commercial aviation, as well—conversations that would eventually lead to the formation of Pan American Airways and other air enterprises. At the same time, Cooper returned to his old haunt at the American Geographical Society to pore over maps of southern Arabia and develop the strategy of using a centrally located base from which to explore the vastness—"triangulating it by plane," as Cooper described it.[7]

By March 1927, Bowman was working with Cooper to develop a fund-raising and advisory committee, and John Hambleton was helping raise money—he even told Theodore Roosevelt about the trip.[8] In a one-page breakdown of the costs, the lion's share of the proposed $155,600 budget was for flying equipment: $80,000 for two planes, at $40,000 each, and almost $20,000 for spare motors and parts, oil, and gas. Additional costs included a salary for one scientist at $125 a week (for twenty-four weeks) and $4,000 for photographic equipment.

One line read: "2 pilots (no salaries)."[9]

But then, in a confidential letter to Bowman, Cooper suddenly announced that he was going to Ottawa "on a hunch that I might make a picture of the American Indian." He hastened to add that he wasn't giving up on Arabia—his friend Hambleton was in the midst of securing bids for the expedition's airplanes. The American Indian film was to be another stopgap project before the real adventure, one that would earn enough money that Cooper could personally finance the Arabia trip, and not be forced to beg from the rich and powerful. "I could ask for money easily for something which was not so definitely my own work and for my own self-glorification," he confessed.[10]

It's possible that this proposed American Indian film was a project his friend and fellow adventurer W. Douglas Burden was undertaking at this time. In fact, Burden had been inspired by *Chang* and had sought Cooper's counsel for his own documentary adventure film on the vanishing culture of the Ojibwa tribe. Regardless, nothing came of it.

Worse, Cooper would recall in a letter to Mabel Ward, Bowman's former secretary at the AGS, that in 1927, "Dick Byrd (Adm. Richard Evelyn Byrd, USN) beat me out of the aircraft which I wanted for The Empty Quarter job and which he wanted for Polar work."[11] Once again, Cooper had to put his Arabian dream on hold.

BUT THE *FOUR FEATHERS* expedition continued to take shape and promised the solace of adventure with a trip to Sudan—the very region in which Harry had been redeemed. There were the prospects of corralling wild animals and filming native tribes. The expedition would include Schoedsack's new wife, and the production would be making movie history by cutting together African location footage with Hollywood sets. This despite the fact that studio president Adolph Zukor was distrustful from the start of this "new kind of picture," as Cooper called the production. "Zukor thought Lasky was crazy for backing me," Cooper observed.[12]

As with *Chang*, Cooper began by dreaming up potentially crowd-pleasing "chariot race sequences," including a brush fire to stampede jungle animals and battle scenes featuring tribal warriors massing for a savage attack on a British fort. On location they'd plunge into the "natural drama" philosophy of first studying the native culture and wild animal life.

Once they were acquainted with every aspect of the native environment, their filming would begin.

For the Hollywood portion, Cooper and Schoedsack's first foray into fiction would feature professional actors, and their cast included Richard

FAY WRAY IN COSTUME, FROM *THE FOUR FEATHERS*. ALTHOUGH MERIAN COOPER WAS ALWAYS DISCREET, HE WAS SOMETHING OF A LADIES' MAN. FAY WRAY, IN CONVERSATION WITH THIS AUTHOR, DENIED A LOVE AFFAIR BETWEEN THEM, EXPLAINING THEY WERE GOOD FRIENDS. COOPER DID SIGN FAY WRAY'S *KING KONG* PREMIERE PROGRAM WITH THIS TANTALIZING NOTE THAT ALLUDES TO THEIR MUTUAL AFFECTION: "TO: ONE OF THE LOVELIST [*SIC*] OF THE FAMOUS MERIAN C. COOPER'S 'WOO'S'—FAY WRAY WITH AFFECTION FROM THAT OLD EX-WOLF HIMSELF 'COOP,' MERIAN C. COOPER." PROGRAM NOTE PROVIDED BY JUSTIN "BUD" CLAYTON. *Cooper Papers, BYU*

Arlen as Lieutenant Harry Faversham, with Harry's three comrades-in-arms played by William Powell (as Captain Trench), Theodore von Eltz (Lieutenant Castleton), and Clive Brook (Lieutenant Durrance). Ethne,

Harry's fiancée, would be played by a young actress who'd already starred in such Paramount films as Erich von Stroheim's *The Wedding March* (1928) and would become a memorable addition to subsequent Cooper-Schoedsack productions. Her name was Fay Wray.

But even as they arrived in East Africa, the dream of the Empty Quarter haunted Cooper. Once, on night watch at the expedition's camp on the Rovuma River, situated on the border of Tanganyika and Portuguese East Africa, he scribbled a "Merry Christmas" letter to Bowman, reporting that he was in fine shape, having walked eighty miles in thirty-two hours a couple of weeks before. But he'd rather be flying, he confessed: "I don't like to write of aviation," Cooper noted. "It makes me forget my present works, and for me that is all that counts at present. When this job is finished I hope to sing a different song."[13]

Bowman responded on January 23, 1928, encouraging Cooper to keep dreaming his dreams but also gently reminding him of the task at hand: "Your undated letter makes me sigh for the wilderness," Bowman began. "Time stands still when one is in the field. . . . I welcome it [news on the current expedition] for the hope there is in it and for your conclusion that the job is difficult.

". . . All good luck, and with assurances that there will be food on the table for you when you get back, believe me."[14]

RUTH ROSE'S BRAVERY and gutsy spirit was a plus in Africa. She took charge of the administrative side of the expedition, managing the commissary, the native help, and the payroll, and handled both a gun and a camera when needed. It was said she fired only one shot, killing a crocodile who was about to make someone its dinner.[15]

Unlike *Chang*'s elephant stampede, the wildfire itself was the easiest piece of business, as the crew took advantage of the season when the natives burned jungle and brush to clear the ground to plant crops. Because of the heavy rainfall, it was hard to get a fire going but the filmmakers managed to film an inferno that burned off twenty square miles.[16]

Lions had originally been planned as the primary creatures in the stampede, but once on location the filmmakers settled on hippos—a seemingly unlikely replacement. It was an idea inspired at their camp on the Rovuma River, when Cooper saw a hippopotamus tuck its squat legs under itself and dive off a twenty-foot-high bank. The image of girth and grace stuck, and the filmmakers decided to capture a herd of hippos and run them over a bank for Schoedsack's camera.[17]

But the inherent danger of hippos was conveyed by a district commissioner who showed the filmmakers a photo of a woman who had been bitten in half by one of the beasts.[18] The danger was to be magnified because the filmmakers had to round up an entire herd and drive them over a riverbank. Cooper and Schoedsack's strategy—seemingly lifted from their elephant work on *Chang*—was to have native boys brandishing flaming torches drive the hippos into a massive corral built with five-foot walls and baited with food. Once they were penned in and pressing against the walls, a restraining barrier of logs could be cut loose, sending the herd falling into the river for Schoedsack's camera, and emulating the story point of animals fleeing the wildfire.[19]

Cooper later estimated that they trapped some forty-nine hippos and ran them over the riverbank for five successive days, making dozens of animals appear "like thousands."

Once, during the trapping phase, Cooper discovered that the native helpers he had recruited from two nearby villages had inexplicably gone home. He didn't tell Monty or Ruth, but, furious, went alone to the villages armed only with a bullwhip made of rhinoceros hide. Seemingly forgetting the painful consequences of the slap he'd given the native chief in Siam, he stormed into the villages and lashed every native he could find. He reasoned that charging in with gunbearers would have gotten him a spear in the back but a fearless man alone would put the fear in the natives, and win back his help.

Whatever his logic, the chastened villagers returned to work and helped trap the hippos.[20]

Cooper had several brushes with death during filming of the dangerous river sequence. Once, he was standing under the logs of the corral when Schoedsack called out, "Coop!" The native assigned to cut loose the restraining logs mistook the call for "Cut!" The man severed the rope, and only an agile leap kept Cooper from being crushed as logs and hippos cascaded over his head.[21]

Another time, Cooper was dressed in Arab clothing and acting as the stunt double for Richard Arlen's character. He was in a boat with an interpreter who was similarly dressed in Arab costume when a hippo swam by and capsized the boat. The interpreter, who had assured the filmmakers he could swim, instead began drowning. Cooper tried to save the man, his task made all the more difficult because the heavy costume dragged him down in the crocodile- and hippo-infested waters. "I got way across with that fool with no help from anybody," Cooper recalled. "Ruth couldn't swim, and certainly none of the boys were coming in to help us. We'd never have gotten out if Monty hadn't waded out to his neck and hauled him in. Monty is one of the bravest guys alive."[22]

The fire sequence also called for a stampede of baboons, and these they found close to the Abyssinian frontier, in a dry wadi where a tribe of several hundred of the creatures lived. Cooper's study of the baboons was more ambitious than their usual research for natural dramas, more akin to scientific fieldwork. He'd been fascinated with primates ever since childhood, when he'd read about a hunt for wild gorillas. Here he had the opportunity to immerse himself in his studies, spending day after day recording his observations of baboon behavior, amassing what would become an eight-hundred-page monograph. They captured several hundred baboons and ran them across a suspension bridge, which was then cut, dumping the baboons into a flowing stream.

The sequence required some three months for a few minutes of final film, Cooper would recall, but it was worth it, and they didn't lose a single baboon.[23]

ONCE THE ANIMAL work had been completed, the *Four Feathers* expedition set off for the domain of the Messeria—a people of western Sudan—and onward to meet the Amarar of the Red Sea Hills, one of the fierce warrior people whose bristling, bushy hair earned them Rudyard Kipling's nickname of "Fuzzy-Wuzzies."

The route into the tribal territories of Sudan had once been a long trek by camel or horseback, but now the filmmakers made it by modern motorcar. It was still rugged and dangerous; though the region lay under the flag of British administrators, it had recently been under the sword of warring tribes. But the government policy left as much power as possible with the native chiefs, including their right to sit in judgment over their people for certain offenses, and allowed the *nazir,* the chief of the Messeria, to continue the tradition of having many wives.

MERIAN COOPER,
DOUBLING FOR ACTOR
RICHARD ARLEN,
WITH TRIBESMAN ON
LOCATION IN AFRICA
FOR *THE FOUR
FEATHERS*.

Cooper Papers, BYU

The filmmakers arranged to meet the Messeria chief, who embodied the bloody reality of recent history. As a lone British official in the area told them, in the dervish days the *nazir* had commanded a hundred men at the battle of Omdurman, killed many enemies with his own hand, and was a notorious slave raider.

It was while motoring into the Nuba Mountains that the filmmakers received word that the Messeria were gathering. They drove for two days over a rough trail until they came to a deep gorge and the sight of the conical thatch-and-earth huts of a Nuba village built along the slopes. They parked in the shade of a grove of trees and Ruth Schoedsack saw to setting up camp while Coop and Monty awaited the Messeria. It was an uneasy wait among the Nuba, Cooper later wrote.

"They are distrustful of everybody and everything, as well they may be, because during many years the Messeria raided their villages, killing every man who made resistance and carrying off the other as slaves. They are to this day dirty, savage, and suspicious."[24]

The second morning in camp, the Messeria made their dramatic entrance, a procession that awakened the filmmakers, who emerged from their tents to see "as strange and picturesque a cavalcade as one could hope to find in long traveling," as Cooper recalled. A column of men in white turbans and flowing robes rode past on ponies, sitting tall in high-pommeled saddles with their spears and bridle chains glittering in the sunlight. There followed a column of horned bulls outfitted with saddles and framework piled high with the chief's rugs, clothing, pots and pans, and household possessions. The beasts of burden were decorated with leather tassels across their wide foreheads, and the framework was adorned with streamers and fluffy ostrich feathers. Atop the horned beasts sat the women of the almighty *nazir*—his wives, daughters, and other female relations—each adorned with robes and anklets and necklaces of gold and silver. The heavy, shifting loads of the beasts were delicately balanced by female attendants walking alongside the bulls as the warriors dashed along the line, howling and waving their spears.

The *nazir* himself soon appeared, sitting tall on a saddle covered with white sheepskin, dressed in a white turban and a blue robe fastened with golden bands and glittering with gold and silver embroidery, a long sword with a hilt of gold hanging from his shoulder. The old chieftain had a white beard and mustache and carried himself with an aura of command.[25] The man who had commanded a hundred men at the battle of Omdurman bestowed upon the Westerners a beneficent smile that made him the very image of the "gentle patriarch," Cooper observed.

Alongside the *nazir* came his bodyguards, also on horseback, each armed with guns and dressed in heavy mail down to their ankles. "It seemed strange to see nomad warriors clad in armor such as our own European ancestors wore in the Middle Ages," Cooper marveled. "As a matter of fact, this custom, in many parts of this region, is directly handed down from the Crusades, as is the type of straight-bladed, cross-hilted sword so much like that of many a European knight who left his bones to bleach in the sands of Syria and Palestine."[26]

The filmmakers spent many days at the chieftain's camp, frequently joining the *nazir* at his campfire. "It was pleasant living with this old chief and his nomad people," Cooper wrote. "At night Schoedsack and I often used to say that, judging from our own experiences, most of the warlike tribes of savage peoples were the easiest to get along with. Among such tribes we have always found fine hospitality, a keen sense of humor, and freedom from petty sulkiness. Thus were the Messeria. It was hard to believe that all of the middle-aged and older men who were treating us with

**PROCESSION OF
MESSERIA IN SUDAN.**

Cooper Papers, BYU

**THE MESSERIA
WOMEN AS THEIR
PROCESSION
ARRIVED AT
THE COOPER/
SCHOEDSACK
MOVIE EXPEDITION
CAMP.**

Cooper Papers, BYU

so much courtesy had been noted savage warriors of the dervish empire, killers and slave raiders."[27]

In the bloody days before British rule, the best defense the Nuba had found against the Messeria had been to retreat to the caves and mountains, where they'd built their conical-shaped thatch-and-mud huts. One day, the *nazir* took Cooper to one of those cliffside villages, looked up at the conical-shaped mud-and-thatch houses dotting the cliffs, and noted that he and his men had once attacked this very village. "They had surprised it and, dismounting at the foot of the cliff, picked off the Nuba men with their rifles before they could escape," Cooper wrote. "'We took back with us many, many slaves,' said the old Nazir, and smiled his gentle, sweet smile."

It was Cooper's idea to ask the *nazir* of the Messeria and the "sultan" of the Nuba if they would arrange a mock Messeria raid on the Nuba village, all for the benefit of Schoedsack's camera. The two tribal leaders were intrigued, particularly with the visitor's offer of sugar and cloth. The *nazir* promised to keep his warriors under control, but Cooper finally decided that such a raid wouldn't fit into the picture and called it off, much to the disappointment of the *nazir*. In fact, Cooper's change of heart had been prompted in part by the Nuba men, who were unconvinced that their former enemy would simply "play" at war games.

"Play!" one of the Nuba men had cried. "These Messeria will not play. They will kill us. We know them."

Cooper again noted the slumbering martial blood when he stood at attention alongside the *nazir* and watched a column of his spearmen riding into camp. The old chieftain sadly missed the bloody ways of old, and knew he was now living in "degenerate times," Cooper recalled. As his men rode past, the old warrior chief offered up a chilling memory: "When we used to ride like that the vultures would gather and fly along to accompany us. They knew they could expect food."[28]

EVEN THOUGH THE mock battle never took place, the filmmakers bestowed a parting gift of sugar and cloth on the Messeria before motoring hundreds of miles into eastern Sudan and the territory of the most notorious of Sudan's fighting tribes: the Hadendoa, the Beni Amer, and the Amarar, which, collectively, were Kipling's Fuzzy-Wuzzies. Back when the British had maintained a foothold on the coast, at the old slave port of Suakin, the tribes had earned that nickname for their great bushy hair, but the silly label belied the respect the British had for these warriors who defiantly charged into hails of bullets armed only with swords and shields, expecting victory but accepting death. Even Kipling's celebrated verse hailed the Fuzzy-Wuzzy as "a pore benighted 'eathen, but a first-class fightin' man" who broke the vaunted battlefield formation of the British square.[29]

Some twenty miles from Port Sudan, on the edge of a hilly range, the filmmakers pitched camp and awaited the arrival of the Amarar warriors. The chief who had conferred with the British deputy governor and district commissioner at Port Sudan had promised that a hundred men of the Amarar tribe—always friendly to the British, even in dervish times—would come, but more than five hundred arrived on camels. Cooper would remember them "as fine-looking a crowd of fighters as I have ever seen." Every man was dressed in white robes, and nearly all carried a cross-hilted Crusader sword and a heavy shield of elephant or rhinoceros hide.[30]

And the swords and shields weren't for show. It was a rite of passage for every boy to learn how to fight, and men regularly settled major disputes by the sword. Even lesser quarrels were settled with a "stone duel," as adversaries stripped to the waist and entered a circle piled with rocks, using only a shield for protection. "A stone duel between two men can be serious," Cooper noted, "but not nearly so bad as when two entire tribes start stone-throwing." It was while trying to film the British-square scene that the violent passions of the assembled warriors almost became inflamed.[31] "They got so excited that when they got past the camera they started hacking each other with swords!" Schoedsack recalled. "So I was very busy going around and disarming and swearing at them—a kick they could understand."

Cooper would recall that he had been up on a platform directing the battle scene and that during the ensuing "race riot" he had leapt off, landing atop two of the men who had started the outbreak. "I was beating them with my megaphone and I stopped the race riot," he said.[32]

"These were very tough fellows," Schoedsack recalled. "They were the real thing, with shields and swords, and we had [hundreds] of them assembled and one interpreter. Well, when the high-mucky-muck [British official in charge in the area] heard we had so many of these fellows, he darn near had a stroke! The whole idea was to keep them apart because they fight."[33]

COOPER AND SCHOEDSACK POSE WITH TWO OF THE "FUZZY-WUZZIES," AS KIPLING CALLED THE WARRIOR TRIBES OF SUDAN. DESPITE THE SILLY NICKNAME HE HAD BESTOWED, KIPLING HAILED THE FUZZY-WUZZY AS "A FIRST-CLASS FIGHTIN' MAN."

Cooper Papers, BYU

"But, despite these reputed qualities, we found the Fuzzies to be good fellows, and the six weeks or so we spent with them were very happy ones to us," Cooper concluded.[34]

WHEN COOPER AND Schoedsack completed their movie expedition, they returned home to Hollywood, where they assembled a production crew that re-created Sudan in the arid landscape of Cathedral City, California, near Palm Springs. "Reality" and "authenticity" were the watchwords of the location work in the "desert camp" at Cathedral Hills. Not only would the terrain itself match Sudan; the Fuzzy-Wuzzies were re-created with a cast of African-American extras. Or, as Schoedsack put it, "All the boys from Central Avenue wearing wigs to charge around in."[35]

Paramount also attached a rising young studio executive as associate producer on *Four Feathers:* David O. Selznick. The man who within a decade would be producing *Gone With the Wind* had grown up in a New York show-business family. His father, Lewis J. Selznick, had run Selznick Pictures and had been one of the giants of the industry until various business reversals had led to his bankruptcy in 1923. David, eager to make it on his own, had come to Hollywood in 1926 as an assistant story editor at Metro-Goldwyn-Mayer (MGM) before moving over to Paramount. When he took on *The Four Feathers,* Selznick also was supervising such pictures as *Forgotten Faces, Chinatown Nights,* and *The Dance of Life.*

Merian Cooper had one caveat for studio executive B. P. Schulberg: that Selznick not bother them on the set. Cooper would soon discover that young Selznick was a brilliant producer—and he would always be grateful that Selznick respected the request and not once intruded on the set.[36] It was the beginning of an eventful partnership between Cooper and Selznick, although there were hard feelings that resulted from *The Four Feathers.* The problems wouldn't come during filming at the Cathedral Hills set but in the editing room. Although their contract required the

DESPITE THEIR PIPES, COOP AND SHORTY HAVE TONGUES FIRMLY PLANTED
IN CHEEK AS THEY POSE AT THE ENTRANCE TO *THE FOUR FEATHERS*
DESERT CAMP SET IN CATHEDRAL CITY, CALIFORNIA.

Cooper Papers, BYU

filmmakers' approval for any changes or additions, they wouldn't be around to make them. On the advice of John Hambleton, Cooper had been putting his movie earnings into a private mutual fund restricted to aviation stocks, and *The Four Feathers* was in postproduction when he departed for Manhattan to become a player in the nascent field of commercial aviation.

Meanwhile, Ernest and Ruth Schoedsack were preparing for a movie expedition of their own, a *Chang*-style jungle adventure for Paramount called *Rango* that featured an old tiger hunter, his son, and the boy's pet orangutan (the Rango of the title). The studio had been anxious for another adventure epic from the Cooper-Schoedsack team, but this time Coop wasn't moving from his setup in New York.[37]

So it was left to Selznick to address the problems that had emerged when the film was shown to preview audiences. For example, the hippopotamus stampede, he reported, had elicited laughs. The revised cut included placing the Fuzzy-Wuzzy battle, which was to come earlier, near the end of the picture. The recut hippo stampede "got gasps as now cut instead of laughs as previously," Selznick explained in a wire to Schoedsack.[38]

Monty and Ruth had already gone overseas when Jesse Lasky called Cooper about having director Lothar Mendes shoot a few new scenes.[39] Cooper agreed, but the final results, from Selznick's editing to Mendes's stagy footage, ultimately infuriated him.[40] He was most upset at the studio for releasing *The Four Feathers* as the last great silent epic, not as the first great "talkie."

"The animal effects, indeed all the African stuff, was a cinch for sound," Cooper later wrote, "but both Lasky and Zukor said sound was an impractical dream, and they didn't wake up until Warners made 'Jazz Singer.' We had just returned from ten months in Africa with the spectacular stuff for 'Four Feathers,' and it was not too late to dub and loop the sound. Zukor turned me down cold, and I had to go ahead and finish 'Four Feathers' as the last big silent picture ever made. It was a hit and made a lot of money, but it would have been a *revolutionary hit* except for Zukor's stubbornness."[41]

Thus, the picture was already a disappointment by the time Cooper attended its premiere at the Criterion Theater. "I made up my mind as I came out of the theatre that I wouldn't make another picture until I could be the boss," he declared.[42]

MERIAN COOPER'S
NEW YORK
ADVENTURE

CHAPTER FOURTEEN

FLYING HIGH

*During this meeting we discussed at length the feasibility of
pioneering, in the near future, Latin American commercial routes
to be created by Pan American. It was then that Hambleton
proposed, for the more distant future, his vision of intercontinental
Polar Flights—a dream in those days more fantastic than today's
prospect of passenger flights to the Moon.*

—Merian Cooper, recollecting the discussions that
inspired the formation of Pan American Airways[1]

ERIAN COOPER HAD ALWAYS DREAMED OF BECOMING A SOLDIER AND AN
explorer; "New York business executive" hadn't been on the short list of
childhood ambitions. But working in the early aviation industry was a logical progression for the grown man who had thrilled as a ten-year-old to
the first manned flight. As a pioneering airman in war, he also felt that the
military and commercial possibilities of flight were synchronous.

"I consistently fought for air power," Cooper once said, "though most
people I knew then thought the airplane was an over-rated toy."[2]

In a way, Merian Cooper had grown up. He was dreaming adult dreams
now, dreams of power and commerce. And he was sharing those dreams as
a valued member of an inner circle of ambitious young men, a new breed
of entrepreneurs, many of whom had fought in the Great War and pursued
their postwar ambitions with a relentless, sometimes ruthless drive. One
such enterprise was Pan American Airways, and Merian C. Cooper was
there at the beginning.

The founding players for Pan Am included fellow World War I veteran
Robert Thach, who would draw up the organization chart for the seminal

Aviation Corporation of America and serve as future vice president and counsel.[3] But, arguably, of all the ambitious young dreamers, the wartime flying ace and visionary who shone the brightest was John Hambleton.

Among his many interests, Hambleton headed up the Federal Aviation Corporation, whose key players included Cooper and his good friend David Bruce, the future confidant of presidents, John F. Kennedy among them. Their private venture included the purchase of land in Washington, D.C., for establishing a Washington airport, experiments in the use of dirigibles and parachutes, high-altitude photographic apparatus, and "other affairs at that time viewed with considerable skepticism by [Hambleton's] less imaginative competitors," as Bruce wryly noted.[4] The Federal Aviation Corporation also invested in such advanced aviation enterprises as Pan American Airways.[5]

It was appropriate that the first discussion of the potential of commercial aviation between Cooper and Hambleton occurred on Christmas Eve 1917, the holiday that had provided so many memorable touchstones in Cooper's life. Cooper knew from the start that he was talking to that rare youth who was both visionary and practical. Hambleton "was on fire with the idea that man would eventually span the oceans by air, and with the direct idea of playing a part in the future of the then unknown civil aviation," Cooper later wrote.[6]

By spring of 1922, Cooper and Hambleton were discussing the future of domestic and American-owned foreign airlines while wandering a deserted, shut-down sawmill in Flat Rock, North Carolina. The following year they debated the potential of domestic airlines versus American-owned foreign commercial airlines, and Cooper shared his memory of the pilot in Jidda who had taken Schoedsack aloft to photograph the holy city of Mecca. By 1926, Cooper and Hambleton had come to a crossroads: One path led to aerial exploration, including Cooper's obsession with conquering the Empty Quarter, the other to an emerging vision of an American-owned foreign airline. "John Hambleton finally chose Pan American Airways instead of Air Exploration," Cooper noted. "I concurred. I believed that his personal choice was wise because I believed in his dynamic and far-seeing vision."[7]

In remembering, Cooper would place the discussions that led to Pan American Airways as coming in late 1926 or early 1927, a time period fixed in his mind because he had just returned from Siam and the making of

Chang. During this period a few insiders—including Cooper and young Juan Trippe, the future president of Pan Am, who had been toiling away on Wall Street—joined Hambleton at the Hambleton family home in the Green Spring Valley area outside of Baltimore, Maryland, to discuss financing for the commercial air operation that would become Pan American Airways. The long discussions ranged from the practical pioneering of Latin American air routes to Hambleton's truly visionary idea for intercontinental polar flights.

Cooper enthusiastically embraced the bold idea of flying the polar routes, while Juan Trippe was more cautious. "In my mind's eye I could envision—as John Hambleton talked—the exact distances between capitols and the time to be saved by a Polar route," Cooper recalled. ". . . Hambleton expressed this idea as a great future for Pan American at that meeting between him, Juan Trippe and me, though all plans for the next few years were aimed at the Caribbean, Central America and South America."[8]

The true genesis of Pan American Airways came in May 1927, when Trippe, Hambleton, and Cornelius Vanderbilt "Sonny" Whitney (also known as "C.V.") formed the Aviation Corporation, which acquired a 50 percent interest in Pan American Airways. Heading the ambitious aviation enterprise were Trippe as president and Hambleton as vice president. In 1928, Cooper, Trippe, and Hambleton took an airborne meeting, with Hambleton at the controls, and they discussed the development of Pan Am's "safety first" policy, the guiding principle that the feasibility of commercial flight was dependent upon safety and a minimum of risk taking.[9]

Hambleton and Charles Lindbergh, who had returned from his historic solo flight across the Atlantic in 1927, both flew the "epochal exploratory routes" over Central America, each skilled pilot taking turns flying as they plotted out the air routes and bases that would open the region to commercial aviation.[10] One of the flights that opened Pan America's first airmail route to the Panama Canal zone was undertaken in an amphibious S-38. This trip met with enormous publicity because of the celebrated Lindbergh. However, John Hambleton had secretly flown the route several weeks before.

"There were no airways or facilities set up, so John Hambleton flew it on the condition that his flight be secret," recalls George Hambleton, the Pan Am pioneer's son. "He set up the fueling [stations] and logistics for where the plane would be landing and then, a few weeks later, accompanied Mr.

Lindbergh as copilot. They landed on the water outside the southwestern tip of Cuba, where Hambleton had arranged to have fuel available in fifty-five-gallon drums, and then they went over to Cozumel, down to Belize and Nicaragua, Panama. All those facilities had been arranged in advance of the flight that got all the publicity."[11]

Meanwhile, although Cooper had left the movies for a time, a potential film idea struck his fancy. In 1929 and 1930, in his apartment on East Seventy-third Street in Manhattan, he began writing "a number of outlines" for the mythic tale the world would come to know as *King Kong.* "I did not devote all my time to it," Cooper recalled in a letter to W. Douglas Burden, "because my good friend, John Hambleton, had got me to go with him into what was then a fascinating new world—commercial aviation!"[12]

By the spring of 1929, the Federal Aviation Corporation had made an initial offer of one hundred thousand shares of stock. With Hambleton as president, Cooper joined the board of directors, a prestigious group that included David Bruce, Anthony H. G. Fokker, George S. Franklin, R. K. Mellon, Brooks Parker, William H. Vanderbilt, and Cornelius Vanderbilt Whitney.[13] By 1931, Cooper was vice president of the Federal Aviation Cor-

MERIAN COOPER'S
VISIONARY FRIEND JOHN
HAMBLETON (RIGHT)
POSES WITH CHARLES
LINDBERGH ON THE
FIRST AIRMAIL FLIGHT
FROM THE U.S. TO
PANAMA. (THE PHOTO
IS AUTOGRAPHED BY
LINDBERGH TO MRS.
FRANK HAMBLETON,
JOHN'S MOTHER.)

Collection of George Hambleton

poration, a director of Western Air Express Corporation of Los Angeles, and a director of Pan American Airways.[14]

Cooper *seemed* to be settling down to the life of a businessman. He held executive positions in a variety of aviation interests, played the stock market, and graced the fashionable clubs around town. But it didn't come as a big surprise to his family when, in 1929, they heard that he was among the twenty-two select passengers of the *Graf Zeppelin* as the German dirigible floated eastward over the Atlantic on a flight around the world. Cooper's trip was celebrated in the Jacksonville paper with a subtitle that said it all: "Adventurous Spirit of Local Man Can *Not* Stand Idleness . . . Merian Cooper Has Looked into Death's Face on Many Occasions."

"Lately, he decided to settle down, he said in letters to relatives here," noted the newspaper account. "He became vice president of the Federal Aviation Lines. Not until today was it known that he had again turned to adventure when, at the last minute, he booked a round-the-world passage on the Graf Zeppelin."

The *Zeppelin* trip was typical Merian, his older brother told the *Jacksonville Journal* reporter. "That's just like him," John said. "He makes up his mind to go on adventures and away he goes."[15]

By 1931, though, Cooper's thoughts were again turning toward Hollywood. That he would soon depart the boardrooms of Manhattan for the soundstages of Hollywood was hastened by one of the great tragedies of his life.

WHILE COOPER WAS busy with his aviation interests, Ernest and Ruth Schoedsack did proud the motto of "distant, difficult, and dangerous." To make *Rango* they journeyed into northwestern Sumatra and the mountain jungles where dwelt a tribe so fierce the Dutch colonial government couldn't guarantee their safety. But the couple won the confidence of the Atjehnese natives. They were in the monsoon belt, but the high, cool elevation was a welcome change from the sweltering heat and malarial conditions of Siam. Monty, anticipating serving solely as director, had hired a cameraman who turned out to be the production's only major problem—an alcoholic tortured by delirium tremens and fears of being devoured by tigers. He was quickly dismissed, and it was a small matter for Schoedsack to resume his normal position behind the camera.

———

WITH SCHOEDSACK OFF in Sumatra, Cooper looked forward to sharing the long-delayed Empty Quarter adventure with John Hambleton. In the late spring of 1929, Cooper and Hambleton were staying together at the Garden City Hotel on Long Island. On June 8, 1929, Cooper and Hambleton saw each other off on separate flights from New York, Hambleton flying to Wilmington, North Carolina, to meet his wife, Cooper heading elsewhere in his little Fleet airplane. Hambleton's plane, which belonged to Consolidated Instrument Company, a maker of aeronautics instruments, also had on board J. Von Der Heyden, a director of sales and promotion for the company, and Von Der Heyden's wife. Their flight endured rough weather, and Von Der Heyden was at the controls when they briefly landed at Logan Field in Baltimore.

The Consolidated plane was in sight of the landing field at Wilmington when it inexplicably circled the field, then crashed. The disaster occurred in view of Mrs. Margaret Elliott Hambleton, who was pregnant with their son George, and she was one of the first to reach the wreckage. John had already been pulled from the plane, and his wife tried to revive him. But both Hambleton and J. Von Der Heyden had died instantly. Mrs. Von Der Heyden was still breathing, but she died in an ambulance on the way to the hospital.

Reportedly, the wings and controls appeared in functioning order, and it wasn't known who'd been piloting the plane. Hambleton's friends would maintain that John *could not* have been at the controls. If this was true, it was one of the few times, other than when he'd shared flying duties with Lindbergh, that he'd relinquished the pilot's seat, and tragically so.[16]

The Baltimore *Sun* eulogized Hambleton as "the victim of the very instrument whose future he had done so much to advance and broaden. . . . He was one of those young men emerging from the World War into maturity of plan and spirit for whom aviation constitutes not merely sport or career but one of the major problems and symbols of the modern world."

C. V. Whitney wrote, "In looking about for comfort from such acts of God we are apt to become depressed. We grope blindly for meaning, for something on which to hang our hats."[17]

George Hambleton recalls that his mother was so shaken by the tragedy that she burned most of her husband's papers, her grief consigning to the flames an irretrievable perspective on the genesis of commercial aviation.

"She'd wanted to put it all behind her, and there were boxes and boxes of early correspondence related to Pan Am, and there must have been letters to and from people like his good friend Merian Cooper—all destroyed," George Hambleton said.

George himself would become a pilot, inspired by the father he never knew. His mother, understandably, was firmly set against it, and he had to earn his own way—which he did, using summer wages earned spreading blacktop to pay for flying lessons. A subsequent career at Pan American World Airways included being named Pan Am's director for the USSR and opening the first direct air service between New York and Moscow. With a smile, Hambleton noted that he and his two brothers were proverbial chips off the old block. "I was flying helicopters and fixed-wings in Korea, my brother John was flying jets, and my half brother George Gibson Carey joined the paratroopers. My mother was fit to be tied with all three children up in the air."[18]

Cooper would recall that, to the end, John Hambleton's visionary mind had been focused on commercial air travel over the oceans and polar routes. The death of his friend, whose vision had so entranced him, seemed to sour Merian on commercial aviation. "With his death," he confessed in a 1964 letter to Burden, ". . . I made up my mind to get back into pictures and to do it with the story I had previously entitled 'Kong' and [later on] 'King Kong.' "[19]

For Cooper there would be one more blow—if not a tragedy, then a crushing disappointment—that would provide the final nudge, if he needed it, to return to moviemaking.

BY JUNE 1930, the Schoedsacks had returned to New York and were cutting *Rango* at Paramount's studio in Astoria. In a rare promotional interview, Schoedsack noted that he and Cooper had proven with *Grass* and *Chang* that a "love interest" wasn't the vital ingredient of a successful picture. "We focus our lenses, not on silly close-ups of love-sick females, but on the elemental clashes between nations and their fundamental problems, between man and nature."[20] This revulsion at the thought of cinematic celebrations of romance would become one of many in-jokes layered into *King Kong*, the epic fantasy in their near future.

Rango, which premiered in New York on February 18, 1931, was a hit with the critics and, reportedly, a favorite of Jesse Lasky's. While Schoed-sack was enjoying his solo success, Cooper suffered one of the great disap-pointments of his life.

Five days after the *Rango* premiere, Cooper learned that the Empty Quarter had been crossed by Bertram Thomas, vizier to the sultan of Mus-cat. The explorer had also come across an unknown tribe, one of the dis-coveries Cooper himself had hoped to make in the vast wasteland of the "Abode of Loneliness." Cooper, ever willing to salute true gallantry, cele-brated Thomas's courage in a public statement: "I consider it the greatest individual accomplishment, and the bravest one, in our day."[21]

It was a gracious comment, but probably the last straw for a man whose philosophy of living dangerously was at odds with the epic folly known as "civilization." At that crossroads he'd find a familiar face: David O. Selznick, who was making a fresh start in the picture business.

"I am getting terribly fed up with civilization again and more particu-larly straight business life and anxious to get away, or at least to make pic-tures myself rather than fool around in the business end of things," Cooper confessed to Selznick in a letter of June 19, 1931. "You have never had to do it or you would realize what a bore it can get to be. It has about as little romance as a fish."

In a postscript, he added: "I talked with Paramount about the possibil-ities of my making a gorilla picture for them and to tell you the truth that is what I am personally very anxious to do. I really have a great idea along this line and if you think any of the companies would be interested or that Myron [Selznick, David's older brother and a Hollywood agent] could get one of them interested I, on my part, would be delighted if you would let me know."[22]

The monstrous gorilla had been gestating in Cooper's imagination since 1929, but after John Hambleton's death Cooper had focused on the emerging story line with a new passion.[23] Film historian Ronald Haver es-timates that Cooper's pivotal moment came sometime in February 1930 when he was leaving his midtown office, heard an engine overhead, and looked up as an airplane, gleaming in the setting sun, passed over the New York Life Insurance Building. "Without any conscious effort of thought I immediately saw in my mind's eye a giant gorilla on top of the building," Cooper recalled.[24] Civilization, Cooper realized, could be symbolized by the "mightiest building in the world," with nature personified in the giant gorilla brought low by the guns of "the most modern of weapons, the airplane."[25]

Cooper had been fascinated by the lower primates all his life, and Rudy Behlmer pegs *The Four Feathers* and Cooper's many hours studying baboons in their native habitat as having "rekindled [his] interest in gorillas. It was this interest that led him to conceive the idea of a gigantic, semihuman gorilla pitted against modern civilization."[26] The urge might have been spurred on by an unfortunate bit of housecleaning, when a too tidy maid inexplicably decided to toss into the fire Cooper's only copy of the massive, handwritten eight-hundred-page monograph on baboons he had begun during the *Four Feathers* expedition, and was still working on in New York. He never returned to the aborted study.

Cooper's dream had also sparked memories of the gigantic "spirit" gorillas of Africa who kidnapped native women and of the giant lizard creatures he'd encountered on a remote island while sailing on the *Wisdom*. But the chief catalyst for his mercurial imaginings was his friend Douglas Burden's voyage to Komodo Island, which legend claimed was populated by "dragons," descendants of a prehistoric past.

CHAPTER FIFTEEN

SIGH FOR THE WILDERNESS

*With its . . . giant pinnacles that bared themselves like fangs to the
sky, it looked more fantastic than the mountains of the moon.*

*As we drew ever nearer, now jamming through dangerous
straits, now skimming past strips of glistening sand that stretched
out tantalizingly into the blue translucence of the water, we
seemed to see a prehistoric landscape—a lost world—unfold before
us. Everywhere, great gubbong palms stood outlined against the
blue. It is a melancholy land, a fitting abode for the weird creatures that lived in the dawn of things, and, as such, it seemed to be
a suitable haunt for the predatory dragon lizards.*

—W. Douglas Burden, describing his
arrival on Komodo Island[1]

IN LATE 1929, COOPER, THE RISING YOUNG AVIATION INDUSTRY EXECUTIVE, CON-
tacted W. Douglas Burden, a trustee of the American Museum of Natural
History, seeking information about different species of gorilla for a picture
he contemplated making in Africa. The two men already enjoyed mutual
respect: Burden for Cooper's achievement of *Chang,* Cooper for Burden's
published account of his adventures tracking the Komodo dragons.

Burden invited Cooper to the museum and introduced him to "the old
African hunter" Jimmie Clark and curator Harry Raven, an authority on
gorillas. He also facilitated an introduction to Harold Coolidge, who had
been hunting gorillas for the Museum of Comparative Zoology in Cam-
bridge and was an expert on the Kivu gorilla species.[2]

Burden's own "lost world" voyage also docked with Cooper's haunting
memory of the mysterious island in the Andamans where Dresser the
Dane had shot the scaly black "devil" Cooper had measured at fourteen

feet. That incident had triggered thoughts of a prehistoric island populated by gigantic creatures, but the dark, scaly lizards that fed on turtle
eggs hadn't struck a thrilling nerve the way the dragons that W. Douglas
Burden encountered on his expedition had. "Your island of Komodo
sounded to me much more thrilling and exciting," Cooper once confessed
to his friend.[3]

William Douglas Burden was an adventurer, an explorer, a dreamer—a
man much like Merian C. Cooper. He was born in Troy, New York, on September 28, 1898, the son of James A. and Florence Stone Burden, whose
family had based its fortune in the ironworks industry.[4] Burden would tell
Kevin Brownlow that a formative experience came at age nine, when he was
taken into the woods of Quebec to meet the native Ojibwa Indians. Burden
would always remember watching the Indians move silently through the
forests, their senses focused and alert to any shift in the wind or movement
of the clouds, speaking only when necessary and then only a few words, always softly uttered.[5] They inspired within him a lifelong reverence for wild
places and a desire to preserve the wilderness.

Burden also appreciated the ancient struggle between man and wild
beasts, and became a celebrated hunter whose treks took him from the Himalayas to the jungles of Indochina. In 1926 he added to his Harvard degree a master's in geology from Columbia University, and was subsequently
appointed a trustee of the American Museum of Natural History in New
York. That year he mounted his expedition to Komodo Island, the account
of which was published in 1927 by G. P. Putnam's Sons, the company that
had released Cooper's previous books.

The year 1927 was also notable because something happened that
spurred Burden's desire to make a movie depicting the Ojibwa tribe before
the white man's coming. "That something was Merian Cooper's *Chang,*"
Burden recalled. "Somehow *Chang* electrified my mind to the possibility of
an Indian picture along similar lines. To be sure, we did not have elephants
or water buffalo or leopards and tigers and gibbon, but we did have wolves
and bear and mountain lion and foaming rapids, and the hardness of deep
frost and long, tough winters." Burden realized time was slipping away, for
the tribe was already succumbing to the white man's diseases. Burden
knew Jesse Lasky had championed *Chang,* so he secured the mogul's enthusiastic support, won a distribution deal with Paramount, and after producing the film under the banner of his own Burden Pictures company, saw

the film premiere of *The Silent Enemy* on May 19, 1930, at the Criterion in New York.[6]

Burden would recall that while planning *The Silent Enemy* he sought Cooper's advice on shooting in the wilds, in the style that Cooper called "natural drama." "After *Chang* came out, I made it my business to get in touch with Merian Cooper. And it was fun, because he was so secretive. He wouldn't tell me how he had done anything. He would just laugh. But then, more and more I had the sense of what he *must* have done, and so gradually, by his not saying, 'No, I didn't do it that way,' I realized he had done it the way I was suggesting. Then I knew I could do the same thing."[7]

Burden would return the favor as his own adventure in Komodo Island became part of the magical alchemy created when true-life memory and imagination bonded like atomic particles, forming the synthesis of dream stuff in Cooper's mind out of which *King Kong* and all its wonders were born.

KOMODO ISLAND LIES west of Timor and east of Java, one of the smallest of the Lesser Sunda Islands. A mysterious, twenty-two-mile strip of volcanic land, it had discouraged European exploration and settlement because of monsoon winds and tidal currents around its coral reefs that roiled to upward of thirteen knots. In 1912 Malay pearl divers risked the currents, hoping to reap a rich haul from its untouched oyster beds. They would anchor in a safe harbor on Komodo, then return to report fantastic visions of giant lizards roaming the island. P. A. Ouwens, director of the Zoological Museum in Java, heard the astounding tales and sent out an expedition, which killed and brought back nine-foot specimens that were christened *Varanus komodoensis*.[8]

Fourteen years later, W. Douglas Burden made his successful expedition proposal to the American Museum of Natural History's president, Henry Fairfield Osborn, promising to bring to the West the first live Komodo dragons. Osborn asked Burden to record the expedition on film, making the 1926 sea voyage not only a scientific research trip but a moviemaking expedition.[9]

Burden hired F. J. Defosse, who had hunted dangerous game in the jungles of French Indochina, as the expedition's herpetologist, along with a Chinese cameraman named Lee Fai, whose services he secured through

Pathé Frères, and some fifteen Malay assistants. Their ship, the S.S. *Dog*, was provided by the Dutch colonial government. The wealthy young adventurer also brought along his attractive young bride, Katharine, affectionately known as "Babs."

After a voyage of approximately fifteen thousand miles, the *Dog* finally came within sight of the twenty-two-mile volcanic island, which Burden later wrote felt like a "lost world." The expedition landed, scouted out the alien terrain, and camped near a pool marked with the tracks of the monsters. "With its fantastic sky line, its sentinel palms, its volcanic chimneys bared to the stars, it was a fitting abode for the great saurians we had come so far to seek," Burden wrote.[10] The visitors also quickly discovered that Komodo Island was teeming with deer, wild boar, water buffalo, and game birds.

Burden knew that the gigantic, carnivorous lizards, a link to creatures sixty million years removed, usually attained lengths of ten feet and weighed up to 250 pounds. The giant lizards were soon spotted, and Burden characterized the dragon as "a primeval monster in a primeval setting."[11] The explorers also discovered that the fearsome creatures—which could swallow a deer's entire hindquarters in a single gulp—were thankfully slow moving and easily shot.

But capturing a "primeval monster" alive was a different story. They set a trap where dragons had been sighted, placing a fat boar carcass in an enclosure. Across the narrow entrance a tree was bent and lashed into place. A noose was tied to the bent end, laid at the entranceway, and covered with grass and leaves. A release string for the trap led to a hiding place where Burden, Defosse, and some of the Malays waited.

At one such trap, several lizards slithered and sniffed around while Burden patiently waited. Finally, a giant lizard with battle-scarred skin like black armor appeared—"a real monster," Burden recalled, the kind of creature they'd been hoping for. After the suspicious creature nosed around the trap for long, agonizing minutes, it leapt for the bait. Burden cut the line, and the trap was sprung. The beast was yanked into the air, but its weight broke the spring pole, so instead of being securely tied in midair, the monster ended up frantically flopping on the ground.

As the giant lizard struggled and vomited, the Malays backed off. Defosse approached with a lasso, then tossed and looped the rope tight around the monster's head and lassoed its tail. After a struggle, the lassoed creature was tied to a pole, hoisted up, and taken to camp, where it was deposited in a steel cage. But, come morning, the expedition would discover that the dragon was gone, the steel mesh of the cage torn open.[12]

Incongruously, the "lost world" included a small village populated by approximately forty convicts brought over by the raja of Sumbawa. "They are a degenerate lot of diseased people, they have reached such a degraded state that they don't even seem capable of curiosity," Burden wrote in contempt. ". . . Komodo is a place 'where every prospect pleases, and only man is vile.' "[13]

Burden also wrote of a hike he and Defosse took to a mountaintop, where they watched the setting sun color the wide sea a blood-red. They saw *Varanus komodoensis* tracks and the evidence that one of the great dragons had earlier stretched out in the sunshine. An evening mist drifted from the nearby woods and the moon rose as the explorer and the hunter talked. "I would like to bring my whole family and settle here," Defosse declared, "and be King of Komodo."[14]

The two men returned to camp, Burden still under the island's spell. Everyone was asleep, except for two natives playing bamboo flutes by the campfire. The white moon glistened on the damp grass; he heard murmuring voices coming from the darkness of the nearby jungle. "I could hear the gentle rustle of a sleepy forest talking to itself," he recalled. "Never was night more enchanting! There was the rattle of green bamboo, the rich fragrance of the 'orchid-scented glade,' and a pleasurable feeling of how little importance here is man. 'The spirit of the place' was sighing on the night wind, with every breath of air that stroked those ancient hills. Now there was a ghostly murmur reminiscent of aeolian music in a pine forest. What magic the moon makes."[15]

It was with poignant reflection that Burden subsequently recorded his emotions upon leaving the lost world with his prehistoric prize. "In a very short time we were sailing away from one of the most charming and romantic islands in the world. Already Komodo was far away, a great shadow that loomed up weird and indefinite in the distance, and it was not without deep regret that we left her lonely shores behind."[16]

The expedition film documented the baiting and capture of a dragon and brought back two live lizards along with fourteen *Varanus komodoensis* carcasses. The dead specimens would be studied and mounted for exhibition in the new Hall of Reptiles of the American Museum of Natural History. The two live dragons were exhibited at the Bronx Zoo, where they drew thousands until they took sick and died. The end came quickly, and Burden would recall how painful it was to see the great dragons wither away in captivity. Their cages had broken the spirits of the mighty beasts who had once known only the freedom of the mountains and rugged jungles of Komodo Island.[17]

MERIAN COOPER'S DREAM of a gigantic gorilla and its primal home of Skull Island took form during conversations he shared with Burden in 1929 and 1930, the same time he was developing his *Kong* treatments. The two adventurers entertained themselves with the ultimate tall tale, and their mutual experiences made for a combustible combination as they let their imaginations roam, blending true-life adventure with bombastic fantasy. "At first we tackled the problem of just how moving pictures might be obtained in heavy jungle," Burden recalled during an extraordinary exchange of letters he had with Coop in 1964, recalling the genesis of *Kong*. "In fact, we explored in considerable detail your ideas on how this could be done, for having just completed *The Silent Enemy* for Paramount, I was at that time most interested in animal films.

"Then we went on to broader things. I remember, for example, that you were quite intrigued by my description of prehistoric Komodo Island and the dragon lizards that inhabited it. . . . You especially liked the strength of words beginning with 'K,' such as Kodak, Kodiak Island, and Komodo. It was then, I believe, that you came up with the idea of Kong as a possible title for a gorilla picture. I told you that I liked very much the ring of the word . . . and I believe that it was a combination of the King of Komodo phrase in my book and your invention of the name Kong that led to the title you used much later on, *King Kong*."[18]

Burden stressed that those early talks had gone into "the whole *King Kong* concept," as he further elaborated: "In fact . . . I recall describing to you Komodo as a remote, hard to reach volcanic island, the very elements that you used in the setting of your picture. And I told you that I had taken my young wife there which could possibly have led to your use of a young girl in King Kong. . . .

"Even my description of how the Komodo dragons were destroyed by civilization when I brought them back to New York was duplicated by you in the way civilization destroyed King Kong, and I hope I am not boasting if I suggest that your leading character, Carl Denham, was a composite that included something of me."[19]

Cooper didn't argue with a bit of Burden's remembrance when he responded in his own letter a week later: "Thanks a thousand for your letter of June 15, 1964 concerning the conception and birth of *King Kong.* What memories it brings back! Everything you say is right on the nose. Boy, what a memory!"[20]

Cooper's long reply noted that he'd conceived a "Giant Gorilla" prior to reading Burden's *Dragon Lizards of Komodo,* which reminded him of his own voyage to the Andaman Islands and the gigantic lizards there. He'd contemplated a cinematic battle between apes and lizards and had become "intrigued with the possibility of photographing and capturing a giant gorilla (or two or three of them) in the hopes of getting one back alive to the United States. But as I began to think over your Komodo island, I wondered how I could get my Gorilla to face your Dragons. There were no airplanes; by boat it seemed a really tough proposition."[21]

What Cooper had in mind was an actual movie expedition that would pit live gorillas and live Komodo lizards, natural drama style, using the intercutting techniques he and Schoedsack had pioneered on *The Four Feathers.* "Back projection had not yet been fully developed (but it was in the air) so in *Four Feathers* Schoedsack and I did it [combined African locations with studio sets and back lot] merely by intercutting," Cooper recalled for Burden. "Then one day, after one of my conversations with you, I thought to myself, why not film my Gorilla—either a Kivu Gorilla in the Congo or a Spanish African Gorilla, or both, and then go back to your Komodo island and film your Dragons and for the purposes of the picture tie them both together in the same way as I had tied together the elements of *Four Feathers.* I also had very firmly in mind to giantize both the gorilla and your dragons to make them really huge. However, I always believed in personalizing and focusing attention on *one* main character and from the very beginning I intended to make it the Gigantic Gorilla, no matter what else I surrounded him with."[22]

Cooper agreed with Burden's memory of the theme of nature versus civilization: "When you told me that the two Komodo Dragons you brought back to the Bronx Zoo, where they drew great crowds, were even-

SIGH FOR THE WILDERNESS · 195

tually killed by civilization, I immediately thought of doing the same thing with my Giant Gorilla. I had already established him in my mind on a prehistoric island with prehistoric monsters and I now thought of having him destroyed by the most sophisticated thing I could think of in civilization, and in the most fantastic way."[23]

It soon became clear that Cooper's fantastical and ever-expanding premise couldn't be achieved by intercutting. He was also dead set against the typical "gag" of a man in an ape suit. So how could he conjure a gigantic gorilla? He began contemplating traveling-matte composite techniques and other "trick work," as special effects was called.

But there would be one last great exploit before Cooper left New York for California: a rescue mission to save the life of Varick Frissell, another colleague and friend in filmmaking adventure.

VARICK FRISSELL, LIKE Shorty Schoedsack, was another young giant, wealthy, handsome, and popular. Like Cooper and Burden, Frissell became fascinated with man's struggle against nature, and he sought to document that primal theme on film. He found his particular subject in the sealers of Newfoundland, who boarded ships bound for the vast ice floes. It was more than a job; it was a rite of passage, as a sealing ship ventured miles from shore, deep into the frozen ice fields. If the crush of ice caught a vessel, the store of explosives a ship carried would blast them free. Once anchored for the seal hunt, the men traversed vast stretches of frozen, undulating ice that lay between them and the abyss of the sea.

Frissell's film was to be a natural drama of sorts, a fictional story personalizing the astounding footage as he followed a sealing expedition of the *Viking*. The melodramatic elements of *White Thunder* (as Frissell originally titled his epic) would be directed by George Melford—whose directorial work included the 1921 Rudolph Valentino drama *The Sheik*—and feature a love triangle involving two sealers contending for the woman who awaits them upon their return from the ice fields.

But the real drama lay in the images of sealers under an overcast sky, looking like smudges against the white expanse, the ice fields rolling with the sea waves. The men were often forced to leap across breaks in the ice, while those stranded on broken ice blocks had to steer the floating fragments like boats back to the main ice mass. At one point, the sealing ship became caught in the ice, and Frissell's camera documented the process of the ship being dynamited free.

Kevin Brownlow, in his *The War, the West, and the Wilderness*, noted that although Frissell was said to have worked with Robert Flaherty, his true mentor was that other pioneer of the documentary adventure film: Merian Cooper. "He had asked for Cooper's help in editing the footage, before returning to shoot additional material," Brownlow reported.[24] Frissell and the *Viking* shoved off from St. John's in Newfoundland to shoot that additional material. But on March 15, the supply of explosives aboard the ship mysteriously exploded, sinking the craft and stranding survivors on that alien terrain of ice, miles from the rugged shore.

Merian Cooper was hurriedly summoned to the New York apartment of Dr. Lewis Frissell, the explorer's father. It had been reported that some survivors had made it across the ice fields to safety at Horse Island, but his son was among the missing. Would Merian lead a rescue mission to try to find Varick and any others who might still be clinging to life on the coastal ice floes?

Cooper agreed and hurriedly organized an expedition that featured Bernt Balchen, who had piloted Admiral Byrd's first Antarctic expedition and was an all-around expert "ice flyer," as Coop characterized him. The rescue team also included Roy Gates and Randy Enslow, a pilot and an experienced "amphibian man." The plane itself, a Boeing amphibian, had been borrowed from one of Cooper's powerful friends in New York, C. V. Whitney.[25]

Stormy weather threatened the mission at the outset, but on March 20 the rescue plane, loaded with 433 gallons of gasoline and hundreds of pounds of food and emergency supplies, managed to lift off from Boston under gray skies and into a sixteen-mile-an-hour headwind. The plane passed over the sea where pieces of ice had broken off and were drifting away with the currents. It was terrible to contemplate whether the lost men had instantly gone down with the *Viking* or had desperately clung to life on rafts of ice, only to be swept out to sea.

"Balchen was wonderful—the greatest Arctic pilot who ever lived," Cooper recalled. "We flew in bad weather low among icebergs, dropped supplies—blankets, food, etc., to scattered survivors, and guided them to

shore—three or four days' desperate work. Balchen made incredible land-
ings in broken ice—we should have been killed a dozen times. We saved the
lives of a lot of survivors."[26]

But of young Varick Frissell there was no trace; nor was there any way
of knowing whether his end had been mercifully swift or if he had lingered
on a flotsam of ice. Frissell's family and friends chose to believe his end had
come swiftly. He was twenty-seven years old when he vanished.

The explosion that sank the *Viking* and the daring rescue attempt made
headlines, and the studio capitalized by changing the picture's name from
White Thunder to *The Viking*. "I've never seen *The Viking*," Cooper once sighed
to Brownlow. "I remember it fell into the hands of some damned 'sharpies'
for distribution—all those dreadful kind of people."[27]

Merian Cooper rarely talked in detail about the Frissell rescue expedition. For a "fortunate soldier" who had scoured the French countryside to
learn the fate of missing comrades, it had been a devastating personal blow
to have been asked by the parents of his young friend to come to their son's

MERIAN COOPER AND FAMED AND FEARLESS "ICE FLYER" BERNT BALCHEN AT
NEWFOUNDLAND BASE FROM WHICH THEY FLEW OVER THE ICE FLOES TO RESCUE
VARICK FRISSELL AND SURVIVORS OF THE *VIKING* DISASTER.

Cooper Papers, BYU

rescue and to have failed them. The Frissell family didn't see it that way, of course. It was a million-to-one shot from the start, and Cooper and his rescue party had put their own lives on the line in the bargain.

"It is a great pleasure to Mrs. Frissell and me to give even this slight remembrance to one so unselfish as to devote his whole time regardless of personal risk in the endeavor to clear up the fate of a friend," Lewis Frissell wrote Cooper. "To me you will always stand out as a type of man of whom there are too few. Our own Varick had many of your qualities."[28]

THE JOURNEY TO *King Kong* was somehow inevitable. The Cooper-Schoedsack formula of "distant, difficult, and dangerous" moviemaking had evolved into pure storytelling. Although the once inseparable partners had struck out on their own, when Cooper returned to Hollywood to make *Kong* he called upon Schoedsack. The ultimate true-life movie expedition team would be making a picture about the ultimate movie expedition, which is how Schoedsack had once characterized *King Kong*: "What we talked about was, suppose we were planning an expedition and you could have anything that was loud and exaggerated and terrific as possible—this is what it would be!"[29]

Cooper would tell Rudy Behlmer that when Schoedsack went overseas to make *Rango,* he was happy to stay behind and "get into the aviation business *and then I got the itch to go exploring again* [emphasis added] and that's how *King Kong* was made."[30] Instead of wilderness, they'd be entering a world of soundstages and back lots. But there was also a limitless world to conquer—the realm of the imagination.

In May 1931, some seven months before he left for Hollywood, Cooper was profiled by Gilbert Seldes in an article celebrating him as a soldier, an adventurer, and a leader in commercial aviation.

Seldes noted that Cooper had a new picture in mind but was feeling secretive. Cooper also alluded to a wanderlust that still burned in him; if he ever got bored he could take a thousand dollars and go become a chief of the Bakhtiari, content with herds, tobacco, and a wife—or two. In such a manner he could live out the rest of his days, Cooper revealed. "He feels that he hasn't quite finished with migrations," Seldes noted.[31]

THE EIGHTH
WONDER OF
THE WORLD

**"THUNDERING INTO HOLLYWOOD!"
BOMBASTIC NEWSPAPER AD
ANNOUNCES THE COMING OF KING
KONG TO GRAUMAN'S CHINESE.**

Cooper Papers, BYU

CHAPTER SIXTEEN

CREATION

*They were adventurers—Cooper, the voluble visionary, Schoed-
sack, the self-styled "strong, silent one."*

*Now, for the first time, they would be adventuring within the
confines of a Hollywood production lot. It was compelling to think
that this newest project would have all the flavor and excitement
of their personal experience.*

—Fay Wray on the start of KING KONG production[1]

I N THE SUMMER OF 1931, DAVID O. SELZNICK WAS A PRODUCER WITHOUT A STUDIO,
and a man without immediate prospects in Hollywood. The 1929 stock
market crash and ensuing Depression had hit Hollywood hard, particularly studios with poor financial management. Paramount's own healthy
profit margin had evaporated between 1930 and 1931, the studio coffers
drained by a number of financial burdens, including the technological
conversion to sound and the acquisition of new movie houses for the studio's theater chain.

The resulting cost-cutting measures, which included slashing executives' salaries, irked Selznick. He also had a dream of a system of individual
production units and independent producers, so one producer wouldn't
have to shoulder a crushing slate of films. He therefore resigned from Paramount in June 1931 and moved to New York, where he settled in at the
Pierre Hotel with ambitious plans to form an independent production
company.

Selznick called upon Merian Cooper, who was now running in elite circles of wealth and influence. Selznick's hope was that Cooper would connect him with the investors he would need to launch his new company.
Merian obliged, introducing Selznick around, notably to the well-connected

cousins Cornelius Vanderbilt "Sonny" Whitney and John Hay "Jock" Whitney. Cooper also saw a chance to advance his giant gorilla story, and that summer he and David Bruce, already intrigued with the *Kong* idea, "pitched" the story to Selznick at a meeting on Long Island.

By then, Cooper had developed a beauty-and-the-beast plotline. It was summed up by his fake Arabian proverb that would eventually open the picture: "And lo! The Beast looked upon the face of Beauty, and it stayed its hand from killing. And from that day, it was as one dead."[2]

Meanwhile, Selznick's dream of an independent company ran into powerful opposition from the likes of MGM mogul Louis B. Mayer, who saw it as an assault on the hierarchy of the studio system. Even if he raised the necessary capital, the studio powers could cut off top-flight talent and prevent his imagined company from arranging adequate distribution and exhibition deals.[3]

So Cooper switched gears and turned his energies to finding a new studio home for Selznick. In addition to working on his *Kong* treatment, Cooper had been contemplating the entire Hollywood film industry from afar. During the summer of 1930, while relaxing on a friend's yacht, he had discussed "the big revival" in the movies generated by talking pictures and what he felt was the studios' potentially disastrous decision to base their financial structure on ownership of theater chains. Ever looking to the future, Cooper had argued that "the day of the large theater was past and that the introduction of the home motion picture and television would eventually ruin" the studios.[4]

His attention turned to Radio-Keith-Orpheum (RKO), also known as Radio Pictures. RKO was technically one of the newer Hollywood studios, even though its origins could be traced back to a nickelodeon in Milwaukee that had opened in 1909. That fledgling business had grown and evolved through mergers and acquisitions until it had emerged as a full-fledged production and distribution company whose parent company was the mighty Radio Corporation of America (RCA). RKO's profits for 1930 had been an estimated $3.5 million, but those numbers were deceptive, inflated by the novelty of talkies. Like everyone enmeshed in the Depression, the studio was struggling, its financial woes exacerbated by the expensive dreams of William LeBaron, vice president in charge of production, who was attempting to put RKO on par with Paramount, MGM, and the other "majors." But LeBaron's high-cost productions were doing lackluster box office, and the studio's head office in New York finally had enough when their stock fell to seventy-five cents a share.[5]

Cooper later stated that through "his various connections in the big money world," he was intimately aware of RKO's financial troubles and the concerns of David Sarnoff, the president of RCA. Cooper maintained that he got things rolling on Selznick's behalf at RKO through his influential friend David Bruce. Selznick, however, would recall that he had himself contacted the head of RKO's parent company.[6] Regardless of how it happened—Cooper's intercession or Selznick's initiative—discussions between Sarnoff and the twenty-nine-year-old producer led to an agreement in October 1931 that installed Selznick as RKO's vice president in charge of production. The RKO studio resources included the base of filmmaking operations on Gower Street in Los Angeles and the old Pathé lot, with its sprawling back lot, in Culver City.

But despite the resources he now had at his disposal, Selznick recognized that RKO was in trouble, with expected losses for 1931 estimated at more than $5 million.[7] Already entangled in Selznick's endeavors, Cooper became further drawn into Selznick's affairs when, at the suggestion of David's talent-agent brother Myron, he attempted to buy the rights to Tarzan, although MGM production head Irving Thalberg had already purchased the renowned jungle-man character for an estimated $20,000. "I think Myron Selznick offered Thalberg $50,000 for me, which Thalberg declined," Cooper later recalled of Myron's negotiations on his behalf. "Anyhow, at the suggestion of Dave Bruce, I later came out to Hollywood to talk to David Selznick. I found RKO in a turmoil, as this was in the depression, but Selznick was taking hold with a firm hand. He asked me to help him and I told him I was interested only in my [gorilla] adventure picture . . . but nobody in Hollywood in the depression was willing to tie up considerable money in what seemed to them a hazardous trip to foreign wilds."[8]

Rudy Behlmer pinpoints September 1931 as the month Selznick asked Cooper to join the team he was forming at RKO.[9] Selznick had instituted a "supervisory system" of production management featuring seven associate producers, two of whom he named as his executive assistants: thirty-nine-year-old Merian Cooper and twenty-six-year-old Pandro Berman.

Although Cooper had only three pictures to his credit prior to his arrival at RKO, he was well versed in the arts and a natural storyteller. Merian resisted being praised as an artist and an intellect, but his son, Richard, will have none of that. "He could pull that on somebody else, but not [his family and close friends]," Richard chuckled. "He was the smartest guy I ever knew.

"The thing about my dad that was a little unfair was that he had a photographic memory. Most people are linear thinkers, but he was parallel-processing all the time, he always had this great mental database to lean on. He had also read classic literature; he knew the basic plots. He'd always studied art and the great masters, so from a visual standpoint he knew basic lighting techniques. When he and my mother went on vacations they'd go to museums and study all the great art. His education in the arts was an ongoing process."[10]

Cooper also had his trademark boundless energy, and he threw himself into his new responsibilities as a studio production executive in charge of a slate of films. He'd also returned to the business as a man with a mission, so at Myron Selznick's suggestion he deliberately refused to take any salary or become an RKO employee until he was satisfied that he firmly retained all rights to the character and name of Kong.[11]

By mid-December, Cooper had sent Selznick his first written treatment of the giant gorilla story.[12] But the million-dollar question was still *how* Cooper would bring his giant gorilla to life. The fake Arabian proverb prologue posed a major creative problem: It set a poetic tone that wouldn't be satisfied by either a real gorilla or the traditional man in an ape suit.[13]

The answer to that dilemma would be found in the southeast corner of the RKO lot on Gower Street, behind the camera department, in an old wooden building that had a sign that read: AUTHORIZED PERSONNEL ONLY.

"It was called the *Creation* building," recalled RKO executive Vernon Harbin, who was a messenger boy on the lot at that time. "We were all very curious, of course."[14]

THE ROOTS OF *Creation* stretched back to early 1930, when a story outline came across the desk of William LeBaron. The outline, from Harry O. Hoyt, who directed the 1925 silent-era classic *The Lost World*, which was based on Sir Arthur Conan Doyle's novel and released by First National studio, proposed a new dinosaur adventure featuring the latest advances in trick devices and cinematic illusion.

"In no other branch of the industry has there been greater improvement than in trick work and this, singularly enough, has not been exploited to the extent of its possibilities," his proposal noted. ". . . The stage cannot attempt it—the novel must leave much to the reader's imagination. On the screen we have the perfect illusion—these terrible monsters breathing, fighting and bleeding in mortal combat among themselves and with the people."[15]

The master of the illusion proposed for *Creation* was Willis O'Brien, a pioneer in the art of three-dimensional stop-motion animation who had done the honors for *The Lost World*.

O'Brien, affectionately known as "Obie," had been born in Oakland, California, in 1886. As a young man, he had knocked about as a cowboy, a freight train brakeman, a surveyor, and a prizefighter. He was also a naturally gifted artist, and one of his many early jobs was at a San Francisco design firm. During a carefree moment at that firm, he fashioned a miniature prizefighter from modeling clay. Another worker noticed, quickly modeled his own clay boxer, and challenged O'Brien to a "duel," much to the delight of their coworkers.

It was then, while adjusting his clay figure into a succession of poses, that the idea of stop-motion animation came to O'Brien.[16]

But it was while working as a wilderness guide that O'Brien found the subject he would focus upon as a filmmaker. He once had led a group of scientists from the University of Southern California to Crater Lake, in northern California, in search of prehistoric fossils. There in the lava beds, where the Modoc Indian tribe of northern California once held out against the whites, O'Brien listened as the scientists discussed the prehistoric past. Their discovery of the fossilized remains of a saber-toothed tiger sealed O'Brien's fascination with prehistoric creatures, and he became determined to bring to life the lost world of the past.[17]

The process O'Brien went on to pioneer remains one of the most exacting crafts in all visual-effects artistry. Typically, a puppet constructed with movable parts is positioned in a succession of poses, which are filmed one frame at a time. When the final film is projected, the perception is that the puppet is moving with continuous, seamless motion. Unlike hand-drawn animation, stop-motion allows three-dimensional puppets and objects to be realistically lit, and thus conveys a magical sense of physical reality.

206 - LIVING DANGEROUSLY

In addition to the animator's skill, the process from the beginning became dependent upon the craftsmanship of the animated object. By the time *The Lost World* was to go into production, O'Brien knew that stop-motion figures would require a sophisticated new approach, and he hired a young sculptor named Marcel Delgado. After a period of careful research, each stop-motion creature for *The Lost World* was endowed with a complex skeletal armature, totally articulated and designed with complex ball-and-socket joints, then built up with sponge and cotton; latex was used for their skin.

While Delgado developed the models, O'Brien oversaw the construction of the miniature landscape sets at First National's Hollywood studio, creating a tabletop world of sculpted mountains and foliage made from sheet metal that would stay constant during the laborious animation process.[18]

An early reel of O'Brien's dinosaur footage was shown to Sir Arthur Conan Doyle himself and he was so impressed that he screened it, without explanation, to Harry Houdini and other conjurers assembled at the annual gathering of the Society of American Magicians in New York. The group was astonished, and the next day's *New York Times* headline noted: "DINOSAURS CAVORT IN FILM FOR DOYLE; Spiritist Mystifies World-Famed Magicians with Pictures of Prehistoric Beasts; Keeps Origin a Secret."[19]

When LeBaron gave the go-ahead to *Creation,* O'Brien was determined to lead another advance in stop-motion technology, technique, and artistry. The equally ambitious LeBaron saw the proposed prehistoric adventure as another chance to outshine other studios in Hollywood.

Hoyt, who would direct, began developing the *Creation* screenplay in April 1930, while O'Brien went to work with a team that included Delgado, puppeteer Orville Goldner, and artists Mario Larrinaga, Byron L. Crabbe, and Ernest Smythe. *Creation* came with a huge price tag: an estimated $652,242 budget and a twenty-week shooting schedule. Film historian George Turner notes this was "about triple the cost and time allotment for a typical 'A' picture of the time." By early 1931 the budget had risen to an eye-popping $1,201,000, a rarefied budgetary realm occupied by only a few previous films.[20]

By the time Selznick took charge of studio production and halted *Creation,* an estimated $200,000 had already been spent on the animation test reel. Ironically, the studio had too much invested to put *Creation* on the shelf, so in early December 1931, Selznick asked Cooper to look at the test footage and see if the production should proceed.[21]

The screening was a disaster. Cooper would later characterize *Creation* as "a reel of pretty badly done animation of a very bad story."[22]

However, O'Brien biographer Don Shay gives Obie credit for the initiative that marked the production breakthrough for *Kong.* O'Brien, who learned of Cooper's dream of a giant gorilla picture, had Byron Crabbe prepare an inspirational oil painting for Cooper showing a towering ape in the jungle menacing a scantily clad, exotic jungle woman and a modern-day explorer.[23]

It may have been Cooper himself who had seen *something* in that test reel—something about the stop-motion technique that convinced him that he *could* create his giant gorilla picture, without ever having to journey to wild locations or snare real gorillas.

Soon after the screening, on his own initiative, Cooper ordered two new sophisticated animation test scenes designed to be used in a new production. He formally proposed this production in the one-page report to Selznick, written on December 18, 1931, that put the kibosh on *Creation,* criticizing its story construction and animation as "entirely wrong." He suggested, however, that a new production might make better advantage of stop-motion. "The results of animation show that the animals will always be somewhat mechanical, but if kept in motion and the speed slowed down about twenty-five percent, real effects can be realized.

"... The whole secret of successful productions of this type is startling, unusual sensation. But that sensation must be of something new, and must have character. Animals can be made into new, sensational story characters, as well as people. This has been proved on the screen in the use of Bimbo in *Chang,* Rin-Tin-Tin, etc. My idea then is to not only use the prehistoric animals for their novelty value, but also to take them out of their present character of just big beasts running around, and make them into a ferocious menace. The most important thing, however, is that one animal should have a really big character part in the picture. I suggest a prehistoric Giant Gorilla, fifty times as strong as a man—a creature of nightmare horror and drama."

Cooper recommended a budget for construction of a stop-motion gorilla and two more test scenes for the new production. He also proposed that four new test scenes could be achieved "by using an animated figure against a projection background, all played against a Dunning foreground [a traveling-matte composite process that allowed two separate images to be combined on one strip of film as, hopefully, a single, seamless image], with close-up work of full sized head mask, and hands and feet. So far as I know, this method has never been done on the screen, and should prove sensational. . . . The Giant Terror Gorilla should give character sensation."[24]

The *Kong* story hadn't yet coalesced into a screenplay, but Cooper planned his test-reel shoot as if this production had been given the green light, and he began hiring principal actors and building full-scale sets to match O'Brien's tabletop miniatures. In a way, he *had* to pull out all the stops—if he didn't impress the RKO executives in New York, they would never agree to authorize the expensive production. O'Brien's stop-motion magic would be featured, including the giant ape model and such *Creation* models as the triceratops.[25]

In addition to a test reel, the presentation for the RKO chiefs would include a series of production sketches produced by O'Brien, including the seminal drawing for one of the most famous images in screen history: the giant gorilla gripping a woman in one fist atop the Empire State Building as fighter planes attack. Cooper imagined other dramatic components, and most formed a virtual template of the final film, from the Skull Island scene of Kong shaking the men off the jungle log to the giant ape's climactic rampage through the streets of New York.

Cooper had always imagined Kong as a fantastical but physically accurate depiction of an ape. Just three days after his *Creation* memo went to Selznick, Cooper fired off a telegram to Harry Raven at the American Museum of Natural History, asking for the basic physical dimensions of a large male gorilla. The next day, he received a Western Union reply from Raven delineating the dimensions he had requested.[26]

"I had to start the test reel and everybody thought it was nuts," Cooper recounted to Kevin Brownlow. ". . . Everybody wanted me to put a man in a gorilla suit and it would have been just horrible and I resisted all pressure. All the financial guns wanted me to do it. We could have done it in a tenth of the time but it wouldn't have been any damn good."[27]

WRITER DAVID THOMSON sums up the making of *King Kong* as "that great testament to collaboration, serendipity, and blind chance."[28] That fragile alchemy also included casting. Fay Wray was the perfect choice to be the virginal Ann Darrow, the romantic interest of Bruce Cabot's John Driscoll. In the story, Driscoll himself was initially angry with Carl Denham for bringing a woman on their expedition, thus recalling Ernest Schoedsack's frustration when Marguerite Harrison joined *Grass*. The stocky, tough-talking Robert Armstrong was cast as Carl Denham, the stubborn and reckless movie producer embarking on the ultimate moviemaking expedition, and he was the very image of Merian Cooper—more than one observer noted their physical resemblance.

There was another way in which the film reflected actual events. The pitch Denham gives Darrow for his mysterious movie project was first enacted for real when Wray visited Cooper in his office. " 'You will have the tallest, darkest leading man in Hollywood.' Those were the first words I heard about *King Kong*," Wray later recalled. "Although I knew the producer, Merian C. Cooper, was something of a practical joker, my thoughts rushed hopefully to the image of Clark Gable. Cooper, pacing up and down in his office, outlined the story to me . . . about an expedition going to some remote island where a discovery of gigantic proportions would be made. My heart raced along, waiting for the revelation. I enjoyed his mysterious tone, the gleeful look in his eyes that seemed to say, 'Just wait until you hear who will be playing opposite you!'

"Cooper paused, picked up some poster-size sketches, then showed me my tall dark leading man. My heart stopped, then sank. An absolutely enormous gorilla was staring at me. 'We're going to make him look about 50 feet high. All in animation.' There were sketches of the big ape, who would be captured and brought back to civilization. . . . Cooper was delighted at my amazement, especially, I think, at the look of shock and apprehension on my face."[29]

A happy addition to the production was Ernest Schoedsack, who rejoined his old partner in January 1932 after months in India shooting location footage for the Paramount production *The Lives of a Bengal Lancer*. The credits for *King Kong* would be emblazoned with the legend of old: "A Cooper-Schoedsack Production." Novelist Edgar Wallace, who at about the same time joined the production from England, would write in his diary about the reunion: "There was a conference on *Kong* which, however, I couldn't attend. I met Cooper afterwards. He was as happy as a schoolboy. He had met the man who was his partner and who had acted as camera man in *Chang*. He'd just returned from India, and 'Coop' was overjoyed to meet him. It was a tremendous revelation of his genuineness. He said he had worked with him for seven years and never had a quarrel."[30]

Thus, it was full speed ahead for Merian C. Cooper. His new assistant, Zoe Porter, would always remember how hard Cooper drove everyone, including (and especially) himself. Those in Cooper's orbit sustained themselves on crackers and milk as workdays often became work nights, and Zoe, for one, loved it all.

"I can still see him energetically striding around his office, pipe in mouth, crackers and cheese in one hand, script pages in the other, while I furiously took shorthand notes trying to keep up with the spontaneous flow of his ideas. It wasn't always easy to understand him through the handicap of pipe and cracker crumbs, but some way I made it. No one could be around him and not be infected with his energy and enthusiasm."[31]

"Cooper was bigger than life and his showmanship seemed to come naturally to him," reflects Ray Harryhausen, a stop-motion protégé of O'Brien's. "There was a theatricality that came, I guess, from his experiences in the war and going into Persia and the jungle with Schoedsack to film *Grass* and *Chang* at a time when there wasn't that much traveling."

Harryhausen recalls an original cartoon made for Cooper during the *King Kong* production that he saw, years later, hanging in Cooper's office when the young stop-motion animator was working on Cooper's 1949 gorilla picture, *Mighty Joe Young*. To Harryhausen it summed up Cooper's hard-charging persona.

"This cartoon showed Cooper jumping up and down screaming, 'Make it bigger, make it bigger!' That's what Cooper always said: 'Make it bigger, *make it bigger!*'"[32]

CHAPTER SEVENTEEN

THE DANGEROUS GAME

> *I used exactly the same methods for strong [story] construction in both* Chang *and* King Kong—*deliberately slow, intriguing, intimate beginning so that the audience would know my characters well before I went into rapid action. In both pictures we tried to establish what Schoedsack and I used to call our 3 D's: difficulty—distance—danger.*
>
> *. . . I knew it to be essential to make it seem within the realms of probable imagination that* King Kong *could exist—that such an island as Skull Island could exist and that it was both difficult, distant and dangerous to get to Skull Island. Indeed, I used five reels to do this. I set up the whole theme and story before the audience ever saw King Kong.*
>
> —Merian Cooper[1]

KONG WASN'T THE ONLY ITEM ON COOPER'S PLATE AT RKO. ONE OF HIS EARLIest projects was *The Marines Have Landed,* a two-fisted tale he had conceived, with Jane Bigelow assisting on a treatment. Even more dramatic—and full of the violence and intrigues he'd eventually experience in China during World War II—was *Roar of the Dragon,* with Cooper and Bigelow sharing story credit on the eventual release.

Set in a river town in central Manchuria, *Dragon* tells of a hotel compound under siege by cutthroat bandits, their murderous leader eager to kill the hero, a brave but dissolute riverboat captain named Carson, played by Richard Dix. The treatments and scripts evolved beginning in early 1932 and on into springtime, including first drafts that set the stage in the peaceful Chinese river town and introduced the main characters, who were awaiting riverboat repairs and destined to be menaced by the bandits roaming the countryside.

"HE'S NOT BIG ENOUGH!"
KING KONG **"MERRY XMAS"**
CARD FOR MERIAN COOPER.

Cooper Papers, BYU

By June 4, added scenes had changed the opening to a montage of newspaper headlines and teletype reports chronicling the brave riverboat captain's battle with the bandit Veronsky, and revealing how his murderous gang had crippled the boat. At the start Veronsky is suffering a bloody wound—an ear bitten off by Carson—and he cries for a hot iron to seal it, even as he bellows, "Carson! Get him, oil him and burn him alive. . . . I'll make him pay for the loss of my ear. . . . Understand? Torture him!"[2]

The machine-gun pace of the editing and the melodramatic action in *Roar of the Dragon* was characteristic of the spare, no-nonsense storytelling inherent in Cooper's earliest work at RKO. Another of these early productions, which served as a bridge to the world of *King Kong*, was the 1932 RKO release *The Most Dangerous Game*. Produced by Cooper and directed by Schoedsack (with Irving Pichel as codirector), it marked the duo's first talking picture, a tautly paced adventure featuring an insane big-game hunter whose fortress island is his personal hunting ground as he pursues the "most dangerous game": man.

It is also a psychological thriller, with the mad General Zaroff (played by Leslie Banks) getting sexual kicks from the hunt as he exclaims, "One passion builds upon another. Kill, then love! When you have known that, you have known ecstasy!" This was wild stuff in 1932, with metaphors for madness—a scar slashing the side of Zaroff's forehead indicates his fractured personality, while his tapestry of a satyr carrying off a woman illustrates his psychosexual bloodlust. And there are overt horrors, such as a dungeon where the general keeps the severed heads of his victims mounted on walls and floating in liquid-filled jars.

The heroic counterpart to Zaroff is the famed, handsome hunter Bob Rainsford, played by Joel McCrea. The cast included two other characters shipwrecked on Zaroff's island: Martin Trowbridge, a likable drunk played by Robert Armstrong, and his beautiful sister Eve, played by Fay Wray. *Dangerous Game* principals included screenwriter James Ashmore Creelman, editor Archie S. Marshek, and composer Max Steiner, all of whom also worked on *Kong*. Best of all, historian George Turner writes, was the title credit for *The Most Dangerous Game:* "A Cooper and Schoedsack production." This was "good news for the many 1932 movie goers who were bored with the overly talky talkies then dominating the screen," Turner contends. "It meant that two men who always made *moving* pictures were back."[3]

Dangerous Game was also layered with inside references to the two partners' own experiences, a flourish that would soon thereafter dramatically
texture *Kong*. The shipwreck that delivers Joel McCrea's celebrated hunter
to Zaroff's island was based on the pirates who wrecked the lighthouse
that briefly sent the *Wisdom II* aground, while the deadfall and other animal traps used during Zaroff's hunt were based on Schoedsack's knowledge of traps he used in Siam.

Dangerous Game, which began production on May 16, 1932, would over-
lap with Production No. 601: *Kong*, which began filming under the working
title of *The Beast*. Cooper was shrewdly getting a double bang for his buck
by using the Zaroff jungle set for the Skull Island scenes he was simultaneously shooting for the *Kong* test reel. The *Dangerous Game* set, built on Stage
12 at the RKO-Pathé lot in Culver City, included a swamp, a trail and a
cave, the Malay deadfall trap, and a ravine bridged by a fallen tree, all of
which could be rearranged to expand the illusion of a wild, rambling landscape.

By May the "Log Set" was on the *Kong* schedule for the Pathé Studio
Stage 11, and the "Jungle Set" by early June on Stage 12.[4]

Dangerous Game channeled tremendous creative energy straight into
Kong. Orville Goldner and George Turner write that with *The Most Dangerous Game*, Cooper and Schoedsack reached an apotheosis in setting a
"thrilling pace" that recalled *Chang* and was to become forever emblematic
of the Cooper-Schoedsack style. Their last outing together had been *The
Four Feathers,* and the duo were determined to avoid the stagebound scenes
and static photography the studio had added to that film. So their initial
talkie celebrated the fluid camerawork and cutting techniques of the best
silent-film storytelling, with the dialogue designed to complement the
action.[5]

Editor Archie Marshek recalled that during the filming, Schoedsack literally timed the actors to the second; a thirty-second scene in rehearsal
might be speeded up to twenty for the final take. It would become the
model for the cutting of *King Kong*.[6]

Reportedly, Cooper sometimes came to the jungle set between takes of
filming *Dangerous Game,* to grab Armstrong and Wray for his test-reel
scenes. Armstrong would shed the suit he wore in General Zaroff's mansion and don a soiled and ripped safari outfit for Skull Island; Wray would
fit a blond wig over her brown hair. There was still no *Kong* script, so

Cooper and James Creelman improvised a chase through the *Dangerous Game* jungle area, where Leslie Banks's Zaroff and his dogs had just tracked Joel McCrea and Fay Wray. While Schoedsack would shoot on one side of the set, Cooper would shoot on the other. "We'd just leap-frog over," Cooper recalled.[7]

RKO PUBLICITY SHOT OF SCHOEDSACK AND COOPER WAS
RELEASED WITH THIS EXCERPTED COPY: "ADVENTURERS PAUSE IN
HOLLYWOOD. . . . COOPER IS THE HEAD OF THE DEPARTMENT FOR
SPECIAL PICTURES AND SCHOEDSACK IS DIRECTING HIS FIRST
STUDIO-MADE PICTURE *THE MOST DANGEROUS GAME*."

Cooper Papers, BYU

The *Kong* test scenes were sometimes perplexing to performers who had to act against nothing, since any action involving Kong and the other stop-motion creations was created separately, in O'Brien's personal production domain. One of the live-action tests was to show the famous scene of Kong shaking Carl Denham's crew off the log that bridges a chasm. When Armstrong was positioned at the far end of the famous log, Cooper asked the actor to "take it big," imagining a monstrous gorilla on the other side of the imaginary chasm. "I've been in this business a great many years," Armstrong replied to Cooper, "but *you* tell *me* how to take a fifty-foot ape *big*!"[8]

Fay Wray performed against a process screen for the scene in which Kong places Ann Darrow in a tree before fighting off the challenge of a ferocious allosaurus. This was the closest the picture came to the original idea of Coop's giant gorilla battling Burden's giant lizard.

(Though many assume that Kong's prehistoric adversary in this battle is a Tyrannosaurus rex, Rudy Behlmer noted in conversation that during his interviews with Merian Cooper, Coop stressed that the creature was an allosaurus.)

The battle scene was itself a vital test of "rear projection," as footage of completed stop-motion animation was projected onto the big screen behind the actress. Wray recalled that filming the scene took a marathon twenty-two hours because of the complexity of synchronizing cameras and lighting with the projected image. They would stop only for brief periods, for food and a little rest for Fay—with two director's chairs pushed together to make a makeshift cot. The filming was surreal for the actress, as she was on the same plane as the big screen behind her. She would be up, sitting in the branch of the prop tree where Kong had ostensibly placed her, the primal battle behind her a blur on the rear-projection screen. "I reacted to the blurs and responded to Cooper's calls of 'Scream, Fay! Scream for your life!' " Wray recalled.[9]

It was during the *Kong* work on the *Dangerous Game* jungle set that Archie Marshek came onto the picture. Marshek would graduate from film editor to production assistant on *King Kong,* along with Walter Daniels. His new responsibilities came to him in spite of the fact that he had stood up to Merian Cooper—or perhaps *because* of it.

Marshek recalled that he had been editing *The Phantom of Crestwood,* a 1932 RKO release being directed by J. Walter Ruben, with Cooper as producer. Without telling the director, Cooper asked Marshek to cut down a particularly wordy scene. While they were watching a rough cut, the director asked what had happened to the dramatically edited scene. Cooper innocently looked at Marshek and put the question to him. When Marshek just as innocently replied that Cooper had asked him to cut it, Cooper got furious and Marshek left, certain his days at the studio were over.

A short while later his phone rang. It was Cooper, calmly asking him to come back and restore the footage.

It was two weeks later that Cooper again sent for Marshek—*this* time the editor was sure he was done for. Cooper was waiting in his office, his pipe in his mouth. He asked if Marshek would be his assistant. "I guess he liked the way I stood up to him, as he would have done," Marshek concluded.[10] Marshek would have the run of *Kong,* supervising the editing work of Ted Chessman, and checking in with Max Steiner on the film's music and the sound-effects work of Murray Spivack, while also serving as a liaison between the production and the Frank Williams lab on Santa Monica Boulevard, where some of the visual-effects composite shots were done.

FOR *KONG,* THE moment of truth came when Cooper flew to New York with concept sketches and the test-reel scenes, which included Kong shaking the sailors off the log and the battle between Kong and the allosaurus.

"The footage met with great enthusiasm at the sales meeting and the project was given the go-ahead," Cooper recalled for Rudy Behlmer.[11] It was also the concept art of Kong holding Ann Darrow atop the Empire State Building, Cooper would recall, that captured the imagination of some wary studio chieftains and sold them on making the picture.

DAVID O. SELZNICK once summed up his personal contribution to *Kong:* "The picture was really made primarily by Cooper and Ernest Schoedsack, under my guidance; and one of the biggest gambles I took at RKO was to squeeze money out of the budgets of other pictures for this venture."[12] Selznick also hired Edgar Wallace, a famous and prolific English writer, and assigned him a number of RKO projects, including Cooper's gorilla picture, reasoning that the writer's name would add luster to the final credits.

Wallace arrived from London on December 5, 1931. In the ensuing week, he was introduced to O'Brien and visited the animator's workshop, where he saw the miniature jungle sets, gorilla models, and some of the full-scale physical "practical" model pieces of Kong, which included a giant mechanical hand, a foot, and Kong's head and upper torso.[13]

Wallace wrote the first screenplay, based on Cooper's treatment, and delivered it to Cooper in early January 1932. That first rough script opens with a monkey holding a rose in its hand, plucking petals while sitting on a packing case on the deck of a tramp steamer. A fifty-year-old man named Danby G. Denham, dressed in an old checkered suit and a peaked sailor's

RKO PRODUCTION HEAD DAVID SELZNICK ADMIRES MERIAN
COOPER'S SELECTION OF *KONG* CONCEPT ART.

Stephan Pickering Archives, BYU

cap, sits in a canvas chair smoking a pipe. The ship's doctor asks Denham what he hopes to find on their voyage. "Something colossal," Denham replies, "something you could show in the Polo ground or Madison Square Garden and pack the place at a dollar a head: Something that's never been seen before."[14]

Wallace's draft lays out the basic sketch of Cooper's idea, beginning with the sea voyage to a mysterious island, in this version called Vapour Island because of its volcanic steam. Enduring elements include Kong spiriting away a woman while a band of men give chase; Kong shaking some of his pursuers off a tree bridge and into a ravine; Kong leaving the woman in the fork of a tree while he battles and kills an approaching dinosaur; Kong retreating with the woman to his cave, where he plucks at her dress, much as the steamer's pet monkey plucked at the petals of a rose; and the hero daring the giant ape's wrath to rescue the woman.

But in many ways, Wallace's script is so different from the final film that it forms a parallel-universe version of *Kong*. In Wallace's draft, Kong's island is visited not only by the tramp steamer but by a band of convicts—perhaps inspired by the penal colony on Komodo Island—and by a lifeboat bearing love interests named John Lanson and Miss Shirley Redman. Shirley Redman is no innocent Ann Darrow, explaining in Wallace's script that she "had too many expectations and not enough money. Then I got the money and no expectations."[15] It's also a fearless and virile Captain Englehorn—not the older, steady sea captain of the final film—who knocks out Kong with gas bombs. When Englehorn approaches with a rifle pointed at Kong's head, ready to finish him off, Denham stays his hand. "He's colossal—he's marvelous. He's worth a million dollars to me." The script fades in to a close shot of a big poster of Madison Square Garden that celebrates the ape: "The most amazing and terrifying being that nature has produced, the super beast, Kong!"

Wallace's script digresses further when Kong is unveiled in New York as a circus attraction. A female lion tamer named Senorita Delvirez is jealous of the attention the press and photographers pay to Miss Redman, who feeds bananas to a caged Kong, much to the delight of the newshounds. So the scheming Delvirez lures her rival into an animal enclosure, where a tiger knocks her down, causing the enraged Kong to break out of his cage. The giant ape runs rampant, looking for Shirley, and, as in the final film, pulls a girl out of a hotel-room window and, when he realizes she's not Shirley, tosses her to her death. Finally, Kong finds the object of his affections and moves from roof to roof with Shirley gripped firmly in his mouth as police searchlights sweep the buildings.

An undated RKO interdepartmental memo from Cooper to Wallace suggested the following for the big end scene: "When ape has girl near end of picture . . . see if you consider it practical to work out theme that John attempts single handed rescue on top of Empire State Building if police will let off shooting for a minute. Then when he fails, air plane attack, or something along this line."[16]

In Wallace's final script, it's night and a lightning storm rolls in as Kong makes it to the Empire State Building. Airplanes arrive with the thunder and lightning, to buzz the giant ape. The girl is below Kong on the pinnacle of the skyscraper as Kong grins "fearfully" and grabs the flagstaff—which becomes a lightning rod. A flash of electricity jolts the creature, and he's mortally wounded. The story ends:

> *EXT. TOP OF BUILDING—NIGHT*
>
> *CLOSE SHOT of Kong with his head against the wall.*
> *Kong opens his eyes, picks the girl up,*
> *holds her to his breast like a doll, closes his eyes,*
> *and drops his head.*
>
> *THE END.*

ON FEBRUARY 19, 1932, not long after delivering the screenplay, Wallace died suddenly of pneumonia.[17]

"The present script of *Kong*, as far as I can remember, hasn't one single idea suggested by Edgar Wallace," Cooper noted in a July 20, 1932, memo to Selznick. "If there are any, they are of the slightest."[18] But Cooper had promised Wallace a cowriting credit, and felt he was honor bound to keep his word. There was also the practical concern that having the famous writer's name on the credits would be good publicity.

Meanwhile, RKO memos to Cooper began suggesting alternatives to the working title of *The Beast*. A title championed by Selznick in a January 22 memo was *Jungle Beast*. But Cooper felt any reference to "jungle" would suggest "an animal travel picture instead of a mystery, adventure, novelty." He favored a "mystery word" that'd be "the name of the leading mysterious, romantic, savage creature of the story" in the manner of *Frankenstein* or *Dracula*.[19]

An RKO memo to Cooper a month later proposed combining *Jungle Beast* and *Kong*:

> KONG, KING OF BEASTS
> KONG, THE JUNGLE KING
> KONG, THE JUNGLE BEAST[20]

On February 24, 1933, RKO finally registered the copyright name *King Kong*.[21]

IN 1932, WITH the *Kong* script still in need of work, Cooper brought in James Creelman, who was also scripting scenes for *The Most Dangerous Game*. By March, Cooper had requested script changes in anticipation of sending the final version of the script to the New York office, including a rewrite reflecting Denham's darker side.

"Please re-write scene in *Kong*, after fight between Kong and meat-eater. Have Driscoll and Denham enter after Kong has exited with girl, and have them see dying meat-eater on ground. Denham has the idea that if Kong could do that, he is off—and goes back. Driscoll goes on." Cooper also noted that he and Kenneth MacGowan, a production supervisor, both agreed that there "should be a closer relationship" between the end of the Skull Island jungle scenes and the beginning of the New York sequence.

"I, too, have always felt we should have some kind of lines in there which show that the ape and the girl are going to be exhibited as 'beauty and the beast,' " Cooper added. "Think we ought to have Denham make some such remark."[22] Other plot points and scenarios changed. Cooper mused about having Kong exhibited in a zoo, but Schoedsack convinced him it was more practical to have Denham exhibit Kong on a theatrical stage. Thus, the venue where Kong breaks his chains would be a Manhattan theater as staged in the Shrine Auditorium in downtown Los Angeles.[23]

A HUGE CREATIVE breakthrough for Cooper came during a fateful stroll through RKO's facility in Culver City and its famed forty-acre back lot. There he saw a native village set that had been built for *Bird of Paradise* and was reportedly present when the inestimable showman and choreographer Busby Berkeley was staging an exotic native dance sequence. It was night, and something of the atavistic energy of the illusion tugged at Cooper's imagination; it may have reminded him of the savage displays of warrior tribes he had seen firsthand, and of the spirit-possessed African gorilla he'd read about as a boy.

A bold idea dawned. King Kong would be a supernatural figure to the natives, the center of a primitive religion full of mysterious ceremonies and rituals designed to appease the primordial terrors that lurked beyond the ancient walls of Skull Island village.[24]

Cooper saw other fresh possibilities during his wanderings around the "Forty Acres," as the back lot was known. He found the old Temple of Jerusalem set from Cecil B. DeMille's 1927 biblical epic, *The King of Kings;* its crumbling columns and walls would become the centerpiece of Cooper's village wall, its massive gate standing between the superstitious natives and Kong's primordial jungle. And what better way to appease the natives' savage god than with a human sacrifice? In Wallace's initial script the giant gorilla simply snatches up Shirley Redman during a mindless rampage against the island interlopers; in the final production, the golden-haired and fair-skinned Ann Darrow would be kidnapped from the *Venture* by the natives and offered up to their god in a ritual sacrifice.

But Creelman found himself having a devil of a time handling the feast of fantastical situations Cooper demanded. "An expedition invading a village filled with hostile natives who sacrifice women is in itself a large premise," he wrote in a three-page letter to Coop. ". . . I can't seem to build to this and also to the prehistoric monsters at the same time." Creelman called the village an "intrusion" and the "human sacrifice angle" another huge complication.[25]

He did, however, produce what Cooper considered the first real script based on his treatment, but there were still problems, particularly with the dialogue.[26]

Cooper had the pick of in-house writers to complete the screenplay but made a surprise selection: Ruth Rose, who'd only dabbled in writing and had never written a screenplay. Nevertheless, Cooper hoped Ruth could make Carl Denham's movie expedition ring true. After all, she knew first-hand what it was like to voyage to mysterious islands, she understood the nature of explorers drawn to the unknown, and she had experienced the dangers of wilderness. She also knew the two partners who were bringing to life the ultimate fantasy movie expedition.

"Put *us* in it," Cooper told her. "Give it the almost Victorian kind of dialogue that it needs to make the fantasy stand up. Establish everything before Kong makes his appearance so that we won't have to explain anything after that. Give it the spirit of a real Cooper-Schoedsack expedition."[27]

Ruth was a natural, and she captured the spirited pace of a Cooper-Schoedsack adventure. Some would even consider Ann Darrow an extension of Ruth Rose herself.[28] Cooper would always hail the sparkling new lines as Ruth's major contribution, estimating that 90 percent of the final dialogue was hers.[29] The finished script, with the byline of James A. Creelman and Ruth Rose, would have the beauty-and-the-beast textures, and Denham would be the man of action. *Venture* captain Englehorn would be less the heroic young figure of the Wallace draft, and more the wise old navigator of the seas. Kong would be captured and delivered as entertainment for the masses, and the most audacious stunt in the history of show business would end in the tragic rampage, followed by Kong's final act of defiance atop the Empire State Building.[30]

Because of the scale and logistics inherent in the *King Kong* production, Cooper and Schoedsack each directed their own units and divided the scenes between them. Years later, in a letter to an inquiring fan, Cooper recalled that Schoedsack had shot all the boat sequences for the *Venture* voyage, including the famous scene where Denham has Ann scream at the unseen monster. He also helmed much of the action in the native village and the New York theater sequence where Kong breaks his chains.

Cooper personally focused on the jungle scenes and Denham's pursuit of Kong, nearly all of Kong's rampage in New York, and "the Empire State finish." Cooper also made it clear who was in control: "In this particular picture I was the Creator and Boss."[31]

THROUGHOUT, FAY WRAY endured being the object of Kong's affections. Whether acting against a process screen or flailing in the grip of the gigantic mechanical hand, she spent long, exhausting hours made all the more demanding by having to scream on cue at the various terrors her character was experiencing. Wray recalled one particular day when she spent eight hours "screaming up and down the scale with a wide variety of inflections and the studio chose the one that produced the most ice up and down the spine; I couldn't speak even in a whisper for days."[32]

BY AUGUST OF 1932, Cooper was able to report on the status of the production to RKO President B. B. Kahane. His two-page letter opened with the projected budget: $517,000, some $115,000 more than anticipated. Cooper assured Kahane that he was "fighting costs on this picture" and that Schoedsack, Walter Daniels, and several other production personnel had labored hard during the previous weeks, cutting out any extraneous trick shots and reducing the number of bit players.

Cooper then slipped in the news about the *Bird of Paradise* brainstorm, which had led to creation of the Skull Island village set, the sacrificial ceremony, and Kong's rampage. It was a recent addition to the story line and, Cooper added, was being economically integrated thanks to their judicious use of the old *King of Kings* set, which in its day had reportedly cost over $100,000 and which they had remodeled for their own purposes for a mere $14,000. The village set recalled a bygone production, he explained, which itself served the story line of the mysterious walls and gate being "the great ruins of an old civilization upon which the village is built," adding that in his and Schoedsack's opinion, the village would "give a really great introduction to the character of *King Kong,* and make the great ape important. The destruction of the village by him will be at least comparable, if not better, than the destruction of the village by elephants in *Chang.* It is the sequence by which Schoedsack and I hope to make this a really big picture."[33]

The production's success depended on the visual-effects work, Cooper stressed to Kahane. It had been impossible to make an accurate budget estimation until the revolutionary trick shots—including animation, development of traveling-matte composite techniques, and process screenwork—had been established through experimentation.

"As you know," Cooper added, "it is only because *King Kong* has this unusual and entirely new series of trick processes that it is possible to make such an unusual picture."

King Kong, put into production only a few years after the film industry had been transformed by sound, would be a giant leap in the art of illusion. But at the time it remained a huge unknown, and Cooper took great pains to reassure Kahane that the risky stop-motion process would pay off.

"My opinion of the picture is unchanged from the first day I was asked to work on it. Animation will always remain animation because the action will never be perfectly smooth. Nevertheless, I think we have introduced such startling trick shots, and unusual value in *King Kong* that everybody will want to see it."[34]

CHAPTER EIGHTEEN

THE HOMUNCULUS

> I've always felt that RKO at the time of Kong was like a labora-
> tory from the days of the old alchemists who wanted to create the
> perfect homunculus. Kong was the perfect homunculus, this figure
> that was injected with life through the stop-motion process.
>
> —Ray Harryhausen[1]

EVEN WHILE THE PRINCIPAL PRODUCTION FOR *KING KONG* PLAYED OUT ON THE
soundstages and at Forty Acres, Willis O'Brien and his crew were busy producing the animation work on a closed stage. It was grueling work under
tremendous pressures, and O'Brien's personal life didn't provide a refuge
from the intense professional demands. O'Brien had two sons he loved
deeply, but his marriage had failed. Marcel Delgado, who met Hazel
O'Brien just after *The Lost World*, would recall that she seemed "under high,
nervous tension."[2] Indeed, it was around the time of *The Lost World* that
Hazel made the first of several suicide attempts. Although O'Brien didn't
actually obtain a divorce, he finally and forever separated from his troubled
wife in early 1930. Although he'd constantly dote on their two boys,
William and Willis, Hazel had formal custody of the children.

A few years after their separation, horrifying tragedy struck. Hazel was
suffering from tuberculosis and cancer, and William, their oldest, became
permanently blinded from tuberculosis in both eyes.[3]

Despite his troubles at home, O'Brien and his *Kong* team continued
forging breakthroughs in the art of motion-picture illusion, advancements
that would forever change the movies. They used every trick in the book
and invented some new ones to breathe life into their "homunculus": state-
of-the-art stop-motion figures, elaborate tabletop miniature sets that uti-

BILL CLOTHIER (CENTER), ASSISTANT CAMERAMAN FOR *KING KONG* ON THE SKULL
ISLAND SET. FILMMAKER CRAIG BARRON RECALLS, "CLOTHIER TOLD ME ABOUT A
FIGHT HE HAD WITH COOPER DURING THE FILMING OF *THE LOST SQUADRON*."
UNION STRIKES WERE CLOSING DOWN PRODUCTIONS IN HOLLYWOOD, BUT COOPER
WAS QUIETLY BRINGING IN CREWS ON LOCATION. THE UNION KNEW CLOTHIER WAS
A PILOT, AND HAD HIM BUZZING THE *LOST SQUADRON* SET, DIVING OVER FRIGHT-
ENED FILM CREWS. ON ONE SUCH OCCASION ANOTHER PLANE FLEW OUT OF THE
SUN, AND ITS PILOT GESTURED FOR CLOTHIER TO LAND AT THE OLD VAN NUYS AIR-
PORT. BARRON NOTES, "IT WAS ONLY WHEN HE WAS FORCED DOWN ONTO THE
RUNWAY AND WAS EXCHANGING PUNCHES WITH THE PILOT THAT CLOTHIER REAL-
IZED IT WAS MERIAN COOPER!" EVENTUALLY THEY TIRED, AND COOPER SAID, "BILL,
WHAT THE HELL ARE WE DOING FIGHTING? WE'RE CUT FROM THE SAME CLOTH."

COOPER ACTUALLY HIRED CLOTHIER TO APPEAR IN *THE LOST SQUADRON*,
PLAYING A CAMERAMAN WORKING FOR THE ERICH VON STROHEIM CHARACTER.
"IN THE SCENE, VON STROHEIM WHACKS CLOTHIER IN THE BACK WITH HIS RIDING
CROP—HARD. BILL ALWAYS FELT THAT WAS COOP'S LITTLE PAYBACK FOR TAKING
UP THAT PLANE AND TRYING TO RUIN HIS SHOTS."

Craig Barron collection

lized multiplane glass matte paintings, miniature and full-scale rear-screen projection, the Dunning traveling-matte process and other compositing techniques, and fusion techniques integrating live actors with full-scale mechanical effects.

The test-reel prototype Kong armature went through a major redesign to become another Marcel Delgado masterpiece. The armature was based on the exact male gorilla proportions Harry Raven had sent Cooper, scaled up to the character's imagined height of fifty feet.

Cooper himself estimated that as many as six eighteen-inch-tall Kong stop-motion figures were created in addition to the prehistoric denizens of Skull Island, which included a stegosaurus, a brontosaurus, and a winged pteranodon. (Marcel Delgado would estimate that only two Kong armatures were crafted.) They also created a number of six-inch-tall, articulated human puppets, scaled to the dinosaurs.[4] Delgado, with the assistance of his brother Victor and other craftsmen, built the full-scale models of Kong's head and shoulders, his paw and a foot, and the talons of the pteranodon, which nearly snatches Fay Wray away from Kong's cave at the summit of Skull Island. The massive, full-scale bust of Kong took forty bearskins for the fur and needed a team of six men to operate its mechanical controls.[5]

Cooper constantly reflected back on *Chang* as an ideal of natural drama and the model they would invoke for everything from story structure to pace. *Chang* had made Cooper and Schoedsack intimately aware of the physical nature of jungle and its almost supernatural ambience. Cooper needed the miniature Skull Island set to reflect a jungle's "quality of receding mystery . . . the semi-darkness, the shadows, and the sense of hidden dangers." He also wanted reality enhanced with a fantastic "dawn-of-creation feeling," an aesthetic inspired by the work of Gustave Doré, in particular his illustrations for Milton's *Paradise Lost*.[6]

The ambitious multiplane setup for the miniature jungle sets—what Cooper called "aerial perspective"—provided the illusion of perspective, depth, and atmospheric haze. To accomplish this, vertical sheets of glass were painted with dramatic jungle details by Mario Larrinaga and Byron Crabbe, then placed one in front of another, at specific distances, to give the illusion of foliage receding into the distance.[7]

Additional breakthroughs for *Kong* were made possible through the work of such in-house units as the camera-effects department, which was headed by Vernon Walker and was responsible for the opticals master-minded by Linwood Dunn. His arsenal featured a machine-age device known as an optical printer, which allowed separately filmed elements to be rephotographed and combined on a fresh strip of celluloid. Dunn, with his assistant Cecil Love and engineer Bill Leeds, built a printer that made RKO opticals state of the art. The rephotographing process was also aided by new fine-grain film stocks, which didn't degrade as badly as earlier film had done.[8]

The production's inventive use of rear-screen technology would become the industry standard. Tiny rear-projection screens concealed in the miniature sets allowed previously shot footage of actors to be integrated during the actual animation and stop-motion photography. O'Brien had already experimented with rear-projection screens on *Creation,* but by 1930, advances in motors allowed the filming camera to be synchronized with the projection shutters. And, just in time for *King Kong,* RKO's own Sidney Saunders, the paint department supervisor, came up with a new cellulose-acetate rear-projection screen, which was first successfully used in *Kong* test shots.[9]

Archie Marshek, who saw the resulting footage from O'Brien's unit as it came into Ted Chessman's editing room, knew how slow stop-motion was to produce; at twenty-four frames a second, which had become the new industry standard with the advent of sound, even a few seconds of animation was a huge task. To help Cooper, Schoedsack, O'Brien, and others review the daily footage, Marshek made loops of the short films so they could run continuously, without forcing the projectionist to keep rethreading.[10]

One masterful sequence from O'Brien's unit was cut despite the fact that it worked brilliantly. It happened after Kong shook the *Venture* men off the log. At the bottom of the chasm, the seamen were set upon and devoured by giant spiders and lizards. It was *too* effective, and made it hard for horrified preview audiences to continue with the story.

"It . . . just stopped the picture cold," Cooper said with a shrug. "It broke every rule that Monty and I knew about picture making. . . . Our whole thesis, which we did on *Chang . . .* is to start a picture slow and get everybody to know the characters and to get the feel of what we're going to tell. And once you start moving, never let it stop, just drive it on."[11] The proven formula of *Chang* would be cited by Cooper when nervous studio executives kept insisting that the picture open with Kong. Cooper wanted a slow, dramatic buildup that would establish everything, from characters to mood, and he assured them that the action would naturally, relentlessly, roll on out of its own creative momentum.

Cooper never backed down on that point, and he won the creative battle.

Marshek recalled that as "Cooper's brainchild" evolved, he and film editor Ted Chessman edited and recut as they went along, until the time came when they were pulling 238,000 feet of footage into a final cut. Marshek finally produced a cut that filled thirteen reels—which horrified Cooper. "No picture of mine is going out in thirteen reels!" he bellowed, and ordered a new sequence to bring it up to fourteen reels. The new sequence would be Kong's destruction of the elevated train, which required construction of an elaborate scale set and weeks of animation.[12]

Years later, Cooper's wife explained to Marshek that her husband had a phobia relating to the number 13. Coop had been shot down in World War I on the twenty-sixth day of the month—the deadly "double 13"—and during the Russo-Polish War, he was shot down and captured on the thirteenth day of July, 1920.[13]

Murray Spivack, RKO's resident sound-effects genius, would remember that while working on the soundtrack for Kong's attack on the elevated train—"a confusion of sounds" to begin with—Cooper noticed a car in the shot and wanted to hear its horn honking. This was a tall order in those days, when there were only three tracks total for dialogue, effects, and music.

"I told him it would lower the quality of the recording," Spivack recalled. "He got mad. I said, 'Be sensible, Merian; you couldn't hear a car horn in all that noise if we did it.' He insisted he wanted it. Pretty soon we were shouting at each other, and right in the worst part of it I started to laugh. He looked surprised and asked, 'What are you laughing at?' I told him, 'Do you know that when you get mad your forehead turns a bright red?' He started laughing then and finally he said, 'Okay, have it your way,' and left."[14]

IN 1965, WHILE working with Bantam Books on a new edition of the original *King Kong* novelization, Cooper revealed to his editor that when he'd showed studio executives his test reel and original-concept art illustrations "it was the 'Empire State' sketch that finally sold the RKO 'hold-outs' on the idea of *making* the picture. . . . The 'Empire State' scene actually contains the central theme of the story: Civilization (the planes) overcomes the Beast (King Kong) made vulnerable by his fatal fascination for Beauty (Fay Wray). This scene also climaxes the element of Pathos I introduced into the story . . . that has, in my opinion, possibly contributed more to the success of *King Kong*, over the years, than any other single element. It was in fact, the first complete scene I visualized during the creative birth of *Kong* back in 1929."[15]

ORIGINAL RKO PUBLICITY PHOTO COPY READS: "THIS IS ONE OF THE GRIPPING SCENES TO BE VIEWED IN THE FORTHCOMING RADIO PICTURE, *KING KONG*. THE HEROINE, PLAYED BY FAY WRAY, IS BEING RESCUED FROM A DIZZY LEDGE OF THE TOWERING EMPIRE STATE BUILDING IN NEW YORK CITY, WHERE SHE HAS BEEN PLACED BY HER CAPTOR, A GIANT FORTY-FOOT APE. POLICE BULLETS ARE POWERLESS AGAINST THE BEAST AND THE PURSUIT PLANES ARE COMING TO ATTACK THE HUGE KILLER." *Cooper Papers, BYU*

Kong's defiance atop the Empire State Building is one of the most memorable images in movie history—but it almost didn't happen. The plug was nearly pulled on the New York sequence in February 1932 because of copyright concerns that *Kong* might be too similar in story construction to *The Lost World,* in which a dinosaur is brought to civilization from a timeless land.

Cooper agreed that it was "a tangled mess" and recommended that they "give up the New York sequence, and end the story on the island. This will apparently obviate all legal difficulties. We will not have as good a picture, but we will have a good picture, I believe."[16] Thankfully, RKO headed off potential lawsuits by buying the rights to *The Lost World* from both Warner Bros., which had absorbed First National in the late 1920s, and the estate of the late author Sir Arthur Conan Doyle. The latter agreement even exempted RKO from having to list *The Lost World* in the *Kong* credits. By March 12, with the legal issue being addressed, Cooper's rewrite notes to Creelman again emphasized the New York sequence.[17]

Cooper always claimed he had never seen *The Lost World* or been influenced by it before making *Kong.* Regardless, it's inconceivable to imagine *King Kong* without its mythic parallels between Skull Island and Manhattan Island. The cityscape used to such iconic effect had been made possible by a 1916 New York zoning law stipulating that city towers be stepped back, an approach that would be adapted by other cities, which resulted in mountainlike buildings with wide bases and soaring towers.[18] Kong's final destination changed with the skyscrapers that soared ever upward: Cooper had originally contemplated the New York Life Insurance Building, then the 1,077-foot Chrysler Building, which became the tallest building in the world in late 1929.[19]

But it was as if the Empire State Building and Kong were meant for each other. Cooper was writing his *Kong* treatments and developing his story in tall-tale talks with Burden even as the skyscraper began rising. The construction started in February 1930 on Thirty-fourth Street as workmen began blasting through fifty-five feet of solid rock to lay the skyscraper's foundation. By August, an estimated 3,439 men were working and welding into place fifty thousand steel beams and columns, each weighing more than a ton. Those workers weren't representative of the "soft" civilization Merian Cooper had once excoriated in comparison to the hardy nomads of *Grass.* The construction crews were straight out of American folklore, tough modern icons fearlessly hanging from beams and striding plank walkways at death-defying heights, hammering into place red-hot rivets, cutting through tons of steel, and pausing to use acetylene torches to light their cigarettes—all of these men climbing into the sky along with the tower as it soared a quarter mile into the heavens.[20]

The Empire State Building opened on May 1, 1931; the world's tallest building had been completed in less than a year.[21] Years later, Fay Wray would muse that Cooper had to have witnessed the completion of the Empire State Building because it was in New York that he'd imagined his gigantic gorilla. "Big! Big! He always thought big," Wray wrote.[22]

When Cooper and Schoedsack began crafting the scene of the fighter planes shooting down the defiant Kong, Cooper made a dramatic suggestion.

"We should kill the sonofabitch ourselves."

Thus the old aerial warrior took up his accustomed pilot's position, and Shorty took the observer's rear cockpit in a mock-up aircraft erected on a studio stage. It's the two partners audiences see firing away in the final film, the creators destroying their creation.[23]

CHAPTER NINETEEN

KONG, KONG, KONG!

> *Why, the whole world will pay to see this. . . . He's always been*
> *king of his world but we'll teach him fear. We're millionaires, boys,*
> *I'll share it with all of you! Why, in a few months it'll be up in*
> *lights on Broadway: "KONG: The Eighth Wonder of the World!"*
>
> —Carl Denham, on the beach of Skull Island
> before setting sail for New York

WITHIN RKO THE BUZZ AND BALLYHOO OVER *KING KONG* WAS FANTASTIC. IN the mercurial world of movies, it seemed that rarest of imminent releases: the sure thing. "We knew we had a hit even before it was previewed," Marshek recalled. ". . . Before the year was over we had a sequel ready for release, *The Son of Kong.*"[1]

The *Radio Flash*, the in-house sales and publicity newsletter, trumpeted the impending release as "The Greatest Sensation of the Age! . . . Breath-Taking! Staggering! Powerful!"

"Because *King Kong* is the most spectacular piece of film merchandising we, or anybody else has ever handled, everything about it must be SPECTACU-LAR to measure up to it," read the breathless *Flash* copy regarding the poster and "accessory sales" campaign. ". . . And those of us who don't measure up to the tremendous proportions of the show in putting it over, may consider themselves spectacular flops!"[2]

Despite the prospect of good times ahead, there was a changing of the guard taking place at the studio. As the new year came rolling in, production head David O. Selznick was on the way out, heading to MGM as a vice president and producer. "I stayed at RKO until my contract expired in early 1933," Selznick recalled. "My new contract . . . was about to be signed when

'Deac' [Merlin Hall] Aylesworth became head of the company, succeeding Hiram Brown. Aylesworth insisted upon the new but still unsigned contract being changed to the extent of giving him approval of everything connected with production. I refused to accept this."[3]

The question of who would replace Selznick as RKO production head became obvious: In the reflected glory of *King Kong,* the one star who shone brightest was the dreamer himself, Merian C. Cooper. A month before *King Kong* was released, an item in Hollywood gossip columnist Louella O. Parsons's syndicated column, dateline Los Angeles, February 5, announced: "B. B. Kahane, who has been counting the pennies and passing on all expenses, has appointed Merian Cooper to take the place left vacant by the Selznick resignation. . . . He has just completed *King Kong* which Radio admits is good. Cooper, who will act in conjunction with Kahane, will be in complete charge of all Radio productions with the exception of the independent units functioning at Pathe Studios."[4]

On February 14, 1933, Kahane officially announced Cooper as the studio's new head of production. Cooper in turn picked Pandro Berman as his executive assistant.[5] Meanwhile, Cooper had put Schoedsack back on the road to adventure, sending him to Arabia to shoot second-unit footage for "a kind of Lawrence of Arabia" production, as he later recalled for Rudy Behlmer.[6]

Selznick, who would be credited as executive producer on *Kong,* was in attendance at the preview in San Bernardino. Cooper later recalled for Kevin Brownlow that Selznick met him after the screening and suggested that Cooper cut the opening and go straight to Kong, and also cut the scene on the boat where Denham implores Darrow to scream for her life.

"To hell with you, David," Cooper recalled saying. "You go make those fancy pictures of yours at Metro [MGM], this is going to run!" It was a harsh and uncharacteristic statement, given the gratitude Cooper always expressed for Selznick's unflagging support of his dream picture, as well as Selznick's presumed knowledge of the creative battles Cooper had already fought. But the spirit of the retort probably illustrates Coop's cocky confidence in his moment of triumph—for a self-taught filmmaker, *Kong* was supreme vindication.

"We blueprinted the whole damn thing," Cooper added of his and Schoedsack's work, reiterating that the "three D's"—"distant, difficult, and dangerous"—had to be emphasized if Kong was to be believable.[7] In addi-

SCHOEDSACK SHAVES IN FRONT OF HIS TENT WITH A NOMAD,
IDENTIFIED AS ONE OF SHEIK FUAZ'S SLAVES, WHO HAS BEEN
ASSIGNED TO BE ONE OF THE ASSISTANT CAMERAMEN DURING
SHORTY'S SECOND-UNIT WORK IN ARABIA. *Don Shay collection*

SCHOEDSACK AND BILL REINHOLDT, HIS ASSISTANT CAMERAMAN, OUT IN THE
FIELD, ASSISTED BY MORE SLAVES OF SHEIK FUAZ, A BEDOUIN CHIEFTAIN WHO
AGREED TO HELP SCHOEDSACK (FOR A PRICE). "ABRAHAM LINCOLN'S
EMANCIPATION PROCLAMATION MEANT NOTHING TO ARABIA," SCHOEDSACK
WAS QUOTED IN RADIO PICTURES' PUBLICITY. *Don Shay collection*

tion, every successful picture had to have a "single strong thought," Cooper later wrote, and the key to *Kong* was the beauty-and-the-beast theme, which ranged from the opening prologue to the last scene, where the policeman and Denham gaze upon the fallen body of Kong.

"Well, Denham, the airplanes got him," the policeman mutters. Denham replies, "No. It wasn't the airplanes. Beauty killed the Beast."[8]

Cooper was presiding as production head when the promotional campaign for *King Kong* was unleashed, beginning with a tease of newspaper ads showing Kong's stomping feet and radio ads crackling with gorilla roars and a woman's screams. RKO historian Betty Lasky, daughter of Jesse Lasky, wrote of the emotional buttons being pushed in New York radio and newspaper advertising as the premiere neared: "The sound effects grew noisier and the ads grew more explicit, until March 1, when RKO made the monster's dread intentions known. 'King Kong, of a former world, comes to destroy our world—all but the soft, white female thing he holds like a fluttering bird!' At last New York was treated to the sight of the snarling ape balanced on top of the Empire State Building, tearing an airplane out of the sky with one giant paw and clutching a flimsily clad Fay Wray in the other."[9]

King Kong arrived with the new American president, Franklin Delano Roosevelt. During the weekend of his inaugural, FDR kicked off the whirlwind "Hundred Days" of legislative action against the Depression by declaring a four-day bank holiday, beginning on March 7. This came on the heels of the suspension of banking in thirty-three states on March 2, the date *King Kong* had its world premiere with simultaneous openings in New York at Radio City Music Hall and the new, nearby RKO Roxy Theatre. Despite the bank closure, by the week's end an estimated 180,000 moviegoers had flocked to the theaters and paid more than $100,000 to see Kong rampage through a mythic version of Manhattan.

King Kong invaded Hollywood a couple weeks after the New York premiere, taking up residence at Sid Grauman's famed Chinese Theatre, on Hollywood Boulevard. Cooper himself was on hand at a special premiere on March 16 with a young lady on his arm, his fiancée, the beautiful actress Dorothy Jordan. Cooper would later ruefully recall, "She liked me better than she liked my picture."[10]

Coincidentally, the film that had premiered when the Chinese first opened was *The King of Kings,* the production whose old set provided the

Skull Island village wall of *Kong*. During that initial run at Grauman's Chinese, a young boy named Ray Harryhausen fell under the spell of *Kong*. "I'd seen gorilla pictures before, with gorillas carrying native women off into the jungle screaming," Harryhausen recalled, smiling. "But *King Kong* struck a note in me that has lasted for years—I haven't been the same since I came out of that cinema. It changed my life."[11]

For the wide-eyed Harryhausen, the exotic movie palace was the most wonderful place to experience the first run of *Kong*, with its forecourt featuring frozen-in-time hand- and footprints of movie stars, a tradition since 1927. The entrance to the theater foyer was guarded by two traditional stone lions warding off evil spirits. "My aunt worked for Sid Grauman's mother, who was an invalid, and Sid had given her free tickets to see this strange film called *King Kong*," Harryhausen recalled. "That's how my mother and I got tickets one Saturday afternoon. And Sid Grauman was a great showman. In the foyer he had the big, life-size bust of Kong that'd been used in the film. It worked by compressed air and the mouth worked and the eyes opened and closed—it was wonderful. And bushes were arranged around it with a little pool, so it looked like he was peeking over the bushes. Oh, it was just staggering the showmanship that went on.

"And when we went into the cinema, they had a half-hour prologue show with live performers on stage dressed in native costume and flying trapezes over the audience. Then, the picture opened with Max Steiner's Wagnerian-type score, which was very unusual at the time, and you saw: 'KONG: The Eighth Wonder of the World.' It was just overwhelming. Half the charm of it was I didn't know how it was done. It was obvious it wasn't a man in a gorilla suit, but I didn't know a thing about stop-motion. But it wasn't just the technical expertise, it was the structure of the story. For the first half hour it took you by the hand from the mundane world and into the most outrageous fantasy that's ever been put on the screen."[12]

KING KONG TOOK in nearly $2 million in its initial theatrical run. Its legion of admirers included such famous (or infamous) fans as Adolf Hitler, who had a print in his private cinema and considered it one of his favorite films.[13] One who was disappointed was Cooper's friend and fellow explorer Lowell Thomas. The man whose book had helped immortalize Lawrence of Arabia had been inspired by *Grass,* and he lamented that Cooper and

Schoedsack became "lost to the factual film. . . . Cooper and Schoedsack gradually went Hollywood." Thomas saw the erosion of veracity coming full circle, from the complete authenticity of *Grass* to the 100 percent Hollywood of *Kong*.[14]

But Cooper and Schoedsack had been on a narrative path from the start, with the spirit of their early natural dramas transmuted into mythic proportions for *King Kong*. Indeed, there was a strange truth to the fantastical movie expedition of *Kong*. Archie Marshek noted that during the production, they could see something of Obie's personality coming through in *Kong*. And, of course, Carl Denham was clearly modeled after Cooper and Schoedsack—it was practically autobiographical. "Audiences sense the underlying reality behind the deliberately outrageous story so that any but the most cynical viewer will forget any tendency to scoff," Marshek wrote.[15]

THE PHOTOGRAPH OF WILLIS O'BRIEN SNAPPED AFTER THE TRAGIC MURDER OF HIS TWO SONS.

Don Shay collection

DESPITE THE SUCCESS of *King Kong*, there was a horrible tragedy awaiting the alchemist who brought the homunculus to life. During the first week of October 1933, Obie brought his two sons to the studio where *The Son of Kong* was being readied for release. It was a thrill even for his fourteen-year-old William, who, though blind, enjoyed handling the stop-motion puppets.

On October 6, around midnight, Hazel O'Brien's neighbors heard gun-shots coming from her home. The police arrived to find Hazel lying on her porch, still alive but bleeding from a bullet hole in her chest, a .38-caliber revolver and five spent cartridges by her side. Inside the house the police discovered William dead from two shots to the chest. Young Willis was alive but had two chest wounds; he died on the way to the hospital. Hazel O'Brien had murdered the two boys. She was rushed to Santa Monica Hospital and informed that she would survive her self-inflicted wound. "I just couldn't sleep, and there was no one to leave the kids with," she repeated in anguish.[16]

There's a photograph of Willis O'Brien taken shortly after the tragedy. He is wearing a hat and holding a miniature human figure in front of a stop-motion triceratops. His face is turned and looking at the camera, al-most as if the photographer has surprised him. The surviving print shows the lines where the photograph had been ripped in two by O'Brien, "who despaired at the anguish reflected in his features," publisher and O'Brien biographer Don Shay wrote.[17]

THE PICTUREMAKER

RADIO PICTURES
PRESENTS
H. RIDER HAGGARD'S
SHE
A MERIAN C. COOPER PRODUCTION

CHAPTER TWENTY

THE EXECUTIVE

David Selznick's heir apparent stood ten feet tall in the estimation of the RKO directorate. . . . The crisis-ridden company needed a man in Hollywood who could work miracles, and the New York office was in complete agreement that Merian Coldwell Cooper was that man.

—Betty Lasky[1]

KING KONG WAS A DREAM COOPER BROUGHT BACK FROM THE WILDERNESS, A dream that took root in the concrete-and-steel hothouse of civilization and was then transplanted into a dream factory. The dream grew into a mythic creature, wonderful to behold, and lifted up its creator and enthroned him as the master of dreams.

But it wasn't just the epic potential and success of *Kong* that attracted RKO executives in New York to "the short, burly, personable executive with a sparkle in his eye and a well-chewed pipe clamped between his lips," as Betty Lasky wrote. "Cooper moved with ease in the world of the rich—*their* world—appearing as much at home in El Morocco or the St. Regis, chumming with young John Hay 'Jock' Whitney and his cousin, C.V. 'Sonny,' as he was in the jungles of Siam with his lanky partner, cameraman 'Monty' Schoedsack."[2]

King Kong was testament to the visionary showman who kept the circus act of movie production under control, a man with leadership qualities that attracted other powerful men. Juan Trippe and Sonny Whitney, the masters of Pan Am, had turned to Cooper even while he was in the midst of *Kong* production, asking him to be their emissary to the powerful Chandler family of Los Angeles, owners of the *Los Angeles Times*. "We want to

COOPER PLAYS WITH BUCK,
HIS ST. BERNARD, ON THE RKO
LOT AS MAX STEINER LOOKS ON.
Cooper Papers, BYU

bring some 'Pacific Coast' influence into the Pan American picture," Juan Trippe wrote Cooper. It was a plan linked to Pan Am's foothold in Alaska, which Trippe noted was vital to the nation's defense, and to opening markets in Asia, which, in turn, would politically strengthen the airline in Washington.

Trippe gave Cooper full authority in the matter, including offering Harry Chandler a generous "financial participation" in the company for his support.[3] It was during the summer of 1932 that Cooper, finding the senior Chandler in ill health, made his overtures to his son Norman Chandler—the "Crown Prince," as Cooper called him—and got the heir to the Chandler fortunes interested in the expansion of commercial aviation.[4]

Cooper had become accustomed to traveling in circles where a simple conversation might start a company, earn the promise of a fortune in investment capital, or plant or pollinate the seed of a brave new idea. Such would be Cooper's style as he became a movie mogul, and his behind-the-scenes maneuvers would have a lasting impact on the movies, from star making to being a force behind such classic films as *Stagecoach,* and helping push the entire industry toward color.

Cooper was at the helm at RKO when the survival of the film industry was at stake. During the nation's bank-holiday crisis, the Roosevelt Hotel in Hollywood was the setting for meetings between studio heads that included Cooper, Louis B. Mayer from MGM, producer B. P. Schulberg, and Harry Cohn from Columbia Pictures. The meetings often became heated, particularly over such proposals as an across-the-board 50 percent pay cut. Cooper took a strong stance against cutting the salary of anyone making less than $50 a week, a position that was backed by Harry Cohn.[5]

As if to underscore the volatile atmosphere, a devastating earthquake, centered in Long Beach, killed an estimated 120 people and caused $50 million in property damage. The shock waves rumbled northward and shook up the movie moguls during their last scheduled meeting on Friday, March 10. "We all had the scare of our lives with the earthquake," Cooper wrote his parents. "I was in a meeting with the heads of the other studios, on the fourth floor of a very rickety building, when the first shock came. A safe came sliding clear across the room, and it didn't take any of us very long to get downstairs. There was no actual damage in Hollywood, but everyone is sitting on needles and pins every time the building shakes from a passing truck. The theaters have been practically empty ever since Friday night. All danger is past now, and people are beginning to lose their fright."[6]

The tremor that rocked Hollywood, from executive suites to studio soundstages, seemed to have a cathartic effect. The following Monday, the day FDR announced that the nation's banks would begin phasing back into operation, there was a one-day walkout by studio workers, but by evening a compromise had been reached: For eight weeks all employees would have a 50 percent wage cut *except* those making under $50 a week. Cooper had gone to bat for workers on the low end of the pay scale and won.[7] "When the banks closed, we weren't able to get any of the company's money from New York, and were afraid we would have to close the studio," Cooper summed up in his letter home. "However, everything is pretty well straightened out now, and looks rather hopeful, in spite of the fact that I have had to take a fifty percent salary cut."[8]

Film historian Rudy Behlmer has characterized as myth the belief that *King Kong* saved RKO from bankruptcy, since the studio had fallen into equity receivership prior to the film's premiere.[9] Other studios were in similar financial straits, with 1933 marking the lowest ebb for the entire industry. "Between 1930 and 1933, the combined stock value of the five 'majors'—RKO, Paramount, Metro-Goldwyn-Mayer, 20th Century Fox, and Warner Brothers—had gone from about a billion dollars to less than $200 million," noted Great Depression historian T. H. Watkins. ". . . Of all the five majors, only MGM was able to stay in the black and its profits had sunk from $14.6 million in 1930 to $4.3 million in 1933."[10]

But *King Kong* led the box-office recovery that raised the foundering ship of RKO and all of Hollywood. In fact, the movies—which had already evolved from the epoch of the silent era to the talkies—were now more than a novelty, a passing curiosity. Whether in a humble neighborhood theater or a grand movie palace, audiences found thrills, comfort, inspiration, and escape. Dark movie halls, pierced by projected light flickering with the illusion of life, became a refuge during the cold years of the Depression, ushering in the Golden Age of Hollywood.[11]

"I'VE NEVER MADE a successful picture unless I was let alone to make it," Cooper declared in an early interview as production head of RKO, announcing that he was giving executive Pandro Berman, producer Kenneth MacGowan, and others creative freedom in his larger plan for "decentralizing authority." He also outlined a program that featured dramas and romances, action movies and topical "headline pictures." "I looked at Merian C. Cooper with increased respect," wrote reporter Jerry Hoffman, the man to whom Cooper outlined his strategy. "Such remarks are unprecedented in Hollywood history. Particularly coming from a studio head. It was then that I began to understand the new spirit and invigorating mode that has become so evident in the Radio studios since Cooper has been placed in charge of production."[12]

Cooper had noticed that Selznick had suffered from studio overhead attached to his productions—even the price tag for *Kong* was inflated by the estimated $200,000 in *Creation* expenditures the studio had tacked onto the ledger. Cooper reasoned that, instead of tying the studio's fortunes to a few prestigious productions, overall costs would be lower and final profits higher if a studio released more pictures into the marketplace. Cooper accelerated production to "an assembly-line pace," Betty Lasky wrote. "In April [1933], Cooper's zeal placed RKO in the forefront of the majors in the purchase of stories and plays. The little studio acquired eighteen properties, eight more than the giant Metro absorbed."[13]

Cooper's strategy favored female stars. Cooper was even quoted in the *Hollywood Herald* as calling women "the life-blood of the box-office." He maintained that female patrons came to see their fellow sex exalted and romanticized on the big screen—"it's an envious interest and a desire to study these glamorous ones," he explained. Indeed, the *Herald* article was headlined "COOPER STAKING JOB ON FEMININE STARS." Cooper had already discovered one of them when he'd noted the potential of a certain Broadway actress and sent an urgent night wire to Selznick on June 7, 1932: "Please have New York office make a test of Katharine Hepburn, now appearing [on Broadway] in *Warrior's Husband,* for part in *Three Came Unarmed.*"[14]

Hepburn signed an RKO contract, although instead of *Three Came Unarmed,* her debut film would be the 1932 release *A Bill of Divorcement.*

Herald reporter Lin Bonner, a self-admitted "Hollywood hooey hunter," had met, with some trepidation, the new RKO head of production. Was Cooper going to be a Moses leading Hollywood to the box-office promised land? Was he the "rank egotist" and publicity-mad character described in so many Hollywood rumors? "But whatever else he may be, he's a rebel, with the zeal and determination of a Savonarola," Bonner concluded. ". . . I'll offer that Cooper impressed me as a man aware that he has a big job on his hands; that he made personal requests of me which threw out the egotist and publicity mania charges; that in my presence he settled the problems of five subordinates in as many minutes."

He'd either be "chump or a champion," the *Herald* concluded. "Right now, he's in the toughest spot he ever encountered."[15]

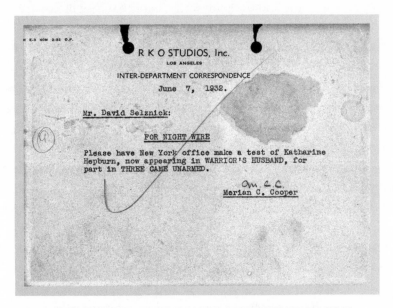

AS STUDIO PRODUCTION HEAD, COOPER EMPHASIZED FEMALE STARS. HE'D ALWAYS BEEN ON THE LOOKOUT FOR COMPELLING ACTRESSES— THIS COOPER MEMO PROMOTES A SCREEN TEST FOR THE THEN LITTLE-KNOWN KATHARINE HEPBURN.

Cooper Papers, BYU

ONE OF COOPER'S earliest decisions was to order the *King Kong* sequel, *The Son of Kong*, rushed into production. Cooper was credited as executive producer, but he wasn't involved in the day-to-day production, leaving it to Ernest Schoedsack to direct and Ruth Rose to script, Willis O'Brien to do the stop-motion animation, with Marcel Delgado and Mario Larrinaga among the *Kong* animation veterans. Archie Marshek was the associate producer, Murray Spivack orchestrated the sound effects, Max Steiner did the scoring, and Robert Armstrong returned as Carl Denham. They were asked to re-create *King Kong* magic on a tight budget and tighter time schedule, while Cooper's interest seemed less the passionate dedication lavished upon the original than a mogul's bottom line.

"I gave Schoedsack $200,000, I think it was, and said, 'Make *Son of Kong* and I don't care what you make because anything made called *Son of Kong* will make money,' " Cooper once explained.[16]

The production secrecy that had shrouded *Kong* carried over into *The Son of Kong,* beginning with the sequel's cover title of *Jamboree.* The plot was summed up by Ruth Rose in a two-page typed synopsis: "Theme: Carl Denham, discoverer of King Kong, returns to Skull Island, finds a fortune in diamonds, discovers the son of Kong who gives his life to save Denham when the island sinks in an earthquake, and [Denham] lives to share his fortune with the girl who has gone through these adventures with him."[17] *The Son of Kong* had the kind of self-conscious irony that, decades later, would become common in popular culture, as the short summary section in Ruth Rose's synopsis elaborated: "The death of King Kong left Kong's discoverer and exploiter, Carl Denham, penniless. Moreover, he is forced to go into hiding to avoid the innumerable suits being brought against him for the damage done in New York City when the great beast went berserk." Captain Englehorn also found himself in the same predicament.[18]

The Son of Kong was released toward the end of 1933, mere months after audiences had seen Kong shot off the Empire State Building, and suffered terribly by comparison. Film historian David Thomson alluded to a lack of creative potency owing to the absence of the franchise's creator and prime mover: "*Son of Kong* was a dismal failure: perhaps significantly, it had O'Brien still, but no Cooper."[19]

But the *Kong* sequel was a rare misfire in 1933, a year when RKO released forty-nine pictures.[20] In addition to *King Kong,* another hit was *Little Women,* which starred Katharine Hepburn and was directed by George Cukor. Although the production hadn't originated with Cooper, as executive producer he'd put his mark on another classic. Rudy Behlmer wrote, "Selznick had selected *Little Women* for production before he left [RKO], and when Cooper became involved with it, he insisted that the picture be based on the book, not only on the play adaptation. *Little Women* emerged as a true picturization of the Alcott novel and started a vogue for faithful screen adaptations of literary classics."[21]

The golden year also marked the beginning of an important new professional and personal relationship for Cooper. He'd later reflect that he'd had three great partners throughout his moviemaking career, the first two being Schoedsack and Selznick. In 1933 he began working with the third: John Ford.

Born in 1895, the son of Irish immigrants, Ford had been directing since 1917, but it was in partnership with Cooper that he created some of the classic films that established him as one of the greatest American directors. It all began when Cooper was taking a break from *King Kong* production and had gone to have dinner at the home of Winfield Sheehan, production chief at Fox.

After dinner, Winnie screened *Air Mail,* a 1932 John Ford picture, and at its conclusion the Fox executive shook his head over poor "down and out" Ford, whom he considered a relic of the silent era. But Cooper calmly headed home, and although it was 1:00 in the morning, he telephoned his business assistant, asking him to call Ford and have him at Cooper's office, if possible, the next morning.

Cooper recalled that Ford arrived "with a chip on his shoulder which I immediately put at ease." Within an hour, Cooper would recall, they had mutually agreed to the two productions Ford would direct—*The Lost Patrol* (1934) and *The Informer* (1935).[22]

It wasn't Merian Cooper, movie mogul, who impressed Ford but the unassuming man of action, the decorated military man and globe-trotting adventurer. For Cooper's part, he saw the superlative cinematic storyteller, not the hard-drinking and sometimes self-destructive director who was often a pain to work with.

"[Cooper] was one of the few executives and producers who ever managed to work comfortably with Ford, allowing the director to feel creatively unfettered while still keeping tight rein on production details," Ford biographer Joseph McBride wrote. "Working with Cooper, Ford felt relaxed and confident enough that he did not need to assert his autonomy by acting rebellious or, as he sometimes did, by sabotaging his own work as a form of passive resistance. Ford's drinking problem, which threatened to disrupt his career in the early thirties, became more manageable after he began working with Cooper."[23]

Merian Cooper also had more than moviemaking on his mind during the spring of 1933. The restless man who'd once vowed eternal bachelorhood had certainly not been a monk—he'd been in the social whirl from

Manhattan to Hollywood—but it was surprising to hear that Coop had been felled by Cupid's arrow: Merian C. Cooper had fallen in love, and would be married before the golden year was done.

"ALLEY OOP!" SO OPENED THE CAPTION FOR THIS MGM PUBLICITY SHOT OF STARLET DOROTHY JORDAN. THE PETITE ACTRESS ALWAYS EMBODIED AN ALL-AMERICAN VITALITY. *Cooper Papers, BYU*

ONE OF THE holdover projects from LeBaron's regime that the new Selznick regime scrutinized and green-lit was *The Lost Squadron,* a drama based on a *Liberty* magazine story by Dick Grace, who'd once headed a group of motion-picture stunt fliers dubbed the Squadron of Death. The 1932 release starred RKO leading man Richard Dix as a stunt-flying daredevil and the notorious Erich von Stroheim as a megalomaniacal film director who keeps his cameras rolling in hopes he'll catch a fatal crash. The production included Robert Armstrong as Woody Curwood, a hard-drinking stunt flier, and handsome Joel McCrea as Red. A pretty, petite young actress named Dorothy Jordan played Woody's kid sister, nicknamed "The Pest" for her admonitions about her brother's hard-drinking ways.

Dorothy caught Cooper's eye, and before long he was squiring his new love around town during breaks in the making of *King Kong*. The actress reportedly had also gotten the attention of swashbuckling pilot and producer Howard Hughes, but it was Merian who won her heart. On May 27, 1933, the couple eloped to Williams, Arizona, and were secretly married. Cooper decided to postpone their honeymoon until the fall because of Dorothy's impending productions, which would include playing the dance partner to a Broadway star named Fred Astaire in *Flying Down to Rio,* a picture the trades dubbed an "aerial musical."[24]

The marriage was kept secret for more than a month, until it finally became front-page news on July 8, when the *Los Angeles Examiner* ran the headline "SH! DON'T TELL A SOUL!" above a fetching portrait of the actress holding a raised finger, as if gesturing for silence. "The only witness to the ceremony from Hollywood," the article revealed, "was Miss Jordan's mother, Mrs. E. P. Jordan, who intimated last night the elopement was kept secret the last six weeks for fear announcement of the marriage might hamper Miss Jordan's career."[25]

In a subsequent *Los Angeles Times* article, Dorothy and Merian's union was compared to other marriages between actresses and powerful Hollywood executives, notably Norma Shearer's marriage to MGM's Irving Thalberg. Cooper was the "big boss" at RKO, and as such Dorothy's rivals on the lot might expect her to get the best scripts and leading men, the best directors and cameramen at the studio's command. "But Dorothy Jordan . . . is perfectly aware of the pitfalls that await her as Mrs. Cooper," the article added. ". . . In fact, talking with Dorothy, it is very clear that she wishes us to know she has no intention of prima-donna-ing as Mrs. Cooper. All the same you may watch for new scintillations in that quarter."[26]

But Dorothy Jordan was as good as her word; she never forgot her roots as the small-town girl from Clarksville, Tennessee. Jordan's down-home, all-American charm was part of her appeal, and was celebrated in a fan publication devoted to her, the *Jordan Journal.*

"It has been rumored that Dorothy went high-hat after her marriage to Merian Cooper," went an item in a March 1934 issue. "It so happens she recently saw one of her old friends that worked with her a long time ago, as she was driving down the street. Dorothy nearly fell out of the window waving to her. She has always been known to be kind, and level-headed, even though she has met with good breaks. That's why she is loved so much."[27]

Dorothy had a slate of films released in 1933—*Strictly Personal, Bondage,* and *One Man's Journey*—but her anticipated role in *Flying Down to Rio*

AS A MAJOR PLAYER IN HOLLYWOOD, COOPER AND HIS WIFE FLEW IN
A RAREFIED ATMOSPHERE, AND A FAVORITE PLACE TO UNWIND WAS ON THE
SKI SLOPES. HERE DOROTHY JORDAN COOPER POSES WITH FAY WRAY.
Cooper Papers, BYU

wasn't among them. The film, designed as a vehicle for Dolores Del Rio, launched the most famous dance team in film history: Fred Astaire and Ginger Rogers. Astaire had been a friend of John Hay Whitney's, who'd suggested the Broadway dancer to Cooper. Before Selznick had departed RKO, he and Cooper had arranged a screen test for Astaire, and Cooper had decided to use Astaire for the musical numbers in *Rio,* with Dorothy Jordan as his partner. But Merian's marriage made him change his plans.

He selected the little-known Ginger Rogers to dance with Astaire, and the rest, as they say, is history.[28] Dorothy Jordan Cooper, then in her mid-twenties, essentially retired from the movies and wouldn't emerge again for the cameras until the 1950s.

IN 1933 MERIAN Cooper had reached the apex of power in Hollywood, and his lucrative RKO contract guaranteed a 20 percent profit participation on every picture the studio released. But RCA president David Sarnoff—the great power behind the powers at RKO—felt that restrictions should be placed on Cooper's lucrative percentage deal.[29]

So although Cooper had been embraced by the studio bosses, the successor to Selznick soon came to realize that his power had its limits. The relationship between the production head and the studio bosses was also strained by Cooper's quixotic struggle to interest RKO in color film-making, a daring—and expensive—proposition at the time.

As early as 1932, Cooper had already become an enthusiastic advocate of Technicolor's revolutionary three-strip process, which emulated nature's primary-color palette. The Technicolor company was struggling at the time, and Edward Curtis, a friend of Cooper's at Eastman Kodak, proposed that RKO purchase one hundred thousand shares of Technicolor stock at three dollars a share. Cooper contacted other industry heavyweights and got them interested in Technicolor's new process, including Walt Disney, who asked Cooper if RKO would put up the money for a full-color animated feature of *Babes in Toyland,* the celebrated operetta composed by Victor Herbert and first staged in 1903. Cooper brought both the Disney and the stock-purchase proposals to his board of directors—and both were rejected.[30]

Undaunted, Cooper did an end run around the obstinate studio executives and approached the Whitney cousins, convincing them to be partners in the purchase of the one hundred thousand shares of Technicolor stock, with options to purchase more. Then, in May 1933, while Cooper was under contract to RKO, he and the Whitneys formed Pioneer Pictures, a company dedicated to producing Technicolor movies. As the trailblazing name implied, Cooper and John Hay "Jock" Whitney (who would become a head of the new company) wanted Pioneer to lead the film industry into the next revolutionary step. Although reluctant to commit to its own in-studio color productions, RKO did agree to release the first color pictures created by Pioneer.

Then, in September 1933, came shocking news: Merian Cooper had suffered a heart attack.

The Douris Corporation; image courtesy
Cooper Papers, BYU

THE PRODUCER

My empire is of the imagination.

—Hascha-Mo-Tet ("She-Who-Must-Be-Obeyed"),
ruler of Kor, in SHE

THE MAN SCHOEDSACK WOULD CALL "OLD INDESTRUCTIBLE" HAD BEEN TWICE shot out of the sky in war, toughed out prison camps, made a nomadic march, faced down man-eating tigers and leaping leopards, survived a cholera epidemic in the jungle, and led a death-defying rescue mission to the ice floes. Such a man didn't have a heart attack at forty. So when Cooper took a "vacation," the Hollywood rumor mill whispered that he'd suffered a nervous breakdown.

Years later, talking to Rudy Behlmer, Coop laughed it all off as typical Hollywood gossip. He'd been in *fine* health, he chuckled, and had briefly re-linquished the reins of power simply to take Dorothy on their long-delayed honeymoon, a whirlwind, around-the-world trip during which he in-dulged his beautiful young bride as if there were no tomorrow. In his old age, Cooper estimated that his honeymoon had probably cost him about $1.2 million in salary, percentages, and lost time.

"I decided a man only gets married once," he wrote Margaret Corcoran, "so despite the protests of my Board of Directors, I resigned and went on what my business advisor called 'Cooper's million dollar honeymoon.' I took the whole front of the Royal Hawaiian Hotel in Honolulu—the biggest suite in St. Moritz."[1] But all that money didn't buy him and his bride true happiness. That didn't come until they ventured far from ostentatious re-treats. "Staying at little German villages and farms, we couldn't spend over a couple of dollars if we tried," Cooper wrote. "There I found happiness.

"When I was completely broke, I had to get my young wife to kick in $5,000 out of her hard-earned savings as an actress to get us home. I told her we would go home right away and make another fortune."[2] According to Cooper, it was upon his return to Hollywood that he officially resigned as RKO production head.

And despite his protestations to Behlmer, Cooper *had* been stricken by illness, probably a heart attack. He took another leave from his duties in early 1934, and his continuing bad health finally forced his resignation. In fact, an October 1934 *Fortune* article referred to Cooper as having had a "nervous breakdown" (as well as making a rumored $500,000 a year at RKO, including box-office profit participation). Pandro Berman, who had filled in during Cooper's first reported absence, was officially installed as the new RKO production head.[3] In 1934, Cooper himself was so concerned about his health that he feared he wouldn't be able to pass a health exam needed to maintain an insurance policy, and sought help from his old World War I comrade Edmund Leonard, who had made a career in the insurance business.[4]

Cooper obliquely referred to the pressures of being a studio head when, in a 1934 letter extolling the virtues of David Selznick, he endorsed the producer's "healthy vitality and energy" and added, in a revealing aside, that "with the tremendous burden which heading a production studio lays on any man, this is a very necessary factor."[5]

Pleading ill health and his responsibilities in Hollywood, Cooper also resigned from the various boards he sat on in New York—all except Pan American Airways. Despite the distance and his studio responsibilities, he had closely followed the company, and kept in communication with Trippe, Whitney, and Robert Thach. Finally, in 1935, he felt compelled to resign from the Pan Am board as well, noting "my long illness and my inability to attend past Board meetings."[6] That same day he sent a personal letter to Juan Trippe, referring to his resignations from other boards and confessing, "I have always hated to resign from Pan Am for sentimental reasons." But his illness and his life out in California had finally forced the issue, and he regretfully tendered his resignation.[7]

Cooper still retained the respect and confidence of the Pan Am brass, an affirmation that was poignantly illustrated when Juan Trippe personally *returned* Coop's letter of resignation. "Naturally I received this note with a great deal of regret for I have always considered your having 'carried on' on our Board in John Hambleton's place as one of his oldest friends," Trippe wrote. ". . . If, however, you still feel you wish to act immediately, have your secretary again forward it to me and I will present it at the next meeting of our Board."[8] Cooper didn't change his mind, and his resignation was finally approved, effective May 21, 1936.[9]

But as one Cooper was leaving Pan Am, another arrived: Merian managed to get his brother John into the company, and a 1936 *Fortune* article on Pan Am would hail him as "the newest of the vice presidents, specialist on international aerial law."[10] John Cooper would enjoy a long and distinguished career; ultimately, as manned flight began moving into space travel, he would pioneer the unfolding field of outer-space law.

Even as Merian was cutting away the extraneous demands on his time and energy, his old, resilient self almost immediately began reasserting itself. Even in his letter to Edmund Leonard, full of fear that he wouldn't pass a health exam, the indomitable optimism came shining through. "I'm really feeling better all the time, and hope to get back all my old vim and vigor," he wrote.[11]

Cooper did indeed regain his "vim and vigor," and began devoting his full energies to Pioneer Pictures, where he was vice president and held a substantial financial investment. Through this channel, he could pursue his Technicolor dreams, and the future looked bright, as Pioneer contracted with RKO to release their first three Technicolor productions.[12] Cooper also agreed to settle his contractual obligations with RKO through a two-picture deal, personally producing what would be two patented Cooper adventure spectacles.

First into production would be a big-screen adaptation of H. Rider Haggard's *She,* followed by Sir Edward Bulwer-Lytton's *The Last Days of Pompeii,* which he tapped Schoedsack to direct.

Cooper wanted to make both productions in Technicolor, but once again, he was plagued by studio intransigence. Worse, the studio waited until *She* was deep in preproduction, with effects artists ready to build miniature model sets, before informing Cooper that the budget for both *She* and *The Last Days of Pompeii* had been cut in half—instead of a planned $1 million for each production, that sum had to cover the costs for *both* pictures.[13]

Still, Cooper had signed to do both pictures before he went on his honeymoon, and that agreement came back to haunt him. "I thought

SHE PROMOTIONAL MATERIAL. THE FINAL FILM WOULD HAVE IRVING PICHEL AND LANSING C. HOLDEN AS CO-DIRECTOR, WITH HELEN GAHAGAN STARRING AS THE INDOMITABLE SHE, RANDOLPH SCOTT AS LEO VINCEY, AND HELEN MACK AS TANYA, LEO'S LOVE INTEREST. THE PRODUCTION TALENT MERIAN COOPER ORIGINALLY HOPED TO SECURE PRESENTS AN INTRIGUING WHAT IF?—JAMES WHALE AS DIRECTOR, GRETA GARBO OR MARLENE DIETRICH AS SHE, JOEL MCCREA AS LEO, AND FRANCES DEE AS TANYA.

The Douris Corporation; image courtesy Cooper Papers, BYU

they held me back too much on money and that was partially my fault because the costs in 1935 were much higher than the costs in 1933. I frankly misfigured the costs and when they said that [a million dollars] was all I'd have to spend I said, 'What the hell, we'll make it for that.' And did, both of them. I'd have made twice as good pictures spending a couple hundred thousand more on each. . . . Unfortunately, I'd signed a contract when money was very cheap at the bottom of the Depression.

Then I was away with my young bride and when I came back money didn't buy as much. So Monty said, 'Let's take all the money and put it in *Pompeii.*' It would have been better if we could and I tried to do it. They wouldn't let me, they insisted on having two pictures. So I really cheated a lot on *She.*"[14]

SHE WAS A perfect fit for the ethos of "distant, difficult, and dangerous." The original Haggard tale describes the mysterious Ayesha, a woman who's lived thousands of years, the embodiment of eternal youth thanks to the

The Douris Corporation; image courtesy Cooper Papers, BYU

"flame of life" she's discovered in Africa. Her title is Hascha-Mo-Tet—
"She-Who-Must-Be-Obeyed"—and she rules the hidden kingdom of Kor
through terror and brute force. Into her domain comes young English explorer Leo Vincey, a man the all-powerful ruler believes is the reincarnation
of the lover she once murdered and has been pining for across the centuries.

Cooper's production made major changes in the story, including relo-
cating She's hidden kingdom from Africa—which Cooper felt had lost
much of its old mystery—to the frozen wastes of the Arctic. Ever the "bigger is better" producer, Cooper pushed production values—almost defiantly, given his tight budget. When Ruth told him the film had everything
in it but a saber-toothed tiger, Coop reportedly replied, "Why didn't I think
of that? A saber-tooth tiger! Write it in!" The end result of that brainstorm
is a giant, centuries-old saber-toothed tiger the intrepid explorers find preserved in the ice. Cooper also imagined a herd of woolly mammoths attacking the explorers and wanted his visual-effects wizard, Willis O'Brien,
to create the thundering herd with stop-motion animation. This idea he finally abandoned, as this vision went far beyond his budgetary limits.[15]

In the film, She comments, "My empire is of the imagination." And it
truly was, a fantastic realm that could be reached only by journeying beyond the Frozen Wastes to a ring of mountains where lived the savage
Amahaggar cave dwellers, and then into Kor's fertile Valley of Smokes,
where She's royal palace stood. The grand palace and its mighty walled
gate were actually the Skull Island gate from *Kong* re-dressed for Kor. The
Hall of Kings—where She had her throne and the sacrificial well of the Sacred Flame—encompassed two stages at RKO's Culver City lot, with set
walls some forty feet high. These were extended even higher using matte
paintings that created the illusion of giant statues representing past kings
of Kor.[16]

THE LAST DAYS *of Pompeii* was another promising spectacle: Pompeii had been
a vibrant town of twenty thousand citizens, until it was transformed into a
living mausoleum by the eruption of fire and lava that burst from Mount
Vesuvius in A.D. 79. The film was named after the Sir Edward Bulwer-Lytton
novel, but the only resemblance Ruth Rose's script had to the book was the
title. And Cooper promised the RKO board that the volcanic destruction

would top Kong's rampage through Manhattan.[17] It was on his honeymoon trip to Europe that he actually walked the ruins of Pompeii, and contemplated producing the epic disaster movie in Technicolor.

Willis O'Brien again would oversee the effects, even as a horrific chapter in his life finally closed with the death of Hazel O'Brien, who passed away in January of 1935 from her various illnesses—mercifully, before she could be brought to trial for the murder of their two sons. O'Brien had found a new love, a young woman named Darlyne Prenett from Santa Barbara, who was blissfully oblivious to the movie business. Introduced to O'Brien after the release of *King Kong,* she hadn't even realized that O'Brien had worked on the film, much less understood stop-motion animation.[18] Darlyne did like *Kong* when she finally saw it—after she and Willis were wed on November 17, 1934. The couple enjoyed a happy honeymoon in Mexico before returning to Los Angeles and Obie's work on *The Last Days of Pompeii.*[19]

Cooper viewed the completion of *She* and *Pompeii* with mixed feelings. Both were financial disappointments, although when rereleased as a theatrical double bill they were a hit. Even that surprising success didn't change Cooper's disappointment in the productions. He was hardest on *She,* once dismissing it as "the worst picture I ever made."[20] Although he felt that *The Last Days of Pompeii* was good, he lamented the studio's refusal to allow him to make it in color. "I almost got RKO to go for it," he once wistfully recalled. "It would have been a perfect color subject. If it had been in color we'd have had a big hit!"[21]

She and *The Last Days of Pompeii* completed Cooper's contractual obligations to RKO, and he could finally turn his full attention to Pioneer Pictures. In the process he once again dedicated himself to his dream of pushing the entire picture business into the realm of color filmmaking.[22]

THE PIONEER

The future of full-color Technicolor motion picture is promising,
indeed seen through the eyes of Merian C. Cooper, who,
as Executive Vice President in Charge of Production for
Pioneer Pictures, Inc., sits in the hub and directs the heart
of Hollywood's color endeavor.

—COMMENTATOR, April 4, 1936[1]

IN 1935, WHEN MARGUERITE HARRISON'S AUTOBIOGRAPHY, *THERE'S ALWAYS Tomorrow,* was published, the expedition of *Grass* and Cooper's dreams of exploration seemed a lifetime ago. She would wonder whether her old partner's life in Hollywood compensated for the life of an explorer he had once pursued.[2]

Cooper was essentially channeling his spirit of exploration into moviemaking, and his great crusade during Hollywood's Golden Age was to make color films. He had already found the future in the new three-strip Technicolor process, a revolutionary leap over previous color systems, including Technicolor's two-color system. And one of Cooper's greatest converts was David Selznick.

It was on March 26, 1932, that Selznick, at that time still RKO's head of production, dashed off a teletype to the New York office, enthusiastically sharing Cooper's vision for a jungle picture. *King Kong* was *not* this unidentified jungle picture, Rudy Behlmer notes. The teletype read "Please advise reaction to idea of Cooper's, which I think has great merit, of adventure jungle picture on next year's program, to be made in what I understand from Cooper, who has seen it, is sensational new secret three-color process . . . if process is as superb as he says, my previous objections to color would be removed, as I feel that it isn't that public doesn't want color so much as it doesn't want the illusion-destroying bad colors which have been foisted upon it. Cooper brings out that we could build artificial jungle splashed with brilliant colors such as usual artist's conception, and that selection of animals such as tigers, leopards, white monkeys, etc., would all lend themselves to sensational results."[3]

In a sign of what was to come, RKO's New York office rejected the color proposal.

She and *The Last Days of Pompeii* were to be the last of Cooper's color disappointments at RKO. Cooper had also wanted to make *Flying Down to Rio* in color.[4] In early 1934, Cooper even hoped to make a Technicolor epic based on the story of Joan of Arc, with Katharine Hepburn in the starring role—and again the studio powers said no.[5]

In retrospect, the studio's caution was somewhat understandable. Color was expensive, and no previous process had been able to produce consistently high-quality images. But color had been a Holy Grail of moviemaking practically from the beginning, and a major breakthrough came during World War I, when Herbert T. Kalmus and Daniel F. Comstock invented the Technicolor process.

Kalmus unveiled what was originally a two-color system in February 1917, at a lecture at Aeolian Hall in New York (incongruously, at the invitation of the American Institute of Mining Engineers). "We were . . . introducing the color by projecting through two apertures, each with a [red and green] color filter, bringing the two components into register on the screen by means of a thin adjusting glass element," Kalmus later wrote. The demonstration was not successful, as the projections had to be perfectly adjusted, and the resulting "fringes" convinced Kalmus that he had to move from projection to what eventually became an "imbibition" process that utilized "two-component cameras." (Imbibition refers to a dye process that, in this case, combined the two colors of red and green during the process.)[6]

Despite its imperfect launch, by 1922 the Technicolor company was incorporated, with Kalmus installed as president. As a small endeavor, Technicolor moved forward deliberately and cautiously, keeping an eye on quality control for its seminal system. Then came the advent of talkies, and it seemed as if Technicolor's time had come. There was a rush of rental requests for Technicolor cameras, and the company labs became busy with

THE PIONEER PICTURES TOP EXECUTIVES CONVENE:
COOPER (LEFT), JOCK WHITNEY (MIDDLE), DAVID O.
SELZNICK (RIGHT). THE MEANING OF WHITNEY'S
BLACK ARMBAND IS UNKNOWN, ALTHOUGH AT THE
TIME IT WAS THE FASHION TO WEAR ONE WHEN IN
MOURNING. *Cooper Papers, BYU*

orders for color-processing work. And with increased demand came the long-feared loss in image quality.

"The result," film historian Ronald Haver wrote, "was a series of garishly tinted pictures that did Technicolor more harm than good, and by 1931 the color boom had turned bust. Kalmus, seeing fifteen years and several million dollars' worth of work and experimentation about to be wiped out, decided on one last Herculean effort to overcome Technicolor's basic shortcoming, the lack of a three-color image. A new camera was designed with three strips of film and the process now included the all-important blue [and yellow] component."[7]

The three-strip process was expensive and cumbersome.[8] But this was no obstacle to Merian Cooper. Despite its drawbacks, he became excited about the potential after test footage was screened for him by his friend at Eastman Kodak, Edward Curtis, who was director of motion-picture sales. In one mad dash, Cooper got the Whitney cousins to come aboard as investors in Technicolor stock, which was a bargain after the two-color process went bust. And he and the Whitneys forged Pioneer Pictures, intent on making three-strip productions. H. T. Kalmus would hail Merian Cooper, who became a good friend, and Jock Whitney as among the first to show a "practical interest" in three-strip color.

But Cooper and Whitney also had utilitarian concerns. Could Technicolor capture the different shades of green in wooded forests and dense jungle? Could the process properly depict a blond actress when she was filmed against pale backgrounds? And, all the while, the Pioneer partners were searching for the right feature property to showcase Technicolor. Reportedly, two hundred stories were considered.

While the search for a feature property was still ongoing, Pioneer Pictures released a test short that showcased the new process, and it was enthusiastically received.[9] *La Cucaracha,* which revolved around a Mexican fiesta, won a 1934 Academy Award in the category of short subjects, comedy.

Despite the award, Cooper was impatient with the progress of color filmmaking. Then he noticed that while Kodak was going through a rough time, an unhappy David Selznick was ready to leave MGM. Cooper decided to see if he could make the twain meet, and in a letter to Edward Curtis, he further mused: "How can the industry be forced into color? Pioneer is well on its way, but it can be done more quickly." Coop put his cards on the table: "Always being your good friend, I am now writing you a way to pull that poor Eastman Kodak Company out of the red, and make a decent showing of it.

"Who will benefit most if the industry goes all color? Why, the poor old crippled Eastman Kodak Company. . . . Seriously, this is the idea I have. David Selznick is quitting Metro. He wants to produce independently. He is willing to form a unit to make four color pictures a year for two years, using the highest grade stars, etc. He hasn't got finances. I think it would be a terribly smart thing for you to finance him. His pictures will be big ones and distinguished ones, and whether you like David or not, he surely goes out after quality and, in my opinion, is really one of the top quality producers in the business." Cooper proposed a $2 million loan, which, he argued, would be quickly returned to Kodak "in your increased sale of negative to the industry as a whole."[10]

Meanwhile, the honor of the first full-length production to utilize three-strip Technicolor would go to the first of Pioneer's three-feature deal with RKO: *Becky Sharp,* a period piece released in 1935 and inspired by the lower-class, social-climbing heroine of the novel *Vanity Fair.* The film was the talk of the industry; many felt the picture would be the make-or-break chance for color. The great experiment reportedly cost $1 million, which didn't hurt the buzz as New York high society turned out in force for a midnight premiere at Radio City Music Hall. The crowd was hoping to be part of film history, just as the awed audiences had been when they'd heard pictures talk at the opening of *The Jazz Singer.*[11]

Actress Miriam Hopkins would win an Oscar nomination for her portrayal of the title character, but the film, considered by many to be too highbrow, suffered lackluster box office, and seemed to prove that the novelty of color wasn't enough to guarantee success.

Cooper relentlessly remained as passionate about color filmmaking as he had once been about the potential of movies to popularize exploration—basically, both passions were about seeing the world in a new way. One of his arguments for color was obvious: Black-and-white films were but shadows of the colorful world moviegoers lived in. "Color renews the world for us, a world of which even the farthest places have been photographed to a turn," Cooper exulted in an interview feature for *Commentator,* a Hollywood publication. "We can now re-invade Africa, Australia, Hawaii, China, even the poles and bring them to fans in the full-glory of reality. Very few of our millions of patrons have seen these places as they really are."

The *Commentator* feature, published in 1936, hailed Pioneer—and Cooper himself—as leading Hollywood's expansion into color production, describing the company as having "the world's most elaborate color production program," with nine major color features planned within the next two years. The article also provided an opportunity to promote what Cooper hoped would be a crowd-pleasing follow-up to *Becky Sharp*, a swashbuckling musical adventure about a dancer shanghaied by pirates, called *The Dancing Pirate*. During the *Commentator* interview, Cooper observed that the new production would showcase color film's unsung ability to re-create the past and provide a time-traveling sensation for audiences.

"Through infinite research we have recreated the costumes, buildings and backgrounds of that time, and in color," Cooper said. "That strikes me as something of a miracle, no less—an actual picture of the past in natural, lifelike colors of the past; something no one would ever see but for color in motion pictures."

Cooper felt that color's expense would soon diminish, just as the costs for sound technology had gone down when the industry had converted to talking pictures. In a stunningly prescient statement for the 1930s, Cooper added that color would make movies stand apart from its coming rival: television. "It will prolong Hollywood's world-wide prestige," he told *Commentator*, ". . . and it will distinguish motion pictures from television, our industry's greatest threat."[12]

But *The Dancing Pirate* also failed at the box office, and it was the final Pioneer three-strip color production RKO would distribute. Outside of the acclaim accorded *La Cucaracha*, Pioneer's color features hadn't ushered in the promised golden age of color. Except for the most astute film historians and students, the world has virtually forgotten those films today.

But the trailblazing connotations of Pioneer Pictures were still apt. They were pioneers headed into unknown territory, often the first to suffer hardship and defeat, and the ones who paved the way for the settlers to come.

IN 1935 DAVID Selznick formed Selznick International Pictures. It was a short walk from MGM to his new headquarters in the colonial-style mansion building on Washington Boulevard, adjacent to the Pathé-RKO back lot. The mansion, appropriately fashioned for a master of illusion, had not only been the administrative building when movie pioneer Thomas Ince ruled the lot, but it had also served as a set for a 1924 Thomas Ince production, *Barbara Frietchie*.[13]

And just as Cooper once hooked his dream of *Kong* to Selznick's rising star, he now saw a chance to advance his ambitions for color film. With the support of the Whitney cousins, he pushed for a merger of Pioneer and Selznick International. "Cooper was helpful," Selznick later described, "and for a time the Whitneys had money in with both Cooper and myself. . . .

"Cooper kept insisting that Pioneer would do better if he worked under me, and finally, at the insistence of C. V. Whitney, I took over the operation of Pioneer, along with Selznick International. To all practical purposes, they were one operation, except as to ownership."[14]

Prior to the release of the ill-fated *The Dancing Pirate*, Cooper made a bold prophecy: "Color films will dominate the entire industry within five years, and within three years, every major feature will be screened in color."[15] Cooper's dream would come true, although his time line was off the mark.

But color *would* grow in popularity, thanks to his own efforts and those of his old friend and Technicolor convert David O. Selznick, whose own creative journey would soon lead to one of the great triumphs of motion-picture history.

WARTIME

WAR EAGLES

> EXT. STATUE OF LIBERTY (MIN. PROJ.)
>
> FULL SHOT Perched on its shoulder is White Eagle. . . . Above,
> the circling, screaming eagles, and behind a magnificent sky of
> broken clouds. O.s. [offscreen] a huge roar of motors. The Ameri-
> can pursuit ships flash through squadron after squadron, headed
> out to sea. Suddenly the last flight has swept past. As the thunder
> of motors diminishes, and the steady victory roar of New York
> City, punctuated by steamer sirens, becomes audible below,
> BOOM INTO A CLOSER SHOT . . . a big magnificent
> CLOSEUP WHITE EAGLE, as he screams in triumph,
> and wildly beats his great shining wings.
>
> FADE OUT.
>
> —WAR EAGLES production draft notes[1]

PIONEER PICTURES MERGED WITH SELZNICK INTERNATIONAL IN JUNE 1936, WITH
Jock Whitney installed as chairman of the board and Cooper as vice president. It was an eventful summer as David Selznick sent his galley-proof
copy of the Margaret Mitchell novel *Gone With the Wind* to his special photographic effects department, the unit he'd entrust with developing the
technology and techniques needed to make Mitchell's epic of the Civil War
in Technicolor.

"So all our future plans were for planning a department that could handle whatever would be required for *GWTW*," recalled Selznick effects cameraman Clarence Slifer. ". . . With each color production that we made before
the start of *GWTW* we gained in experience, equipment, and personnel."[2]

Cooper and Whitney arrived at Culver City in time to be involved in the
making of Selznick International's inaugural Technicolor feature. *The Garden of Allah*, a romance set in the Sahara, had previously been made in 1917

and as an MGM silent film in 1927. This new version starred sultry Marlene Dietrich and debonair Charles Boyer.

Cooper promoted an aesthetic that would emulate the Dutch and Flemish painters of the sixteenth and seventeenth centuries, and this set off a creative struggle with Natalie Kalmus, Herbert's estranged wife and the "color director" for Technicolor, who favored a bright, almost monochromatic color scheme. But Cooper prevailed, and the Technicolor labs gave *The Garden of Allah* a rich, luminous look.[3]

The Garden of Allah was also the first three-strip color production that would match color matte paintings with live-action color photography, an advance that would soon prove vital, given that *Gone With the Wind* would feature more than one hundred matte shots.[4]

Cooper had what he wanted: a partnership with Selznick in an ambitious and independent production company at the forefront of color filmmaking and control of his own productions; in addition, he had John Ford signed to a two-picture deal. It looked like everybody would be making beautiful music together.

But this story wouldn't have a happy ending. Selznick retained ultimate story approval, and a dustup was coming over a project that had first come to Ford's attention as a *Collier's* magazine short story titled "Stage to Lordsburg." The story told of a dangerous stagecoach journey through Indian territory. Ford and Cooper would rename it *Stagecoach,* and by the summer of 1937 they had received verbal commitments from Claire Trevor to play Dallas, a hopeful prostitute, and young John Wayne to star as the outlaw known as the Ringo Kid.

Ford and Cooper charged ahead, but Selznick was already wary of the feisty, independent Ford, and what he felt was the noncommercial nature of many of his films. Selznick clearly wanted to keep Ford on a short leash, as he noted in a June 29, 1937, memo to Whitney and company treasurer John Wharton: "The only other story that I would be willing to have Coop and Ford make is *Lafayette Escadrille,* which I think could be outstanding in color without stars."[5]

Cooper and Ford met Selznick at his house to discuss *Stagecoach* over dinner—and a heated dinner it was, emotionally. Cooper personally was surprised that David seemed unimpressed with their choice of the western genre and of Trevor and Wayne as the leads. But the duo stuck to their guns, stressing that they were planning a film that was sure to become a classic. By the time coffee was served, Selznick was giving them the go-ahead.

But by the next morning, Selznick had reconsidered. He told the startled filmmakers that their western wouldn't even earn its print costs back unless there were two major stars in the lead roles. He proposed Gary Cooper as the Ringo Kid and Marlene Dietrich as Dallas. Both were bad casting, Merian felt.

"We argued all morning, but I couldn't shake him and he couldn't move me, so right then and there I resigned," Cooper said, summing up the encounter. "... I was vice president of both companies [Selznick International and its Pioneer division] and owned a piece of each, but I threw the cash and the long-term contracts overboard on what was to me a point of honor. After I left, Jack [Ford] told David that he'd made a contract with me personally to make *Stagecoach* regardless of what company made the picture, so he left too."

Cooper's dramatic resignation and Ford's departure left Selznick emotionally stretched between genuinely hurt feelings and his business instincts, which told him Ford had no legal right to walk out. The immediate result of Cooper and Ford's departure was that Pioneer Pictures "ceased to exist except as legal caretaker" of its few Technicolor properties, film historian Ronald Haver noted.[6] Cooper and Ford, partners in honor, formed their own company and christened it Argosy Pictures, with Cooper as president and Ford as chairman of the board. *Stagecoach* went into production, although Cooper refused credit for the expertise he'd given it. He had originally envisioned making it in color, but it was famously shot in black and white, and this turned out to be perfectly iconic for the setting in Monument Valley, an expanse of primordial rock formations in the Southwest that would become *the* archetypal backdrop for much of Hollywood's western mythology.

For Selznick, *Gone With the Wind* began production the chilly night of December 10, 1938, on the venerable RKO-Pathé lot in Culver City. It was an evening that would go down in movie history, not only because Selznick's Technicolor cameras were rolling on the burning of Atlanta sequence, but because the fire would clear out old, crumbling sets, making way for the antebellum mansion of Tara, the Atlanta railroad station, and other sets that would be built for the new production. It was a purging of the past, and the centerpiece of the inferno was the massive set that had stood for years as the

Temple of Jerusalem, the gates of Skull Island, and the great doors that led to the lost kingdom of Kor. The seventy-five-foot-high walls that had once kept out King Kong were prepared with sprinklers that alternately stoked the fires with blasts of gasoline and controlled the inferno with sprays of water. Cables ran from the wall to trucks that, at a signal, helped pull down the flaming structure.

Selznick's effects cameraman, Clarence Slifer, was filming with a new high-speed Technicolor camera capable of shooting seventy-two frames per second when the oil-soaked wooden sets ignited, and flames shot hundreds of feet into the sky, blanketing Culver City with smoke.[7]

The year 1939 marked an apex of success for both Selznick and Ford, as both were vindicated by the critical and commercial successes of their respective productions in what many film historians feel was Hollywood's greatest year. Cooper would credit *Gone With the Wind* as the production that "put over color, in my opinion."[8] *Stagecoach* would ride into film history as the classic Coop and Ford had argued it would become, laying the foundation upon which the tall, laconic John Wayne built his future screen persona, particularly in his famous westerns, many of which would be John Ford and Merian C. Cooper productions.

IN JUNE 1937, Cooper moved to Metro-Goldwyn-Mayer, considered by many to be the ultimate Golden Age dream factory. It was a time when Merian and Dorothy were starting a family: In 1934, Mary Caroline was born, and Richard was born two years later. At MGM, Cooper was hired to produce, and his first assignment was to find the next appropriate vehicle for Academy Award winner Luise Rainer. The result was *The Toy Wife*, released in 1938, which, unfortunately, did not ignite her career (bad career choices and a stormy marriage to and divorce from Clifford Odets would lead to her premature retirement). MGM also allowed Cooper to busy himself with outside interests, which included contributing extensive preproduction work for famed British director-producer Alexander Korda's *Jungle Book*, released in 1942, and *Eagle Squadron* for Walter Wanger, also released that year. Cooper was also heavily involved in Argosy's *The Long Voyage Home*, a 1940 release inspired by the plays of Eugene O'Neill, directed by Ford, and "presented" by Walter Wanger.

But Cooper was also looking to make another fantasy epic that would equal, if not top, *King Kong*, which was enjoying its widespread theatrical rerelease in 1938. The domestic rereleases suffered the censor's scissors on some of the more controversial moments, including Kong's rampages on Skull Island and in Manhattan and the scene where a curious Kong strips away Ann Darrow's clothes and sniffs his fingers.[9]

Still, *King Kong* retained its beguiling power, and in those days, when movie magic was created in secret and effects artists were generally anonymous, one of its thrills was the mystery of *how* it had been done. A typical fan letter of the period read, "I recently saw your movie entitled 'King Kong' at a local theater. This picture was so thrilling and mysterious that it aroused in me a desire to know the full particulars of its filming. Would you be so kind as to send me these particulars, giving special emphasis to the parts where the ape held the woman in his hand. What I mean is, was the picture drawn, or acted by a person in a costume?"[10]

Cooper had always contemplated potential *Kong* projects, starting with the rushed sequel. In fact, in 1935, when Cooper and Jock Whitney formed Pioneer Pictures and assumed management of the company, Cooper had asked Selznick for a suggestion for a picture his new company might develop and the next day the canny producer shot back a suggestion: *Tarzan vs. King Kong*. MGM wouldn't allow their jungle man to play opposite the most famous ape in movie history, but a flurry of legal activity about *Kong* rights gave Cooper pause as he came to realize that he might not have full control over the figment of his own imagination.

Indeed, decades later, Cooper would engage in a legal battle as he tried to regain ownership of his creation. In the meantime, he decided to do the next best thing to a remake: produce a "*King Kong* type picture."[11]

The project would be known as *War Eagles*, and it turned out to be his great quest at MGM.

THE STORY LINE for *War Eagles*—which also had the working title *White Eagle*—outlined another lost-world scenario. In a 1938 proposal, Cooper imagined a "warm volcanic valley twenty thousand feet deep" in the south polar ice fields, where members of a lost tribe ride gigantic flying eagles. They live on a plateau that is like paradise, the outline explained, except they have no food and to replenish supplies they must fly their eagles into a fertile "prehistoric valley," which would become known to the production as the Valley of the Ancients. This valley is the flip side of paradise, primal and full of terrors, from prehistoric monsters to a "race of savage apelike men" who trap monsters for their bloody arena battles and covet the "women of the bird people" for use in sacrifices to the prehistoric monsters. Cooper conceived the adventure as "a super-Western of the air in which, instead of riders of the plains on horseback, we will have wild riders of the air on giant prehistoric eagles."[12]

THE *WAR EAGLES* PRODUCTION, WHICH ENDED WITH THE COMING OF WORLD WAR II, IS THE GREAT *WHAT IF?* FOR FANS OF COOPER AND O'BRIEN. IT COULD HAVE USHERED IN A NEW ERA OF VISUAL-EFFECTS ADVANCES, JUST AS *KONG* HAD IN 1933, AND A RENAISSANCE OF WORK FROM THE COOPER-O'BRIEN TEAM. "ONE OF THE MYSTERIES IS WHY COOPER AND O'BRIEN NEVER RETURNED TO IT," *WAR EAGLES* EXPERT DAVE CONOVER MUSES. "THE WILL TO DO IT DIDN'T SEEM TO BE THERE AFTER WORLD WAR II."

Art by Duncan Gleason; from the collection of Dave Conover

The hero of the tale, who had come from the outside world, was another alter ego for Merian Cooper. But while Carl Denham was the movie expedition leader incarnate, this hero—unnamed in Cooper's 1938 outline—recalled Cooper's own reckless youth and his early adventures as an aviator. "Our hero is a young, athletic, daring army flyer. He is considered wild as a March hare, though a great aviator. One day he goes too far on some daring foolish stunt. He is court-martialed and thrown out of the army. He puts a bold face on the matter, but under this careless exterior he really is deeply hurt. Army aviation has been his life. He considers himself disgraced—a man without a country." In "a reckless gesture towards Fate," the hero flies around the world and while crossing over the polar region crashes in the prehistoric valley, where he is rescued from a monster by a group of eagle riders led by a "beautiful, exotic girl."

Cooper envisioned a great "showmanship spectacle scene" that would rival King Kong atop the Empire State Building. After hearing a radio broadcast announcing that a nameless enemy has threatened to destroy New York, the hero mounts White Eagle, his own giant eagle, and leads hundreds of war eagles to the rescue in a clash with enemy bombers over New York. "After the destruction of the enemy airplane fleet, our hero, on his great White Eagle, will land on the Statue of Liberty for his last triumphant farewell to the country of his birth," Cooper outlined. It was a smashing scene, straight out of the triumphant superhero comic-book imagery of the war years to come. Indeed, superhero comic books were emerging as a new medium, with Superman born in 1938, the year this *War Eagles* outline was written.

"I think it has greater box-office appeal than *King Kong,* and will make more money," Cooper declared.[13] Since he planned to make the film in Technicolor and hoped to re-ignite the magic of *Kong,* he called upon Willis O'Brien, the indispensable architect of miracles, to helm an effects effort that would include *Kong* veteran Marcel Delgado. (Schoedsack would not be involved and had gone on to his own projects, including directing the 1940 Paramount horror thriller *Dr. Cyclops.*) By the time Cyril Hume was into a third draft of the script, Delgado was crafting detailed armatures and puppets for the eagles and an allosaurus for the Valley of the Ancients.

As was done in *Kong,* scale miniature stop-motion sets of the mountainous lost land were built, with projection screens placed into the rock formations to integrate live-action footage of Viking warriors. Ray Harryhausen, the ultimate *King Kong* fan, met O'Brien for the first time on *War Eagles* when the master was working on the test-footage animation, and marveled at the production art O'Brien showed him, particularly an oil painting of the war eagles perched on the spikes of the Statue of Liberty's helmet.[14]

A four-hundred-foot stop-motion animation test was produced in 1939 featuring warriors on eagles battling the allosaurus in the Valley of the Ancients. "For O'Brien, the animation was even more painstaking than usual since the war eagles had to be manipulated on invisible, but sturdy wires," wrote publisher and O'Brien biographer Don Shay.[15]

ANOTHER IMAGE FROM *WAR EAGLES*.

Art by Duncan Gleason; from the collection of Dave Conover

"*War Eagles* was to be the next step after *Kong*," notes Dave Conover, programming director for the annual Wonderfest convention held in Louisville, Kentucky, a lifelong fan of animation and special effects, and an expert on the *War Eagles* production. "The scope of the project was tremendous—it was going to be the ultimate pulp adventure movie. The villains were clearly Nazis; 'Nazis' or 'Germany' is never referred to in the script, but there are words like 'Teutonic.' There was a strong science-fiction element because the villains have a ray weapon that knocks out all electrical capabilities—radar and targeting systems, engines—which leaves New York defenseless so they can bomb at will. Cyril Hume developed this idea of a giant zeppelin armed with the ray which, at the end of the battle, is blown up and crashes into New York harbor and short-circuits the ray."[16]

War Eagles clearly foreshadowed America's emerging wartime fears as the Axis powers of Germany, Italy, and Japan began their ominous march of conquest. In 1935 the Italian Fascists invaded Ethiopia, displacing Cooper's powerful acquaintance Haile Selassie; in 1937 the Sino-Japanese war began; in 1938 came Hitler's annexation of Austria. The world war officially began in Europe when Nazi Germany invaded Poland on September 1, 1939.

Because of the impending war, *War Eagles* was shelved. Merian Cooper couldn't wait through the two years it would take to make the picture—he was going back to war![17] Cooper was turning his back on a number of promising projects, including a film about Lawrence of Arabia that Alexander Korda wanted him to produce.[18] "In 1937 I firmly believed the United States would be at war by late 1941," Cooper elaborated years later. "Though I was still in the Air Force Reserve as a Captain, I requested and was reinstated as a pilot. If we went to war, I wished to see combat."[19]

Conover, and a number of fantasy fans and movie memorabilia collectors, lament that lost dream of *War Eagles*. "It could have been the biggest fantasy epic ever made," Conover concludes. "The whole aerial combat sequence at the end would have been unlike anything that had been done. But I think MGM was skittish about the material, such as New York being attacked, and shy about openly using Nazis as villains. When Germany attacked Poland, *War Eagles* ran out of steam. The studio realized reality was outstripping fantasy, and Cooper knew he was going back to war.

"For O'Brien, it was a great missed chance. There's some evidence he was to be the director of the film. MGM production logs of the time for *War Eagles* have spaces for the various production credits. Under 'producer,' Merian C. Cooper is listed, and under 'director' it says 'O'Brien.' It's hard to say whether this refers to the tests or the final film.

"One of the mysteries is why Cooper and O'Brien never returned to it. The will to do it didn't seem to be there after World War II."

Decades later, what survives are scraps of the dream, such as production concept sketches and an estimated four eagle armatures. Conover noted that movie memorabilia collector Bob Burns owns six nitrate frames of the Technicolor test footage. A friend of Burns's had plucked them by chance from a garbage can in 1970, the year MGM auctioned off—or threw away—its nearly half-century storehouse of props, costumes, and memorabilia.

THOUGHTS OF WAR were never far from Merian Cooper's mind. He and Edmund Leonard, his old comrade of the air, had been exchanging notes marking each September 26, the date they'd been shot down in flames. Leonard usually wrote in longhand on the stationery of his long-standing employer, Pacific Mutual Life Insurance Company, while Coop generally sent off a telegram or a note dictated to a secretary. A telegram from Cooper to Leonard, sent in 1932, was typical of the messages, and read: "FOURTEEN YEARS AGO TODAY IN FLAMES BEST REGARDS AS EVER COOP."[20] Leonard took to calling the date "our second birthday" or simply the "anniversary." Over the years, the notes would offer a chance to catch up and exchange family news, particularly as each man reported on their young children growing up.

An uncomfortable reminder of war came in the *Los Angeles Times* headline the morning of November 14, 1938: "CRASH KILLS WORLD WAR ACE." Lost was Cooper's friend and Pioneer colleague L. C. "Denny" Holden, who had been flying from New Jersey to Nashville with another fellow aviator from World War I, Captain W. Krout, when their O-46 army observation plane crashed and burned in the foggy hills near Sparta, Tennessee. The handsome Holden had been a Princeton lad and one of the great combat fliers in World War I; it was said that in one day Holden shot down three enemy aircraft, including two balloons, and his decorations included the Distinguished Service Cross and the title, after the death of flying ace Frank Luke, of "balloon buster."

After the war, Holden studied architecture in Paris and became a leading New York architect, but his lust for adventure led him to fly with the French against the Riffs in Morocco in 1926. Cooper subsequently got his old war comrade into the movies, where Holden's expertise with color photography made him a key player at Pioneer, and he was the color designer for some of the earliest Technicolor productions, including *The Garden of Allah* and *A Star Is Born*.[21] Cooper also selected Holden as co-director with Irving Pichel on *She*.

Only three months before his fatal crash, Holden had written Cooper with the news that he had rejoined his squadron. "It seems strange to be back in the Army," Holden wrote on stationery from his New York office in Rockefeller Plaza, "but I find that I can still fly and get by the physical exams. There is so much to do in these new planes what with radio, adjustable pitch propellers and one thousand and one dials that have to be watched, that there is now very little fun in flying except to get from one place to another in the shortest time possible."[22]

At Miller Field on Staten Island, after a salute was fired and taps sounded, the ashes of the two airmen were scattered beyond Lower New York Bay from one of the planes of Holden's old squadron at they flew over in formation. The memorial program included a poem that must have seemed a rallying cry to Merian Cooper:

> *Unto the flush of dawn and evening I commend*
> *This immaterial self and flamelike part of me—*
> *Unto the azure haze that hangs at the world's end*
> *The sunshine on the hills, the starlight on the sea.*[23]

Cooper, ever aware of matters of personal honor, began divesting himself of anything that smacked of war profiteering, including what he described as his "rather extensive" aviation interests. Cooper recalled that he could have gotten permission from the War Department to hold on to those assets "but I didn't think it was proper."[24]

He would also go to Washington to meet with General of the Army Henry "Hap" Arnold, who would command the Army Air Forces in World War II, to discuss the possibility for a movie popularizing air power. Such a movie would be made, but by Walt Disney, and it would be the 1943 feature *Victory Through Air Power,* based on the bestselling book of the same title and dedicated to Cooper's old commander from the Great War, General Billy Mitchell. Coop himself abandoned his proposed propaganda film project, and for a good reason, as he recalled: "I went back on active duty on June 16, 1941. When the first Air Staff of the Air Forces was formed—well prior to Pearl Harbor—I was appointed Executive Officer of A2 under General [Carl A. "Tooey"] Spaatz when General Spaatz was General Arnold's Chief of Staff."[25]

Coop was stationed in Washington, D.C., and would be ordered on a number of special intelligence missions, including one where he was sent by General Arnold to London, to report back on the bombing siege of the Nazi blitzkrieg.[26]

When the United States finally entered the war, Cooper got the news in a setting straight out of the cavalry films he would produce with John Ford in the postwar years. In fact, Ford was *with* Cooper—the two filmmakers were part of an intimate group lunching at the Virginia home of Rear Admiral Andrew C. Pickens and his wife, Harriette. It was a stately residence dating back to colonial times, with a dining room wall literally marked by history—a carefully preserved musket-ball hole from the Revolutionary War. When the admiral excused himself to take a phone call, then returned to report the news of the attack on Pearl Harbor, his guests solemnly rose.

"It's no use getting excited," the general's wife calmly said. "This is the seventh war that's been announced in this dining room."[27]

STRIKE FORCE

> *Come on, hit us, bring us down if you can—if we are going to die,*
> *O.K., but if this crate falls I'm going to put it nose down, full throt-*
> *tle, and bend it around a street. I'll take plenty of you bastards*
> *with me when I hit. And some airplanes were hit by anti-aircraft,*
> *and some by ground machine guns, and some by Japanese fight-*
> *ers—but none fell, no, not one. So now pour on the coal and let's*
> *get going—again through bursting shells, again through fighters, out*
> *over the bay, out over cruisers, out over coastal batteries blazing*
> *away—out—out—away to sea.*

> —Merian Cooper, "unconventional report"
> on the Doolittle Raid[1]

WITH AMERICA'S DECLARATION OF WAR ON JAPAN, COOPER BECAME A MAJOR player in one of the biggest missions of the young war: the bombing of Japan in response to Pearl Harbor, an operation dubbed "Force AQUILA."

One of his comrades, a man he'd brought onto the mission, was Robert Scott, known as "Scotty," a thirty-four-year-old pilot who had never seen combat but whose flying experience and desire to fight had impressed Coop. Scott would remember the shiver of anticipation when he arrived at MacDill Field near Tampa, Florida, for briefing by Force AQUILA commander Colonel Caleb V. Haynes on what seemed a suicide mission: "This could be a one-way trip," Scott later wrote. "Our pistols had the numbers filed off; no names or organization numbers were on our clothing and equipment; 'no accountability' said the papers that we signed." But Scott also noticed—and took strength from—the sight of the unflappable Cooper, calmly smoking his pipe. He was nearly old enough to be Scott's father, but here he was, volunteering for action.[2]

The road to Force AQUILA actually began, Cooper later detailed, soon after Pearl Harbor when General George Marshall, Admiral Ernest King, and General Arnold were summoned to the White House to discuss the potential for a retaliatory air raid with President Franklin Delano Roosevelt. Commander Low, Admiral King's operation officer, drew up a plan for launching B-25s from aircraft carriers to bomb Tokyo and other cities, an approach General Arnold discussed with Brigadier General James Doolittle. The final plans, which Arnold personally shared with Cooper, would call for a two-pronged operation: Doolittle leading a strike from an aircraft carrier, and C. V. Haynes launching a land-based attack from China.

Cooper reported to Colonel Haynes for attachment to Force AQUILA, which was the code designation for the Tenth Air Force, on March 6, 1942, with orders to organize the mission under Haynes's command. Force AQUILA was at the heart of a number of "China air projects," army historians Charles Romanus and Riley Sunderland note, which were under the overall command of Colonel Clayton L. Bissell.[3]

Cooper was in a "unique spot," he'd recall, as his official title was assistant executive officer and intelligence officer, but he was really deputy commander of Haynes's mission and under dual orders from General Arnold, giving him authority to ask any military commander for any aid and "unlimited power" to go anywhere in the world.[4] Cooper outlined the strategy and events in a letter he wrote in 1971 to Doolittle himself: "Thus, General Arnold had two strings in his bow: one, the B-25s from the carrier . . . the other, the B-17s from East China commanded by C. V. Haynes, with me actually running it. All were sure that if one failed, the other would get through to bomb Japan. It was just a question of who would get there first.

". . . Every member of the Haynes mission was a volunteer, only being told that they had a dangerous assignment—nothing more. C.V. and I were the only men on the mission who knew that we were ordered to bomb Japan. I alone knew our mission depended on whether you, or our mission, got there first."[5]

Colonel (later Major General) Caleb V. Haynes was once described by General Claire Chennault as a pilot who "looked like a gorilla and flew like an angel."[6] Haynes had handled some of the biggest planes in the air, including the first B-17s, and had flown experimental long-range heavy bombers and some of the first survey flights of worldwide air routes for the

Air Transport Command, the aerial arm of the wartime supply effort. Cooper simply described Haynes as "the best big ship pilot in the Army Air Corps" to head "this long shot raid."[7]

Ironically, because Robert Scott outranked Merian—he was a full colonel to Coop's new rank as lieutenant colonel—he became Haynes's executive, leaving Cooper as assistant; but Coop would always be number one in Scotty's book. Before the war, the tall, handsome Georgian had become bored with flying training missions. But his thirty-fourth birthday was coming, and his dream of flying combat seemed out of reach—until he attended a party at Cooper's Beverly Hills home around April 1941.

Cooper was the charismatic center of the party, and Scott learned of his host's wartime exploits and how he'd refused to profit from the coming war by divesting himself of any potentially compromising financial interests. Scott was fascinated, and drawn to the middle-aged, slightly stooped figure who seemed to use his pipe like a stage prop as he stuffed the bowl with tobacco and paused, pondering a question about Germany's Luftwaffe. Later, Scott and Cooper chatted and Scott impressed his host, despite the fact that he had never experienced combat.[8]

Merian Cooper personally brought up Scott's case with Haynes, and it was with surprise and delight that Scott found himself ordered to report to the location where Force AQUILA would embark on their mission. There he found Cooper, now wearing the silver leaves of a lieutenant colonel. Scott noticed that Coop looked at least ten years younger than when he had last seen him in Beverly Hills, and was brimming with enthusiasm as he filled Scotty in on the particulars of his planning for what seemed to him "the greatest mission in the world."[9]

The flying arsenal for Force AQUILA consisted of one B-24, seven B-17s, and nine C-47s. It was going to be an adventure just getting the force as far as India. Nobody except Haynes had flown even the first part of the route, which set off by way of Brazil, flew over the South Atlantic to Africa, crossed Sudan to Arabia, and continued on to Karachi, India, where they would await the green light for China. It was a remarkable flight and a tribute to Haynes's leadership and selection of pilots, Cooper noted, that the entire task force arrived safely in Karachi.

Cooper, with his secret knowledge of Doolittle's parallel mission, hoped they would be the first to bomb Japan, and he drove the strike force hard. "C. V. Haynes used to grumble at me and say: 'My God, Coop, why do you have to push everybody day and night?' " Cooper wrote Doolittle. "I was absolutely under orders not to tell Haynes about your mission until we actually got to China. . . . I knew—if the Navy carriers were already at sea—that there was a single code word that would be sent to us in India, on our way to China, which would call off our mission."[10]

Upon landing in Karachi, Cooper stayed with the planes while Haynes flew to New Delhi, where he had been ordered to report to Major General Lewis H. Brereton upon his arrival and to present instructions about keeping the supply route open between India and China in preparation for offensive missions in the China theater. While Cooper awaited Haynes's return he ordered guards armed with .45s to shoot anyone who tried boarding the waiting planes. Three days later, Haynes returned from Delhi and Cooper got the secret code: The navy carriers were already at sea and Force AQUILA had been called off.

The task force was ordered to turn its B-17s and the B-24 over to General Brereton, plus whatever crew he needed. "Haynes and Scott and I and the C-47s were ordered up to Northern Assam to open up a flying route to India," Coop recounted to Doolittle. "We did. It was afterwards called 'The Hump.' "

Doolittle did the honors in the first bombing strike against Japan. In his letter to Doolittle—whose name became forever synonymous with the mission known as the Doolittle Raid—Coop couldn't resist adding a competitive note: "Frankly, I wanted to beat you out and bomb Japan first."[11]

SOON AFTER THE Doolittle Raid, Cooper found himself sitting in the headquarters of the American army in China, looking into the eyes of General Doolittle. He later wrote down his immediate impressions of the man who had just returned from a virtual suicide mission.

"This is what General Doolittle—a sturdy, compact little man, with eyes flashing, every moment radiating energy and strength, a hard-bitten dangerous look to him under a laughing exterior, dressed in torn, muddy wool shirt and trousers, no mark of rank on his shoulders—this is what he told me as he sat astride a broken-down old chair in a bare, white-washed walled mosquito and fly-specked bedroom in the queer ramshackled old house which climbs in broken parts up the side of a hill in Chungking. . . . He had just been flown back that night with some of his men—by an American Army transport pilot who risked his neck to do it—from having been as near death in as many ways as a man can crowd in a few days, yet I have never seen a man more alive."

Cooper himself was interviewing Doolittle and his men about their mission, which, because Japanese patrol boats had been detected, launched prematurely from the deck of the aircraft carrier *Hornet* the dawn of April 18, 1942. Cooper made his ten-page, typed document available to the War Department's public relations branch, and his report served notice in its opening sentence: "An unconventional report of an unconventional mission." Cooper's report was written in a hard-boiled style jangling with a tough-guy stoicism straight out of a James Cagney movie—as produced by Merian Cooper, of course.[12]

"This is the account of how eighty Americans bombed Japan," Coop wrote. The Doolittle Raid had begun as a "suicide take-off ... from the deck of a carrier in a rolling sea." They wouldn't have fuel enough for any kind of return—"every man *was sure* he was going to die"—but they'd made it to Japan, flying so low they were practically scraping the treetops, until they were over the roofs of Tokyo. The only thing off-limits was the Imperial Palace, but everywhere else it was bombs away: "Factories exploding a thousand feet high, gas and oil plants flaming, Tokyo afire, Nagoya afire then down low again, plenty low, machine guns pouring lead into soldiers."

Soon the gas gauges were running low and the planes turned toward China with night coming down and the black sky full of rain and only the sea below. "Then every aircraft captain had to make the decision—and these were his only choices—a wheels-up night descent on that wind-swept sea; or bailing out into the blackness of the night over the wild terrain of Eastern China, surely close to the Japanese lines, perhaps within the Japanese lines," Cooper wrote. "The game was up—for in a few minutes the gas would be finished."

Cooper typified the courage of Doolittle's raiders in the person of Gunnery Sergeant Edward Horton, who had been the first to parachute from his plane over a rough, mountainous area. The view outside the window had been blackness lashed with rain when pilot Lieutenant Joyce called the bail-out order and added: "O.K. fellow, I'll see you in Chuchow. Let me know when you're ready, Horton." Horton had said he was ready, the pilot wished him good luck, and with a final "thanks for a swell ride," Horton stepped out into the void.

Cooper described that night as one that would live among the traditions of the native people, as abandoned planes crashed and burned along the mountainsides and the white bloom of parachutes floated down like ghosts out of the storm clouds. The next morning, for more than a hundred miles around, strange white men trudged into villages muttering in Chinese the words they'd learned by heart: "I am an American." "And they took those strange men—who had landed bruised and shaken among the mountain crags, and who had shivered the cold and rainy night through, wrapped only in their thin, silk parachutes—took them into their homes and fed them, and then guided them onwards, for the word had gone swiftly by mouth to mouth from village to village, 'These men are friends. Bring them to Chuchow.' These simple Chinese peasants will tell [in years to come] of how the Japanese, with impotent rage, flew over Chuchow, day after day, seeking out the Americans with bombs, until American Army transport planes slipped in between bombing raids and plucked them from death's last chance at them and flew them to Chungking and safety."

Before Doolittle departed Chungking for the United States, he discussed the mission with Cooper, revealing that a few of his pilots had been captured in China by the Japanese. He even gave Cooper a map he had marked up with the potential location of his lost crews.

"General Bissell flew back from East China with you, and I can remember you well—open neck, unshaved, dirty clothes, but still full of fire," Cooper later wrote. "You were ordered to fly back immediately to the United States and did so. I told you I would do the best I could for all your men. I did."[13]

In a humorous postscript to a letter to Dorothy Jordan, Doolittle mentioned the sum Cooper had lent him to help him make the journey home. "I am enclosing a personal check for $100 to cover the loan which Merian kindly made me in Chungking," Doolittle wrote from the War Department in Washington. "Had it not been for his kindness—and affluence, I would have had the Devil's own time getting home. As it was, I arrived just about destitute."[14]

Cooper had received full intelligence on the missing raiders from Tai Li, the head of the secret police for embattled Nationalist leader Generalissimo Chiang Kai-shek. He immediately went to Clayton Bissell, who would soon be promoted to brigadier general and air officer in China under General Joseph W. Stilwell. Cooper presented Bissell with an audacious plan: He would *personally* rescue the captured airmen. He declared that he would either return with the freed raiders or not return at all—if Cooper was trapped this would be a one-way trip, and he'd choose death over capture and torture.[15]

Bissell approved Cooper's plan, which was to infiltrate enemy territory in disguise, with the help of two Chinese secret service agents from the generalissimo's police force who were conversant in English. Cooper's travels in Abyssinia, Persia, Siam, and elsewhere had taught him that gold, not paper money, was of universal appeal when it came to bribes or buying information, so he asked for—and Bissell agreed to supply him with—$10,000 in gold coins. Cooper also stated that he would refuse any decoration or award in the aftermath of the mission so that "there be no question of personal aggrandizement."[16]

The morning of Cooper's mission he went into Bissell's office to get the gold and, inexplicably, Bissell did an about-face: The rescue mission was off. Cooper was ordered to remain in Chungking and work with Bissell as a debriefing officer for the Doolittle crews. Cooper was "pretty broken up" over the decision and wasn't informed why his secret mission had been canceled. By December 1942, Coop recalled, he was still pressing his plan at the highest levels in Washington, including a personal appeal to U.S. Army Chief of Staff General George Marshall, who turned him down cold.[17]

Of the captured men, three were ultimately executed after trial, and one died in prison. In the brutal, three-month campaign of retribution for Doolittle's raid, Japanese forces burned Chinese villages to the ground and slaughtered their inhabitants. Anyone suspected of helping Doolittle's pilots was exterminated, including villagers who'd been filling in bomb craters on the runways used by General Claire Chennault's Flying Tigers. But despite the terrible price, the Chinese kept up their efforts to aid American airmen in Japanese-occupied territory.[18]

COOPER WAS ATTACHED to duty with Haynes's Assam-Burma-China (ABC) Ferrying Command effective on April 17, 1942.[19] On April 22, Colonel Haynes arrived at Dinjan with nineteen officers and twenty-two enlisted men from the aborted Force AQUILA, including Robert Scott, whose combat dreams now turned to joining General Chennault's Flying Tigers, which had been fighting the Japanese in China months before Pearl Harbor.

But the new challenges in the Hump of the Himalayas were formidable, including ferrying munitions and supplies into Burma and transporting soldiers and evacuating civilians.[20] The ABC made daily round-trips to far-flung airdromes, and the small force of officers and enlisted men worked tough, sixteen- to twenty-hour days.[21] The aerial supply and transport missions were always at risk from Japanese fighters, but the ultimate danger was the twenty-thousand-foot-high Himalayan range—a route that provided Coop with an eagle's-eye view of the Brahmaputra he'd once dreamed of exploring. The Hump required skill and steely nerves to navigate, for this was a rarefied space where ice could form on the wings, literally changing the shape of the wing and compromising the aerodynamics that keeps the plane up, or spread an icy, obscuring crust over windows. Black clouds often hid the ancient mountain walls, which the transports used as cover to escape the Japanese fighters.

Scott would recall takeoffs from Dinjan and the dangerous, five-hundred-mile flights to Kunming. They would skirt the jagged Himalayas, the treacherous mountains often shrouded in black, stormy clouds. The mists would part, revealing craggy peaks and primordial jungles below. "We'd find ourselves wishing for the clouds to materialize and blot out the hazardous peaks," Scott recalled. "... Whenever I would mention them to Cooper, he'd yell at me, 'Want to live forever, Scotty?... You were afraid the war would be over before you could get here. You're closer to the AVG [American Volunteer Group, known as the "Flying Tigers"] and Chennault today than you've ever been. Chin up, boy! Doesn't that give you a charge?' "[22]

During an April 26 mission to Lashio, Burma, to deliver ammunition and gasoline to Chennault's American Volunteer Group and the Chinese army, Coop and Scott were flying together, with Scott manning a machine gun that he used to keep an enemy fighter at bay. Colonel Haynes was heading the mission, which Cooper had volunteered for in his official capacity as intelligence officer and to perform extra duty as radioman. After eluding the Japanese fighter, they landed at Lashio, where an air-raid alert had scattered the frightened native labor from the airfield. While under threat of an enemy air strike, Cooper helped unload the planes. The

Haynes transport mission, Scott later noted, was "the last Allied Airplane to land at that station before its capture by the enemy."[23]

A similar scenario played out the following dawn when Cooper volunteered to ride a lead plane stocked with ammunition and piloted by Captain Bert M. Carleton. This was a mission bound from Dinjan to the AVG in Loiwing that included three other planes bearing aviation gasoline. First Lieutenant Robert L. Hartzell later reported that they were about twenty flying minutes from their destination when they received radio warning from Loiwing that enemy aircraft were in their area. The pilots hadn't yet encountered air opposition, and they were uncertain what to do: If they continued they would risk death, and if they aborted the mission the vital supplies wouldn't be delivered.

Cooper, as senior air officer, assumed command and ordered the pilots to land at Myitkyina, in northern Burma, roughly halfway to their destination. Once they were safely on the ground, he supervised and assisted in unloading the gasoline planes. The AVG were out of .50-caliber ammunition, and since that was the most vital need, Cooper decided to personally take the lead plane on to Loiwing. He asked Carleton to fly with him.

He waited for a chance to lift off and had the men prepared to disperse the other three planes in case of an enemy attack. After a tense fifty minutes, they received a radio report that the enemy had split off and it was safe for all four planes to continue to China. The ships were reloaded and continued on their mission. As with the Lashio mission, when they reached their destination there was another air-raid warning and the native labor had fled. "When we landed at Loiwing," Carleton recalled, "Colonel Cooper had all ships unloaded as quickly as possible. The other three took off immediately. He held me on the ground to collect and evacuate women and children at Loiwing to Kunming."

Cooper concluded that the Japanese had a shortwave radio station overlooking the field at Myitkyina whose personnel had called back the attack planes, because they wouldn't have time to catch the supply planes on the ground, which had been swiftly unloaded. His suspicions seemed confirmed the next day when other transports from Dinjan that didn't take evasive precautions were hit at Loiwing by Japanese fighters. General Haynes notified the British, who failed to act on the warning; two British transports were destroyed by Japanese aircraft while on the ground at Myitkyina.

Robert L. Scott, as operations officer of the Assam-Burma-China Ferrying Command, wrote a recommendation that Cooper be awarded the Distinguished Flying Cross or the Silver Star for having brought the vital cargo to Loiwing. "His own transport, in constant danger of bombing, he held on the field for two hours until he could carry out the request to load it with women and children for evacuation to China," Scott explained. "His action was above the call of duty as he started the flight as a passenger and senior air corps officer. He assumed command in a critical situation and with a display of cool gallantry saved the four transports loaded with [supplies]. Not content with this act, he looked first to the security of the three accompanying planes and then loaded his own during an air raid alert and evacuated fifty women and children to China."[24]

IN FEBRUARY 1942, General Joseph Stilwell was appointed head of the military mission in China, as well as being named Allied chief of staff to Chiang Kai-shek. In March, Stilwell was in Burma when the Japanese forced his dramatic foot journey with a group of refugees over the mountains to India. Haynes and Scott had earlier landed at Stilwell's embattled headquarters when Japanese forces were within twenty miles, and the sound of their artillery boomed like thunder. They had orders to evacuate Stilwell, but he rebuffed them, insisting on walking out. "The Japanese were fast over-running Burma," Cooper recalled. "I was in one of the last planes evacuating personnel out of Myitkyina and Lashio, before the Japanese captured them. . . . I reported to Chungking, on a second set of orders from General Arnold, then volunteered to join General Chennault when he inducted the A.V.G. into the American Air Corps on July 4, 1942. He made me his Chief of Staff."[25]

Cooper, Scott, and Haynes all threw in on the side of Chennault and his Flying Tigers. When Coop joined the Tigers, arriving at the city and key eastern airfield of Kweilin, he strode in like a man living his own movie, as Chennault himself later recalled for Dorothy Jordan: "His first remark upon landing at Kweilin the first time was, 'A million dollar background.' "[26]

THE FLYING TIGER

> *Cooper and Chennault made a perfect team.... Cooper was probably closer to Chennault than any other man out there. He was completely honest, meticulously loyal, and just about the bravest man I had ever known. He was a staunch pillar upon which the Old Man could lean. His keen analytical mind and his planning knowledge of higher echelons eased many of the problems that were trying the patience of Chennault.*
>
> —Colonel Robert Scott[1]

> GENERAL CHENNAULT: *My ideas about fighting . . . was never give the enemy a chance and kill him as quick as you could.*
>
> INTERVIEWER: *What do you suppose makes a quality like that in a man, General? Early life?*
>
> CHENNAULT: *I haven't the slightest damn idea what makes it in a man. You either have it or you don't have it.*
>
> —Interview with General Claire Chennault[2]

To WARTIME MOVIEGOERS IN 1942, PEARL HARBOR WAS A FRESH AND OPEN wound. The tragedy gave built-in perspective to *Flying Tigers*, a drama set in the days before the Japanese raid and featuring John Wayne, three years removed from the dusty trails of *Stagecoach*, as the leader of a daring squadron of American flyboys battling Japan in the China skies.

It was a drama based on the real mercenaries flying and fighting on behalf of Chiang Kai-shek's government for a paycheck and the bonus awarded for confirmed enemy kills. The American Volunteer Group, popularly known as the Flying Tigers, embodied resourcefulness and fearlessness, had a reputation for *not* going "by the book," and although outmanned and outgunned had been delivering heavy losses to the enemy, their ferocity

CHENNAULT AND HIS FLYING TIGERS.

Cooper Papers, BYU

heralded by the bared shark fangs painted on the noses of their P-40 Toma-
hawk fighters. This fearsome imagery had been inspired by a picture in *India
Illustrated Weekly* of an RAF squadron in the Libyan desert. It would always
mystify Chennault how his squad of shark-fanged P-40 fliers got the nickname "Flying Tigers."[3]

Claire Chennault was the man who'd convinced Chiang Kai-shek's Nationalist government to allow paid American volunteers to join China's air
war against the Japanese invaders. He led the Tigers, taught fighting techniques, and had laid out the strategy that was dealing heavy losses to the
enemy. A retired U.S. Army Air Corps officer who had been in ill health

**THE RUGGED VISAGE OF
GENERAL CLAIRE
CHENNAULT, LEADER OF
THE FLYING TIGERS.**
Cooper Papers, BYU

only a few years before, Chennault was as tough as a mile of country road
and as rough-hewn as the wilderness of northeastern Louisiana, which he
had explored as a boy, crossing the cleared cotton fields to strike out into
the oak woods and swamps. That wild world of wolves and bear, deer and
wild game had become a part of him. Even when he was commanding
deadly missions in China, he would recall the seasons of the wilderness,
could almost hear a big buck deer crashing through the canebrake.[4]

General Chennault's "Huckleberry Finn" boyhood, as Merian Cooper
would later characterize it, made him physically fit, sharpened his mental
faculties, and inculcated a tenacious independence that made him a controversial figure in the straitlaced structure of military high command.
Chennault became a student of war, poring over books describing ancient
battles in Rome and Carthage and Greece, marveling at accounts of ar-

mored warriors and charging elephants and warships burning at sea. He became a pilot during World War I and thereafter chief of U.S. Army Air Corps fighter training. Always an enthusiastic advocate for air power, he had a short fuse when it came to a "penny-wise, pound foolish type of thinking."[5]

By the winter of 1937, hearing problems had left him in an unhappy retirement. His troubled mind conjured a metaphor from those boyhood days when he'd occasionally see the swirling eddies of the Mississippi smash steamboats to kindling or drag down mighty cypress trees. The eddies of life had dragged down many a boyhood friend: river gamblers shot in arguments, swampland inhabitants felled by yellow fever, farmers who failed to scratch out a living farming cotton in a land where it was almost impossible to keep the wilderness at bay. Now the vortex of life seemed about to take *him* down.

It was during this period of soul searching that he began getting letters from friends in China reporting on the Japanese invasion and the seemingly inevitable prospect that the United States was heading for a face-off with Japan for control of the Pacific. Roy Holbrook, now an adviser to the Central Trust Company of China and a confidant of Chiang Kai-shek's government, offered Chennault the chance to train Chinese air force pilots. Chennault, having taken a long look at the swirling eddies of life, was bound from San Francisco to China on May 1, 1937.

Chennault would travel to Yunnan, a province in southern China he would later recall as "a slice of the medieval world nestling in the heart of Asia." It was a dreamlike land of mile-high plateaus and jade-green lakes, surrounded by the snowy peaks that climbed into the world's mightiest mountain ranges and unmarked frontiers leading to Tibet, India, and Burma. Centuries before, Marco Polo had once traveled the old Jade Road through Yunnan; down in its plains, the armored elephants of Burmese kings had battled Kublai Khan's mounted archers. Chennault settled in the province's capital city of Kunming in the summer of 1938. Until the end of World War II, Kunming would be his main base of operations and the nearest thing to home. Then, encouraged by Madame Chiang Kaishek, he began the formidable task of bringing American know-how to the disorganized Chinese air force.

By November 1940, he was back in the States, recruiting American pilots for the American Volunteer Group.[6]

With America's official declaration of war, the AVG was disbanded, and on July 4, 1942, the China Air Task Force (CATF) begun. It later became known as the U.S. Fourteenth Air Force, from March 1943. Chennault's first chief of staff, Merian C. Cooper, was his combative match and shared his vision of airpower—and that short fuse for clueless superiors.[7] Chennault described Cooper as "a character straight from the Hollywood movies he once directed," and in his autobiography related the arrival of his soon-to-be chief of staff: "One day he appeared in the A.V.G. hostel at Peishiyi carrying his bedroll and announced that he was tired of squatting in Stilwell's Chungking headquarters and wanted a job with an outfit that was fighting.

"With his shirttails generally flapping in the breeze, a tousled fringe of hair wreathing his bald spot, a mantle of pipe ashes over his uniform and sagging pants, Cooper would never have passed muster at a West Point class reunion but he was a brilliant tactician and a prodigious worker. He engineered some of the most successful C.A.T.F. forays."[8]

Years later, Cooper would congratulate his old commander on his book, adding, "Of course, I liked what you said in it about me, too. I have long harbored the suspicion that I would not be the most dashing figure at a West Point reunion and I'm not even sure that I'd want to be."[9]

WHEN THE CATF was born on July 4, the unit was made a component of the Tenth Air Force, the overall air unit for the China-Burma-India theater. Although General Marshall had reportedly promised Chiang Kai-shek that Chennault would be the ranking air commander in China, the leader of the Flying Tigers would find himself under the command of then Colonel Clayton L. Bissell. Chennault would trace the bad blood between the two back to 1931, when he was studying at the Army Air Corps tactical school at Langley Field, Virginia. Bissell, a flying ace from World War I and an instructor at the tactical school, was teaching fighter plane tactics straight out of 1918 and the western front, "dawn-patrol and dogfight tactics," as Chennault termed them, which he felt were hopelessly inadequate against modern bombers. In fact, Chennault would later write with disdain that Bissell had even abandoned the idea that fighter planes could bring down bombers.

Bissell, who was in command of the China air projects and had been in

China for the Doolittle Raid, had botched the job, Chennault believed, only reinforcing his low opinion of the man. According to Chennault, Bissell had been so secretive he hadn't even shared details of Doolittle's mission with him and his Flying Tigers. If he had, Chenanult felt, a single AVG ground radio station could have helped guide the American bombers to friendly fields. As it was, the raiders had had to bail out in the dark and the unknown, and some, including Doolittle himself, had landed so near enemy lines they were lucky to avoid capture. Chennault recalled the crew that had even passed up a friendly field and crash-landed in Japanese territory, where they had been taken prisoner, with three of those crewmen eventually executed in Shanghai. "My bitterness over that bit of bungling has not eased with the passing years," Chenanult wrote in 1949.

Thus, Chennault couldn't have been pleased with the way a man he despised was elevated to a superior position of command.

"Chennault was promoted to brigadier general," historian Barbara Tuchman wrote, "but Bissell, his *bête noir,* was promoted a day earlier and named air commander of the theater."

In the shadowy atmosphere of China intrigues, Chiang Kai-shek was left in the dark on the issue, while Chennault was furious at what he felt was a broken promise. But General Joseph Stilwell, who oversaw U.S. and Chinese forces in the China-Burma-India theater, had insisted to General Hap Arnold that Bissell be allowed to outrank Chennault, and Arnold had agreed.[10]

Despite his successes and popularity with the men who bravely fought under him, Claire Chennault was considered a maverick to many officers, a "black sheep" with a habit of playing by his own rules—not the recommended path for military advancement. In China, Chennault would place himself in furious opposition to General Joseph Stilwell, who was his cantankerous match; Stilwell's nickname was "Vinegar Joe." It was a complex situation, from bad blood between Chennault and Bissell to mistrust of Chennault's maverick ways, particularly his supreme belief in airpower. A 1943 *Time* magazine cover article on General Chennault—which proclaimed him "as American as a baseball bat"—summed up the situation: "[Chennault] is essentially a man of offense, and in China, Allied strategy dictates a mission of defense. His job is to give the Chinese armies air support, to bomb strategic points whenever possible and to keep nibbling at Japanese air strength."[11]

Chennault didn't want to nibble; he wanted to *feast* on the enemy. As a leader of a rough-and-tumble mercenary force in pre–Pearl Harbor China, he'd developed a feel for the country and a fondness for its people. As a leader who had enjoyed the freedom of taking it to the enemy without restraint, he chafed at the leash.

Cooper had arrived in the teeth of this political skirmish. Although he would credit General Bissell for doing "a pretty good job," Cooper was on the outs with Bissell from the moment he signed up with the Flying Tigers, as he later told Robert Scott: "Bissell treated me swell when he thought I was a big shot, but when on my own volition—as my orders were open—I went over and joined General Chennault before the AVG disbanded, Bissell was off of me like a ton of bricks."[12]

Despite being absorbed into the army structure and now considered part of the team, Chennault and his men retained an us-against-the-world swagger. They needed it. One of the sore points, they felt, was that they were being starved of the resources they needed to fight the war. It had been rough getting the China Air Task Force up and functioning in the midst of what Chennault remembered as "the gloomy summer of 1942," a time during which the outfit "had to fight, scream, and scrape for every man, plane, spark plug, and gallon of gas." The fleet at Chennault's command included fifty-one battered P-40 Tomahawks from the AVG campaigns, only twenty-nine of which were flyable and all of which would have likely been consigned to the scrap heap back home. Mechanics worked around the clock to keep them operational, with no spare parts and only a few hand tools, suffering buzzing, biting insects while they toiled at night by the light of smoky kerosene lamps or handheld flashlights. Chennault was also saddled with the greenest recruits and he would recall that the first army pilots he got in China matched the sorry condition of his planes.[13]

There were high points, though, and one of them was the formation of the 23rd Fighter Group, heralded by the long-awaited command for Robert Scott. Chennault himself ushered the unsuspecting Scott into the tile-roofed headquarters in Kunming, a building pockmarked with shrapnel hits and bomb damage. Cooper, General Stilwell, and Generalissimo Chiang Kai-shek were among the group who waited to greet Scott. After introductions, an interpreter for the generalissimo asked Scott if he was prepared to take command of the Flying Tigers of the 23rd Fighter Group.

Scott, taken by surprise, looked over at Cooper, who was smiling to himself as he pressed his thumb over the glowing tobacco in his pipe. Though flustered, Scott instantly accepted. He'd recall that on June 30, only the second day of his command, a shortwave radio broadcast from Imperial Japan included a propaganda message from Tokyo Rose that announced that the "American bandits" known as the Flying Tigers were terminating their bloody contracts for green American kids "led by a Hollywood playboy named Colonel Scott."[14]

Colonel Cooper himself proved again to be a godsend. Given the hardscrabble conditions, what could be better than a combat veteran and wilderness explorer whose mind was hardwired to study conditions in the field and adapt to new situations? He made his mark with energy and devotion, inspiring the greenest young pilots as they faced deadly, daunting odds. "When planning a mission for the C.A.T.F., Cooper worked around the clock until every detail was satisfactory and then rode the nose of the lead bomber peering over the bombardier's shoulder at the target," Chennault recalled.[15]

Coop took a cue from Chennault himself, a master strategist who would spend many a long night poring over maps and contemplating how to strike the numerically superior Japanese forces. Chennault made himself a friend of adversity and used aerial guerrilla warfare tactics, keeping the enemy off balance with surprise hit-and-run attacks aimed at widely disparate targets. Being mobile and using a network of airfields allowed them to stay on the offense as well as spread out the enemy, keeping them from delivering a concentrated, lethal blow.[16]

Chennault's complex chain of airfields linked the bases of Hengyang, Paoting, and Lingling and the airdromes of Hengyang, Ch'ing-chiang, and Kweilin. "By using that large number of airfields, the Japanese were never able to find us on any airfield," Chennault wrote.[17]

They blended into the countryside and turned even the most inhospitable conditions to their advantage. One strategic airfield in the south, at Kweilin, for example, was tucked away in a valley among rice paddies, surrounded by black limestone peaks with mountain caves serving as headquarters and bomb shelters. These caves offered the added bonus of providing cool refuge from the summer's heat and humidity.[18]

Chennault taught discipline and teamwork and led by example, flying many missions himself.[19] And the Flying Tigers fought like hell. One trademark incident came the moonlit night of July 29, 1942, when they flew to defend their key airfield in Hengyang. They met Japanese bombers across the Siang River, and Johnny Alison—a wizard at flying a P-40—took on the lead enemy bomber and fired away until he'd crippled his target, even as enemy fire ripped his own plane and he went down, a streak of flame his comrades saw plummeting toward the river.

Alison crash-landed in the river but survived, suffering a head wound that was tended at a nearby Catholic mission. Alison was convalescing there when, the next morning, he watched another battle take place over the embattled airfield—an enraged David "Tex" Hill was leading ten Tigers in P-40 Tomahawks against thirty-five Japanese Oscars, fighting to avenge what he thought was Alison's death. In that battle, Tex focused on the formation leader and, in a deadly game of aerial chicken, accelerated for a head-on collision. Both pilots kept firing away as they maintained a crash course, closing at six hundred miles an hour. Chennault, watching from the ground, was reminded of a pair of western gunmen shooting it out on a frontier main street, neither giving an inch—until the Japanese pilot blinked first, dropping into a steep dive as Tex's plane practically grazed his cockpit.

But the Oscar was seemingly damaged and trailing smoke, and after circling the field, the Japanese pilot made what seemed a suicide move: He suddenly went into a vertical dive and crashed in flames into a row of decoy bamboo P-40s parked on the airfield. Tex landed and swaggered over to the smoldering plane. The dismembered body of the pilot, along with his samurai sword, had been thrown from the wreckage. Tex poked the toe of his cowboy boot at the blackened, severed head.

" 'You tried to kill me, you little bastard,' " Tex drawled coolly. " 'Two can play at that game.' "[20]

BY LATE SEPTEMBER 1942, C. V. Haynes was off to India on a new assignment and wrote a fond letter from Kunming, which he sent to Cooper at Peishiyi, China. "Will be over from time to time when the planes are ready and a nice juicy target is ripe," he declared. "Will see you then and when you come to India will have a place for you."[21]

But October 1942 was to be the turning point for Coop in China. Early that month, Cooper's intelligence confirmed Chennault's estimate that

Japan was planning to attack the western terminus of the CATF supply route in Dinjan area. On October 25–26, with Chennault away from Kunming headquarters, the enemy struck, unleashing two coordinated attacks on Dinjan and Kunming. Cooper, on his own initiative, directed a successful defense of Kunming that intercepted and turned back two large enemy formations one hundred miles from the base.[22]

Meanwhile, the other war—the political war—had been heating up behind the scenes. Chennault and Chiang Kai-shek had ultimate faith in offensive airpower and were committed to strengthening the aerial supply route over the Hump, but the military command wanted to reopen the Burma Road and oppose the enemy with land-based strategies. Chennault and Cooper also felt that the Communists in China posed a tremendous threat and that they would make their move in a postwar power struggle. It didn't help Chennault or Cooper's cause that many, including General Stilwell, were distrustful of Chiang Kai-shek's government. Stilwell even feared that the United States had been "forced into partnership with a gang of fascists under a one-party government similar in many respects to our German enemy."[23]

John Alison recalled that the enmity between the Chennault and Stilwell camps was so bitter that the old AVG boys taught Chinese coolies who unloaded supplies along the Hump the English phrase "Piss on Bissell." The Chinese took the mysterious words as a special American salutation, and the Flying Tigers hoped that one day the loathed Bissell would be so greeted by the Chinese.[24]

Cooper himself had the audacity to draw up his own plan for winning the war in Asia. Alison, who would become a brigadier general, later explained that Cooper's plan was to take Hong Kong with a coordinated attack from air, land, and sea that would begin with a bastion formed across the Japanese supply line, using several thousand paratroopers dropped at strategic points on land while navy submarines set up a blockade.

"[Cooper] felt a bold stroke like this would wrest Hongkong from the Japanese and severely limit their capability to fight a war because it would prevent them from supplying the homeland. He felt that under the shield of U.S. airpower and with U.S. naval support we could not only take Hongkong, but we could hold it. So this was the difference in military philosophy between Stilwell on the one side, and Chennault and Cooper on the other." Alison noted that Chennault went so far as to fly to Washington to gain support for "Cooper's plan of a vertical envelopment of Hongkong," but nothing came of it. Stilwell retained General Marshall's confidence.[25]

Colonel Cooper finally wrote a letter to a friend from his World War I days, Major General William J. "Wild Bill" Donovan, chief of the Office of Strategic Services (the OSS was the forerunner of the CIA). Robert Scott characterized the letter as Coop "letting his hair down about the restrictions placed on the Old Man."[26] Cooper's letter made the rounds in Washington, and raised eyebrows and blood pressures. "Cooper was no diplomat," Chennault later wrote, with classic understatement. "He made no secret of his contempt for the Stilwell-Bissell policy of timid defense in India and complete neglect of the strategic possibilities of China. It wasn't long before Bissell was suggesting Cooper's removal on grounds of ill health and offering a West Pointer in exchange."[27]

The simmering frustration finally boiled over, and Cooper huddled with Chennault to outline a strategy that would finally make good on the aborted promise of Force AQUILA, and hit Japan from China. The two men spent a long, fevered night crafting a letter historian Barbara Tuchman calls "one of the extraordinary documents of the war . . . the self-annunciation of a military messiah."[28]

THE CHENNAULT LETTER, dated October 8, 1942, proposed a bold strike to accomplish Japan's downfall within six months, a year at the outset. The general declared that a force of 105 modern fighter planes, 30 medium bombers, and 12 heavy bombers could deliver the knockout blow. The plan included a dedicated effort to increase the aerial supply line between India and China, with Cooper's hand evident in an assertion that this aerial route would be "child's play" compared to the difficulties Pan American Airways had faced in establishing its South American and transoceanic routes.

Chennault would follow the example of Scipio Africanus's defense of Rome when Hannibal was at its gates and Scipio struck at Carthage, forcing Hannibal's forces to defend a new front. He proposed striking Japan's supply lines in the southwest Pacific and hitting Tokyo as well. By forcing the enemy to fight on two fronts, the plan would stretch the limited capacity of the Japanese air force, the letter reasoned. By choking off the supply line and hitting industrial centers in Tokyo, Kobe, Osaka, and other cities, the Chinese army could assert itself while American naval forces could close in on Japan and allow General Douglas MacArthur to advance from his stronghold in Australia.

Japan would fall, and America would win the gratitude of China in the postwar world. Chennault concluded that it was essential that he be given "complete freedom of fighting action" and that he be the personal representative dealing with the generalissimo.[29]

The letter was addressed to "Mr. Wendell Willkie, Special Representative of the President," and it would be hand delivered. The former Repub-

COLONEL COOPER (LEFT) AND GENERAL CHENNAULT INSPECT A
CAMOUFLAGED PLANE. THE DYSENTERY THAT AFFLICTED COOPER
THROUGHOUT THE WAR IS EVIDENT IN HIS GAUNT FEATURES.

Cooper Papers, BYU

lican presidential nominee was now FDR's personal emissary, and during an October tour he met with Chennault for two hours and left with the letter on October 11. Robert Scott later wrote that Willkie's visit had been precipitated by Cooper's earlier letter to Bill Donovan: "Conjecture is that it was through Cooper's letter that Wendell Willkie knew what to investigate most carefully when he came to China.... No sooner did Willkie reach Chungking than he telephoned CATF headquarters at Peishiyi with the request that he visit and chat confidentially with the commander [Chennault]."[30]

Finally the letter was delivered to the president, who forwarded it to the War Department, "where it created a major scandal," Chennault noted.[31]

DESPITE THAT "MAJOR scandal," the general would hang on to his command. Whatever some of the military higher-ups thought of him, Chennault had powerful backers, from Chiang Kai-shek to President Roosevelt. Merian Cooper, however, took the fall for his own end-run letter to Donovan. "Ill

SMOKE 'EM IF YOU GOT 'EM. COOPER AND CHENNAULT TAKE A BREAK FROM THE ACTION. IN PLANNING AERIAL MISSIONS FOR CHENNAULT, COOPER WAS GUIDED BY A DICTUM HE LEARNED DURING HIS DAYS STUDYING MILITARY STRATEGY AT THE NAVAL ACADEMY. "I LEARNED ONE THING WHICH I BELIEVE IN," HE ONCE WROTE. "IN WAR ONLY A SIMPLE PLAN CAN SUCCEED. THIS IS HOW NAPOLEON BEAT EVERYONE UNTIL HE FOUGHT WELLINGTON AT WATERLOO." *Cooper Papers, BYU*

health"—as General Bissell had suggested—was the official reason given for his transfer out of China. Cooper *had* been suffering from dysentery, but that was endemic among Americans in China. Men had flown and fought while suffering from malaria or dysentery, and Cooper was no exception.

Before leaving China, Cooper gave the enemy one last taste of his theories. He drew up the plans and flew along for a series of daring raids over Japanese strongholds in Hong Kong and Canton. Observers estimated that during the Canton raid alone, the China Air Task Force downed twenty-nine Japanese pursuit planes, destroyed forty-two enemy planes on the ground, and sunk two ships. There were some wounded among the Americans but no losses in the Canton raid, although Cooper had a narrow escape. Colonel Scott, the pursuit commander, was watching his back and shot down a Japanese fighter that was closing in on Cooper's plane.[32]

C. V. Haynes joined them for the air strike over Hong Kong, which met his definition of a "nice juicy target." It was also personal with him, since Japanese radio propaganda had proclaimed that there was no reason to fear the China-based American bombers because they were led by "an old broken-down transport pilot named Haynes." At his own expense, Haynes printed leaflets in English and Japanese, declaring that "these bombs come with the compliments of the old broken-down transport pilot Haynes."

Cooper himself prepared for the offensive in a marathon ten days, laboring day and night despite suffering "overwork and fatigue," Scott recalled. He was untiring in briefing the pilots and providing superior intelligence data and insights into the enemy mind.[33]

The Hong Kong strike began with a rendezvous at Kweilin—Coop's "million dollar background"—on October 24, with Chennault directing combat operations out of their limestone cave headquarters. By midnight the Kweilin valley airfield was crowded with twelve B-25s and ten P-40s, and in the morning they took to the sky for the first Allied bombing attack on Hong Kong. " 'Tex' Hill led the fighter cover with Caleb Haynes heading the bombers," Chennault wrote. "Colonel Cooper was in the nose of Haynes's B-25 squinting over the shoulder of Harold 'Butch' Morgan, the lead bombardier. The attack was a complete surprise. The B-25's dropped their load of Russian-made bombs into Kowloon, and Haynes's rice-paper leaflets were fluttering down before the enemy fighters attacked."[34]

Captain Everett W. Holstrom later commended Haynes's piloting skills. Immediately after the bombs had been released, the CATF had come under attack from at least twenty enemy fighters. "General Haynes maneuvered his formation with such consummate skill that all the fighters were denied a favorable position for attack," Holstrom reported, adding that at least six

enemy fighters were shot down in the process by the gunners of the
bomber planes.[35]

Tex Hill also helped them break free when Japanese fighters began pursuit. Scott later reported that six Japanese planes had climbed to the left of
the bombers, while other Japanese planes began closing in to attack from

VIEW FROM A B-25 BOMBER. ON BACK OF PHOTO IS STAMPED:
"COUNTRY—BURMA; CITY: LUNGLING; DATE: 11-20-42; ALTITUDE: 11,600."

Cooper Papers, BYU

the right. Tex suddenly turned his fighter "on its back" and went into a
speed dive, maneuvering between the enemy planes and bombers—and
launched headlong into the thick of the enemy fighters, just as he had
done in the deadly chicken fight above Hengyang, forcing the enemy
planes to turn away and shooting one down in flames.

"In this first attack Major Hill held his fire on the enemy so relentlessly
that had his plane not gone into a spin I am certain he would have rammed
the Japanese," Scott described. "He recovered from this spin and in spite of
the lost altitude he succeeded in delivering fire on several enemy ships and
turned them from the attack." Hill's aerial daring and fighting skill in-

spired the younger pilots, giving them courage in the face of superior enemy numbers.

Even after the mission's bombers and escort fighters had fought through to the clear, Hill and another pilot kept up a vigilant rearguard action. They shot down "at least eighteen enemy planes," Scott estimated, and he recommended the Texan for the Distinguished Service Cross.[36]

"The C.A.T.F. was probably the smallest American air force ever to be dignified by the command of a general," Chennault later wrote. "It certainly was the raggedest. Its paper work was poor, and salutes were scarce, but when the signals were called for combat, it never missed a play."[37]

THE WAY OF A FIGHTER

*In my best judgment, not only is he a superior Chief of Staff for an
Air Force in combat but is entirely qualified for high command of
large Air Force units in combat. . . . Colonel Cooper has demonstrated his fitness for promotion through the hard school of war.*

—General Ennis C. Whitehead, promotion recommendation
for Merian Cooper[1]

COOPER WAS FINALLY ORDERED TO LEAVE KUNMING FOR KARACHI—"FOR THE
purpose of hospitalization"—on November 24. But the colonel didn't immediately respond to the order, as a CATF headquarters report noted;
when the directive was made, "Colonel Cooper was absent on duty in the
Eastern China Theater, in connection with operations being conducted
there, and . . . he remained on this duty through November 28, 1942."[2]

But even Cooper couldn't postpone the inevitable, and by December he
was in New Delhi, where he publicly maintained a diplomatic silence about
his dismissal, even when an Associated Press reporter caught up with him.
"To look at him you would never guess that he is one of the toughest, can-
niest fighting men the Japanese have to face in this theater," said the AP report. "He is slender, of medium height, with mild brown eyes and a bald
head (about which his wife is sensitive)." The article noted that Cooper had
joined Chennault when the American air force "was ludicrously outnumbered" and that he had fulfilled the duties of practically an entire staff for
Chennault. Colonel Robert Scott was quoted as having said that Cooper
had "pulled off his last big job" before leaving China, an eastern offensive
with seven raids in five days.[3]

By the end of the month Cooper was back in Washington, where he

**BACK HOME, COLONEL COOPER MAKES A
REPORT ON THE CHINA SITUATION FOR
ROBERT LOVETT, ASSISTANT SECRETARY
OF WAR FOR AIR.**
Cooper Papers, BYU

began recovering from his dysentery and pushing to get back into the fight as soon as possible. He took the opportunity to vacation with Dorothy, but he also set up shop in the Pentagon office of an old friend, Lieutenant Colonel Laurence Stallings, and his return was celebrated in an issue of *Shipmate,* the U.S. Naval Academy alumni association magazine, which seemed proud of the former senior classman who'd once been mustered out of Annapolis. All was forgiven and forgotten as the article saluted "Cooper, class of '15" and summed up his restless state of mind: "He itches for his next assignment."[4]

Behind the scenes, Cooper was again in a combative mood, confronting a military leadership he believed was failing Chennault and was oblivious to the danger of China falling to the Communists. Indeed, he would later recall that he had spoken up for Chennault and Chiang Kai-shek and against communism in China before the assembled military brass in the War Room in Washington.[5] He also claimed to have engaged in a "heated two-hour conversation" with General Marshall during which he lambasted the despised Stilwell.

"I *gloried* in it," Cooper recalled. "[Marshall] tried to get me to retract one word of my belief that General Stilwell was communist-minded. I refused to retract one goddamn word. General Marshall then said, 'Cooper, so long as I have anything to do with the U.S. government in an executive capacity you shall never receive another promotion nor decoration.' He kept his word."[6]

However, Cooper still had powerful friends in the political and military establishment, and letters of commendation attested to his indefatigable energy and devotion to duty. Robert Scott, writing to Cooper in November 1942 from his 23rd Fighter Group headquarters command in Kunming, summed up the sentiment: "That you have either accompanied each dangerous raid or made efforts to accompany it has been an inspiration to every pilot in this group. We know that intelligence obtained by you has made possible the accomplishment of much destruction to the enemy. . . .

"In my opinion your presence on dangerous bombing missions, your observation of enemy tactics when you yourself was subject to enemy fire and bombing, your untiring efforts to maintain the offensive all have been acts of bravery above and beyond the call of duty."[7]

———

COOPER FLEW DOWN to Florida for rest and relaxation, and while there he received word from the Polish embassy in Washington that both he and his old comrade Colonel Cedric E. Fauntleroy had been honored by the president of Poland with the order of Polonia Restituta, III Class (Commandoria).[8] Back in Washington, Cooper also met up with John Ford, who was taking a break from his duties as chief of the Field Photographic Branch of the OSS, with a rank of lieutenant commander in the navy. Ford had many interesting experiences ahead of him, not the least of which would be command of a film crew that recorded, in color, the D-day landing at Omaha Beach.

"The discussions between Ford and Cooper . . . laid the groundwork for their postwar reactivation of Argosy Pictures," historian Joseph McBride noted.[9]

Finally, on May 3, 1943, Cooper was posted to New Guinea. He was still stateside while en route to his post when he learned that Ernest Schoedsack had suffered a serious eye injury while in the United States, flying a high-altitude mission to test secret new photographic equipment. Cooper later explained to Rudy Behlmer that Schoedsack's mask had somehow come off at a high altitude, and when the plane made a bad landing, it damaged Schoedsack's retina. Cooper saw to it that Schoedsack got to a hospital, but his restless friend immediately resigned from the military and left the hospital. He hadn't entirely recovered when he accidentally bumped his head—an inherent danger for a man six feet, six inches tall— and reinjured his retina. For the rest of his life, Ernest Schoedsack would be plagued by failing eyesight.[10]

The New Guinea campaign would prove to be a mirror image of Colonel Cooper's experiences in China. Cooper was again a chief of staff, this time to General Ennis C. Whitehead, and he again won praise from his immediate supervisors. He was in the direct line of strategic operations, from General MacArthur and General George Kenney at the top to the day-to-day work handled by General Whitehead, with Cooper acting as his immediate assistant. As in China, Cooper was given a young, inexperienced staff, and, in Whitehead's final opinion, he molded them into a smoothly efficient organization by virtue of his leadership, devotion to duty, and knowledge of modern air warfare.

New Guinea also provided another opportunity for him to put his theories of airpower into practice, since he supervised the Fifth Air Force offensive in the Markham Valley, a hazardous mission that covered some two hundred miles, from Port Moresby to Nadzab.[11] As usual, Cooper wasn't just planning missions but seeing them through—between May and August 1943 he participated in nine recorded operational combat missions.[12]

General Whitehead hailed chief of staff Cooper as a "key figure" and "a vital and driving force" in the logistical planning and tactical maneuvers involved in "the destruction of the bulk of massed Japanese airpower assembled on the left flank of the New Guinea theater." One of the major tasks for the Allies was establishing air superiority in the Lae area, which would allow Allied fighters to strike the main Japanese base at Wewak. They accomplished this by establishing an airdrome at Marilinan in the Waiput Valley, some forty miles from Lae. Cooper had to move quickly to build the strategic airdrome and bought time by a diversionary ruse—a "bold outflanking stroke," Whitehead called it—that wasn't noticed by Japanese reconnaissance flights until twenty-four hours before the Americans opened up their aerial offensive against Wewak.

The premise of the bold stroke was to basically come in *behind* the Japanese forces, Richard Cooper explains. "Airplanes were used to bring in the artillery; they'd break down the howitzers. The Japanese didn't think they could get that far—they were surprised. The whole war [in the Pacific] was outflanking and outsmarting the Japanese. Dad always thought strategically and had MacArthur's ear."[13]

By the time the Japanese forces *did* realize what was happening, the Marilinan airdrome had been established, with four runways and a tactical force of 2,500 men, 84 aircraft, and enough gasoline to support all planned Allied air operations. Cooper also established a liaison between the air force and other Allied armed services engaged in New Guinea, laying the foundation for future coordinated operations against the enemy.

"The entire force at Marilinan was carried 200 miles from Port Moresby by air transport alone, marking the first time in history a major air base had been developed entirely by airborne move," Whitehead recalled. "This move was accomplished in the face of consistently adverse weather conditions and during a peak period of Japanese airpower strength in the Southwest Pacific."[14]

Despite continuing bouts with dysentery, Cooper remained a dynamic force in New Guinea. *Cosmopolitan* magazine correspondent Lee Van Atta wrote of Cooper as "the keen-bladed scalpel utilized by General Douglas MacArthur to push the Japanese nearly 2,000 miles northwest from their 1942 stronghold at Burma on the northern shores of New Guinea. . . . [Cooper is] a top member of the air team which has evolved a new, devastating and already proven technique of sky warfare."[15]

A U.S. Air Force Who's Who published after the war confirmed that Cooper's devotion to work in New Guinea had become legendary, as had his eccentric persona, which included the affectionate nickname "The Pipe." It was said that his top priorities, in order, were: winning the war, his pipe, and his field telephone. The Cooper entry noted, "His staff could follow him into any given point in New Guinea simply by scouting his tobacco trail. He in turn could follow them, at any given time and usually at God-forsaken hours, by his deft maneuvering of the standard field telephone which have driven stronger men to insanity but on which Cooper flourished."[16]

CHENNAULT FOLLOWED COOPER'S progress throughout the war. In a letter he sent Dorothy Jordan Cooper on May 10, 1943, the general revealed: "Just between you and me, Coop was the finest fellow I ever had associated with me. I have had numerous requests to have him sent back to China, but all were disapproved for reasons which you undoubtedly know about. If I ever have the authority, I am going to have him back, regardless of the loss to some other field commander. We agreed that *we* had a job to do in China, and that *we* could do the job better than anyone else. I certainly look forward to finishing it up with Cooper's assistance. . . . I am still determined to have him back with me."[17]

By 1943, Dorothy was expecting her and Merian's third child, Theresa. After the birth, Chennault wrote Dorothy his congratulations, adding that he'd heard Merian was doing great work. He also revealed his own intimations of career mortality. "I am still laboring under the same difficulties that existed when Coop was here and, apparently, only an act of God can change the situation," he explained. "We are still winning battles, however, and, as Coop says, 'They can't kick out a winning general.' "[18]

Richard Cooper and his older sister, Mary Caroline, grew up during the war years with an absent father. But Richard never felt cheated that his dad sought combat duty, even though he was already a decorated veteran and pushing fifty. "He always felt age didn't matter when the country went to war," Richard acknowledged. "That was part of the code of honor." This code was exemplified by the war heroes Richard grew up with, men like Robert Scott, Tex Hill, John Alison, and the others who dropped by the Cooper home in Hollywood, where the family spent most of the war years. When they were stateside these men brought news from the front, and accounts of his dad's latest exploits. They held back the dark side of war. "I was impressed with their honesty," Richard Cooper recalled. "They were young, yet they'd taken on the mantle of responsibility. They were an impressive group."[19]

Cooper's post-China service continued to elicit recommendations for promotion. General Ennis Whitehead, in a letter to Lieutenant General George C. Kenney, noted that Colonel Cooper deserved to be made a brigadier general but alluded to the political pressure that cut off such promotions. "I know that all [the recommendations] went to the Senate excepting Colonel Cooper's nomination," Whitehead wrote. "You are undoubtedly familiar with the reason for this. I would certainly appreciate it if this can be cleared up in Washington. By every standard I know of, Colonel Cooper is qualified for promotion . . . he knows how to fight modern war. . . . So far as I know, he has not made a tactical or strategical error in his thinking and recommendations in more than a year of war in New Guinea." Whitehead added that when he was away in Townsville, in Australia, Cooper had particularly shown his worth; the execution of attack bombers against the Japanese attempt to evacuate their stronghold at Rabaul was without fault. "Cooper stopped the Rabaul evacuation," the general declared.[20]

By October 15, 1944, when Cooper was finally relieved from duty with the Fifth Air Force, an award recommendation estimated that more than seventy thousand troops were under his direction. "Colonel Cooper was a key figure in the destruction of Japanese air power in New Guinea," the June 26, 1945, recommendation for the Distinguished Service Medal concluded, "which cleared the way for the occupation by Allied Forces of the whole north coast of that island."[21]

The New Guinea campaign was recalled in 1966 when Cooper received a Western Union telegram from a famous movie star of his close acquaintance. "A fellow in my business gets to know a lot of people. I thought I knew you until I went to New Guinea. There I heard generals, young men for that rank, openly praising you behind your back for your thoughtful, dedicated and selfless work for others during World War II. You have set an example that is hard to follow. My congratulations and compliments, sir. You are a man." The telegram was signed "Duke"—John Wayne.[22]

IN THE FALL of 1944, General Kenney sent Cooper to Europe and out of the tropics, where, "having burned out a number of young operations officers under me, I burned myself out by dysentery, sinus, etc.," as Cooper wryly admitted. Anticipating victory in the European theater, the Allies had decided to move American units from there to the Pacific, where they would take part in the anticipated assault on Japan. Cooper was charged with drawing up a plan for these troop movements.[23] However, his health was at risk the entire time; in addition to the dysentery that had plagued him since China, his bad heart put him at risk when he flew along on high-pressure and high-altitude combat missions.

"MacArthur finally had to put a stop to [Merian's] flying—but he'd still sneak off and fly," Richard Cooper revealed, smiling.

Cooper never returned to Chennault and China. Despite his amazing fighting record, Marshall and Arnold forced Chennault to resign his command of the Fourteenth Air Force on July 6, 1945, replacing him with Lieutenant General George E. Stratemeyer.[24] Robert Scott would write that the Old Man left with cheers ringing in his ears during the official farewell, when a car provided by Chiang Kai-shek drove Chennault along streets crowded with Chinese waving flags of both countries, firecrackers bursting to chase away evil spirits, and bomb-marked buildings decorated with Flying Tigers banners and buntings.[25]

Scott, who went from Force AQUILA to the Hump to command of the 23rd Fighter Group in China, returned to the States and wrote *God Is My Co-Pilot*. This autobiographical account of his wartime exploits not only became a 1943 bestseller but almost immediately went into production as a Warner Bros. movie starring Dennis Morgan as Colonel Scott and Raymond Massey as General Chennault. A miniature set of the air base at Kunming reportedly made Scott, an adviser on the picture, "a little homesick." Wartime scenes, such as those showing P-40s strafing Japanese convoys, were re-created at the Warner Brothers ranch and rural hills outside Los

Angeles. The war was winding down when *God Is My Co-Pilot* had its New York release, on March 23, 1945.[26]

Always preferring to be where the action was, Merian Cooper personally saw peace proclaimed, standing among the dignitaries on the deck of the U.S.S. *Missouri* in Tokyo Bay during the official Japanese surrender on September 2, 1945.[27] Cooper was looking forward to a glorious postwar world. "We are entering the most interesting period in the history of the world," Cooper said to International News Service reporter Rupert Hendricks. "Just look what we have ahead of us. Commercial aviation is just beginning to be born, electronics is opening a vast new field, television promises a great new medium of entertainment and communication, and plastics are certain to be employed in thousands of ways not yet even thought of.... It's a great world ahead."[28]

By the end of 1947, Claire Chennault had his own happy news. He'd

CLAIRE AND
ANNA CHENNAULT.
Cooper Papers, BYU

been married on December 21 to Anna, a young Chinese woman. "I suppose you have seen the stories about my marriage," Chennault wrote Dorothy Cooper. "I was very fortunate in finding a nice little girl who is intelligent, energetic, and very sweet. Naturally, I call her my China doll."[29]

But the prospects of a peaceful postwar world were still to be threatened by the Communist menace, Chennault and Cooper believed. In *Way of a Fighter,* Chennault concluded his book's opening passage with an extraordinary vision: "As a practicing warrior for many years, I am convinced of the complete futility of war." Nationalism sparked war, he wrote, and the ease by which planes could now move around the planet, loaded with peaceful commerce or atomic destruction, only underlined "the folly of the artificial borders of political states."

The intrigues between the West and the Communist-bloc nations had their fulcrum in China, which Chennault likened to a fuse burning down to the powder keg of a third world war. "I am convinced that the people of this planet must ultimately and inevitably move toward a single form of world government if civilization is to survive. . . . In this struggle there are still many battles that cannot be avoided. The most critical of these now is to prevent the Communists from organizing the vast and rich land mass of China under their whip and turning its weight against us and the other free peoples of the world."[30]

Chennault wrote those words from Shanghai in January 1949. That very month, Communist forces took Peking, and Chiang Kai-shek and the remnants of his political party fled to the island of Formosa. In October, a triumphant Mao Tse-tung proclaimed the establishment of the People's Republic of China.

COLD WARRIOR

*I believe that psychological warfare is the only way to combat
Communism and I believe that one of the best weapons in such
psychological warfare is motion pictures.*

—Merian C. Cooper[1]

COOPER HAD ALWAYS TAKEN TO HEART THE ADAGE ABOUT KNOWING ONE'S
enemy, and he *believed* the Communist declarations that threatened global
domination—had believed them since 1919. He also believed that airpower
would provide the decisive weapon.[2]

Cooper was also an advocate of psychological warfare, and he viewed
postwar cinema as a battleground all its own in the global struggle against
communism. As a filmmaker, Cooper pursued patriotic themes at Argosy,
which he and Ford resurrected in 1947, including the trilogy of so-called
cavalry pictures starring John Wayne: *Fort Apache* (1948), *She Wore a Yellow
Ribbon* (1949), and *Rio Grande* (1950). These Ford-Cooper films celebrated a
romantic vision of the settling of the West and America's grand military
tradition. "When some postwar resentment to the Armed Forces was being
directed against the Officer Corps and was destroying respect for it, my
partner in civilian life, rear Admiral John Ford USN Ret., and I, made such
pictures as *She Wore a Yellow Ribbon* and *Rio Grande*," Cooper wrote. "These
pictures stressed the high moral character and devotion to duty of our officer corps."[3]

In 1950, with the impending retirement of his nemesis General George
Marshall, Cooper finally received his long-delayed promotion to brigadier
general, U.S. Air Force. On March 31, 1953, he received a permanent commission as brigadier general, U.S. Air Force Reserve, and marked the auspi-

MACIEJ SŁOMCZYŃSKI
AND HIS FIRST
WIFE, BARBARA, IN
1943, BEFORE HIS
INCARCERATION
IN A GERMAN
PRISON CAMP.

*Collection of Malgorzata
Słomczyńska-Pierzchalska*

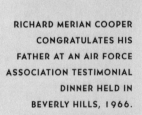

MACIEJ IN PARIS WITH
UNIDENTIFIED MAN, 1956.

*Collection of Malgorzata
Słomczyńska-Pierzchalska*

RICHARD MERIAN COOPER
CONGRATULATES HIS
FATHER AT AN AIR FORCE
ASSOCIATION TESTIMONIAL
DINNER HELD IN
BEVERLY HILLS, 1966.

Cooper Papers, BYU

cious occasion with a note to his old comrade Buck Crawford. "And as you were my deep and great friend in the Kosciusko Squadron, and have been a tried and true friend ever since, I want to remember you this day," Cooper wrote. "You are one of the few men in my life that I have always known I could call on in good times or bad."[4]

In the early 1950s, Cooper was convinced that he had found the perfect medium on which to wage his psychological warfare against communism: the revolutionary widescreen format known as Cinerama. This would provide a sprawling canvas upon which to paint a patriotic vision of a bountiful land of freedom worth fighting and dying for. Working with Lowell Thomas, who was trying to develop the new format as a commercial enterprise, Cooper helmed the inaugural 1952 production, *This Is Cinerama*, which included an "America the Beautiful" sequence dreamed up by Cooper to present a new kind of American propaganda and to counter the insidious influences of Communist doctrine. "The last twenty-four minutes of this picture consists solely of aerial shots of the United States," Cooper wrote. "Lowell Thomas and I ended it in this manner for one—and only one—purpose—to arouse the innate patriotism of the people of the United States."[5]

"If we want to save our way of life and civilization, I think I am one of the men most capable of helping to do it," Cooper stated in a 1958 letter to his old Flying Tigers comrade Colonel Tex Hill. "The whole trick is to do something strong and great and beautiful and American that will arouse the emotions of the audience—to tell great stories which are devoid of violence, sex, crime, etc., and still are fine entertainment. *If they are ever recognized as a subtle kind of American propaganda, then I will have failed*" (author's emphasis).[6]

Cooper sometimes protested, sometimes embraced the excesses of the witch hunt for Communists at home. He'd signed an October 20, 1947, telegram from the Special Committee of the Screen Directors Guild to Joseph W. Martin Jr., speaker of the House of Representatives, and J. Parnell Thomas, chair of the House Committee on Un-American Activities, that argued the constitutionality of smearing the good name of citizens without giving them the right to defend themselves. "IF THERE ARE TRAITORS IN HOLLYWOOD OR ANYWHERE ELSE, LET THE FEDERAL BUREAU OF INVESTIGATION POINT THEM OUT," the telegram read. "... BUT AS CITIZENS, LET THEM HAVE A FAIR TRIAL, PROTECTED BY THE GUARANTEES OF THE CONSTITUTION. SUCH IS THE

BILL OF RIGHTS." The telegram's other signatories were George Stevens, president of the committee; John Ford, chairman; John Huston; George Sidney; and William Wyler.[7]

But Cooper also supported Senator Joseph McCarthy, who'd eventually be disgraced, with "McCarthyism" becoming synonymous with reckless accusations against innocent parties. In 1954, a month before McCarthy's Senate colleagues censured him, Merian and Dorothy together sent the senator a telegram of support that proclaimed, "WE BELIEVE THAT YOU HAVE FOUGHT COMMUNISM THAT YOU HAVE STOOD FOR THE CONSTITUTION. . . . WE OPENLY AND FRANKLY WILL STAND BY YOU."[8]

That year also marked the death of Marjorie Crosby-Słomczyńska, the woman with whom Cooper had had an out-of-wedlock child in Poland in 1921. Their son, Maciej, survived his own adventures during World War II, as Maciej's daughter Malgorzata "Daisy" Słomczyńska-Pierzchalska recalled in 2003:

My father didn't talk much about it, but probably his worst experience from wartime was when he was in the most dreadful place, the Gestapo prison in Warsaw known as Pawiak, a place which has a horrible infamy in Poland—many Poles were murdered there during World War II. He was a member of an underground army known as Armia Krajowa, or AK. It was one of the biggest underground organizations in German-occupied Europe. My father was arrested by chance—the Germans often arrested young people for unimportant reasons. He didn't have a gun in his pocket, which is why he probably survived the Gestapo prison. He spent three months there and was sent to a slave labor camp in Austria. He later told me he always believed in his good luck and thought, "I'll survive, they can't kill me. I'm too young, I want to live."

At the end of the war there was heavy bombing of the area of my father's camp by American and British air forces because it was a heavily industrialized area; there was a tank factory there, so it was an important target. During one of these bombings he and some other prisoners escaped and made it to France through Switzerland. My father got in touch with Cooper from France and they exchanged letters. . . . There are many letters between the end of the war and when he came back to Poland. At first, his attitude was very positive: "Father is so good to me . . . he sends me a lot of money and arranged a job for me in the American army." He told me he was attached to [General George] Patton's army as a translator. My father had gotten married early in the war and had a child in Poland, which he wanted to bring to France, which was extremely difficult because there were zones [divided up between Russian, American, British, and French forces] that were impossible to get through. But in letters you find Cooper arranging the passport for [his son] and his wife. So, it was obvious the contacts were frequent.

In the postwar years, however, this already tenuous relationship became strained—then snapped. "My father once told me, 'I had a terrible argument with my father in France just after the war and that's why I came back to Poland.'" What was the argument about? "I don't know." Daisy shook her head. "I can only suspect."[9]

Merian Cooper had kept up contact and financial support with Marjorie over the years, and Maciej would always remember Merian Cooper as the great love of his mother's life, that she loved him until the day she died. Over the years, Maciej Słomczyński contemplated coming to America to visit his father, but after that terrible argument in France they never saw each other again.

IN 1958 GENERAL Claire Chennault died, after a valiant battle with cancer. "Now that stolen moments from Heaven has come to an end, I see so little for me to go on," Anna Chennault wrote Cooper from Washington, D.C. "When he died, half of me died with him.

". . . The Chinese used to say husband and wife shouldn't love each other too much, otherwise they will get the jealousy of god and they wouldn't have long lives together. Maybe we did love each other too much, and had used up all the time and happiness that heaven allowed."[10]

One of the great creative obsessions that took hold of Merian Cooper in the postwar years was a big-screen feature celebrating the life of his former commander, a man Cooper believed might have saved China from communism. Merian C. Cooper Enterprises began developing the biographical feature as a key component in his psychological offensive against the Red menace. In a 1959 treatment, Cooper even proposed the Chennault story as "the first true drama in Cinerama." The picture would boast stunning scenes of aerial and ground battles and "exotic and beautiful backgrounds and strange peoples" perfect for widescreen, but at its heart would be dramatic adventure and a love story—"a human picture," Cooper declared.

He elaborated on his dream in a letter to Tex Hill, who expressed an interest in helping raise private capital for the project. The Chennault story would feature "a Huckleberry Finn–Tom Sawyer type of opening, which was Chennault's boyhood," Cooper wrote, and continue on through the general's war experiences and romance with Anna—"which I think will be one of the most beautiful love stories ever put on the screen"—then to Chennault's brave fight against cancer.

"And in the end," Cooper concluded, "I intend to lift it into the clouds, as I did in the end of 'This is Cinerama,' and introduce a high spiritual note to show that Chennault's spirit still carries on."[11]

Cooper lined up the rights to Robert Scott's book *Flying Tiger: Chennault of China* and produced a treatment on the work. On August 22, 1958, a Western Union telegram from Anna Chennault and Thomas G. Corcoran, who had been a former insider with the Flying Tigers operation, officially authorized Cooper on behalf of the Chennault estate to produce *Chennault of China* as a movie.[12]

Cooper bowed to postwar realities by emphasizing that the production wouldn't stir up old animosities, as he noted in a treatment section headed "*Non-Political:* No reputations will be assailed. . . . The Japanese market is important. The Japanese will not be shown as villains, but as impersonal enemies, as they were in *Bridge on the River Kwai*."[13]

In his flurry of fund-raising letters, Cooper placed the planned Chennault movie squarely in the context of the struggle against communism. A November 1958 letter to Richard K. Mellon—whose powerful uncle, Andrew Mellon, Cooper had associated with during his years in the aviation industry—pitched the project in no-nonsense terms: "I WANT TO REPEAT TO YOU THAT I THINK THIS COUNTRY IS IN MORTAL DANGER NOW, WITHIN AND WITHOUT. The only thing that can save it is to combat the Communists with the same subtleties that they use. They are masters of psychological warfare.

"I not only think that you ought to back *Chennault of China,* but I think—if I may be permitted to say so—it is your duty to do it. . . . With your help—or men like you—I think I can do as much as any man alive to save this country.

"In my best and long-considered judgment, the United States will either be in a hydrogen war by 1961 or will have turned Communist, unless some men like you use men like me to fight it."[14]

In 1959 and into 1960, Cooper spent $62,000 in preproduction and entered into a contractual arrangement with veteran director John Farrow to helm the production. By then, Cooper envisioned shooting in Formosa, Burma, England, and Spain.[15] On September 15, 1960, a letter from Cooper to Farrow concluded, "You are going great. Let's hit 'em!!!"[16]

But a year later the project's momentum began to slow. Cooper was running into trouble dramatizing Chennault's wide and varied life, and he had promised Anna that he would make a good picture or none at all.

In 1961 he would report to a friend that he was "still in there pitching." At one point, Merian enlisted his old friend David O. Selznick in the effort, and Selznick's wife, actress Jennifer Jones, was seriously considered for the part of Anna Chennault, as was Rex Harrison for the role of General Chennault.

But for all the effort and dedication, this planned feature on the original Flying Tiger would prove to be one of Cooper's unrealized cinematic dreams.[17]

BY LATE 1958, when air cadet Richard M. Cooper was busy at the United States Air Force Academy in Colorado Springs, Colorado, his father was addressing letters and attachments to chief of staff of the United States Air Force and onward "through channels" for the eyes of the president of the United States. These communications constituted "an official report" on past and future communist intentions, particularly in the Far East. Cooper detailed his personal experiences and presented himself as both a combat-hardened soldier and a master of media who could play the game of psychological warfare as good as or better than the Reds.

The attachments included an October 12, 1953, letter, written prior to his retirement from the armed forces, in which he expressed his belief in the continued importance of airpower and the coming space age. The space age had arrived when the first artificial satellite, Russia's *Sputnik,* was launched into orbit on October 4, 1957. A new world was dawning, one of rockets and guided missiles and a potential struggle for outer space—and all of these were concerns Cooper felt were being ignored, as usual, by clueless decision makers.

For Merian Cooper, the fight against communism would never end; in some ways it was the great idealistic crusade of his life. Coop—stubborn, hard bitten, and battle hardened—would never give up the fight. His stoic resolve was reinforced by the fact that he had been right so many times: Cooper had been one of the dreamers of commercial aviation, had championed breakthrough innovations in the movie industry, and had seen America's involvement in World War II as inevitable, years before Japan's attack on Pearl Harbor. (He would later claim he had anticipated that as well.) Unlike those who claimed that the Commies had burrowed deep within the U.S. government or were hiding under every bed—positions taken out of real conviction, paranoia, or for blatant personal political gain— Cooper's fervor could be traced to his own torturous experiences in the Moscow prison camps. Although he was naturally combative and drawn to war—even after he had experienced its terrors and sorrows—it was not his need to fight but the *cause* that mattered. He truly and passionately believed that Communists were hell-bent on world domination, an obsession of his that objective observers might characterize as either pure, selfless patriotism or complete egomania: *I think I can do as much as any man alive to save this country.*

Cooper's anti-Communist resolve sometimes obscured his good sense, as in his support of Senator McCarthy. He was sometimes flat-out wrong; mercifully, the fateful year of 1961 came and went without America becoming a vassal state of the Red empire or suffering the nightmare hydrogen war he'd predicted. But Cooper's anti-Communist beliefs didn't make him part of a political fringe group in the postwar world—powerful political insiders and military leaders shared his crusade, not to mention a wide swath of the American public.

In a taped monologue Cooper sent Kevin Brownlow in England during the 1960s, he alluded to his involvement in a shadow network that was working to stem the Red tide: "Kevin, I want to tell you that I'm probably one of the leading anti-Communists in the world and control more than several hundred people, some working on large pay and some working on small pay, to see that we keep the best form of government, which we inherited from England [and which] took a thousand years for the Anglo-Saxon race in England to get—the individual freedom of man. . . . I'm prepared to die now or have my son die for anti-Communism, if you want to call it that."[18]

Otto C. Doering, an intimate of General Bill Donovan's, once wrote W. Douglas Burden confirming Cooper's ties with the major players behind the intelligence network that became the Central Intelligence Agency. "I know that Coop was consulting with then Colonel Donovan . . . and I am sure that he made a substantial contribution in the early beginnings of what later became the Central Intelligence Agency."[19]

"Bill Casey [CIA director during the administration of President Ronald Reagan] was a good friend," Richard Cooper added. "All these people knew each other. But I think it was more a group that discussed what needed to be done [in the Cold War struggle against communism]; I don't think they organized any activity."[20]

One of Cooper's personal heroes in the struggle was a man he considered the better of Alexander the Great, Napoleon, Hannibal, Caesar, and every military leader on through to Stonewall Jackson and Robert E. Lee. That man was General Douglas MacArthur. On October 5, 1958, Cooper wrote his son at the Air Force Academy, detailing an extraordinary two-hour private meeting he'd had with MacArthur at the general's apartment at the Waldorf Towers in New York.

They'd talked of many things, he wrote. MacArthur had approved of young Richard's choice of a military career, and shared Cooper's respect for their mutual friends and fellow officers from World War II, particularly General Claire Chennault, for whom Cooper said MacArthur used the term "genius." But their long conversation, most of which Cooper admitted he spent in rapt attention, was MacArthur's vision of the future. "Europe had passed its peak," MacArthur reportedly said, and "the future of the world was in the Far East." The Chinese had evolved from Confucian precepts into "warlike, strong people." MacArthur, Chennault, and Merian Cooper himself were among the few who'd seen the gathering danger in China; they had been voices howling in the wilderness.

America had to be strong and "stand our ground and not compromise"—that was the belief MacArthur expressed that day, Cooper noted. "Both he and I—old soldiers that we are—dislike war, but he said to me, 'Cooper, on the deck of the *Missouri* I made my preachment against war.

Nevertheless, I was forced to fight the Korea war and not allowed to win it, which I easily could have. The Americans and the Communists, both Russians and Chinese, are arming themselves to the hilt. In all history this has never happened to two great opposing powers that they have not employed their arms against each other.' He added, 'I do not know when it will come, but the inevitability of conflict is a certainty.' "[21]

Indeed, the Cold War was never an easy battleground for Merian Cooper. The "police action" in Korea would give way to the hard slog of the Vietnam War. At least his son would make the old man proud, flying over five hundred combat missions, including two hundred combat missions over North Vietnam; Lowell Thomas would call Richard Cooper's survival a 100-to-1 miracle. One brush with death came when his plane was hit by a .37-millimeter shell, which damaged one engine but didn't explode.

"If that shell hadn't been a dud I wouldn't be here today," Richard Cooper said. "But I never thought about it; that was just part of the deal. You just go and fly your best. I had an advantage because I'd heard about war growing up. I was around people who'd fought in World War I, World War II, the Korean War, and there are certain things that never change in war. It wasn't a great leap from hearing about it to doing it. It felt pretty comfortable flying through flak because I'd already pictured it in my mind.

"The thing I got from my dad was that while he did dangerous things, he wasn't totally reckless," Richard added. "He used to say, 'Check, check, check,' to make sure everything was covered. His high code of honor also dictated that you never command others to do anything you wouldn't do yourself."[22]

Before Richard Cooper left for war, his father gave him a lesson in the art of living dangerously, reciting the stoic philosophy taught him so many years before by the fearless Arctic explorer Vilhjalmur Stefansson. "I can mention any number of men who were killed on what we used to call 'coconut missions' in war," Merian Cooper explained in a taped monologue for Kevin Brownlow. "They'd chosen the easy missions and they got bumped off. My son lived because I didn't have to spell it out in ABC's to him. He knew what I meant. He knew that if you went on a hazardous mission, you thought not only of yourself but of the value of your men and everything that could happen to them. . . .

"When my son went off to fight in Vietnam he was age twenty-eight or twenty-nine. He'd never taken one dime from me nor one word of advice since he was seventeen and I never asked him to. But before he went off to war he asked, 'Dad, you've been to three wars. What advice have you to give me?' As near as I can remember—and my memory is pretty accurate—I said, 'Son, everybody will tell you not to volunteer. I, on the contrary, tell you to volunteer for *every* dangerous and hazardous mission. You'll either come back thinking well of yourself and disregard all the [medals] they put on your chest, which means nothing, or you'll come back in a pine box. In which case I will see that you are properly buried as your mother would desire.' And thus I sent him to war."[23]

EMPIRE OF THE
IMAGINATION

ARGOSY

The name of the firm that Ford and Cooper head, Argosy, was chosen by them only after careful consideration. Consult your mythology, and you'll find that Argosy was a boat, and that its cargo, if one isn't too literal, was adventure.

—Argosy Pictures news release, circa 1949[1]

Argosy's post-world war II reorganization was helped by seed money invested by Washington and Wall Street power players, including Cooper's old friend David Bruce, a future ambassador to France, West Germany, and Great Britain, OSS chief Bill Donovan, and Otto C. Doering, Donovan's right-hand man during the war.[2]

Doering, a lawyer, had known Cooper from when he was counsel for the Irving Trust Company, the receiver of RKO during the troubled economic times of the early 1930s, and he became the prime contact for the Argosy investment group.[3] While Doering worked with Cooper on the postwar capitalization, Ford focused on preproduction for *My Darling Clementine,* a picture he owed Darryl Zanuck.[4]

Argosy set sail into a world and industry that would be dramatically transformed in the postwar decades. The Golden Age of the old studio system, with its in-house operations and individual studio culture, was in its twilight; the new Hollywood would sell off its back lots and move toward providing financing, facilities, marketing, and distribution expertise to independent producers who would bring in projects. RKO entered into such an arrangement with Argosy, a four-picture distribution deal settled on September 27, 1946. The contract, which would be extended to a fifth picture, generally split costs and profits while allowing Argosy full creative control and ownership of the properties.[5]

COOPER AND ASSOCIATE PRODUCER EMILIO FERNANDEZ
TAKE A BREAK FROM WORK ON *THE FUGITIVE* IN A NATIVE
STORE AT TEPOZTLÁN, MEXICO. *Cooper Papers, BYU*

PORTRAIT OF AN ICON,
DIRECTOR JOHN FORD.
INSCRIBED ON
PORTRAIT: "TO
DOROTHY & COOP
IN MEMORY OF AN
EXCITING, EVER-
LASTING FRIENDSHIP.
JACK."

Cooper Papers, BYU

The partners wanted to make *The Quiet Man,* a romantic tale set in Ireland, but decided that *The Fugitive* would be the first postwar picture of the new Argosy. The film, based on a Graham Greene novel, was set in Mexico and centered on the betrayal of a Catholic priest. With its religious theme and undertone of spiritual anguish, it would prove a hard sale at the box office.

"If *The Fugitive* had made ten million dollars, we probably wouldn't have had any trouble making *The Quiet Man* at RKO," Argosy vice president and

REDBOOK MAGAZINE PICTURE OF THE YEAR AWARD TO *THE FUGITIVE.* LEFT TO RIGHT: COOPER, UNIDENTIFIED MAN, GREGORY PECK, JOHN FORD, AND EMILIO FERNANDEZ. ALTHOUGH THE FILM WON CRITICAL ACCOLADES, ITS POOR BOX OFFICE WASN'T AN AUSPICIOUS START FOR THE POSTWAR ARGOSY PICTURES.

Cooper Papers, BYU

general manager Donald Dewar recalled. "But *The Fugitive* didn't make ten million dollars."[6]

Indeed, Ford biographer Joseph McBride calls *The Fugitive* "a quixotic, self-defeating gesture for someone trying to launch a new film company." By 1951, the RKO ledger listed worldwide returns for the picture of $1,158,870 on a negative cost of $1,124,326, which didn't include marketing costs. To keep the company viable, John Ford turned to the bankable western genre, and the result was the celebrated and enduring trilogy of cavalry pictures.[7] Richard Cooper noted that while Ford was a brilliant director, his father's contributions to the Argosy productions—particularly the cavalry pictures—has often been overlooked. "He had a lot to do with the authenticity, the story," Cooper explained. "One thing Dad did for John Ford was he'd get the stories together; every scene was tight. He'd lose even a good scene if it didn't advance the story. And when my dad came onto a project and came up with a budget, he'd know *exactly* what it'd cost—he never padded or pared down the books."[8]

Argosy's postwar plans included a global "outdoor motion picture operation," which Argosy publicity couldn't resist linking to the exploits of the company president. "Visit Cooper's office, and you'll find a camel saddle," a 1949 company news release observed. "Cooper has ridden in it for close to 1,000 miles. On his wall is a photograph of swarming, spear-throwing savages. He took it himself in Africa 28 years ago. Behind glass is a message in what appears [to be] cuneiform symbols. It's an official clearance for him from a tribal chieftain. It was used to get Cooper through a danger-infested area of the Persian mountains."[9]

A seven-page, uncredited proposal titled "Memorandum Exploitation," dated March 31, 1948, laid out the globe-trotting production philosophy: "Showmanship and the constant element of adventure are the two fundamentals concerned but economy of production cost has been a guiding factor in the mapping of the outdoor-adventure scheme." The "outdoor program" divided the planet into moviemaking regions that included Malay-Siam, Africa, Tahiti, Persia, the South Seas, and Saudi Arabia. The pictures would either be produced entirely abroad or, taking a time-honored cue from *The Four Feathers*, utilize prefabrication to integrate distant locations and Hollywood studio work. Potential projects included *African Cowboy*, featuring American cowboys roping wild lions, and *Revenge*, a proposed offering from the "Malayan-Siam program" that imagined the ultimate melding of the major elements of *Chang*: "a tiger charging a circle of elephants."[10]

The Argosy map of the world also staked out a piece of territory marking a bit of unfinished business for Merian Cooper, as a company memo described: "The fourth geographical region is Persia where it is planned to make . . . the story of a tribe's unceasing hunt for grass land and their torturous navigation of the forbidding ranges of Zardeh-Kuh. The Bakhtiari migration is one of the least known and most epochal struggles for survival by man. Probably the cheapest to make of all pictures on the Argosy schedule. It is also one of the most photographically beautiful and thematically a challenge."[11]

Grass had always been the "damned half picture" to Cooper, and now he saw a chance to finally make it whole. A 1947 production outline was not only titled *Grass* but detailed one element Cooper felt had been missing from the original: "One man and one woman, and their children, will exemplify for the audience the whole of this struggle for survival which breeds a race that is proud and strong, rugged individuals all, meeting bravely the moods of natural forces seemingly bent upon their destruction."[12]

Although Cooper, now in his mid-fifties, wasn't planning to personally make the trek, he organized the crew for the expedition. Finally came the day when Ernest Schoedsack got the call from his old partner announcing that the new adventure of *Grass* was on. "He called me up and said, 'I'm sending a camera crew over to Persia to make *Grass*. I wish you to brief them,'" Schoedsack recalled for Kevin Brownlow. "I said, 'I'll brief them. I'll tell the silly bastards not to go!'"

Things had changed. Persian friends of Ernest and Ruth's had informed them that the Persian Gulf region was being built up, that a railroad now traversed that country, that trucks and cars were being used in the migration. Even the mighty Karun was no longer braved by tribesmen—no longer were they pushing off into the treacherous currents on rafts and inflated goat skins. A bridge now spanned the river.

Schoedsack saw the expedition as a soft bunch who wouldn't have lasted a day roughing it as they had back in the 1920s. The new expedition had even enlisted the help of government soldiers, toward whom the tribes maintained a natural antipathy. "And they had to have their beds and tents and guards and their vodka and their sun-kissed orange juice and they wouldn't get up until eight o'clock [in the morning] and then they had to have their eggs and bacon," Schoedsack scoffed. "By that time, of course, any tribe you're under are gone and [the filmmakers with their] tents and junk and heavy Mitchell cameras—nothing." By the time they returned, Schoedsack estimated they had spent thirty times what the original *Grass* had spent, with absolutely nothing to show for it.[13] For Cooper, the expedition's failure represented a door that had closed, forever, on one of the great dreams of his life.[14]

ONE ENDURING DREAM, however, did reach fruition. "As an antidote to the harsh realities of a warring world, we propose specifically to invade the world of the fabulous," Cooper and Laurence Stallings wrote in a proposal titled "Imaginative Films." "... We propose to do these pictures with a sense of reality, rather than make-believe, and to follow the lines of the great creatures of the imagination, such as Chang, King Kong." Cooper contemplated a new gorilla picture in which he would use a live gorilla—for "terrific audience appeal," he noted in his proposal—which, in a reprise of *Kong*, would be captured and raised by a woman, resulting in the gorilla's affection for the woman and the tragic consequences.[15]

The idea was ultimately transformed into the 1949 Argosy release *Mighty Joe Young*, with a young girl named Jill living on a plantation in Africa; her father allows her to keep a baby gorilla as a pet. The girl, played by Terry Moore, and the gorilla grow up together—the gorilla to gigantic proportions. Enter a Carl Denham–like showman named Max O'Hara who comes to Africa and imagines the gorilla, Mighty Joe, as the perfect attraction for his African-themed nightclub in Los Angeles.

But civilization and Mighty Joe are a bad mix, with the inevitable rampage as Mighty Joe wrecks the nightclub and is captured, jailed, and scheduled to be shot as a menace. Jill and Gregg (Ben Johnson), one of O'Hara's hired cowboys, are in love, and with the tough but good-hearted O'Hara assisting, Mighty Joe is broken out of jail. After Joe saves children from a burning orphanage, Jill, Gregg, and Joe happily return to the verdant fields of Africa.

Cooper ultimately decided to bring this new giant gorilla magically to life as a stop-motion figure and turned to Willis O'Brien, with whom he'd last worked on the ill-fated *War Eagles*.[16] This pet project of Cooper's, which included coproducer credit for John Ford, reunited O'Brien and several others from the old *Kong* gang: Ruth Rose wrote the screenplay, Cooper's alter ego Robert Armstrong was back as the bombastic O'Hara, and Schoedsack was installed in the director's chair despite his failing eyesight.

(Ray Harryhausen, who did most of the stop-motion animation, would re-member Schoedsack as being nearly blind and having to rely heavily on assistants.)

Mighty Joe Young would be of special significance in fantasy film history as the big break for Harryhausen, who was destined to pioneer his own stop-motion techniques and build his own empire of fantasy productions. In the 1930s, Harryhausen had joined the company of other *Kong* enthusiasts and fantasy fans, including two who became lifelong friends: Ray Bradbury, the famed fiction writer whose stories were then suffering rejection slips, and Forrest Ackerman, who coined the term "sci-fi" (for science fiction) and who created the magazine *Famous Monsters of Filmland*. They all attended the weekly gatherings of the Los Angeles Science Fiction League held in the cozy Brown Room of Clifton's cafeteria in downtown Los Angeles. They were an eclectic group of visionaries beguiled by the past, from dinosaur lovers to an Egyptologist, and believers in the future, from a rocket expert to space-travel enthusiasts. They nurtured one another's imaginations, and during these years Harryhausen began his own stop-motion experiments, making little dinosaurs out of rubber, with wooden ball-and-socket joints. "I had to do everything by experiment; there were no books on it," Harryhausen recalled.

Harryhausen's first real breakthrough came while he was still in high school and saw a girl in study period reading a big book—with an illustration of Kong! It was an illustrated *King Kong* script, a bound volume Merian Cooper had given a select few, including the girl's father, who had worked on Willis O'Brien's crew.

"This was quite by chance—the fickle finger of fate!" Harryhausen marveled. "I told her of my intense interest and she said her father was working with Willis O'Brien and he was down at MGM making a film called *War Eagles*." The girl arranged for Harryhausen to visit the set, where he met O'Brien and shared a suitcase of his own experimental stop-motion dinosaurs with the master. "He was very kind, very tolerant: 'Your stegosaurus has legs like sausages, you've got to learn anatomy.' So I studied a lot of Charles Knight's paintings and read anatomy books and I rebuilt a lot of my dinosaurs and gave them good muscle structure. I tried to follow in O'Brien's footsteps."

Finally, Harryhausen hooked up with O'Brien and worked on retainer as his assistant for about a year before *Mighty Joe* got the go-ahead. He had shown Cooper some of his previous animation work and gotten approval to be hired onto the production.

"Cooper would visit [the stop-motion set] every day, and occasionally he wore heavy shoes with taps on them so we'd know when he was coming," Harryhausen recalled, smiling. But Cooper didn't interfere, Harryhausen noted, and even O'Brien left him alone to do the animation, instead focusing on working on story development. "Obie made a lot of [preproduction] drawings and would take them into the story conferences with Cooper, Schoedsack, and Ruth," Harryhausen recalled. "They'd incorporate his ideas into their script and it became the writer's ideas, so Obie contributed to the script enormously."

Harryhausen helped O'Brien design the armature, which the stalwart Marcel Delgado built up into the muscles of the final puppet form. Harryhausen recalled that he worked with four Mighty Joe puppets, each fifteen to sixteen inches tall, with other puppets including a tiny figure for long shots. Harryhausen's first animation was a moody scene of Mighty Joe in his jail cell. As the production progressed, Harryhausen's responsibilities as primary animator grew.

"I was the only one who seemed to be turning out any footage that was usable!" Harryhausen commented. "I was left alone; I started to eat celery and carrots, so I'd get into the mood of the gorilla. I'd time some of the movements with a stopwatch. I did nine-tenths of the animation, but it was Obie's picture because he designed the thing. He'd made detailed storyboards of the broad bits and that was my guide . . . we'd talked it over during the sketching period."[17]

Cooper remained the very image of a Denham/O'Hara showman, the producer who always wanted things big—*bigger!* He pushed the spectacle of the picture's crowning moment, Joe's rescue of the children from a burning orphanage.[18] And while Harryhausen claimed he was left alone, Cooper was relentless with other aspects of production, including the work of costume designer Adele Balkan, who noticed that Cooper was sensitive to posterity. "One day he looked at me when I was showing him [Terry Moore's] clothes for another scene, and he said, 'But Adele, you know my pictures show for years. They're ageless, they're going to show forever. What lengths are skirts going to be that many years from now?' "

Toward the end of the production, Balkan came to work to discover a room full of orchids, compliments of Cooper. "I wore an orchid every day," she later related. "And when I talked to Terry, I said, 'Orchids?' She said, 'A houseful of orchids!' It was his appreciation. He knew we had done a good job. But as I told my boss at RKO, this man drives me crazy, it was day and night, day and night. But I understood him, I knew what he wanted, and I achieved what he wanted, but he didn't let me alone do it. He let me alone to originally design it, but from there on out he had to put his two cents in. But they all ended up as my designs."[19]

**TERRY MOORE AND SCHOEDSACK ON *MIGHTY JOE* SET
WITH DISTINGUISHED VISITOR GENERAL GEORGE KENNEY.**
Cooper Papers, BYU

In the end, though, Cooper would decry his failure to make good on his bold ambitions for *Mighty Joe Young*.

"I wanted to do something close to a true cartoon strip with unreal dialogue in a black-and-white style—no shadings. But I lost my nerve and didn't do what I had intended. It was a child-like picture, but it should have been done more broadly and been played more for laughs."[20] The film, nevertheless, made peace with Cooper's own mythology: Instead of a gorilla bloodied by bullets and shot off civilization's tallest skyscraper, a big, good-hearted gorilla was finally left alone and content with his human friends in a pastoral, peaceful Africa.

Because of his failing eyesight, Schoedsack's last movie production would be *Mighty Joe Young*. But he clung to what was left of his indomitable spirit, leaning on his self-deprecating humor for support. In a postscript comment on *Mighty Joe*, Schoedsack wrote a page of doggerel that opened: "The times are bad, inflation grows, the world is full of sordid woes. The cold war's daily growing colder And daily we are growing older. So, let us take you by the hand And lead you back to Cooper-Land." The poem imagined the audience in rapture, metaphorically letting the years fall away with every antic of Joseph of Africa:

> *Oh! How much younger can we get?*
> *Hold on! You ain't seen nothin' yet!*
> *You don't believe it? Here's the proof!*
> *Our Joe, high on a blazing roof*
> *First saves his girl friend,*
> *Then a child! The audience is going wild!*
> *For if there's much more of this corn*
> *They'll get so young they won't be born!*
> *Alas, at last the show is done,*
> *It's dark and silent on stage one.*
> *Reluctantly we must return—*
> *Again the world is cold and stern.*
> *However much we may begrudge it*
> *We have to think about the budget,*
> *And even though Joe has no equal*
> *We wonder who'll finance the sequel. —E.B.S.*[21]

One of the last great Argosy films was the one Cooper and Ford had pushed for years, the tale of an Irish-American boxer escaping his past who returns to the bucolic home of his forefathers and falls in love with a fiery Irish lass. *The Quiet Man* was released in 1952, starring John Wayne as Sean Thornton and Maureen O'Hara as Mary Kate. Of its inspiration, Cooper revealed, "We simply adapted [Shakespeare's] *The Taming of the Shrew* and laid it in the late 1920s in Ireland."[22]

The film was released through Republic Pictures, a small studio headed by Herbert J. Yates where John Wayne was the biggest in-house star. *The Quiet Man* was a strong box-office performer, but its foreign receipts weren't as good as anticipated. Cooper and Ford eventually filed a legal claim charging Republic with improperly crediting Argosy on foreign box-office receipts. Ford was furious with Cooper over the financial troubles and even blamed John Wayne for getting him involved with Republic. Wayne, disgusted with Yates's treatment of Ford, left the studio, his contract having expired with *The Quiet Man*.[23]

Argosy was running out of steam by the time of *The Quiet Man*, and the talk around the office was of financial cutbacks, not hot production prospects, Donald Dewar recalled. He also characterized Argosy as, basically, John Ford's company. "If Ford wanted to make a picture he made a picture. . . . The original idea being that Cooper would handle the business and Ford would make the pictures . . . but Coop didn't want to handle it. Coop wanted to make pictures and we ultimately made . . . *Mighty Joe Young*."[24] Instead of Ford first going through Cooper before presenting a matter to Dewar, the director began communicating directly—not so much an end run as "exercising his prerogatives," claimed Dewar, who felt as if he was caught between the two high-powered partners. "I saw that it was time to leave . . . the place around me was very strained . . . it was just not pleasant."[25] Argosy limped to its last landfall with its formal dissolution in January 1956.

Meanwhile, Cooper had become involved in Cinerama, that bold widescreen enterprise that Lowell Thomas was championing. Merian and Dorothy were living in Pacific Palisades, California, with their three children—Mary Caroline, who was almost twenty, Richard Merian, two years younger, and Theresa, who was about ten years old—but his family would see little of him during the whirlwind months when Coop crisscrossed the country by air, alternating between *Quiet Man* work in Hollywood and the Cinerama project in New York. He was convinced the picture business was in a rut and needed a good shaking up—and Cinerama was just the ticket.

THIS IS **CINERAMA**

帝 國 劇 場

COVER FROM MERIAN COOPER'S SOUVENIR PROGRAM
FOR THE PREMIERE OF *THIS IS CINERAMA* AT THE
IMPERIAL THEATRE IN TOKYO, JAPAN. THE COVER
IMAGE CELEBRATES THE DRAMATIC ROLLER-COASTER
OPENING AND IS SIGNED "COOP."

Cooper Papers, BYU

THIS IS CINERAMA!

> CINERAMA, PROPERLY EMPLOYED, IS NOT BASICALLY A
> MEDIUM OF ENTERTAINMENT, THOUGH IT IS THE GREATEST
> FORM OF ENTERTAINMENT YET DEVISED. IT IS ESSENTIALLY
> SOMETHING OF THE SPIRIT AND SOUL.
>
> —Merian Cooper, telegram to Lowell Thomas[1]

CINERAMA WAS THE BRAINCHILD OF FRED WALLER, AN EFFECTS GENIUS Cooper had known during the early Paramount days who had done a couple of special-effects shots on *The Four Feathers*. Waller had spent years devising a way to bust open the traditional, almost square borders of the conventional movie screen—to allow moving pictures to go *wide*.[2]

The breakthrough came when Waller realized he had always been thinking in terms of a *flat* screen, not a curved screen that emulated the three-dimensional way an individual sees the world. At the 1939 World's Fair, Waller unveiled a system he called Vitarama, featuring eleven matching projectors.[3] The final breakthrough, however, was his experimental Waller Gunnery Trainer, which was used to train World War II combat pilots. Trainees sat in front of a gigantic, spherical screen upon which five synchronized projectors displayed films of enemy planes, creating a three-dimensional effect emulating a gunner's point of view.[4]

This in turn led to the Cinerama system, which synchronized image and sound on a grand scale. The special Cinerama camera was in fact a three-camera unit that simultaneously shot three separate films of a subject. Exhibition of the resulting film required a special theater and three synchronized projectors, all projecting an image onto a curved screen almost three times as wide as it was tall. The effect would be heightened by seven-channel stereophonic sound, another breakthrough in a time when sound recordings were largely monophonic.

For the first Cinerama film feature Lowell Thomas brought aboard pioneering documentary filmmaker Robert Flaherty to direct. But within a few weeks of the start date, Flaherty died. Thomas, according to Cinerama publicity, then turned to his friend and fellow adventurer and filmmaker Merian Cooper.[5] A 1951 letter from Cooper to Thomas, however, indicates that the reverse might be true, with Cooper writing that he had read that Thomas and Mike Todd, the famed Broadway and film producer, were planning a new venture into "Waller's system of dimensional picture making and exhibition." Cooper explained that he had been interested in the idea for years, and pitched himself for a "hot idea which I think would really show off the medium.

"As you know," Cooper added, "when nobody else except Walt Disney believed in Technicolor, I was one of the people who really got major productions going into Technicolor.

"If Waller's system is as good as I think it is, I am really interested."[6]

Thomas coproduced the inaugural Cinerama production with Cooper and served as vice chairman of the new board of Cinerama Productions Corporation, matching his partner in visionary zeal for Waller's invention. "What if I could have turned the Cinerama camera on the tremendous pageant in India, on the elephants and brilliantly attired maharajas and the more than a million people whose faces appeared in my second feature-length film?" Thomas wrote. "What if I could have opened the three lenses of the miraculous Cinerama camera on Allenby and his men as they swept the Turks from the Holy City of Jerusalem, and the Bedouin Camel Corps under Lawrence in Arabia?"[7]

Thomas and Cooper met to discuss the first Cinerama production, and their brainstorming lasted several days. They agreed that the new medium's future fortunes couldn't be sacrificed on the judgment of movie critics, who would inevitably focus on the subject matter of the first feature. "This advent of something as new and important as Cinerama was in itself a major event in the history of entertainment," Thomas wrote in the premiere program for *This Is Cinerama*. "The logical thing to do was to make Cinerama the hero."[8]

Their approach was to demonstrate Cinerama's potential through a variety of vignettes, most of which were shot before Cooper became involved.

The "European Sequences"—as the premiere program called it—included selections ranging from Venetian boatmen rowing along the canals of Venice to scenes from *Aida* at the La Scala theater in Milan. Those sequences were supervised by Todd and his son, Michael Todd Jr., along with dramatic roller-coaster footage they shot at Rockaway Beach in New York.

In addition to Thomas and Todd, production principals on the seminal Cinerama feature included coproducer Robert L. Bendick, a combat cameraman with the First Motion Picture Unit from Cooper's old battleground of the China-Burma-India theater. Cooper himself was the perfect choice to take on "the final and ultimate responsibility," as Cooper once characterized his work.[9]

WHENEVER MERIAN COOPER discussed an idea, whether tackling a new production idea for *King Kong* or drawing up a battle plan in China, he was a human dynamo—restless, pacing, stoking his pipe, his machine-gun patter trying to keep pace with the ideas that were firing in his brain. He was in fine form when he met with Mike Todd to elaborate on the "hot idea" he had for Cinerama. In a letter to Lowell Thomas recounting the meeting, he described how he had been "on fire with my idea. Walking up and down, I poured out my idea to him. I think visually and, as I talked, scene after scene flashed across my mind with mounting power. . . . Scarcely ever in my life had I been so confident that I had a great idea that I was sure I could execute. Even as I write this now, once more I am on fire with the thought of it.

"What I wanted to do was tell a story in Cinerama of the beauty and power and glory of these United States and its people, in sweeping and dramatic terms."[10]

What Cooper had in mind would be the big finale: his "America the Beautiful" sequence, featuring the Mormon Tabernacle Choir and uncredited music by Max Steiner. Cooper arranged the dramatic sequence with Hollywood stunt pilot and speed flier Paul Mantz, who would pilot a converted B-25 bomber from New York to California while outdoor photographer Harry Squire sat in the nose of the plane with the three-camera Cinerama unit. It was the first thing Cooper shot, a triumphant ode that would span the continent and soar into the clouds on the music.[11]

The final movie showcased contrasting visions, an intermission establishing the demarcation point after a first half featuring often staid footage, much of it shot with a stationary camera. The exception was the opener itself, which featured the Mike Todd images taken from a Cinerama camera mounted to the front car of the Rockaway roller coaster, which gave audiences a vicarious experience of every thrilling, gut-wrenching dip and turn. Then came the second half—Cooper's major directorial contribution—which *moved*. This included the grand "America the Beautiful" finale and a Cooper segment shot in Florida's Cypress Gardens water park featuring lean, young, crew-cut men and beautiful girls dressed as southern belles who doff their billowy dresses for bathing suits to perform water ballets on water skis (coincidentally, one of Fred Waller's inventions).

MERIAN AND DOROTHY AT *PHOTOPLAY* AWARDS DINNER. "MY MOTHER WAS A BEDROCK," SAYS RICHARD COOPER. "THERE WERE A LOT OF UPS AND DOWNS—MY DAD WOULD BE AWAY IN WAR, OR WORKING ON THINGS THAT WERE VERY DRAINING, SUCH AS *THIS IS CINERAMA*—BUT SHE WAS ALWAYS THERE, SOLID AS A ROCK. SHE WAS AN EXAMPLE OF [THE TRADITION OF] SOUTHERN WOMEN WHO WERE SINGLE-MINDED IN COMMITTING TO A RELATIONSHIP. THERE WAS A LOVE STORY THERE."

Cooper Papers, BYU

The famous opening sequence came together some four months before the film's targeted New York premiere of September 30, 1952. Cooper had proposed an opening showing "the growth of life and light," a traditional 35-millimeter sequence featuring Thomas as narrator tracing the evolution of moving pictures, from magic-lantern slides to early silent flickers to modern images—"and now the audience gets hit in the face with *Cinerama*," Cooper outlined.

"Immediately over three spectacular Cinerama shots—and they should be very spectacular—I suggest that Mr. Thomas repeat some simple phraseology such as '*This is Cinerama*,' each time on a rising note."[12] Cooper deemed the roller coaster the most spectacular introduction to Cinerama, but he first had to win over Cinerama board members who wanted the sequence at the end, if used at all. "One of the directors, who shall be nameless, said, 'If you open with that roller coaster at least six women will faint or run out of the theater,'" Cooper once revealed. "And I said, 'If they don't, we got a failure! This is a shock opening and then I'm going into something slow and beautiful.'"[13]

It was a rush to the end—Cooper recalled he had received the print of wheat fields for the "America the Beautiful" sequence only some twelve hours before the opening in New York. "When I opened that picture I had cut it together, it was in my brain, but I never had time to [screen it before the preview]," Cooper told Rudy Behlmer. "It was the biggest night I ever saw in the theater for a picture . . . I knew we'd revolutionized the business."[14]

The audience for the premiere of *This Is Cinerama* was a distinguished group that included RCA head David Sarnoff; William Paley, founder of CBS; Louis B. Mayer, the recently dethroned head of MGM, who was now an adviser to the Cinerama corporation; former presidential candidate and New York governor Thomas Dewey; and *New York Times* publisher Arthur Sulzberger. As promised, the opening prologue appeared on a conventional movie screen, featuring Lowell Thomas and shot in black and white. Then the atmosphere became electric—and the contrast in color, scale, and sound was instantly apparent—when Thomas announced, "Ladies and gentlemen, *this is Cinerama!*"

The curtains slowly parted, revealing the wide, surrounding screen and what writer Bruce Handy, in a retrospective article on Cinerama, hailed as the most famous point-of-view shot in film history—the front-seat view of the roller coaster beginning its thrilling run.

"This was virtual reality 1950s-style," Handy wrote. "Audience members, their fields of vision nearly filled by the image, felt as if they too were rushing down the track . . . and, if we are to believe press accounts of the day . . . [would] leave the theater at intermission to buy Dramamine."[15]

The year 1953 was a big one for Cooper. The highlight was the Academy of Motion Picture Arts and Sciences awarding him an honorary Oscar for his "many innovations and contributions" to the movie business.

That year Coop also turned sixty and he relinquished his pilot's license. "I'll never put hands on an airplane's controls again," he said in an article in the *Minneapolis Sunday Tribune* celebrating his achievements and his ties to this city where he'd once been a newspaper reporter.

"I learned elsewhere that a lot of Hollywood minds are watching to see which way Cooper will move next—his moves generally have been followed by revolutions, major or minor, and more money at the box-office," *Tribune* reporter Bob Murphy wrote.

"Maybe it will be color television," Cooper mused.[16]

MEANWHILE, OLD FRIENDS and colleagues were passing away. In 1954, the year his old love Daisy died in Poland, Cooper lost his observer from the Great War. Edmund Leonard passed away on March 4 at the age of sixty-two, leaving behind his wife, Grace, and his grown daughter, Emily, whose passage to adulthood and marriage had been chronicled during Leonard's long correspondence with Cooper. The two had kept up their exchanges of

MERIAN COOPER: THIS IS YOUR LIFE! A LINEUP OF SURPRISE GUESTS JOINED HOST RALPH EDWARDS IN HONORING COOPER ON A 1949 BROADCAST OF THE POPULAR RADIO PROGRAM. PICTURED HERE IS GINGER ROGERS, WHO SHOT TO STARDOM WHEN COOPER PAIRED HER WITH FRED ASTAIRE.

Cooper Papers, BYU

"second birthday" greetings on each anniversary of the date they'd been shot down in flames, years stretching into decades of "borrowed time," as Leonard called it. Leonard had even been one of the surprise guests honoring Merian in a 1949 radio broadcast of *This Is Your Life*. "When you walked out from behind that curtain," Cooper later wrote, "I just couldn't believe my eyes and there's nobody in the world I would rather have seen."[17]

In 1953, for his final second-birthday message, Cooper had written, "September 26, 1918, when you and I faced death together."[18] In November of that same year, Cooper had sent Leonard a photostat copy of the letter he'd sent his father on January 23, 1919, detailing their ancient battle in the air. "As you know, a lot of people have given me, in my opinion, a lot too much credit for this fight," Cooper wrote. "I think my story shows that you were the better man."[19]

A friend of Leonard's told Cooper that one of the last things Leonard did, before entering the final stages of the cancer that killed him, was go to a local movie palace and watch *This Is Cinerama*.[20]

TELEVISION ARRIVED AFTER the war, but it truly emerged as a popular medium in the 1950s, and Cooper began contemplating productions for the small screen. One proposal returned to the mythic font of H. Rider Haggard for *The Alan Quartermain Adventure Series*, featuring an adventurer for hire. Episode ideas ranged from Quartermain smuggling a rare orchid out of the territory of a savage tribe in South America to his capturing the Abominable Snowman for the British Museum.

Another series idea was *The Golden Palace*, set in the days of San Francisco's bawdy Barbary Coast and starring popular entertainer Burl Ives as "the lusty, likeable rogue" who owns the Golden Palace, where mingle whalers and sea captains, gold miners and fur traders, showgirls and figures of high finance.[21]

The movie industry responded to television by stressing the spectacle of the theater experience. There were genuine breakthroughs, such as Eastman Kodak's single-strip Eastman color process, which ended Technicolor's monopoly on full-color theatrical film processing, and curiosities like 3-D, which required that the viewer don special glasses to appreciate a three-dimensional effect; that craze soon went the way of all fads. But the major and lasting innovation was the widescreen format, and Cinerama encouraged other studios with its miracle box-office returns. Despite playing in only fourteen converted theaters by 1954, *This Is Cinerama* was one of the highest-grossing films by then. "*This Is Cinerama* would change movies forever," Bruce Handy concluded.[22]

From the start Cooper had anticipated competition, and in short order Paramount ushered in VistaVision, advertised as "Motion Picture High Fidelity." Even Cinerama investor Mike Todd left to form a new company, which pushed a new seventy-millimeter widescreen single-projection process dubbed Todd-AO; it was used in such films as *The Sound of Music*. But the first widescreen answer to Cinerama was Twentieth Century–Fox's Cinema-Scope, unveiled in the 1953 biblical epic *The Robe,* advertised as "The Modern Miracle You See Without Glasses!"

CinemaScope was an anamorphic process, something Cooper and Schoedsack had considered and rejected for the elephant stampede in *Chang,* having disliked the format's aspect ratio. The anamorphic lens literally squeezed images onto film, then unsqueezed them when they were projected.[23] For theater owners, the beauty of CinemaScope and other anamorphic processes was that, other than a larger screen and a stereophonic sound system, the costs were minimal; a new lens could be fitted to a theater's existing projector. Cinerama, on the other hand, was practically a new medium, requiring massive capital investment and special theaters equipped with three projectors, special sound systems, and a wide, curved screen.

Thus financial problems became worrisome, and on February 24, 1953, Cooper wrote Dudley Roberts, the president of the Cinerama corporation, with his concerns. Cooper saw Cinerama in visionary terms; it was frustrating to him when others, especially those ostensibly committed to the new medium, did not grasp its potential. In some ways, his efforts recalled his struggles to inspire a cautious RKO studio leadership to embrace the potential of Technicolor. In his letter to Roberts, Cooper wrote that to finance the company—from opening and equipping theaters to training personnel—they needed $20 million, a figure he claimed was comparable to what Twentieth Century-Fox was spending on its CinemaScope productions. In March, Cooper and Thomas visited Cornelius Vanderbilt Whitney, one of a number of potential investors. C.V. came aboard with an offer of $5 million for Cinerama stock—which went unanswered by the board.[24]

Cooper and Thomas kept pushing for the survival of Cinerama. In a telegram Coop sent Lowell Thomas in the summer of 1953, he outlined a vision of the future that would build on the foundation of *This Is Cinerama.*

IT IS URGENT THAT WE IMPRESS ON ALL OUR ASSOCIATES BOTH OLD AND NEW SOMETHING THAT THE PUBLIC IS TELLING THEM AND US OVER AND OVER AGAIN EVERY DAY. THE MOTION PICTURE AS WE HAVE KNOWN IT ALL OUR LIVES IS DEAD. THE PUBLIC IS SICK TO DEATH OF OVERPOLISHED PHONY PICTURES. THEY BELONG TO THE DARK AGES.

. . . CINERAMA IS A MEDIUM OF EDUCATION NOT ONLY OF THE MIND AND OF THE SPIRIT OF MAN BUT PROPERLY USED IT GIVES MAN A

CONCEPT OF HIS RELATION TO THE VAST UNIVERSE. IT IS AS IF ONE
CAN BE TRANSPORTED INTO SPACE AND LOOK DOWN UPON THE EARTH
AND ALL MANKIND. CINERAMA, EMPLOYED WITH BRILLIANT IMAGERY
AND IMAGINATION, IS THE GREATEST MEANS I KNOW OF MAKING UN-
DERSTANDABLE TO THE WORLD, THE PRINCIPLES UPON WHICH THIS
COUNTRY WAS FOUNDED. . . .

Cooper ended with a mutual admonition that both he and Thomas
had "a great trust" to which they must be faithful.

. . . I HAVE PROVED MORE TIMES THAN I CAN REMEMBER THAT I WAS
WILLING TO RISK MY NECK, MY LIFE, AND WHAT FORTUNE I HAVE HAD
FOR IDEALS. . . . A TRULY DRAMATIC UNPOLISHED AND ROUGH-HEWN
USE OF CINERAMA IS PART OF THE EVOLUTION OF A NEW ERA. LET'S
FIGHT FOR OUR IDEALS AND PUSH ON TO THE FUTURE   —COOP.[25]

Cooper had accepted a position as vice president of Cinerama Productions and was elected a member of the board, but it was all dross for him if
the company proved to be going nowhere. He lobbied the board members,
arguing "the danger of the theaters going dark" unless there was adequate
financing and expansion. He proposed aligning the company with Technicolor, Eastman Kodak, DuPont, or some similar technological enterprise,
and developing a skilled staff of "technicians and dramatists" to ensure a
flow of Cinerama productions.[26]

Finally, C. V. Whitney, after failing to buy a controlling interest, left
Cinerama—and Cooper went with him. They announced formation of a
new production company, C. V. Whitney Productions, which would carry
on Cooper's dreams of a new American cinema through a program of films
celebrating American history and outdoor adventure. One proposed production in the American Series was *The Avenging Texans,* a serialized Western that had appeared in prose form in the *Saturday Evening Post.* That film,
which John Ford signed to direct on November 29, 1954, would become
The Searchers.[27]

COOPER LEFT THE original Cinerama corporation, but he never stopped
dreaming up ideas that could exploit the limitless potential of the

medium. In 1962, he prepared various outlines that imagined turning the bulky Cinerama cameras on mountain climbers, rodeo riders, skydivers, and sports car drivers. He noted that "jazz is almost a universal music" and proposed that a Cinerama picture featuring beloved musician Louis Armstrong would make an interesting subject. A proposal titled "Expeditions-Adventure" envisioned Cineramic safaris in Africa, tiger hunts in India, and tracking Kodiak bears in Alaska. Cooper contemplated taking Cinerama underwater and to the battlefields of Vietnam, imagined popular stage plays as properties, and even "Cinerama 3-Dimensional Color Television Without Glasses."

Cooper also saw Cinerama as perfect for transporting audiences into the new frontier through widescreen pictures set in outer space. "When you deal with Space you are dealing with the reality of Tomorrow," he declared.[28] He had shared his dreams of space as a featured speaker at the Fiftieth Anniversary of Powered Flight luncheon on April 15, 1953, held in the Crystal Room of the Beverly Hills Hotel. Before a distinguished audience that included his old World War II comrade Doolittle and Chuck Yeager, who had cracked the sound barrier in 1947, Cooper proclaimed the certainty of space travel and predicted that the "rocket planes" of the near future would fly passengers across the oceans.[29]

By the 1960s, he was seeing those dreams come true and imagined audiences vicariously joining the daring new adventure into outer space. A 1962 Cinerama idea from Cooper titled "Rocketry (Astronauts)" proposed presenting astronauts as "Everyman" and "not some superman or god-like being." That year John Glenn became the first American to go into orbit, and Cooper envisioned Cinerama pictures that would follow astronauts through training and launch, simulating with stop-motion animation a trip into orbit, with actual astronauts such as Glenn providing narration.[30]

By 1962, Cooper even envisioned taking Cinerama global in a chain of Disneyland-like amusement parks: Cineramalands, which would feature the ultimate "Super-Cinerama Theatre." The parks would be built near major population areas but far enough from city centers to allow the company to purchase large tracts of land for parking, the theater, and other attractions. There would be Cineramalands in the metropolitan regions of Los Angeles, New York, Chicago, Detroit, Paris, Rome, Berlin, Munich, and Tokyo, as well as the French Riviera, the Italian Riviera, and central England. He envisioned nothing less than an empire of the imagination.[31]

Cooper imagined an immersive experience at the Super-Cinerama Theatres, with "modern transfer electronics" allowing a surround screen 360 degrees horizontal by 160 degrees vertical. The inaugural production, *Space Picture in Super-Cinerama*, would be as big a hit as *King Kong*, Cooper believed. (He'd contemplated doing a new *King Kong* film in Cinerama, but

COOPER AT THE PODIUM AS FEATURED SPEAKER AT A DINNER CELEBRATING THE FIFTIETH ANNIVERSARY OF MANNED FLIGHT. IN A 1972 LETTER TO RAY BRADBURY, COOPER RECALLED THAT HE'D EXPOUNDED ON A FUTURE OF ROCKET TRAVEL AND OUTER SPACE ADVENTURES, WHICH EARNED WILD LAUGHTER FROM THE AUDIENCE. THE HEAD OF A CALIFORNIA MANUFACTURING FIRM TURNED TO A WOMAN AND ASKED, "WHO IS THAT NUT?" THE WOMAN, DOROTHY JORDAN COOPER, RESPONDED: "THAT IS MY HUSBAND!" COOPER ASKED THE OPINION OF TWO PEOPLE IN THE AUDIENCE, HIS OLD FRIEND JAMES DOOLITTLE AND PILOT CHUCK YEAGER, WHO'D JUST BROKEN THE SOUND BARRIER. "JIMMIE DOOLITTLE THOUGHT I WAS A LITTLE OPTIMISTIC; CHUCK THOUGHT I WAS A LITTLE PESSIMISTIC. THEIR VOCAL STATEMENTS KILLED THE LAUGHTER AND, INSTEAD, I GOT A LOT OF APPLAUSE." *Cooper Papers, BYU*

felt there were too many technical problems to overcome in the short term.) As Walt Disney had done with his Tomorrowland attraction at Disneyland, Cooper wanted Cineramalands to reflect "the far-reaching technological concepts now already moving forward with meteoric speed," including mass-transport systems and a "Cinerama helicopter landing field and a very modernistic Cinerama hotel." He seemed to anticipate the coming computer revolution, explaining that the popular notion of "mechanical brains" as being large, unwieldy contraptions was being overthrown as transistors replaced bulky vacuum-tube technology.[32]

Strangely enough, Cooper betrayed no bitterness when Cinerama failed to take hold and Cineramalands didn't sprout around the planet. He later told Thomas that making *This Is Cinerama* was "one of the most exciting adventures of my life." And for the patriotic brigadier general, the making of the epic "America the Beautiful" sequence was "one of the highpoints of my whole life."[33]

IN THE MIDST of Cooper's Cinerama crusade, C. V. Whitney Productions, which had begun with fanfare and high expectations, ended after only a few productions. Whitney's advisers had persuaded the would-be movie mogul to dream a new dream: investing in a chain of television stations.

Meanwhile, the rights for *Grass* and *Chang* had become entangled in Whitney's ownership interests, a matter that would vex Cooper for years to come. "I bought [*Grass* and *Chang*] from Paramount for him for C. V. Whitney Pictures," an exasperated Cooper wrote his executive assistant, Charles FitzSimons, in 1970. "Sonny has more than once said to me he was a dual personality. He can be a kind and generous friend or just the opposite."[34]

The Searchers, released on May 26, 1956, would be the last film Cooper and Ford would make together, and their only film for Whitney Productions. But it would be a fitting valedictory. It had all the grand trimmings of a Cooper production, from glorious Technicolor to widescreen Vista-Vision and even Max Steiner music. And Ford himself was back home in Monument Valley, where his cinematic vision of the West began. The opening title, "Texas 1868," appears against a blackness that is broken as a door opens onto the wilderness. A silhouetted woman comes into the light, shielding her eyes against the wind as she scans the horizon. It's Dorothy Jordan Cooper, still beautiful but years removed from the wisecracking Pest of *The Lost Squadron*. Her searching eyes locate a lone horse rider, Ethan Edwards, her brother-in-law and a former Confederate army officer, blown in with the wind from many wanderings. Their repressed love, although lost forever, is still smoldering when the homestead is attacked by Indians and the family slaughtered.

Ethan seeks the only survivor, his kidnapped niece (Natalie Wood), but many seasons pass before he has his revenge. And when he captures his niece, the viewer doesn't know whether he'll take this last tribute in blood—until he lifts her into his arms and softly utters, "Let's go home, Debbie." "Home" is his murdered brother's neighbors, the Jorgensens, and as they all go inside Ethan grips his left arm with his right hand (an homage to Western star and John Ford regular Harry Carey) and a voice-over softly sings, "Ride away, ride away," the refrain dying out as Ethan turns to face the wilderness and the door onto the frontier closes.

CHAPTER THIRTY

THE RETURN OF KING KONG

By virtue of imagination and craftsmanship [Cooper and his production team] achieved the truly remarkable feat of turning an eighteen-inch toy gorilla into one of the mythical figures of twentieth-century civilization.

—Ronald Haver[1]

ONE NIGHT IN 1961, FUTURE HALL OF FAME QUARTERBACK Y. A. TITTLE, WHO was moving from the San Francisco 49ers to the New York Giants, was driven to the airport by his wife and young daughter, Dianne. After returning home from the San Francisco airport, Dianne was allowed the special treat of staying up to watch *King Kong* on television.

"Oak branches scraped against the roof, our beagle dog howled, and Kong arrived in New York City about the same time as Y. A. Tittle did," the football star's daughter wrote many years later. "It was hard not to jump to conclusions: from the looks of the situation on TV, it seemed that maybe my father had made a big mistake in leaving. What kind of place was New York, anyhow? And what if my father did not know that gorillas hung out on the tops of the skyscrapers there? This place was different.

"This was New York. This was KING KONG!"[2]

After its many theatrical rereleases, now, with television, the legend of *Kong* was passing on to a new generation; Cooper had lived to see his creation become a cultural icon. Some of the inevitable critical commentary dissected Kong like a laboratory frog, and Cooper personally bristled at any intellectualizing over purported hidden messages and meanings. In a 1966 letter he wrote to an admirer, he took particular issue with the licentious characterization given the scene of Kong plucking off Ann Darrow's clothes. "I played this scene as a great gorilla playing as with a toy—and played it for comedy—and so the 1933 audiences took it," Cooper wrote. "It had *no* decadent 'rape' concept or execution!!!"[3]

Some were drawn to new creative possibilities inspired by the classic film. In 1962, Willis O'Brien proposed further adventures for crafty showman Carl Denham. "In line with the current demand for comedy and more comedy," Obie wrote Coop, "I have a suggestion for one based on the legend of 'The Abominable Snowman.'

"Why not have Carl Denham (Robert Armstrong) *plant* one in the Himalayas??? And we will call Denham 'The Abominable *Show*man.' "

The scenario, Obie wrote, would begin with Denham in a New York office with a view of the Empire State Building, reminiscing about the days of Kong. Suddenly, he and an associate "are startled to see a large, dark object slowly creeping up the side of the Empire State. It is only workmen hauling up a large 'tarp' but it brings back the headaches of 'Kong' even more vividly." When another associate comes in and explains he can't get Denham the giant elephant he wants but can get a giant gorilla, Denham throws the man out of his office. But before the man slams the door, he makes a parting comment—"as a showman, Denham is abominable"—which gets Denham thinking of his new greatest wonder of the world.[4]

Other showmen were moving in on Skull Island to capture the giant gorilla. Two years before O'Brien's Abominable Snowman pitch, former RKO and Selznick legal counsel Daniel T. O'Shea was working out a contractual deal that included O'Brien in the planned production *King Kong Meets Frankenstein*.[5] Cooper had always believed his rights were unassailable, and the rude awakening came in 1962 when the Toho company of Japan, Universal Studios, and producer John Beck released *King Kong vs. Godzilla* which, in the unkindest cut of all, featured the man-in-an-ape-suit gag Cooper had always bitterly opposed. Cooper charged his attorney Richard Goldwater, of the firm of Wright, Wright, Goldwater, and Mack, to file suit to enjoin distribution of the movie.[6]

The Aurora model-making company was also cashing in on the legend, adding the giant ape to their model-kit line of Universal monster creations that included Frankenstein's monster, Dracula, the Wolf Man, and the Mummy. Charles B. FitzSimons, Cooper's executive assistant and the brother of Maureen O'Hara, protested to Aurora Plastics that the company should be negotiating with him and Cooper for such licensed properties.

O'Shea had also been maneuvering on behalf of RKO to sell *King Kong* as part of a liquidation of the studio's assets. "I am apparently in a hassle with RKO, for whom, I am informed, Danny O'Shea is liquidating its literary properties," Cooper wrote Robert Bendick. "My hassle is about 'King Kong.' I created the character long before I came to RKO and have always believed I retained subsequent picture rights and other rights. I sold to RKO the right to make the one original picture King Kong and also, later, Son of Kong, but that was *all*."[7]

David Selznick, whom O'Shea approached in 1963 for help in selling *Kong*, seemed to agree with Cooper in a letter to his former partner: "I don't want to do a single thing in this connection that would prejudice your interests . . . [which] seems to have a great deal of merit."[8]

Cooper and his legal team offered up various documents to bolster their case. One was a 1932 letter Selznick had written a Mr. A. Loewenthal at the Famous Artists Syndicate in Chicago, discussing a potential comic strip based on *King Kong*. "It is much of the quality of 'Tarzan,'" Selznick wrote of *Kong*. ". . . The rights of this are owned by Mr. Merian C. Cooper."[9] Cooper's legal team argued that Selznick, then head of studio production and with all the legal resources of RKO at his command, wouldn't have so clearly attributed ownership of a property if it wasn't fact.

Other documents in Cooper's defense were missing, including his original story and treatments. "Unfortunately, there is a more than thirty year history of lost papers, deaths, and destroyed files—never an easy task to overcome—but I am still working on it," FitzSimons wrote in 1965.[10]

Among the lost papers were two key letters from RKO's head executives. "At the time of 'Son of Kong,'" Merian wrote his brother, John, "I had received an informal yet binding letter from Mr. Ayelsworth, the then president of RKO, and a binding, formal letter from Mr. B. B. Kahane, the president of the RKO Studio Corp. stating that I had only sold the rights for two pictures . . . and that all other rights whatsoever were vested in me. How these two letters were lost or destroyed probably is a matter of fraud and/or perjury." Richard Cooper confirms that his father realized these valuable papers were missing when he returned from World War II and expressed the belief that these documents were, indeed, stolen.[11]

Meanwhile, Cooper scrambled to get letters of support from old and influential friends. It was during this period that Cooper and W. Douglas Burden exchanged letters tracing the genesis and evolution of *King Kong.* David Bruce, writing from his post as U.S. ambassador in London, vouched for Cooper's claims, recalling how he'd read Cooper's *Kong* treatment and discussed it with Selznick more than thirty years before.[12]

The other side was dismissive of Cooper's claims. In a letter addressed to Charles FitzSimons from Gordon E. Youngman of the Los Angeles firm of Youngman, Hungate & Leopold, which was representing John Beck, the Toho company, and Universal Pictures, the attorney gave this withering response: "For the sake of the record, I wish to state that I am not in negotiation with you or Mr. Cooper or anyone else to define Mr. Cooper's rights in respect of *King Kong.* His rights are well defined, and they are non-existent, except for certain limited publication rights."[13]

Cooper pounced on the "Mr. Cooper" comment and directed Fitz-Simons to draft a letter to Gordon Youngman on what seemed a pointed refusal to properly address Cooper as "Brig. General, USAF, Ret." Fitz-Simons's letter noted that this was "as much a slur on the Armed Forces as it is on General Cooper personally. . . . This form of sarcasm, if it be so intended, is to be deprecated." Cooler heads prevailed and, at the request of attorney Richard Goldwater, the letter wasn't mailed.[14]

"It seems my hassle over 'King Kong' is destined to be a protracted one," Cooper sighed in a letter to Burden. ". . . They'd make me sorry I ever invented the beast, if I weren't so fond of him! Makes me feel like 'Macbeth':

" 'Bloody instructions which being taught return to plague the inventor.' "[15]

IN A COMPREHENSIVE article on Merian Cooper's career written by historian Rudy Behlmer and published in *Films in Review* in 1966, the *King Kong* legal imbroglio wasn't even mentioned. The seventy-three-year-old producer was busy, Behlmer noted, with a variety of projects, including an autobiography, of which Cooper said, "The most interesting chapters haven't been lived yet."[16]

It was an optimistic, practically defiant statement, given Cooper's advancing years and the old friends and colleagues who were passing away or in physical decline. Willis O'Brien—only months after pitching the idea about Carl Denham and the Abominable Snowman—had died, in November 1962. Merian and Dorothy had sent red roses to Darlyne, Obie's widow, and Coop had posted a tribute in the *Hollywood Reporter:* "He will live long in my memory . . . as my friend, and to the world as a genius." Rudy Behlmer recalls a phone call he received from Cooper in 1965: " 'Rudy! Dave Selznick just died. . . .' He just sighed; he was basically delivering a bulletin about this giant of the industry who'd just passed away."[17]

By 1969, Max Steiner had been slowed by age, while Schoedsack was suffering from worsening vision problems. But Schoedsack was channeling his considerable creative energies from visual to aural media and wrote Coop about the showmanship possibilities of the "music-color system" he was developing from his "ivory tower" home in Santa Monica.[18]

There were celebrations of life, grand anniversaries, reunions. Cooper missed the 1961 reunion of the 20th Aero Squadron 1st Day Bombardment Group 1917-1919 Association to attend his class's fiftieth reunion at the Lawrenceville School, near Princeton, and thereafter head to Colorado for his son's graduation from the U.S. Air Force Academy. Charles D'Olive, a fellow 20th veteran, filled Cooper in on how they'd been honored at Wright-Patterson Air Force Base: "It's too bad you couldn't be there . . . we were treated like kings by the Air Force.

"This creeping awareness of becoming an Historical relic gives one a queer feeling—especially when you see a . . . photo of yourself hanging in a Museum. I, like you, am having a great time with my 'Bonus Period.' I was shot down on Oct. 18 over the Argonne—But didn't get hurt—the Hun pilot pulled up past me + actually waved his hand—why he didn't finish the job—I'll never know."[19]

Cooper had earlier written to association president Dewey O. Tharp, sending his regrets. He'd noted the reunion motto—"It's later than you think"—and had recalled his missions with Edmund Leonard and how Eddy had finally been defeated by cancer only a few years before. "He was a true comrade and I mourn his memory. However, it is *not* later than *I* think, because every day I have spent since September 26, 1918 has been a bonus day. After all, my mother and father received one of those beautiful official messages from General Pershing which read, 'In memory of Merian C. Cooper, 1st Lieutenant, Air Service Signal Corps, who was killed in battle . . .'

" . . . I am having a great time in my bonus period and couldn't feel better. I would appreciate, if you do not think it presumptuous, if you would read this letter aloud at the first *sober* squadron meeting."[20]

TOWARD THE END of his life Merian Cooper kept dreaming his dreams, and in his dreaming he always returned to his greatest creation. One of those dreams was an autobiography he'd planned to title *I'm King Kong.*

In 1969, Cooper even came up with a new idea straight out of his space-picture brainstorms: He imagined King Kong on an asteroid in outer space.

"It is really a brilliant device for updating the whole story and at the same time retaining *all* of the elements," wrote FitzSimons, who felt they could make the film once their legal difficulties regarding *King Kong* were clarified. "The Asteroid becomes Skull Island and King Kong is still brought back to 'world' civilization to meet his end at the hands of more sophisticated weapons in a situation equivalent to the Empire State building scene, still overcome by 'Beauty' as he was in the original." FitzSimons signed off with the news that he'd been assigned by Twentieth Century-Fox to supervise all their TV movies. "So maybe the day is coming when I will have the leverage to help launch the 'King Kong' remake! Nothing would make me prouder!"[21]

The asteroid idea developed during discussions over a comic-book project that would have taken readers back to Skull Island, an idea Cooper rejected—everyone knew Kong had been shot off the Empire State Building! He and FitzSimons mulled other ideas, though, including a new generation of characters.

FitzSimons then proposed a "geriatric substance counteracting the aging process." The idea beguiled Cooper and grew in his imagination to become a "River of Youth," as mystical and eternal as the Flame of Life in *She.* Cooper wrote FitzSimons about "the possibility that Carl Denham has found the 'River of Youth,' so that when we discover him he is unchanged from what he was a generation ago." Cooper then imagined a "billion inhabited planets," some with civilizations a million years advanced from earth's and the possibility of the ultimate lost world in space, teeming with dinosaurs and the greatest creature of all: "There's King Kong reincarnated."

Taking a page from *War Eagles,* he further imagined the planet divided into two sides of existence, one a paradise of beauty and wonder, the other a timeless wilderness of prehistoric terrors and struggle where King Kong lurks.

"This would not be a space comic per se but only use space to get our characters to a new and more mysterious and larger island than Skull Island—in fact a small planet about the size of a large asteroid," Cooper wrote FitzSimons. "... I visualize our young people finding one [asteroid or planet] that is divided one half into a land of mystery and terror ... the other half of the planet a land of rapturous sensual beauty—eternal spring—dominated by the 'River of Youth.'

"... Once we get our people off into space and find a way for them to stay young forever we could go on to one hundred top stories and one hundred other planets if we wished. I have the imagination to do it. ...

"If I am nothing else in this world, Charlie, I am conceited enough to believe I am a good showman."[22]

JOURNEY TO THE UNDISCOVERED COUNTRY

The only true exploration of the future is of Outer Space—perhaps a billion planets with Life on them. Man will explore these billion planets just as surely as he mapped this Little World from the Air. And after basic Exploration, comes Colonization! What fun! I'm sixty-eight, but if I could get a triple shot of monkey glands, a face lift, and a red wig to cover my fringe of gray hair, I would still like to take a shot at it, but if not me, my son's sons will, I hope lead in the exploration and colonization of Outer Space.

—Merian Cooper, 1962[1]

I wish you'd get me a pill that I could take and be transformed back into the 13th, 14th, 15th or 16th century. I loved the jungle and the desert and the undisturbed woods.

—Merian Cooper to W. Douglas Burden, 1972[2]

IN 1967, ANOTHER OF COOPER'S LINKS TO YOUTH AND ADVENTURE VANISHED: Mrs. Arthur M. Blake, the former Marguerite Harrison, passed away. Her last years were tumultuous, if sketchy: another marriage and financial trouble, with Cooper providing a needed loan at one point; a stormy reunion with the son she had abandoned to become a reporter and world traveler; a daughter-in-law who supposedly despised Marguerite so intensely that she burned Harrison's papers after her death.

A year or so after Marguerite's passing, during a get-together that included Ernest and Ruth Schoedsack and Kevin Brownlow, Cooper recalled the woman who had saved him in the Russian camps and had been a partner in *Grass*. "Monty, you and I were damn fools for one thing," Coop drawled. "She dressed pretty—every time she knew she was going to be in a shot she put on these damn white britches and they almost made the picture unbelievable. . . . But looking back on it now, it was a hell of a trip for a woman to be on. She had guts." Cooper added he'd read Harrison's auto-biography, *There's Always Tomorrow,* only a few years before and had been upset at Harrison's descriptions of her old partners, particularly of her characterization of himself as "moody." "I said [to Ruth], here's the description of me and Monty and I read it to Ruth and she said, 'It's accurate on both of ya!' " And Cooper laughed a big, boisterous laugh.[3]

Years after her death, Marguerite Harrison, a pioneering woman of adventure, became the obsession of Patrick Montgomery, who was making documentaries in the 1980s and joined with screenwriter Wesley Moore to film a feature drama on Harrison's life. They followed her ghost into pre-glasnost Soviet Russia, retracing Harrison's footsteps through the peasant villages of the timeless countryside to the very rooming house in Moscow where she had lived when she was engaged in espionage and humanitarian activities and Merian Cooper was starving in the prison camps.[4]

"We worked on this project in the late eighties and throughout the nineties until finally I had no more money or time to spend on it and bowed out of the deal," Montgomery said, reflecting on the chase in 2004. "But we still have hopes." Indeed, Montgomery was still learning that the old legend had new, unexplored dimensions: "There's a CIA guy I know who believes Marguerite was the principal agent for the U.S. government in the thirties! Could be!

"People like Marguerite Harrison don't exist anymore—she was like a classic Cooper movie character," Montgomery noted. "You look at *King Kong* and it's basically about two guys who want to go exploring and one wants to take a woman along and one doesn't—it's what happened in *Grass.* You can say that Marguerite, in some ways, was the inspiration for the Fay Wray character in *King Kong.* Certainly, Cooper drew from all the stuff he was involved in.

"Cooper, Schoedsack, and Harrison lived in more mysterious times. People born in the 1890s grew up reading about places Western man hadn't visited and they could go visit some unknown land or discover a tribe. Theirs was the last great era of exploration, and you combine that with moviemaking, the ultimate fantasy machine. Here were Cooper and Schoedsack deciding they'd explore the world and, at first, they were going to do it with documentaries. Then they realized they could do even more if they did fiction films based on those adventures. They were at the juncture of the nineteenth century, when the world was unknown, and the twentieth century, when you could film those mysterious places and share it with everybody."

AS AN OLDER man, Cooper longed for those days of high adventure, so entwined were they with his youth and a wild world fast disappearing. He hadn't retreated from civilization, although he and Dorothy had moved from the smoggy environs of Los Angeles to the relatively tranquil seaside town of Coronado, outside San Diego. But in a letter to writer Ray Bradbury, Cooper expressed his exasperation with the modern world: "I will give you a ring one day when I am up in that terrible town of L.A.: God help me from smog, automobiles and television!! I might add that I live in Coronado without an automobile or a TV set—which is the secret of happiness . . . that, and being more in love with my wife now than when we were married on May 27, 1933."[5]

Despite the concrete chaos of civilization, Cooper was heartened by the emerging ecology movement and W. Douglas Burden's crusade for wilderness preservation. "I am delighted that you are keeping up your ecology fight," Cooper wrote his friend.

Ecology is a hifalutin word to me. I just think about keeping Nature undisturbed. . . . In fact, I think we ought to destroy most of the automobiles that now exist; maybe I should say commercial airplanes also. Thank God you and I traveled when we had to do a lot of it on foot or horseback or camelback. And I must admit when I spent ten months sailing on a ketch—the Wisdom II—I enjoyed that far more than any steamship trip I ever took. In other words, I am for nonprogress. . . .

I have been a little guilty myself, in my youth, of pushing the use of commercial aircraft, instead of fighting everything mechanical. All those years I spent in the jungle or the desert or the woods were wonderful to me. Thank God I saw Africa, the mountains of Persia, Arabia, etc. before they have been contaminated by the automobile and airplane. Perhaps that is the reason I am so rabid on space travel, as I am sure there are a billion continents, some of them inhabited, perhaps some far more advanced in technology than ours;

but sure as heck some of them are without motor cars or airplanes or freeways or all these other gadgets of our civilization. . . . My concept was—and is—that we will have a vast migration from this little world of ours to more primitive planets—certainly not within our little minor planetary system, but surely in that unknown, infinite, celestial system.[6]

From the vantage point of his years, Merian Cooper looked into his crystal ball and pronounced that the future would be dominated by two things: "the Conquest of men's Minds and Space." He traced his celestial interests to Christmas Eve 1917, in Issoudun, when he first discussed commercial flight with his visionary comrade John Hambleton. In a 1961 letter to a friend, he recalled becoming fascinated, back in 1922, with the writings of rocket-science pioneer Goddard and how, a few years later, while in the jungles making *Chang,* he'd encountered three professors studying the effects of the moon on animal and plant life who believed humankind would one day journey into space. Cooper had gone them one better—he'd said he believed humans would *colonize* the planets.

In his letter, Cooper added a postscript: "Save this for your children. I will either prove—before many years—to be the world's dumbest and most stupid man—or a minor, very minor—Prophet of Space."[7]

(Cooper's 1953 prophecy of rocket travel came true on June 21, 2004, when a privately financed "rocket plane" took an inaugural eighty-eight-minute voyage, shooting up more than sixty miles, just slipping beyond the atmospheric boundary into outer space, before gliding down to a successful landing at the Mojave Airport. The main financier of *SpaceShipOne* was billionaire Paul Allen, whose interests include a Cinerama theater in Seattle, one of the few functioning Cinerama facilities left in the world.)

IN HIS FINAL years, Cooper reflected on his experiences in war, exploration, and the movie business. He was not, by nature, an introspective sort, but occasionally some sage observation emerged in conversation or correspondence. In a long letter to Bosley Crowther, a motion-picture editor at *The New York Times,* Cooper wrote, "What is drama? What is greatness in film making; if there is such a thing? To me, film drama is something that emotionally and spiritually—if you will—moves people of all ages and all races."[8]

Cooper remained a virulent anti-Communist and even claimed that his long crusade had repeatedly put his life in danger. "These Commies are tough fighters and have done their best for many years, to try and destroy me—both my physical life and my personal happiness and my reputation," Cooper revealed in a letter to his old friend Frederick W. Pennoyer Jr. "I have never put this fact on paper—except officially—to anyone else. But it is true. It has been especially true in World War II in China in the Pacific, and after World War II until now. But I still keep on because I have believed since 1919 that the Communists meant to destroy this Republic."[9]

Cooper's musings included a hard look at the strange, internal wiring by which men fight and give their lives in war. In a letter to Captain Frederick W. Pennoyer III, the son of his old college friend Vice Admiral Frederick W. Pennoyer Jr., Cooper looked back on his days as a soldier in three wars, sharing the insights that came from having "looked death in the face." He deduced that he simply hadn't had the sense to be afraid—the trembling and anxiety always came after combat, the scare passing in time for the next death-defying adventure. "The really brave men that I have known are those who have been scared to death all the time—before, during and after—and yet have gone ahead and performed their duty (in many cases in a far more superior manner than have I)," Cooper concluded.[10]

IN THE LATE 1960s, Merian Cooper was diagnosed with cancer; at one point a leading cancer specialist in San Diego informed Dorothy that her husband had only two weeks to live.[11] Merian wrote Ernest Schoedsack a letter about his condition on February 17, 1970: "I just want to tell you, Monte, once more that of all the partners and friends I've ever had, you were the bravest, the finest, and in many ways the most talented. I have always had the deepest admiration for you, and also for Ruth for her bravery on 'Four Feathers' and for the wonderful scripts she did on 'King-Kong,' 'Last Days of Pompeii,' etc.

"This sounds like a farewell note. Actually, I have been optimistic and in high spirits, although I know on the record that this is a tough operation. If I were betting, I would consider it a 50-50 chance. If it turns out on the wrong side of the 50%—hail and farewell, Caesar!

"Again to you and Ruth my true affection and deep friendship—in the truest sense of the word."

Cooper signed the letter "Your old friend and partner."[12]

Richard Cooper recalls that it was July or September 1970 when his father was flown to Houston's St. Joseph Hospital, where Dr. John S. Stehlin attempted a last-ditch operation. After three months of intensive care, Cooper was released from the hospital, cured and without a trace of cancer in his system. In an April 29, 1971, handwritten letter to John Wayne, he noted that his recovery had astounded his medical specialist, who'd told him "it was a miracle, beyond his medical knowledge."

Cooper took his survival as a divine sign that he had been given the grace of even more bonus years with which to continue his mission against the "other side," the Communist forces he felt were as powerful and threatening as ever. "Things are now happening which I can only tell you about face to face—truly dangerous things for our country," Cooper revealed to Wayne.

"I wish to God General MacArthur was still alive—but we are strong still; and so are the other side. . . . Me, I believe God has willed that I should live for the dangerous works I am now called on to perform. I have not felt so well in forty years—I work 14 to 16 hours a day with no feeling of fatigue; and take on a task every day which is beyond my intellectual capacity—but I think God guides me. So be it."[13]

Cooper continued to live as he had always lived, fully aware that his every waking moment was a precious gift of borrowed time. It was a lifelong philosophy he keenly felt in his last days, and he opened a 1972 letter to Kevin Brownlow with the sentiment, expressed in a quote attributed to Lord Nelson before the Battle of Trafalgar: *Waste not a second. Five minutes can mean the difference between victory and defeat.*[14]

The letters and notes he would scribble in his distinctive loopy scrawl for Kathy Ryan, his secretary, had a particular urgency. His notes would record the hour—often to the very minute—as if he were conscious of each grain of sand as it emptied from the once-full hourglass of his life. It was natural, his consciousness of time. Outwardly, it was always "onward and upward" with him, but his true feelings manifested themselves in other ways—hence the dream of Carl Denham discovering the mystical and eternal spring of the River of Youth on a world that encompassed both sides of Merian Cooper's nature: the "land of mystery and terror," as he'd called it in his letter to FitzSimons, which exalted the savage struggle for survival that had always beguiled him, and the "land of rapturous sensual beauty." He'd envisioned such an environment in *War Eagles*—a land divided into darkness and light as neatly as the Chinese symbols of yin and yang—and it represented his dream of ultimate existence, a world where one could relax and recharge in peace and contentment while assured that if things got too boring, a land of death-defying adventure waited over the horizon.

Cooper's thoughts turned to the wild places he had known in his prime years of living dangerously. His mind also fixed on many of the obsessions of his past, including color picturemaking. One concept he explored was a

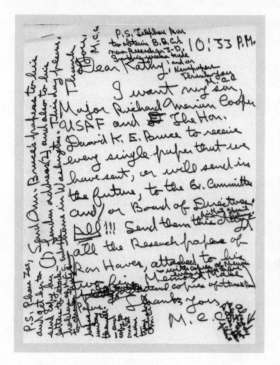

TOWARD THE END OF HIS LIFE, MERIAN COOPER'S HAND-WRITTEN NOTES (WRITTEN IN A LOOPY SCRAWL BECAUSE OF THE WORLD WAR I BURNS THAT LEFT HIS HANDS SENSITIVE) SEEMED TO POUR OUT HIS RESTLESS ENERGY. HE WAS MARKING TIME TO THE MINUTE—"10:33 P.M.," ON THIS NOTE TO HIS EXECUTIVE SECRETARY REGARDING THE BUSINESS OF "ADVANCED PROJECTS."

Cooper Papers, BYU

process for converting black-and-white photographs to color, an idea Cooper discussed with Lowell Thomas and Gilbert M. Grosvenor, editor of *National Geographic* magazine. "If you want me to do a single black and white photograph of which I know the colors, I suggest one of Haile Selassie sitting on his throne, which Schoedsack and I took in 1921," Cooper wrote Grosvenor. "It is unique; his black velvet robes flecked with pure gold would make a magnificent color picture."[15] Cooper even pursued colorizing black-and-white stills from *King Kong,* and with inventor

Wadsworth Pohl he explored the idea with Bob Gibeaut, a special-effects man at Disney.[16]

Cooper's last great obsession was a company he formed and christened Advanced Projects. He installed himself as chairman of the board and named his trusted friend and assistant Charles FitzSimons president, inventor Waddy Pohl vice president in charge of technical development, and Kathy Ryan his executive secretary. The company was not the delusion of an old dreamer going through the motions; the board he was forming attracted too many notable figures, albeit lifelong friends, for that. In addition to his son, Richard, those who accepted directorships included General John Alison, his old comrade from China; W. Douglas Burden; Thomas Corcoran; and lawyer Earl S. Wright.

In a letter to Kevin Brownlow, Cooper outlined the vision of Advanced Projects, which would "revolutionize both theatrical productions and exhibition as well as television." The major focus would be 3-D color television, a venture Cooper felt would either make nothing for his investors or generate a minimum of $100 to $500 million. At any rate, at seventy-eight he was having a good time. "In other words, I'll be the 'big shot' at the top and let Mr. FitzSimons and Mr. Pohl do all the work while I make money in my usual way—lying flat on my back and smoking my pipe. That's the way I've made every penny I ever had. I ration time, and always remember that time is the most valuable commodity in the world."[17]

Cooper built all his plans for a big-business empire on the notion of imminent financial collapse. He later wrote that Nelson Rockefeller had once told him that his brothers, after having estimated the cost of building Rockefeller Center in 1928–29, anticipated and awaited the stock market crash and resulting Depression, during which construction costs fell to half the "book price estimate" of the Roaring Twenties. Similarly, Cooper anticipated that the inflation of the early 1970s would be followed by a rupture in the financial markets and another depression. In a letter to his investors, he wrote, "I personally think that this company should not issue public stock until several years from now, when the Market Break has bottomed out and the general public is extremely 'bearish' and the market itself just beginning the first leg of a new Bull Market."[18]

A few days after this letter, Merian wrote W. Douglas Burden to report his continuing good health. "I've been examined every month since [the successful surgery] by a leading San Diego specialist and he can find no trace of cancer in my system. And six months ago, when I flew back to Houston for a day to be examined by Dr. Stehlin himself, he informed me that I had a complete cure and that I had no cancer."[19]

That day he also wrote David Bruce with his medical update. "I am still able to work twelve to fourteen hours a day, but Dorothy insists (and I am glad she does) that I take a one and a half hour to two hour walk by the sea every morning. It is beautiful beyond compare.... My good health and zest is due entirely to Dorothy's wonderful care of me.... I have never been so happy in my life."[20]

Meanwhile, the dream of 3-D color television began running into daunting technical difficulties. Yet Cooper was enjoying the challenge, happily spending his bonus time smoking his pipe and contemplating Advanced Projects. He always maintained a self-deprecating humor and he was in good spirits, usually signing off a letter with the exclamation: "*Praise be to Allah. That's me!*"

He kept the interests and welfare of his close friends at heart, such as when he asked Lowell Thomas for help in organizing a surprise honor at the Explorers Club for W. Douglas Burden, the great explorer and dragon slayer.[21] On April 14, 1972, in the grand ballroom of the Waldorf Astoria in New York, the Explorers Club had its sixty-eighth annual dinner and Burden was honored. The souvenir program, quoting from a concluding passage in Burden's book *Look to the Wilderness,* noted his plea to "save every swamp and bog and forest and desert and canyon and mountain fastness that we can. It is the garden of inspiration for our total future. It is the elemental heritage of the human race. Let us save wilderness everywhere. It is our birthright."[22]

ON DECEMBER 30, 1971, Cooper was one of those who delivered the eulogy at the funeral services for his old friend and colleague Max Steiner, held at the Church of the Hills at Forest Lawn cemetery in Glendale, California.[23]

In a July 6, 1972, letter to Otto Doering, Coop was still upbeat about his health, the prognosis still good: "The doctor says ... I have the lungs and heart of a man of 30 and the drive and intellect of a man of 25. They are wrong—they should have said a man of 21."[24]

But only a few weeks later Cooper got horrible news: The cancer had returned.

"It was of course a great and upsetting shock to hear of your relapse," Ernest Schoedsack wrote, "but Old Indestructible has bounced back so many times that I expect to hear any day now that you are planning to re-make the Kong for 360 degree screen in three dimensions and color. I won't go along unless you use my 4-channel sound. . . . Had lunch with Fay last week, and I think she will be still available to scream for us."

Monty's own health problems had worsened, his letter adding he had curtailed his activities because of "severe and irreversible degeneration of what little vision I have."[25]

Dorothy made an inquiry about a new cancer treatment that seemed to offer a reprieve, but it was only a false hope. The Man Who Cheated Death could cheat death no more. With his last chance gone, Merian C. Cooper began slipping away. His daughter Mary Caroline was already close by in San Diego; Theresa had come home from England, and Richard was given leave from his duties as combat flight leader in Thailand to be at his father's bedside.

Reportedly, in his final days, Merian remarked to Dorothy, "Death will be a new adventure."[26]

On April 21, 1973, Merian Coldwell Cooper died at Mercy Hospital in San Diego.

LOWELL THOMAS, ON his radio broadcast of April 23, 1973, confessed, "It gave me a jolt" to pick up *The New York Times* and read of Merian Cooper's death. "General Merian Cooper wasn't just a remarkable man, he was incredible," he declared.[27]

Maciej Słomczyński, Cooper's lost son and a successful writer in Poland, got the news in Kraków. He wrote Cooper's longtime assistant Zoe Porter, his letter opening, "I am awfully sorry to trouble you after so many years but the truth is that your person and your 1959 address form the only link I have when trying to get in touch with some of the problems of my youth.

"Few days ago I learned from the Polish press about the death of Merian Cooper. For the last fifteen years or so I did not try to get in any contact with him. To be frank I did not think his death [would] hit me so hard. The last letter I got from him was dated 1954. Afterwards I was perhaps too much concerned with my own career, and as he never wrote I did not write either. I believed that closing the whole affair once and for good would suit him."

The letter had a simple request: If the Cooper family in America found papers or snapshots connected with Maciej's side of the family, could they send them on to him? He added that he was a success, with "millions" of copies of books printed, wealth, honorary degrees—"so they can freely send all this without being afraid they'll contact some poor creature, silly and irresponsible." Maciej had another question: Did Merian have any other children? He simply didn't know.[28]

But his only link to Merian Cooper was a dead end, and his letter to Porter was returned, stamped "not at this address."

Maciej did pour out his heart to his sister Ania, who lived in Canada, and who had written a long letter touching on Cooper and their mother. Maciej responded in a letter marking the nineteenth anniversary of their mother's death. "She loved him very much until the moment she died. . . . But now they have both passed away. But I am still alive and so are my children. . . . And it wouldn't be like that if these two people hadn't met. And there would be no me. It is strange, isn't it? I wanted to go to America to see him but I am not to see him any more. It is too late. This death has carried me back many years, to the time of my childhood, to the things I once dreamed about, wanted to do, change, mend. Maybe it was more my fault than his. But it was as it was. You have thrown me off balance with your letter. You have brought Mother back, her troubles, my twisted affairs, and all this problem of nationality, language and longing. It has all come back to me as the world of unfulfilled possibilities."[29]

THE MEMORIAL NOTICES included the sympathies of comrades-in-arms from the wars Cooper had fought in. The bulletin for the 20th Aero Squadron poignantly announced: "General Merian C. Cooper wanted the members of the 20th to call him 'Coop'; Neither Germans or Cossacks will shoot him down again, nor will more movies show his craftsman's touch, for 'Coop' is gone."[30] A commemorative service at the Polish Air Force Memorial paid homage to the cofounder of the Kościuszko Squadron, while a wreath was laid in his honor by the Association of the Citizens of Lwów, who were always grateful for Cooper's humanitarian efforts during the days of darkness and siege.[31] Cooper's "manhood and patriotism" were saluted by General Chennault's old group, the Fourteenth Air Force Association.

A condolence letter to Dorothy from Ector LeDuc, one of Cooper's doctors in San Diego, was well meant but clinical: "Someday, of course, there may be a better way to treat cancer of the prostate and other cancers in addition, but at present there are certainly limitations both in the treatment and many others, but in the case of General Cooper the response was obviously temporary in nature but it did give him that much more tolerable life after his treatment in Houston."[32]

Dorothy had wanted more than a "tolerable life" for her husband. In a 1974 letter to Thomas Corcoran, she confessed that it still pained her that Merian hadn't been granted a few more years to realize his plans for Advanced Projects. "He never ceased thinking upon the solution of the challenge—last February and March when he was confined to the house his most contented moments were those when he smoked his pipe and pondered the solving step by step . . . the problems of making his visionary values practical. Only a few days before he was hospitalized for his final illness he said to me, 'Chickie, I know, I know just what to do with Advanced Project'—But he was not granted the time."[33]

On May 16, with full military honors, General Merian C. Cooper's ashes were committed to sea. The memorial service, held at St. Alban's Episcopal Church in West Los Angeles, included a reading from the First Letter of Paul to the Corinthians, chapter 13, reportedly Merian's favorite New Testament passage. The scripture's closing sentence told the truth of the man whose dreams had always fixed on exploring the unknown: "For now we see through a glass, darkly; but then face to face: now I know in part; but then shall I know even as also I am known."

COOPER LEFT BEHIND something that endured beyond the grave: a legend. But the legend would lie dormant, as if under an enchanted spell, and decades would pass before his life's story and work, including the epics *Grass* and *Chang,* would be resurrected. But because his great creation, the giant gorilla Kong, lived on, there was that door cracked open onto that life, the personal legend waiting in the shadows.

Cooper's very end had a showman's flourish: After a short illness Robert Armstrong, who played Carl Denham, died in a Santa Monica hospital on Friday, April 20, 1973. It was the next day—only a few hours later—that Cooper followed his surrogate self into eternity.

And there was still one more showman's touch. Randy R. Merritt, a lawyer who'd worked with Richard Cooper, recalled how, years later, he saw Charles FitzSimons tear up when describing the passing of his old friend and boss. "Charles recalled he'd heard a sonic boom, like a plane breaking the sound barrier, at the exact moment, as he later found out, when Merian had died. It was Merian Cooper saying good-bye."[34]

THE ONLY KNOWN PHOTOGRAPH OF MERIAN COOPER'S BURIAL AT SEA.

Cooper Papers, BYU

THE LEGEND

"DISTANT, DIFFICULT, AND DANGEROUS"

*I wanted to demonstrate there was a tremendous arc in
Cooper's career, from being a newspaper reporter to explorer to
financier to aviator to filmmaker to starmaker, that he was
interested in things behind the camera, from Technicolor
to joining Lowell Thomas to do Cinerama. I wanted to show
the great diversity of his life and yet home in on a central
theme which unites all of that, which is summed up in his
famous statement: "distant, difficult, and dangerous."*

—James D'Arc, Brigham Young University film
archivist on organizing a Cooper exhibition at
the 2003 Pordenone Silent Film Festival[1]

IN 1976, ARCHIE MARSHEK, ONE OF THE FEW REMAINING PRODUCTION PRINCI-
pals from *King Kong*, was driving to the old mining town of Telluride, Colorado. He had never heard of the place until he'd received a letter bearing
the town's postmark, inviting him to participate in a *King Kong* tribute at
the Third Annual Telluride Film Festival. The drive took Marshek to the
Wupatki Reservation, where volcanic explosions had once enriched the
soil with ash, through majestic Monument Valley, where his thoughts
turned to John Ford and his late friend Merian Cooper, and past the ruins
of the mysterious Anasazi, who'd once flourished on the mesas and cliffs.
It was a time-traveling journey that culminated in his appearance on the
stage of the Sheridan Opera House with Fay Wray, the last living featured
player from *Kong*; Linwood Dunn; Orville Goldner, who had recently written *The Making of King Kong* with George Turner; Zoe Porter; and Dorothy
Cooper.

During the tribute the house lights went to black and Robert Arm-

"LA JUNGLA MISTERIOSA"—
CLASSIC *CHANG* POSTER
REPRODUCED AS GREETING
CARD AT THE 2003 LE
GIORNATE DEL CINEMA MUTO.

strong's Carl Denham could be heard over the speakers, once again introducing "*the Eighth Wonder of the World!*" A spotlight pierced the darkness and
shone on the curtain, which parted, revealing a model of the Empire State
Building and atop it a mannequin of King Kong.

The crowd, Marshek later wrote, went wild. Then, to the stage came Fay
Wray with effects creator David Allen, who had recently created a special
Kong puppet for a TV commercial. Allen brought onstage with him the
real thing—one of the articulated metal armatures of Kong used in the
film. And then the newspaper and magazine photographers took photos of
Fay Wray and Kong onstage, just as had happened in the movie.

After an intermission, a sparkling thirty-five-millimeter nitrate print of
King Kong was screened, complete with scenes the censors had snipped in
past rereleases. The enthusiastic audience reaction—the purest evidence of
the film's enduring appeal even as it approached its fiftieth anniversary—
reminded Marshek of a prophetic comment regarding *King Kong* that Lloyd
Arthur Ashbuck had made in 1933: "So great was its impact that I venture
to predict it will not be forgotten even in 1960. It's destined to become a
living legend of American filmlore."[2]

That year, the bicentennial of the nation's founding, also marked the
release of a controversial *King Kong* remake. For several years, Universal had
planned a new *King Kong* production set in the 1930s, while producer Dino
De Laurentiis and Paramount were developing a modern retelling. Universal and De Laurentiis would win out in what *Kong* fan Paul Mandell termed
"gorilla warfare" in a scathing open letter to De Laurentiis in a 1976 issue
of *Cinefantastique* magazine. "De Laurentiis has invested huge sums in a
forty-foot mechanical Kong which will actually be placed in the streets of
New York and atop the World Trade Center! It all seems ridiculous—it is!"

In truth, Mandell was irate that the producer wasn't even considering
stop-motion—this was more than a decade before acceptable computer-
generated animation would emerge—and lumped the De Laurentiis production with 1962's *King Kong vs. Godzilla* and other examples of what
happened when classics were "blasphemed by the producers of schlock."[3]
Feelings among *Kong* purists ran so high that Fay Wray refused to sign a
poster for the new movie when it was brought to her by a fan during a Telluride autograph session, Marshek reported, although she offered to sign
another item. The vaunted mechanical Kong, which sought to replicate in
full scale the imagined height of the original, would prove to be a disaster—

a million-dollar creation so wooden it would be used for only an estimated ten seconds of screen time.[4]

In December 1976, the De Laurentiis *King Kong* was released. The production provided the battleground upon which was waged the fight to control Kong. Merian Cooper had fought that battle a few years before, and hadn't lived to see his resolution. But his son, Richard Cooper, would pick up the banner and charge into the legal fray.

THE FINAL FIGHT to control *King Kong* began in 1975 when RKO licensed the Dino De Laurentiis Corporation (DDL) to remake the classic film. Over the years, RKO and fifteen licensees had enjoyed a long string of successes with Kong, producing toys, games, books, and other products.

But the movie-remake deal between RKO and DDL did not go unchallenged. Universal Studios, claiming RKO had promised them exclusive remake rights, sued both RKO and De Laurentiis in California state court for breach of contract and wrongful interference with contractual relations. While pursuing its claim, Universal also began preproduction work on its own *King Kong* remake and instituted a copyright action in federal court against RKO, DDL, and Merian Cooper's heir, Richard Cooper.[5]

Universal's federal action asked the court for a declaration that they could make their version of *King Kong* without infringing on any other rights, claiming the story was in the public domain because the copyright had lapsed. Indeed, although a new, long overdue schedule of rights had been ushered in with the Copyright Act of 1976, *King Kong* had been made under the antiquated Copyright Act of 1909, which placed the burden on copyright holders to renew their rights after twenty-eight years. The original Edgar Wallace–Merian Cooper novelization and serialization—published in 1932, ahead of the film's release—had not been renewed after the initial twenty-eight-year period, and had therefore automatically gone into the public domain around 1960.

RKO and De Laurentiis filed counterclaims against Universal, arguing that Universal's remake would infringe on their copyright rights. Meanwhile, Richard Cooper denied that the story had fallen into the public domain and filed his own cross-claim against RKO. He also continued his father's argument that Merian Cooper's 1932 agreement with RKO was only a limited grant of rights for the original movie and a sequel, and that any other commercial exploitation of Kong was for Merian Cooper's account.

This tangled legal web of claims, counterclaims, and cross-claims was finally presented in the United States District Court of Los Angeles before Judge Manuel Real. For the first time, all possible claimants for the right to exploit King Kong were in the same courtroom.

Meanwhile, O. C. Doering, Cooper's old friend from the RKO and Argosy days, contacted a top Washington copyright lawyer regarding the Kong case and Richard Cooper's claim. In the process, he discovered something that would help Richard tremendously. "Coop could *possibly* have had an interest in the renewed copyright of the movie, itself, jointly with RKO," Charles FitzSimons wrote lawyer Earl Wright, passing on the opinion of Doering's Washington contact. "This could be *enormously* valuable and a simple notification of Dick's rights to Paramount, De Laurentis [*sic*] and Universal might 'smoke' this out by inducing their legal departments to get into it of their own accord without Dick having to adopt a position or do a thing!"[6]

It was a four-day bench trial, which was the same as a jury trial except that Judge Real would make the final decision after hearing the arguments and considering the evidence. Judge Real gave his verdict on November 24, 1976, affirming that the *King Kong* novelization and serialization *were* in the public domain and that Universal could make its movie as long as it didn't infringe on the 1933 RKO release.

But on December 6, 1976—the very month Paramount released the De Laurentiis *King Kong*—Judge Real made a subsequent ruling, which held that all rights in the name, character, and story of King Kong, other than the rights in the 1933 movie and the sequel, *The Son of Kong,* were vested in Cooper. The ruling held that even though RKO hadn't mentioned Merian Cooper when they'd renewed the *King Kong* movie rights, they had been acting, as a matter of law, as "constructive trustee" on behalf of Cooper's rights. As a result, the court ruled that *all profits* RKO had earned through its exploitation of *Kong,* excluding the original film and sequel, should go to Richard Cooper, the legal heir to his father's claims.

The ruling—which would become known as the "Cooper Judgment"—expressly stated that it wouldn't change the previous ruling that the novelization and serialization had gone into the public domain. But it was a huge victory that affirmed the position Merian Cooper had maintained for years.

Richard Cooper sold his Kong rights to Universal in December 1976, while retaining worldwide publishing rights to aspects of the story, characters, and title that were not in the public domain.

After RKO and Universal appealed the district court's opinion, the studios settled with each other. The Ninth Circuit Court of Appeals then directed the case back to Judge Real to determine the effect of the settlements and to enter dismissals and new judgments as appropriate. In November 1980, Judge Real officially dismissed the claims that Universal and RKO had brought to the bench trial four years before. Two months later, Judge Real also reinstated the Cooper Judgment.

Meanwhile, from 1976 through 1979, Paramount, under its licensing agreement with De Laurentiis and RKO, used the King Kong name and character to produce toys and games, wristwatches, and apparel products.

But with the original *King Kong* novelization and serialization in the public domain, was there an opening for more commercial exploitation of what had clearly become a cultural icon? There was, setting the stage for another legal wrangle, this time with Universal and Nintendo squaring off in the matter of King Kong versus Donkey Kong.[7]

Although Universal would create a King Kong attraction for a Universal theme park and by 2003 had embarked with director Peter Jackson on a new remake of the classic film, by 1981 the *King Kong* rights it had exercised were minimal. Universal had dropped its earlier plans for a *Kong* remake, and its merchandising consisted of continuation of a prior license granted to an already existing licensee relating to the sale of Kong masks and costumes.

But, in July 1981, the Nintendo Company and its wholly owned subsidiary, Nintendo of America (collectively "Nintendo"), introduced the Donkey Kong video game to the American market. In the original version of the game, players maneuvered a little character named Mario up a series of girders, ladders, and elevators to save a blond woman from the clutches of an impish gorilla. By 1983, Nintendo had earned more than $180 million from the game. Suddenly, Universal was interested in its rights to Kong.

In June 1982, Universal sued Nintendo in federal court, alleging infringement of its rights to King Kong, and also sent out "cease and desist" letters to many of the Nintendo licensees producing Donkey Kong products. Nintendo filed a counterclaim against Universal, alleging wrongful interference with their licensed agreements.

Ultimately, the district court rejected Universal's claim of ownership of exclusive rights to King Kong, a decision subsequently affirmed by the Second Circuit Court of Appeals. In dismissing the suit, the court ruled that Universal could not claim exclusive trademark rights to King Kong. Even though there had been a judgment in favor of Richard Cooper—who subsequently had sold Universal his rights—trademark rights could not be so easily transferred. The court noted, "Trademark rights are fragile; they do not exist in the abstract, but only because of the public's association of them with a particular product or business."[8]

The court's ruling further noted the name, title, and character of King Kong no longer even signified a single source of origin to potential consumers. The court pointed out that Kong rights were held by three parties: RKO had rights to the original movie and sequel, Richard Cooper owned worldwide book and periodical publishing rights, and the Dino De Laurentiis company had rights to its 1976 remake. "Universal thus owns only those rights in the King Kong name and character that RKO, Cooper, or DDL do not own," the court summarized.[9] In the end, the court determined that there was simply no likelihood of confusing King Kong and Donkey Kong.

THE LEGAL BATTLES continued into 1983 and the fiftieth anniversary of *King Kong*. To mark the half century, a gigantic inflatable Kong figure was hoisted to the ape's famous perch atop the Empire State Building. It was a battle getting it up to the summit, with winds whipping the cables and tearing at the figure's nylon fabric. Finally, the blowers, pumping in air through the figure's toes, filled out the mighty ape to its full size, "producing one of the most striking sights ever added to the Manhattan skyline," *Time* magazine noted. But the wind-whipped peak, which had long ago ended the dream of providing a docking port for dirigibles, created a fatal puncture, and "after only a day of glory, the mighty Kong lay hanging off the building's spire like an old brown garbage bag," *Time* reported. "It was beauty killed the beast last time, mundane nylon failure this outing."[10]

Ray Bradbury and his old friend Ray Harryhausen celebrated the fiftieth anniversary at a lavish event at the venerable Grauman's theater on Hollywood Boulevard. "When Kong fell from the Empire State, he killed two kids with one slam, me and my pal Ray Harryhausen," Bradbury later wrote. ". . . Because Kong crushed us to earth, we arose with fiery souls to strike toward a night in 1983 when we would attend the fiftieth anniversary of Kong at its repremiere at Grauman's Chinese. There, Fay Wray rushed out of the mob to leap and join us in Kong's mechanical arms and give us hugs. Cinema madness, you must admit, pays off."[11]

TOWARD THE END of the 1970s, two more leading members of Cooper's remarkable inner circle, both integral to the creation of *King Kong*, passed away. The bell tolled for W. Douglas Burden in 1978, and Ernest Schoedsack followed a year later.

"Thank you so much for telling me the sad news . . . poor Monte!" Kevin Brownlow wrote Dorothy Jordan Cooper. "He hated being old more than anyone I have ever met, and old age dealt him a series of cruel blows. I am sure you are right—his death was a release.

"I am grateful that I knew him ten years ago, when he still had some of his old vigor and vitality and humour. He was certainly an extraordinary and unforgettable person."[12]

In 1979, Brownlow's *The War, the West, and the Wilderness,* his epic history of the makers of silent movies who ventured "into dangerous and distant places," was published; he dedicated the work to Merian C. Cooper and Ernest B. Schoedsack, who had inspired the book. In a letter to Dorothy, Brownlow underlined his debt of gratitude and added a poignant note: "I regret most that Merian could not see it—for it is his spirit that animates it. . . . But that is how remarkable people like him achieve their immortality—by transferring something of their spirit to so many of those they meet."[13]

That spirit had also been transferred to Rudy Behlmer, who, in 2004, reminisced about his long interview sessions with Cooper in the 1960s. He could still imitate the distinctive southern twang and high-pitched inflection, rising in octaves, when Coop got excited about an idea (which, he recalled, sometimes left Behlmer's wife "shaking" if she answered the telephone and got a burst of Cooper's barreling energy). Behlmer remembered the little things: Cooper always referring to Dorothy as "my bride," his cagey denial of having suffered a heart attack while at RKO, the surprisingly gentle gesture when Cooper once took the hand of Behlmer's five-year-old son to walk him across a street. "He seemed to be a paradox,"

Behlmer said. "But he was an adventurer par excellence, and danger was part of that life. His whole credo, as he told me, was that in the wilds you had to think on your feet and make decisions. I don't think you can ask for more clarification of a true adventurer."

Behlmer noted Cooper's extraordinary impact, beginning with the seminal films that influenced the art of documentary films and even fictional adventure. The dramatic elephant stampede for *Chang*, for example, directly inspired similar sequences in the subsequent MGM *Tarzan* movies, as Behlmer discovered while doing research in the MGM archives. "I think when *Chang* came out there must have been awe in the movie business; people were overwhelmed to think of these two guys shooting this thing by themselves in the middle of nowhere."

Part of Cooper's genius was his farsighted thinking, Behlmer added. "There was the concept of 'natural drama' and the idea in *Four Feathers* of shooting in Africa and intercutting. Cooper realized the potential of stop-motion after seeing what Willis O'Brien was doing on *Creation*—that was Cooper's vision. Then he made *The Last Days of Pompeii*, and that started this renaissance of disaster films like *San Francisco* and *Hurricane*—once again, Coop was the door opener. He was there when things like three-color Technicolor was starting, and he was the visionary, the driving force." Even as an old man, Cooper hadn't lost his visionary eye; Behlmer recalled Cooper walking away from a potential TV series because the network refused to do it in color. "This was in 1965, when the networks all hadn't gone one hundred percent to color yet. But Cooper wouldn't do it unless it was done in color. As usual, he was ahead of his time."

It was "strange," Behlmer added, that Merian C. Cooper's name, unlike those of other legends of cinema, didn't conjure up a specific image, an instant persona. "I think Coop's life was such a mosaic that people didn't put it all together," Behlmer concluded.[14] Only the likes of Kevin Brownlow, Ronald Haver, Rudy Behlmer, and George Turner had kept the Cooper name alive in their books and articles about film.

In the years following Cooper's death, *Grass* and *Chang* had become similarly forgotten, so rarely seen that some people assumed they were among the legendary lost films of the silent era. But a resurrection of interest and an emerging critical appraisal of Cooper's work began taking hold. In 1981, Kevin Brownlow wrote Dorothy Cooper that UCLA had the last thirty-five-millimeter original print of *Chang* but had discovered that it was badly decomposed. "In desperation," Brownlow reported, "they sent it to be printed by the best film surgeon, Karl Malkames. He had always loved the film and was heartbroken when he saw the state it was in. A few fragments emerged in S. Africa . . . but there was no way the film could be properly restored. However, a vast sum of money was spent trying."[15]

But then a miracle occurred: A copy of *Chang* had been preserved in the Natural History Museum, then part of the British Museum. It had been a gift made in 1927 during a formal ceremony in which Paramount managing director J. C. Graham presented the film to C. Tate Regan, the museum's director. It was the first time a copy of a film had been officially accepted by the British Museum, and it had been presented in a hermetically sealed "casket," then placed in a British Museum vault with the stipulation that it not be opened until September 4, 1977. In a September 1927 article in *Kinetograph Weekly* the film had been hailed "as a true account of the animal life of this era" that would be included in a cinematic time capsule for the future, along with gramophone records made by the Columbia Gramophone Company of animal noises recorded in London's Zoological Gardens.[16]

"The Natural History Museum contacted our National Film Archive [in London] and informed them they had an original tinted print of *Chang*," Brownlow wrote Dorothy. "The NFA people rushed over and found a beautiful positive which looked as though it had never been projected. It was shown at a special event at the twenty-fifth London Film Festival, to an appreciative audience.

"So the film has been saved for posterity . . . this time it has been printed on acetate before the showing."[17]

By the early 1990s, *Grass* and *Chang* were once again unspooling in theatrical presentations at prestigious art-house cinemas from New York to San Francisco. The summer 1991 schedule for San Francisco's Castro Theatre hailed its screening of *Chang* as "The Restored Lost Masterpiece by the Makers of *King Kong*."

The theatrical revivals had been made possible by Milestone Film & Video, which made "decent" money, company vice president and cofounder Dennis Doros explained, but they had fallen short of his ultimate goal: triggering a global renaissance of interest in the works of Cooper and Schoedsack. "It was, 'My, aren't these films wonderful—now, what's the next film?' " Doros said, shrugging with resignation. "Nobody put two and two together: Something about those films is art! I think modern audiences should care about those films. Out of the one hundred and fifty to two hundred films we've done, *Grass* and *Chang* are among the ones I'm most proud of distributing. *Chang* is a national treasure in Thailand. *Grass* has images of a race and culture that don't exist anymore; it's been called the greatest migration in modern history, and I agree. The journey of the Bakhtiari is so astonishing, the power of those images is like a dream, the way they're constantly moving and climbing.

"Some of the old [silent-era] adventure films for the public have embarrassing scenes, such as seeing if some native can open a bottle of soda pop or having a pygmy smoke a cigar and choke on it. But Douglas Burden loved the Indians, and Cooper and Schoedsack loved the Bakhtiari and Thai people. They felt these were the lost tribes, and they were going back in time to when men were men, basically."[18]

Despite Doros's chagrin, those early 1990s theatrical releases planted a seed. A retrospective featuring the Cooper-Schoedsack films and other historic adventure films of early cinema highlighted the international stage of Le Giornate del Cinema Muto 2003, the twenty-second annual silent-film festival, held in Italy. Once again, the "distant, difficult, and dangerous" team was traveling overseas.

THE TOWN OF Sacile, Italy, a short drive from the canals of Venice, retains its venerable Venetian character, evident in the aged facades and the shady loggias flanking the town square. The bells in the clock tower still toll the hours, and the gentle Livenza River winds through town, providing romantic views from bridges and grassy banks. Sacile, a counterpoint to the bustle of nearby host city Pordenone, was the 2003 venue for the twenty-second annual festival, which had grown into a prestigious international gathering of fans, filmmakers, and academics. From screenings to panel presentations and collegium talks, the event was in the vanguard of the preservation and celebration of the world's silent-film heritage.

Thus, it was a major event in the rediscovery of Merian Cooper that an entire slate of early adventure films presented under the title "Cooper-Schoedsack and Friends" was one of the featured programs at Le Giornate del Cinema Muto 2003. The adventure series included such rarely seen films as *With Byrd at the South Pole* (Paramount, 1930) and Martin and Osa Johnson's *Simba: The King of Beasts—a Saga of the Africa Veldt* (1928).

Once again, darkened theaters lit up with Varick Frissell's *The Viking* and visions of the undulating ice floes upon which Frissell had lost his life during the mysterious explosion; once again W. Douglas Burden's *Chang-*like natural drama of vanishing Indian life, *The Silent Enemy,* flickered across movie screens. Cooper and Schoedsack's seminal trilogy was featured—*Grass* and *Chang* and *The Four Feathers.* There were also snippets from *Ra-Mu,* the travelogue Captain Edward Salisbury released in 1929 and 1934 featuring Schoedsack's camerawork in Abyssinia, including the massing of Ras Tafari's army—images that had often been presumed lost in the fire that destroyed the *Wisdom II.* (Even Cooper, in a list of his directorial career, wrote that "the film was destroyed by fire in Savona, Italy in 1922.") There were test-footage scenes from *Creation* and Schoedsack's solo feature, *Rango.*[19]

During a late-afternoon break from the hectic cinematic schedule, Milestone vice president Dennis Doros sat on a bench on the bank of the river below the town square. He reflected on Cooper and Schoedsack and the great explorers of their generation who brought back moving-picture documents.

Doros had been working at Kino International when he'd been inspired by Kevin Brownlow's *The War, the West, and the Wilderness,* leading him to forge what he called a "wilderness series" on video, featuring some of the exploration films Brownlow celebrated in his book. Years later, Doros said, Milestone's Age of Exploration series was also surprisingly successful in its video and DVD release. "It struck a nerve with people—it's about seeing lost images of lost cultures. When I was growing up, everything was shot in studios, and even if it was a location, the 'horror' of shooting in Alberta, Canada, wasn't the same as when people knowingly risked their lives to take these journeys and make these films." Doros and his future wife, Amy, set their sights on more than a dozen seminal adventure films but were particularly focused on Cooper-Schoedsack films: "Kevin said they were the best."

Doros's first great buy was *Chang,* which he used his bar mitzvah savings to acquire. The journey to secure the rights had led nowhere until

Doros got a promising lead—an article about a racetrack in which C. V. Whitney played a prominent part. Realizing that the former head of Pan Am and Cooper's old partner was still around, Doros placed a call and discovered that Whitney still held the rights. "Whitney was ninety-five, but sharp as a tack. We offered ten thousand dollars for the rights, and Whitney had this young lawyer who said something like 'That's not enough and you can't have it for perpetuity; we're going to have to make it a five-year deal.' He gets back to Whitney and the quote I heard from Whitney was 'You want to reduce perpetuity to a five-year deal? I'm ninety-five fucking years old—how long do you think I'm going to be living? Make the deal, they're nice people.' C.V., God bless him, saw how much we loved Cooper and the films and sold us the rights."

Milestone's *Chang* was transferred from the negative Cooper and Whitney struck in 1955, when they bought the rights from Paramount. Meanwhile, C. V. Whitney had sold his rights to *Grass* to Films Around the World. Around 1965, as Doros recalls, the owner of that company donated the film and its rights to the Museum of Modern Art, from which Milestone acquired the rights around 1990.[20]

The celebration of Cooper's film legacy at the 2003 festival also featured a collection of artifacts tracing Cooper's life titled Distant, Difficult, and Dangerous: The Life and Films of Merian C. Cooper. The exhibit included a *King Kong* room, where the classic film played continuously on a cutting-edge home television unit. There was also a buzz throughout the festival that there had been an appearance by Malgorzata "Daisy" Słomczyńska-Pierzchalska, daughter of Maciej Słomczyński, who'd broken the silence about Merian Cooper's out-of-wedlock son. She had written a book about her father's life that had been published in Poland, and she had come to Sacile at the instigation of Kevin Brownlow and festival organizers.

These developments particularly pleased James D'Arc, the curator of the Arts and Communications Archives at Brigham Young University, who oversees BYU's Merian C. Cooper Papers collection, the source of many of the items in the festival's exhibition. He had been a driving force behind the "Cooper-Schoedsack and Friends" program.

Cooper had been D'Arc's passion and the focus of his own personal quest ever since his youthful viewings of *King Kong*, which had acquainted him with the names of Cooper and Schoedsack and launched his ever-growing knowledge of their careers. But he hadn't truly been hooked until 1973, when he saw the side-by-side obituaries of Robert Armstrong and Merian Cooper, who had died within hours of each other.

"The delicious irony of it struck me: Where did Merian Cooper leave off and Carl Denham begin, and vice versa?" D'Arc recalled over pizza in a quiet Sacile restaurant. "I'd been reading about how the Carl Denham character was molded off of Cooper, and when I saw the obituaries that left an indelible impression. It just hit me: 'This is a fascinating man.' When I got my job at Brigham Young University I focused my persistent and ongoing attention to Merian C. Cooper. And that's exactly what it took. My first meeting with Dorothy Cooper at her home in Coronado, California, was very nice; she had wonderful southern charm and hospitality—but she wasn't going to give her husband's papers over easily. I kept up contact and a steady stream of correspondence with her for years after that."

During those years, BYU secured the papers of Cecil B. DeMille, Howard Hawks, Max Steiner, and other major figures of film history. The turning point for Dorothy came, appropriately enough, during the fiftieth-anniversary year of *King Kong*, when Jimmy Stewart donated his papers to BYU. "[To celebrate] we invited Jimmy Stewart and his wife, Gloria, up to BYU and they stayed most of the week, and the last night we screened a thirty-five-millimeter print of *It's a Wonderful Life* on campus in a large auditorium that seated twenty-three hundred people," D'Arc recalled, smiling. "It was a wonderful evening, and Stewart was terrific. The event got great press, and I think that's what pulled Dorothy over. In 1986 she said, 'I've made my decision. I want [Merian's papers] to go to Brigham Young University.' "

The massive material that D'Arc and his colleagues received indicated that not only had Cooper himself saved practically *everything*, but his parents had done likewise. "He's Merian C. Cooper; you just save those things," D'Arc noted. "His parents saved everything from the message Merian wrote on a scrap of paper smuggled out of a Russian prisoner-of-war camp to all the diplomatic cables regarding their son. I think his parents had a real pride in their famous son, going from one adventure to another."

D'Arc, a regular at the film festival since 1988, had shared BYU's Cecil B. DeMille collection at the 1991 festival, and soon after, his thoughts had turned toward a similar celebration for the neglected life and works of Merian Cooper. "There'd never been a focus on Cooper *anywhere,* not just the Pordenone festival," D'Arc explained. "I have a strong sense of the collections I take care of, and I feel that if I don't publicize or enhance their profile, I'm falling down in our archival trust. About three years ago I began planting the seed in the minds of the festival organizers, needling them in a very friendly way. I noted the tremendous collection of material at BYU and the fact that there'd never been a dedicated exhibition to Cooper. Finally, the time was right and they indicated they wanted to have Cooper as the focus for this year's festival.

"It's a curious irony that in order to preserve things of worth for the future I'm hurrying to chase down the past," D'Arc remarked wryly. "The past is not some static thing that sits there like a big granite mountain. I see the past as a mirage that's quickly receding and, often, the faster we run toward it the more beguiling and elusive the mirage becomes. What makes it concrete is the 'paper,' the collective term for journals and production files, letters and copies of correspondence, plaques, certificates, photographs. It's like an archeologist who goes to a site and digs up shards of pottery and attempts to reconstruct the life and perceptions of the people who made it.

"For most of us close to the Cooper legacy the Le Giornate del Cinema Muto 2003 is really a pivotal event in the next chapter of the public legacy of Merian C. Cooper. Like the metaphor of a hothouse in which things are always growing, the festival has gathered writers, historians, and filmmakers who figure in the legacy of Cooper to germinate new ideas, new projects, new enthusiasm. It goes without saying, the influence that Daisy's appearance and her revelations have made in this group."[21]

Daisy Słomczyńska-Pierzchalska's book about her father, who died in 1998 from lung cancer at age seventy-six, was published in Poland in May 2003, its title translated as *I Couldn't Be Different: The Enigma of Maciej Słomczyński.* Maciej's own life, his daughter's book revealed, was as momentous as that of his famous father. He survived a Nazi slave-labor camp and became a storied writer in Poland whose work included children's books, plays, a series of wildly popular crime novels, and translations into the Polish language of the works of Shakespeare and James Joyce, notably *Ulysses.*

"I'm a molecular biologist, not a writer like my father," Daisy explained over coffee in a café on Sacile's town square. "But I wrote the book, I think, because I miss him very much, and to sort out my feelings toward him and his death. But writing it, I also realized how interesting my grandparents were."

Daisy had never been in contact with anyone from the Cooper family, although she was hopeful that there might be some future contact. But in her own family, the relationship between Cooper and her grandmother had never been a dark secret. Her father had told her about his biological father; the emotional implications, however, hadn't really resonated until after Maciej's death. It was around 1999, while poring through his personal papers, that Daisy found the old correspondence between her father and Merian Cooper and suddenly realized the complexity of their relationship.

"The problem was, when I could have asked my father a lot of questions I wasn't interested enough to ask," she said, sighing. "He told me things, I just didn't analyze them at the time. Once, we were in London and in front of the Ritz Hotel when my father told me, 'Take a photograph of me because here I used to meet my father.' I took the photo but I didn't ask anything further, you know?"

She recalled the awful years of the war, when her father had been captured by the Gestapo and escaped from a slave-labor camp. And then had come the disillusionment for the son who'd never be fully embraced by his father. "They had a long correspondence [after the war] and were arranging something that failed," Daisy explained. "I have a letter from my father that says, 'I got the letter from my god damn father. Nothing new in them entirely.' He was angry. Why? I don't know. My father was twenty-four and always wanted to be a writer and I think he wanted to go to America and expected Merian would help him settle in Hollywood, something like that. And [Cooper] probably refused because by then he had a young wife and children. My general impression is Cooper wanted to arrange something, but it wasn't what my father expected. He probably wanted to be treated as a son."

Daisy noted that Cooper stayed in touch with her grandmother until her death in 1954, although by then it had become largely surreptitious. "I know that their correspondence wasn't direct—it was through Cooper's secretary, Zoe Porter, a sort of covert operation. Times were tough in Poland, but it was impossible to send money, so Zoe Porter sent on Cooper's behalf parcels of goods like tea and coffee, because there was nothing in Poland at the time. I have letters from Zoe to my grandmother that are like business letters: 'I'm sending something this day and that day,' and so on. But Cooper was interested in what happened to my grandmother. She was ill after the war; she had severe arthritis and was in a wheelchair."

During the festival, Daisy visited the Distant, Difficult, and Dangerous exhibition, seemingly trying to connect with a famous man who was a blood relation but also a figure of mystery to her. "It's a strange feeling," she said. "I knew from my early childhood that he was my grandfather, but he's a complete stranger to me and was probably a stranger to my father. It wasn't a normal relationship."

But she refused to paint her own father as a tragic figure—after all, he'd become one of Poland's great writers. In the end, father and son had much in common. Each had escaped from a wartime prison camp and carved out successful careers in the arts; they had both shared a wry sense of humor, been generally carefree and careless with money, and had a fondness for pipe smoking. "I don't want to give the impression that my father was this sad guy thinking about the father who didn't want him, because it was the complete opposite. He was serious in that he was a specialist in Shakespeare and Joyce and did all this remarkable work, but he was famous for his sense of humor. He was optimistic and always looking toward the future, not the past. It's only when I read those old family letters that I realized how hard this family story was for him."[22]

The Maciej Słomczyński story doesn't reveal an entirely admirable or honorable side of Merian Cooper. Merian Cooper's love child was, perhaps, the last fling of the admittedly reckless youth whose streak of rebelliousness had gotten him kicked out of Annapolis, then put him on the personal path of redemption that brought him to Poland. But, strangely and wonderfully enough, his love affair had given Poland one of its great modern men of letters. For the man who'd wanted to be of help to the Polish people since boyhood—and who brought humanitarian aid and martial ferocity to the cause—it might have been his greatest gift.

WHEN JAMES D'ARC was asked whether Cooper was an anachronism in the twenty-first century, he answered both yes and no. "He had a classic nineteenth-century classical mind as regards chivalry, a romanticism for exploration and doing difficult and dangerous things that made him almost a Kiplingesque character. Yet, he wasn't a Luddite—he embraced modern technology. Aviation was probably his first love; he could operate in the circles of high finance and motion-picture technology. In one lifetime you have this inherently contradictory romantic lover of technology. In my opinion, Cooper could be comfortable anywhere and in any time period because he'd find a way to adapt and channel his energies toward some new invention, a new show, a new investment. He was a cultural chameleon and an astonishing renaissance man, the likes of which we haven't seen since.

"I think Merian C. Cooper is perpetually fascinating and he imparts a sense of wonder and awe to anyone who investigates his life. Lowell Thomas said it best: 'Merian C. Cooper was more than a remarkable man—he was incredible.' "

AS A NEW millennium neared, *King Kong* was still resonating throughout the popular culture. In 1991, *Kong* was awarded preservation priority status as one of twenty-five classic movies added to the Library of Congress's National Film Registry; in 1998, it was named one of the top one hundred American films by the American Film Institute (number forty-three on that list, for those keeping score). By 2003, Merian Cooper's greatest creation was slated to be given new life as *Lord of the Rings* filmmaker Peter Jackson began turning his attention to a *King Kong* remake, a project Jackson had dreamed of ever since he'd seen the original at an impressionable young age.

The original film had struck a creative spark with Jackson, much as it had inspired young Ray Harryhausen, as Jackson explained in a *Time* article preceding the Academy Awards ceremony that saw the final chapter in his *Lord of the Rings* trilogy sweep all eleven categories in which it had been nominated, including Best Picture. As a kid, Jackson loved making Super 8 movies—but he became passionate about film after seeing *King Kong*. The next day he began a remake. "I built a cardboard model of the Empire State Building," Jackson recalled. "And I built a little rubber King Kong out of wire and my mother's fur coat. . . . But hardly any of it got made. I realized that, at the age of nine, a remake of 'King Kong' was a bit ambitious."[23]

The fallout from *Kong* came full circle for Ray Harryhausen on June 10, 2003, when he was honored with a star on the Hollywood Walk of Fame placed directly across the street from Grauman's Chinese Theatre, where he'd first seen *King Kong*. "It's rather a bit of irony that I'd end up with a star almost opposite where the whole thing started seventy years ago!" Harryhausen mused during the ceremony in his honor.

THE KONG MYTH ENDURES. KONG BATTLES SKULL ISLAND DINOSAUR.
Art by Joe Devito, Kong: King of Skull Island (DH Press, 2004)

With a buzz building about the *Kong* remake, it seemed a grand notion to have a reunion of three fabled members of the Los Angeles Science Fiction League, all of them lovers of *Kong* and Cooper lore, all of them having made their mark on popular culture: Ray Harryhausen, Ray Bradbury, and Forrest Ackerman.

For Harryhausen, the reunion in Los Angeles was another stop on a long trip from his home in England. The tall, professorial-looking stop-motion master and wizard behind such fantasy films as *The Seventh Voyage of Sinbad* and *Jason and the Argonauts* was bound for New York for signings of *Ray Harryhausen: An Animated Life,* and a retrospective of some of his famous films at the Walter Reade Theater in Lincoln Center.

That New York visit would also provide him an opportunity to visit Fay Wray, whose performance as Ann Darrow had thrilled and inspired him as a lad. Harryhausen didn't know it at the time, but the visit would include a trip with Wray to the top of the Empire State Building, chasing the mythic ghost of King Kong.

MYTHIC VISION

To leave a mark on New York City, you need an indelible visual: King Kong on the Empire State Building swatting at planes; the Beast from 20,000 Fathoms rampaging through Coney Island; Godzilla biting holes in the Brooklyn Bridge.

—Tad Friend, *The New Yorker*[1]

MOVIE LEGEND FAY WRAY TO MAKE HISTORIC VISIT TO OBSERVATORY OF EMPIRE STATE BUILDING . . . King Kong's Leading Lady to Visit Site of Cinematic Triumph. "No monkeying around" as legendary actress Fay Wray, King Kong's favorite leading lady, will make a historic visit to the Empire State Building, site of the 1933 classic film that thrilled millions and made Wray, King Kong and the Empire State Building instant movie stars, on Saturday, May 15th; 3:00 P.M.; Empire State Building; 350 Fifth Avenue, Main Lobby, Manhattan.

—Empire State Building press release, May 15, 2004

THE CLARION CALL OF THE LOS ANGELES SCIENCE FICTION LEAGUE EVOKED THE sense of Saturday matinee serials and golden age comic books, and of a time when kids played crime busters and were hooked into wireless radios, rocketry, and other technological marvels. Indeed, the people who once crowded the Brown Room on the third floor of Clifton's cafeteria in downtown Los Angeles were a breed apart, dreamers fueled by popular culture and inspired by the latest scientific breakthrough, believers in the future and custodians of the past.

The topics for each of the weekly Thursday-evening sessions might range from rockets and space travel to hydroponics and painless childbirth, from talks on the craft of writing to reports and recommendations for current issues of *Astounding Science Fiction, Thrilling Wonder Stories,* and other periodicals. They were also interested in current events; in 1940, when London was being bombed, league members listened to reports and read letters from the embattled city.

The group's storied alumni included Robert Heinlein, who would earn a name for himself as one of the seminal forces in science fiction literature. It was Forrest "Forry" Ackerman who brought the two Rays to the meetings—"Forry is responsible for all of our lives," Ray Bradbury declared as the three old friends settled in at the reunion at Clifton's. Bradbury had been beguiled by a notice Ackerman had posted about the meetings of the league; Harryhausen, still pursuing the secrets of stop-motion, had gone to a revival of *Kong* and seen beautiful eleven-by-fourteen stills from the film displayed in the lobby. These, he discovered, belonged to Ackerman, who not only let him study the stills but invited him to the Brown Room gatherings.

The three shared a love of primal things—monsters, and dinosaurs, and *King Kong,* of course—and the two Rays would collaborate on one movie project together that touched upon their prehistoric fascination: *The Beast from 20,000 Fathoms* (1953).

The 2004 reunion was a cozy, private affair. In addition to the three guests of honor, a few friends and acquaintances were in attendance, including filmmaker Craig Barron, who made an audio recording for the Visual Effects Society, and Arnold Kunert, who brought a cameraman to videotape the event. The reunion took place on the restaurant's spacious but deserted third floor, in the general area once occupied by the old Brown Room. The space had long since been remodeled, yet Clifton's remained an oasis of tradition in a sea of change. "This used to be Los Angeles; this was the center of everything," Bradbury recalled of the old downtown, which had boasted movie palaces and department stores and nickel hamburger stands, and where on New Year's Eve a million people crowded its streets to cheer in the new year.

But the "good old days" weren't all golden—it was the Depression, after all. Bradbury noted that his family had been on relief and he'd sold newspapers on street corners. "My dad didn't have a job and I graduated in a suit with a bullet hole in the front. My uncle was killed in the suit when he jumped a holdup man, and we couldn't afford to have the suit repaired. So on graduation day I wore the suit he was killed in."

During the reunion, Bradbury was asked why, given those tough times, the people who'd once met in the Brown Room had maintained such optimism and a firm belief in the future. "No, no." Bradbury shook his head. "Optimism is a lying word. Optimal behavior is everything and that's *love*. Love drives you into the future when you have nothing. I didn't realize how bad off I was. Why? I was in love with H. G. Wells and Jules Verne and Edgar Allan Poe and libraries and books and films. *King Kong* might be showing in Pasadena, at a little ten-cent theater, or they might be showing *She,* and Ray would call me up and say, 'Let's go out.' We'd head all the way out to a dime movie at night because we were in love. I used to hang out at Paramount studios because I wanted to go over the wall and be a screenwriter, and I'd know all the people who hung out in front of Columbia studios, and in front of the Brown Derby restaurant on Friday nights after the boxing matches quit when George Burns and Jack Benny and Cary Grant would show up. I was fourteen and I'd go out roller-skating around Hollywood. Why? I was in love, you see. Not optimism. Love. Love is the answer to everything."

Ackerman touched on how close the three of them were to the seminal influences of science fiction and fantasy, describing the day the great H. G. Wells, author of *The War of the Worlds, The Invisible Man,* and *The Time Machine,* came to Los Angeles to deliver a lecture. "I went and Heinlein was in the audience, and it inspired him to write a story called 'Solution Unsatisfactory,' " Ackerman recalled.

"I was afraid to go to the theater—I was afraid I'd have a heart attack," Bradbury exclaimed. "I loved him so much I thought I'd collapse if I ever met him, so I never made it. But I had no money; it cost a dollar to hear the lecture. I had no dollar." Bradbury then recalled the film version of Wells's novel *The Shape of Things to Come:* "That film made me plunge into the future. I came out with a desire to live forever because at the end of that film children go off in a rocket to the moon and [one of the main characters] says, 'It's either the stars or the grave. We have to choose. Do we go to the stars or do we die on Earth? Which shall it be?' "

Bradbury described how he'd recently testified in Culver City on "an interlocking broadcast" to a government commission on space travel. His passionate belief that the future and the destiny of humankind lay in space travel echoed the sentiments of Merian Cooper—after all, hundreds of years ago, European explorers set sail for India and found a New World. "They bumped into a large object—three hundred million people and democracy, that was the large object," Bradbury exclaimed. "And no one predicted it! So, what's going to happen to us on the moon and on Mars? Fabulous things. We can't predict it, but we're going there and we'll prevail and in five hundred years we're going to Alpha Centauri! The human race will be preserved, a whole new frontier."

The talk inevitably turned to *King Kong* and Merian Cooper. "When the Dino De Laurentiis version came out, I referred to it as 'The Turkey That Attacked New York,' " Bradbury recalled with a grin. "The reason the original works is not only the animation—it has a perfect screenplay. There's a couple anachronistic things needing changing, but otherwise it's perfection. If I were doing a new version I'd just take the old screenplay and rub a damp cloth over it, clean out the dust."

"Merian Cooper was a bigger-than-life character who lived a life of adventure—which De Laurentiis didn't live—which comes through in *Kong*," Harryhausen added. "It was a great pleasure to work with him; I was with the [*Mighty Joe Young*] unit for almost three years. He was an unusual man, as he should be, or he wouldn't be Merian C. Cooper. He was vibrant, he had an excessive enthusiasm some people might call eccentric."

"I met Cooper, I did indeed," Ackerman added. "There was a revival of *Kong*, and I was asked to introduce him. I said, 'All I need to say is *bom-bom-bom*' "—here he beat his chest like a gorilla—" '*Merian C. Cooper!*' "

Over the course of the get-together, at a far table and out of the line of sight, sat Bob Burns, a celebrated collector of movie memorabilia who had brought along two prized artifacts. At an opportune moment, they were brought forward: the original skeletal armatures of King Kong and Mighty Joe Young, long shorn of their fake flesh and fur and mounted on solid bases.

As the two iconic objects were placed on the table, Harryhausen's eyes lit up. He pounded his chest, Kong-like, and to the rapturous laughter of his friends evoked the Skull Island chant: "*Oh! Bala bala Kong nna hee . . .*"

"Oh this is Jennifer, *Mighty Joe*." Harryhausen smiled as his long hands went to the armature and instinctively began animating it. "This was the main one, Jennifer, that went through all the gyrations you see on the screen. . . . This armature was based on Willis O'Brien's original King Kong."

A question was posed: Why did you name the big gorilla Jennifer?

"Well, at the time [we were making *Mighty Joe*] they were shooting *Lust in the Dust* . . . what was that movie? *Duel in the Sun!*"

"Same thing," Bradbury deadpanned.

"And we had to wait until the [*Duel*] rushes were finished before we could project our dailies. I remember watching Jennifer Jones being shot at and her little hand quivering over these rocks and I thought I could incorporate some of those motions into Mighty Joe, so I nicknamed it Jennifer. Cooper used to come in and say, 'Ray, is that *Jennifer*?' I don't think Miss Jones would care to know, but that sort of influenced me."

Someone suggested that the two armatures were now talismans of popular culture, practically sacred objects. "They are," Harryhausen agreed, nodding. "We made four of these for Mighty Joe. There's one in London at the British Film Institute that still has the rubber on it, but somebody took the fur off—they skinned it alive."

The three were asked about the notion of uncharted Skull Island and lost worlds, a concept hard to accept in a world of modern global communications and satellite surveillance systems. "It's difficult in that respect," Harryhausen acknowledged, "in the thirties there still was a lot to be discovered. In *Kong*, Captain Englehorn hears the voices of the Skull Island natives in their ceremony and he goes, 'I think that's the language of the Nias Islanders.' Well, Nias Island actually exists, although they're not black but Asian people, and we [Harryhausen and his wife, Diana] thought we'd go there. We arrived early in the morning, in the fog, but there was no skull, no ancient wall. I stepped out on the pier and there was this native guy and I thought I'd try out Ruth Rose's language and I said, '*Bala, bala Kong nna hee.*' And the native put his hands on his hips and said, 'What are you *talking* about?' "

For Harryhausen, there was disappointment that the cinematic work of the stop-motion masters now required hundreds of hands and complex computer technology. "Something that's present in *King Kong* and most of the fantasy films I made with [producer] Charles Schneer is that stop-motion makes things look realistic, but you know it isn't. There's a magic there," Harryhausen said. ". . . You have to fall in love with a character to put life into it. My 'actors' did exactly what I wanted them to do. It's a Zeus complex. Zeus put characters into the arena of life and they'd perform according to the gods; that's what the Greeks believed."[2]

IT'S STILL POSSIBLE to walk the streets of New York searching for the ghost of Merian C. Cooper, decades after his burial at sea, and follow his invisible footsteps back into time. One can walk up Broadway, as Cooper did after he disembarked from the ship that brought him home from Europe after years filled with war, siege, and the horrors of the prison camps, then pause, as young Cooper did that first night home, at the stone lions of the public library and wander over to the tree-shaded oasis of Bryant Park. One can visit the downtown address where Cooper lived when he was reporting for the *Times* and haunting the American Geographical Society, while over on 122 East Forty-second Street stands the Art Deco skyscraper in which he had his Federal Aviation Corporation offices.

There's the American Museum of Natural History, with its dramatic diorama of three stuffed dragons that W. Douglas Burden brought back from the volcanic island of Komodo. One of the creatures is frozen in the moment of gorging on a wild boar, while the foreground dragon raises its scaly head, and the one in the background reveals its forked tongue.[3] In the museum library there is a cassette recording of *The Burden East Indian Expedition*, a short black-and-white silent film of the expedition that remains as dramatic as the *Venture*'s fictional voyage to Skull Island.

But the greatest monument to the memory of Cooper and *Kong* still has to be the Empire State Building, to this day one of the tallest skyscrapers in the world. There Fay Wray became enmeshed in a story that blurred the borders between fantasy and reality, and a famous film transcended the ravages of time. As David Thomson wrote: "Fay Wray is forever the wisp of near-naked woman in the beast's paw. Seventy years later the image is as stirring and as surreal as ever."[4]

Fay Wray passed away in her New York apartment on Sunday, August 8, 2004, a month before what would have marked her ninety-seventh birthday. In March, Peter Jackson had met with her, and over dinner the director had asked Fay if she would make a cameo appearance in his *King Kong*. It would be a surreal touch, with Fay Wray remarking on the death of Kong with a line that echoed one from the original film: "It was beauty killed the beast." Wray had declined, reportedly saying, "How can someone play me when I'm here?"[5]

The day before her death, Justin "Bud" Clayton, a friend, had taken her to Central Park in a wheelchair. Back in 1963, when he was fifteen years old, Clayton had fallen under the spell of *Kong* and had written Fay Wray a fan letter. Fay had answered, and their correspondence had never stopped. They finally met in person in 1983, on the fiftieth anniversary of *Kong*, and became good friends. Since Clayton now lived in New York, he could regu-

FAY WRAY
AT HOME,
NEW YORK CITY,
2004.

*All photos provided by
Justin "Bud" Clayton*

FAY WRAY
AND RAY HARRY-
HAUSEN GAZE OVER
NEW YORK FROM
THE OBSERVATORY
OF THE EMPIRE
STATE BUILDING.

larly visit her. Recently, he had been concerned that Fay seemed frail, but she was full of life during their outing in Central Park. Clayton would re-call how enraptured Fay had been while she watched an artist in the park doing a charcoal drawing of a young girl. That night the two watched a rented video, a classic from 1943: *The Song of Bernadette,* the story of a young girl who sees visions.

It had been a lovely day, but the night was a restless one. Yolanda Tur-cios, one of Fay's assistants, stayed up all night with her, and Bud was called Sunday morning and told of her weakening condition. "I rushed over," he recalled. "She was happy to see me. As a matter of fact, we watched *King Kong* together. It was the last [movie] she ever saw. Fay had been coughing due to fluid in her lungs, and she had a congestive heart condi-tion. But I didn't think the end would come so quickly. I had to leave in the afternoon, and it must have been around eight-thirty that night when she passed away. She was so in love with life. I'll never forget her."[6]

Fay Wray was buried in Hollywood Forever cemetery, its venerable grounds located near her old studio home of Paramount. She joined many of her contemporaries from the early days of the movies who were already buried there, including Rudolph Valentino, Douglas Fairbanks, Jesse Lasky, Cecil B. DeMille, and others who, famous in their day, were now for-gotten names.

The Tuesday night following her passing, on August 10, the Empire State Building paid tribute to Fay Wray by extinguishing the building's lights for fifteen minutes. "This wasn't grandstanding," Caryn James wrote in an online article, "but the recognition of a deep and genuine tie between Wray and the building that helped make her famous."[7]

Only three months before her death, Fay Wray had made her last visit to the Empire State Building.

ON MAY 15, 2004, Fay Wray had returned to the Empire State Building with her old friend Ray Harryhausen. A few days before that event, the actress who had become a living legend sat in her apartment in Trump Tower, the place she'd called home for the past twenty years and had once shared with her third husband, Dr. Sanford Rothenberg, a successful neurosurgeon who had passed away in 1991. She wore a bright pantsuit and her hair was perfectly coiffed. At almost a hundred years old she moved with the slightly stooped measure of the years, but there was a twinkle in her eyes, a smile, a lilting laugh revealing the beautiful young actress who'd long ago achieved movie immortality.

Her apartment included works of Asian art and a dramatic wall-sized reproduction of a *Kong* poster inspired by the seminal concept art of the roaring ape gripping Ann Darrow atop the Empire State Building as fighter planes swoop in for the kill. But she gestured to vases of red roses and white flowers—flowers were on her mind today. "There's a certain beauty to flowers that's unforgettable," she observed, when asked why she liked them so much. "That's it."

When asked about how Merian Cooper came to hire her for *The Four Feathers,* their first film together, Fay Wray laughed. " *'How did that happen?'* Well, it just happened!" She reminisced about those times, and at one point, she lifted both of her arms up, balled her hands into fists, and demonstrated the chest-beating motion with which she said Cooper always greeted her.

She was reminded about an old photograph that had been taken of her and Dorothy Jordan on a skiing trip, and a scene from the past became vivid in her mind: a ski trip to Switzerland with Coop and Dorothy and a load of "swells." "I'll tell you something about myself that's very important," Wray said. "There was a place where people skied and I thought, 'Gee, I don't want to be tangled up with them, I just want to be free.' . . . All these elegant people. . . . So, I said to myself, 'I'll go up on a hill, I'll have a nice little cabin on the hill and nobody will see me.' So after that I went skiing through the trees and onto a plateau where Cooper was and Dorothy was there."

Of that time when *King Kong* burst into the world and they all became famous, Wray commented: "Everything was happening, everything seemed to be happening at the same time."

When Wray was asked if she had a special affection for the Empire State Building, she smiled and replied, "I certainly do. I don't pretend anything different. I'm going to be going there soon, and I'll have a nice time looking at everything there."[8]

THE PLANS FOR Fay Wray's return to the Empire State Building had come together quickly. Wray had talked for several weeks about heading to the top, and Bud Clayton had thought it would be a grand idea to have Ray Harry-hausen join her. Clayton called the Empire State Building to arrange the visit, and the staff asked if Miss Wray would mind if they invited the media to document what would be called her historic return. And so it was arranged.

On May 15, it was a clear but hot and muggy midafternoon when TV news trucks and photographers began arriving at the famed building. Soon after, a taxi bearing Wray and Harryhausen pulled up. Wray moved slowly, one hand on a cane, the other hand holding on to Harryhausen's arm; he was celebrating the occasion by wearing a tie embellished with jungle apes, the nearest thing to an image of Kong he could find. As they neared the Fifth Avenue entrance, some kind of tangible energy preceded them, the aura of a timeless screen goddess manifested in mortal flesh. "Miss Wray, I was in love with you all these years," said a suited member of the staff. He grinned, reaching for Wray's hand as they made their way into the lobby.

Wray and Harryhausen stopped just inside the door. Greeting them, in the center of the long, Art Deco hallway, was a crowd of photographers and television cameramen, some kneeling, others leaning in for a shot. They brought with them the whirring and clicking sound of cameras, just as they had that time onstage, when Ann Darrow had stood in the shadow of the Eighth Wonder of the World. Time itself seemed to slow down.

"How does it feel to be back?" someone shouted. Tourists, drawn by the commotion, began to stop and stare. "They're picking up on it," a building staffer murmured, surveying the crowd as whispers and exclamations carried the news: That's Fay Wray. . . . Fay Wray? . . . *It's Fay Wray!*

It required three separate elevator rides to reach the pinnacle, above the public observation deck, where the top observatory is. There, in an enduring and mythic vision, the giant Kong had once reared and roared his defiance at buzzing fighter planes. Through the sun-glazed windows there was a view of the Chrysler Building, and there lay the ledge upon which Kong had delicately placed Ann Darrow.

"They call it a concrete jungle," Harryhausen commented, gazing out and holding on to Wray as she stepped up to peer through the window. She laughed and began singing in Spanish a song from *Viva Villa!,* one of her films. The lyrics translate as "Because singing the hearts are happy. . . ."

Someone asked if she could see King Kong out there, and one could half-imagine the creature of myth, perfectly perched on these Olympian heights.

Back on earth, in a quiet hallway, Wray and Harryhausen sat and spent some time with reporters and photographers. Harryhausen held up a photograph of Fay Wray, the beautiful innocent from the days of *Kong*. "It was beauty killed the beast," he intoned. Harryhausen then explained how it had changed his life, that first time he'd seen King Kong atop the very building in which they sat. "My wife *still* cries when Kong falls off the Empire State Building," he declared to the reporters.

"Oh! *I do, too!*" Wray exclaimed, looking around at the flash of cameras, craning her head at reporters asking what it felt like to be back in the famed building.

As she left the building she announced, "I'm very happy." A taxi pulled up at the Fifth Avenue entrance and Wray was gently ushered into the back seat, as Harryhausen stepped out into the traffic to get in on the opposite side. "There's a movie star," a building staffer said to no one in particular as Wray waved and blew a kiss. And then the taxi accelerated into the stream of traffic and she was gone.

With nightfall came the roiling clouds of an electric storm. Late that evening the weather report on one of the New York television news programs announced a sudden cold front, thunderstorms, and "vivid displays of lightning" sweeping the region, the electric, elemental forces capping a strange day that had been less springtime than summer, with temperatures just missing the record of ninety degrees, set in 1898. Then came a brief news spot: "Seventy years ago she thrilled moviegoers around the world by dangling from the world's tallest building in the arms of a giant ape. Today . . . Fay Wray returned to the Empire State Building without King Kong. The actress's view of the New York skyline from the famous observatory was indoors this time, and a little less harrowing than 1933."

But it didn't take much imagination to imagine that harrowing day in '33. *King Kong* promotional pictures had once showed Kong towering above a nocturnal Manhattan skyline, the sky ripped by jagged lightning bolts. On this night, amid the lightning and thunder, the rain was a deluge at times. From a distance, the Empire State Building could be seen, its upper floors and antenna lit up in red, white, and blue.

It was a wild, elemental night and appropriately so—mythic events and real time had merged. It wasn't Fay Wray but Ann Darrow who this day had returned to the site of her greatest thrill, the adventure of a lifetime that had begun at the docks opposite Manhattan, with a sea trip to uncharted Skull Island and its primordial wonders and dangers. It was a blessing to know that in 2004, when so much of the world had changed, Ann Darrow hadn't been forever traumatized by the adventure of old, that she had been comfortably retired and content with her memories.

ONE OF THE ENDURING IMAGES OF MOVIE HISTORY IS KING KONG ROARING HIS
DEFIANCE ATOP THE EMPIRE STATE BUILDING. NOTED ARTIST JOE DEVITO
PROVIDES A CONTEMPORARY INTERPRETATION OF THE SCENE, A GLIMPSE OF
KONG WITH ANN DARROW IN HIS CLUTCHES AS SEEN THROUGH THE STRUTS OF
AN ATTACKING FIGHTER PLANE. *Art by Joe Devito from* Kong: King of Skull Island *(DH Press, 2004)*

And what of the man who'd sent her to Skull Island, whose recklessness had put Ann's life in danger? On this magical night, a ripple in the imagination opened a portal to a dimension of possibilities, and out flew a vision of Merian C. Cooper at the controls of his old Liberty plane, flying above the Empire State Building.

KONG ELECTRIC! PERIOD RKO PUBLICITY SHOT.

RKO publicity shot; BYU Film Stills Collection

Once upon a time, Cooper had taken his customary place in the pilot's cockpit to fly into the myth of his own making, there to shoot down his creation, the manifestation of his dreams that he'd transmuted from the spirit-possessed giant jungle ape that had beguiled him as a child.

That killer pilot and the giant ape from Skull Island were, in fact, kindred souls and always had been: aliens on this island of concrete and steel, fellow outcasts of civilization. As the lightning bolts crisscrossed and broke open the storm, it seemed as if the dark, nightmarish form of Kong was illuminated by lightning atop the Empire State Building, and that his roar merged with and became the storm's own booming thunder.

And then the mythic Beast howls in recognition at the Liberty plane soaring overhead. Coop—his goggles on and a grin as big as his heart—performs a barrel roll to the thunderous, answering roar of his creation. He then rides a lightning bolt and with a gallant wave points his ghost plane back toward the Unknown. *Death will be a new adventure.*

ACKNOWLEDGMENTS

A writer never works in a vacuum, and this book is the product of the interest and involvement of a number of talented individuals and institutions. First on the list is editor Steve Saffel, who believed in the project from conception and whose expert editorial guidance was sheer inspiration. The one who ultimately made this book possible is Bruce Tracy, editorial director at Villard, and I thank him for his faith and support. This is the first biography of Merian C. Cooper, and thanks to Bruce and Steve the once inexplicably unsung life of an American original can at last be celebrated. Special thanks to Barbara Bachman for the book's elegant design.

RESEARCH INSTITUTIONS

Brigham Young University, Provo, Utah. L. Tom Perry Special Collections, Harold B. Lee Library. Merian C. Cooper Papers, Zoe Porter Papers, Argosy Pictures Corporation Papers

The Merian C. Cooper Papers at BYU is the mother lode of material on Cooper's life. I'm indebted to curator James V. D'Arc for his enthusiastic and unflagging support—he's the dream of anyone who's ever wanted to dig into an archival collection, a true supporter of serious research. I also appreciate the help of Norm Gillespie and the other BYU staffers who helped guide me through the voluminous material in the collection.

Academy of Motion Picture Arts and Sciences and Academy Foundation; the Margaret Herrick Library, Beverly Hills, California

This is where my journey into Cooper's life began, and I'm grateful for the early information and guidance, particularly the help of Barbara Hall.

American Geographical Society, New York City
Special thanks to executive director Mary Lynne Bird and Peter Lewis.

American Museum of Natural History Library, New York City
A tip of the hat to Barbara Mathé, archivist and head of library special collections.

Explorers Club Archive, New York City
My special appreciation to curator Clare Flemming and Ryan Haley.

Hoover Institution Library and Archives, Stanford University, Stanford, California
Thanks to Carol Leadenham for her help with the collection.

Museum of Modern Art, Department of Film and Video, New York City
My appreciation to Charles Silver and Ron Magliozzi.

New York Library for the Performing Arts, Lincoln Center, New York City
My best, as always, to Kevin Winkler.

Pacific Film Archives, Berkeley, California
Special thanks to the entire staff.

San Francisco Airport Commission Aviation Library and the Louis A. Turpen Aviation Museum
Librarian Christine L. Harris was incredibly helpful in sorting through materials pertinent to early flight, World War I flying aces, Pan American Airways, and other matters pertaining to Coop's aviation interests. I also appreciate the help of curator John H. Hill and consulting curator Dr. Frank Norick.

University of California at Los Angeles, Arts Library Special Collections (the RKO papers)
Special thanks to the entire staff.

SPECIAL RESEARCH

I owe a debt of gratitude to two leading film historians, both of whom had the good fortune to have known Merian Cooper: Kevin Brownlow and

Rudy Behlmer. Both allowed me to transcribe and quote from their personal cassette tapes of interviews with Cooper (Brownlow's tapes also included sessions with Ernest Schoedsack and Ruth Rose). Although some of the material from these tapes has been used in previously published works, it was important for this writer to hear the voices of Cooper and company. I also thank Stephen Pizzello, executive editor at *American Cinematographer,* and John Rutter, at the text division of the National Geographic Image Collection, for their help and support.

INTERVIEW SUBJECTS

A special chest-thumping roar of appreciation to the late Fay Wray and that storied trio from the Los Angeles Science Fiction League: Ray Harryhausen, Ray Bradbury, and Forrest J. Ackerman. Special thanks also go to Merian's son, Colonel Richard Cooper. My best wishes to Theresa Cooper Henderson and the entire Cooper family. The following also provided insights and materials that helped me piece together the mosaic of Merian Cooper's life: Craig Barron, Rudy Behlmer, Dave Conover, James D'Arc, Dennis Doros, George Hambleton, Randy R. Merritt, Patrick Montgomery, Stephan Pickering, and Malgorzata "Daisy" Słomczyńska-Pierzchalska.

SPECIAL EVENTS AND VENUES

Le Giornate del Cinema Muto 2003

The twenty-second annual Pordenone Silent Film Festival saluted Merian Cooper, and I thank the many organizers of this wonderful annual event for their gracious help and assistance. My special appreciation goes to festival president Livio Jacob and director David Robinson. *Grazie* as well to: Federica Dini, Greg Franczak, and Massimo Licandro.

Clifton's Brookdale, Los Angeles, California

Thanks to this venerable restaurant for facilitating the reunion of the Brown Room regulars of the old Los Angeles Science Fiction League: Ray Harryhausen, Ray Bradbury, and Forrest J. Ackerman.

Empire State Building, New York City

For working the logistics of the visit of Fay Wray and Ray Harryhausen, I thank Lydia A. Ruth, director of public relations, and public relations contact Patricia Amerman. And another Kong-like chest-thumping roar of appreciation for Justin "Bud" Clayton, whose brilliant idea it was to take Fay and Ray to the top of the Empire State Building.

SPECIAL THANKS

I'm particularly appreciative of the input of literary agent Joe Spieler, whose early critique of my book proposal inspired the final version, which was embraced by the editor and publisher, and also to Victoria Shoemaker, who was devoted to, and ably represented, the project.

My appreciation to Dana Hayward, who went beyond the call to provide beautifully prepared and bound copies of the manuscript. Editorial assistant supreme Keith Clayton was also superb in handling the demands of this book: Thank *you*, Keith! On the design side, Dave Stevenson did a wonderful job with the jacket, beautifully illustrating the spirit of Merian Cooper. The seamless copyediting—which, sadly, the reader will not appreciate as this author did—put the final polish to the enterprise. The peerless work of copy editor Bonnie Thompson was simply awe-inspiring, as skillful as a scalpel in the hands of a brain surgeon.

A grand chorus of thanks to James D'Arc, Rudy Behlmer, Bob Wyatt, and my parents, August and Elizabeth Vaz, for proofreading my manuscript and providing excellent feedback and suggestions; ditto for my computer gurus Bruce Walters and Richard Friedman. My brother Patrick was my guide into the Internet, where he helped snag me an original edition of *Grass*. And here's a shout-out to the rest of my siblings: Katherine, Maria, Peter, and Teresa: Love you!

The following contributed in a variety of ways, and I thank them, one and all: Jan Blenkin, Joe DeVito, Joe Musso, George and Diana Hambleton, John Michlig, Ted Tsukiyama, Rudy Burwell, James McNaughton, Philip Turner, Don Shay, Lee Wiggins, Mike Wigner, Tom and Vita Blatchford, Victoria Riskin (Fay Wray's daughter, who put me in contact with her mother; thanks also to Victoria's assistant, Kimberly Blagrove), Arnold and Marlene Kunert (Arnold, one of the masters of the universe, arranged the reunion at Clifton's), Bob Burns, Lee Tsiantis, Howard Green, Taylor White, Chris Warner, Brian McLendon, Ned Gorman, and Athena Wickham.

NOTES

DREAMS OF ADVENTURE

Chapter One: The Man Who Cheated Death

1. William O. Douglas, *Of Men and Mountains* (San Francisco: Chronicle Books, 1990), p. 328.
2. Merian C. Cooper, *Grass* (New York: G. P. Putnam's Sons, 1925), p. 141.
3. Kevin Brownlow, interview with Merian Cooper, circa late 1960s; various cassette tapes made available to author by Kevin Brownlow.

Chapter Two: Tales of Exploration and Adventure

1. Paul B. Du Chaillu, *Explorations and Adventures in Equatorial Africa* (London: John Murray, 1861), p. 61. From the collection of the American Museum of Natural History, New York.
2. Rudy Behlmer, "The Adventures of Merian C. Cooper," article from *Register to the Merian C. Cooper Papers* (Provo, Utah: Brigham Young University, 2000), p. 2. James D'Arc, with John N. Gillispie, compilers, Merian C. Cooper Papers, MSS 2008. L. Tom Perry Special Collections, Harold B. Lee Library, Brigham Young University, Provo, Utah (hereinafter cited as Cooper Papers, BYU). Genealogy reference, Merian Cooper letter, May 11, 1965, Merian C. Cooper Papers, box 1, folder 1, Special Collections Harold B. Lee Library and College of Fine Arts and Communications, Brigham Young University, Provo, Utah.

    John C. Cooper would later remarry. His second wife was the former Elizabeth A. Painter. It's not clear whether there was tension between Merian and his father's new wife. As a young reporter and during his years overseas during World War I and the Russo-Polish War, Merian kept up a constant stream of letters home but almost always addressed them "Dear Dad." It was a rare note that mentioned Elizabeth, although those that did were cordial, if not warm. Merian's son, Richard Cooper, recalls only fond memories of "Grandmother Elizabeth."
3. Phil Patton, "Sell the Cookstove If Necessary, but Come to the Fair," *Smithsonian,* June 1993: 40, 50.
4. *Proceedings of the International Conference on Aerial Navigation Held in Chicago* (New York: American Engineer and Railroad Journal, 1894), pp. 5, 309; San Francisco International Airport Aviation Library.
5. Genealogical document; box 1, folder 6, Cooper Papers, BYU.

6. Lynne Olson and Stanley Cloud, *A Question of Honor: The Kościuszko Squadron: Forgotten Heroes of World War II* (New York: Alfred A. Knopf, 2003), pp. 18–19.
7. Ibid., p. 19.
8. Merian C. Cooper, "Guardians of the Lion of Judah," *Asia,* November 1923: 835; box 7, folder 1, Cooper Papers, BYU. "Khedive" was the title of the Turkish viceroys of Egypt from 1867 to 1914.
9. Untitled but ascribed to Merian Cooper, "Untitled Piece," box 28, folder 11, Cooper Papers, BYU.
10. "Col. John Cooper—His Ancestors and Descendants," genealogical document prepared by Nancy Cooper for Merian on Feb. 25, 1922; box 1, folder 2, Cooper Papers, BYU.
11. Behlmer, "Adventures of Cooper," *Register to Cooper Papers,* p. 11.
12. Paul B. Du Chaillu, *Explorations and Adventures in Equatorial Africa,* pp. 56–61, 69–71.
13. W. K. L. Dickson and Antonia Dickson, *History of the Kinetograph, Kinetoscope and Kineto-Phonograph* (1895; facsimile ed., New York: Museum of Modern Art, 2000), pp. 19–20.
14. Ibid., p. 52.
15. Ibid., p. 33.
16. Ibid., pp. 27, 30.
17. Behlmer, "Adventures of Cooper," *Register to Cooper Papers,* p. 2.

Chapter Three: The Road to War

1. Olson and Cloud, *A Question of Honor,* p. 24.
2. Merian Cooper, letter to his father, no date, on stationery marked "Army Y.M.C.A. Fort McPherson Georgia"; box 2, folder 5, Cooper Papers, BYU.
3. Behlmer, "Adventures of Cooper," *Register to Cooper Papers,* p. 2.
4. "C" [Merian Cooper], *Things Men Die For* (New York: G. P. Putnam's Sons, 1927), pp. 44–47.
5. Behlmer, "Adventures of Cooper," *Register to Cooper Papers,* p. 2.
6. Merian Cooper, letter to his father, undated but circa Christmas 1916; box 30, folder 6, Cooper Papers, BYU.
7. Merian Cooper, letter to his father, on stationery of *The Des Moines Register* and *The Evening Tribune,* n.d.; box 30, folder 6, Cooper Papers, BYU.
8. Merian Cooper, letter to his father on *Minneapolis Daily News* stationery, January 10, 1916; box 30, folder 6, Cooper Papers, BYU. This letter also revealed that after three tries he'd been accepted by Stanford's law college. It's intriguing to imagine Cooper settling in for years of study, passing the bar, and setting out on a legal career.
9. W. C. Robertson, managing editor, *Minnesota Daily News,* "To Whom it May Concern," Sept. 22, 1916; box 2, folder 4, Cooper Papers, BYU.
10. Merian Cooper, letter to his father on *Minneapolis Daily News* stationery, n.d.; box 30, Cooper Papers, BYU.
11. Merian Cooper, letter to his father, n.d.; box 30, folder 7, Cooper Papers, BYU.
12. Cooper, *Things Men Die For,* pp. 49–51.
13. Merian Cooper, letter to his father on stationery marked "Company B Second Regiment, Infantry Guard of Georgia, El Paso, Texas," n.d.; box 30, folder 6, Cooper Papers, BYU.
14. "A Country Boy's View of a Great General," in "Voices of the Century" special issue, *Newsweek,* March 8, 1999: 38.

15. "Sergeant Cooper to Be Aviator" (from the *Macon Telegraph*), undated clipping; box 30, Cooper Papers, BYU.
16. M. C. Cooper, "El Paso Greets Company K with Cheers and Affection," *El Paso Herald,* March 26, 1917; box 2, folder 4, Cooper Papers, BYU.
17. M. C. Cooper, "Brave Hearts Keep Eyes Dry," *El Paso Herald,* 1917 (no other date); box 2, folder 4, Cooper Papers, BYU.
18. Merian Cooper, letter to his father on stationery marked "ARMY Y.M.C.A. Fort McPherson Georgia," n.d.; box 2, folder 5, Cooper Papers, BYU.
19. Merian Cooper, letter to his father, dated "1917," marked "True Copy"; box 2, folder 5, Cooper Papers, BYU.
20. Merian Cooper, letter to his father on stationery marked "Army and Navy Young Men's Christian Association," 1917; box 2, folder 5, Cooper Papers, BYU.
21. General Walter A. Harris, letter to Mr. Cooper, Aug. 27, 1916; Hoover Institution Library and Archives, Stanford University.
22. Merian Cooper, letter to his father marked "En route to France 1917"; box 2, folder 5, Cooper Papers, BYU.
23. Major Joseph Tulasne, "America's Part in the Allies' Mastery of the Air," *National Geographic Magazine,* Jan. 1918: 1.
24. Merian Cooper, letter to his father, May 10, 1918; box 2, folder 5, Cooper Papers, BYU.
25. Merian C. Cooper, "My Life in War and Peace," unpublished manuscript dated April 12, 1965, pp. 11–12; box 28, folder 12, Cooper Papers, BYU.

FORTUNATE SOLDIER

Chapter Four: The Test of Steel and Blood

1. Merian Cooper, letter to his father, Jan. 23, 1919; box 2, folder 6, Cooper Papers, BYU.
2. *The U.S. Air Service in World War I,* vol. 1, comp. and ed. Maurer Maurer (Washington: Office of Air Force History, Headquarters USAF, 1978), p. 365, San Francisco International Airport Aviation Library.
3. Walton Rawls, *Wake Up, America! World War I and the American Poster* (New York: Abbeville Press, 1988), p. 182.
4. Emile Gauvreau and Lester Cohen, *Billy Mitchell: Founder of Our Air Force and Prophet Without Honor* (New York: E. P. Dutton & Co., 1942), pp. 24–25.
5. Merian Cooper, letter to his father, n.d.; box 2, folder 5, Cooper Papers, BYU.
6. Photo in Cooper scrapbook, vol. 1; box 49, Cooper Papers, BYU.
7. Merian Cooper, letter to Wolfgang Langewiesche, "Roving Editor," *Reader's Digest,* May 31, 1961; provided to author by George Hambleton.
8. William Mitchell, tribute letter to the editor of the *Sun,* June 12, 1929; provided to author by George Hambleton.
9. Horace Brock, *More About Pan Am: A Pilot's Story Continued* (Lunenburg, Vermont: Stinehour Press, 1980), p. 4; San Francisco International Airport Aviation Library.
10. Edmund Leonard, diary entries from eighteen-page report on his World War I experiences, n.d.; box 2, folder 9, Cooper Papers, BYU.
11. Ibid.
12. *The U.S. Air Service in World War I,* vol. 1, pp. 365–66.
13. Merian Cooper, "My Life in War and Peace," pp. 11–12.

14. Edmund Leonard, diary entry, p. 8; box 2, folder 9, Cooper Papers, BYU.

15. Merian Cooper, letter to his father, Sept. 14, 1918; box 2, folder 5, Cooper Papers, BYU.

16. Special Orders document, Headquarters Service, Chief Air Section, American Expeditionary Force, Aug. 31, 1918; box 2, folder 9, Cooper Papers, BYU.

17. Leonard, diary entry, p. 11.

18. E. C. Leonard, "Description of Aerial Battle," five-page typewritten report on the mission of Sept. 26, 1918, n.d., p. 1; box 2, folder 9, Cooper Papers, BYU.

19. In his January 23, 1919, letter to his father, Merian noted that after this particular mission the maximum bomb load was never more than two hundred pounds, to allow pilots to gain more altitude. Box 2, folder 6, Cooper Papers, BYU.

20. Commanding Officer Lewis F. Turnbull, recommendation for Distinguished Service Cross for Merian Cooper to C.O. 1st Day Bombardment Group, Dec. 8, 1918; box 2, folder 9, Cooper Papers, BYU.

21. In a report from W. S. Bressler of the 9th Aero Squadron, who'd been flying over the lines during the battle, this German officer had been the enemy flier who'd actually fired the fatal bullets that brought down Cooper's plane. The American Red Cross, National Headquarters in Washington, D.C., one-page typed report on "Capt. Merrian [sic] Cooper, 20th Aero Squadron," listed "under date of Dec. 31st"; box 2, folder 6, Cooper Papers, BYU.

22. Robert Thach, office of Chief of Air Service, letter to John Cooper [Sr.], Oct. 9, 1918; box 2, folder 6, Cooper Papers, BYU.

23. Three Western Union telegrams, Nov. 2–3, 1918; box 2, folder 6, Cooper Papers, BYU.

24. Leonard, "Description of Aerial Battle," p. 4.

25. Ed C. Leonard, letter to John C. Cooper, Sr., Dec. 2, 1918; box 2, folder 6, Cooper Papers, BYU.

26. Mrs. Charles M. Garrison, letter to Hedda Hopper, July 19, 1952; box 2, folder 6, Cooper Papers, BYU.

27. R. G. Hutchins report on Cooper case, n.d.; box 2, folder 9, Cooper Papers, BYU. Both Cooper and Leonard recounted in personal and official reports the fateful bombing mission and the deadly aerial dogfight.

28. Cooper, "My Life in War and Peace," p. 15.

29. "Captain Merian C. Cooper, Air Service U.S.A.," unaccredited and undated three-page outline of Cooper's military record (circa 1919), p. 2, and various documents; box 2, folder 10, Cooper Papers, BYU.

30. Cooper, *Things Men Die For,* pp. 53–55.

31. Thomas Rhinelander, letter to Mr. John C. Cooper, February 14, 1919; box 30, folder 9, Cooper Papers, BYU.

32. Captain Merian Cooper, American Red Cross, Inter-Office letter to Capt. Williamson, Dist. Mgr., Jan. 7, 1919; box 2, folder 7, Cooper Papers, BYU. With the support of Mrs. Clarkson Potter and the aid of the American Red Cross, Cooper prepared a January 7, 1919, report on some seventeen cases, including comrades who'd perished in Dun-sur-Meuse.

33. Merian Cooper, letter to his father on stationery marked "American Y.M.C.A. On Active Service with the American Expeditionary Force," Jan. 1919; box 2, folder 6, Cooper Papers, BYU. This letter was written in what looks like Cooper's hand, meaning it was probably composed toward the very end of January, after the letter to his father of January 23, which he'd dictated. In the

letter he'd added, "I am going back to the hospital to have my hand treated some more, but it is practically well so I hope to be flying again soon."

34. Merian Cooper, letter to his father from Paris, Feb. 17, 1919; box 2, folder 9, Cooper Papers, BYU.

   Edmund C. Leonard was also recommended for the Distinguished Service Cross on December 8, 1918, the commendation noting that their plane had taken up "a very exposed position to protect a plane below the formation" and that after being wounded Leonard regained his senses and "continued to fire his guns at the enemy, assisting in bringing down at least one more enemy aircraft" before collapsing again. D.S.C. recommendation from Lewis Turnbull, 1st Lieutenant, Commanding Officer to C.O. 1st Day Bombardment Group, A.E.F., France, letter of recommendation, Dec. 8, 1918; box 2, folder 9, Cooper Papers, BYU.

   Both Cooper and Leonard would be awarded the Silver Star by American Expeditionary Forces in France on June 3, 1919; as noted in letter from Edmund C. Leonard to the adjutant general's office in Washington, D.C., Nov. 5, 1942; box 2, folder 9, Cooper Papers, BYU.

35. Capt. Merian Cooper, letter to Chief Decorations Section, n.d.; Hoover Institution Archives.

36. Death certificate in box 41, Cooper Papers, BYU.

Chapter Five: The Kościuszko Squadron

1. Cedric Fauntleroy, letter to John C. Cooper from Lemberg, Poland, June 20, 1920; box 3, folder 2, Cooper Papers, BYU. Cedric Fauntleroy would be in periodic correspondence with Cooper's father. On June 20, 1920, Fauntleroy sent a letter from Lwów thanking Cooper's father for a charitable donation to a children's relief fund.

2. "Biography of Ernest Schoedsack," *Dr. Cyclops* Paramount publicity release, Feb. 1940; p. 1; Museum of Modern Art Film Archives, New York.

3. Ibid., p. 2.

4. Kevin Brownlow, interview with Ernest Schoedsack from cassette tapes of sessions with Merian Cooper, circa late 1960s; made available to author by Kevin Brownlow. All succeeding Schoedsack quotes, unless otherwise noted, are also from this source.

5. Ernest B. Schoedsack, annotated by George E. Turner, "The Making of an Epic: *Grass*," *American Cinematographer*, Feb. 1983: 42.

6. Brownlow, Cooper interview.

7. Olson and Cloud, *A Question of Honor*, pp. 26–29.

8. Merian Cooper, letter to his father on stationery marked "United States Food Administration Mission for Poland," n.d.; box 2, folder 10, Cooper Papers, BYU.

9. Merian Cooper, letter from Lwów, Poland, to Senator Duncan Fletcher, circa 1920; box 30, Cooper Papers, BYU.

10. Merian Cooper, letter to his father on stationery marked "U.S. Food Administration Mission to Poland," n.d.; box 2, folder 10, Cooper Papers, BYU.

11. Merian Cooper, "Thirty Days," typed list of autobiographical ideas, n.d.; box 28, folder 13, Cooper Papers, BYU.

12. Captain Merian Cooper, letter to Dr. Gerszon Zipper, editor of *Chwila* [The Moment], Lwów, Sunday, April 27, 1919; Hoover Institution Archives.

13. Merian Cooper, letter to his father on stationery marked "American Relief Administration Mission to Poland," n.d.; box 2, folder 10, Cooper Papers, BYU.

14. Cooper, *Things Men Die For,* pp. 87–89.
15. Merian Cooper, letter to his father on stationery marked "American Relief Administration Mission to Poland," n.d.; box 2, folder 10, Cooper Papers, BYU.
16. Translation from *Wiek Nowy,* Sept. 16, 1920; Hoover Institution Archives.
17. Letter, "Subject: Duty," dated Warsaw, May 19, 1919; Attachment of Grove message dated May 20, 1919, and Herbert Hoover on June 2, 1919; box 2, folder 10, Cooper Papers, BYU.
18. Olson and Cloud, *A Question of Honor,* pp. 29–30.
19. Squadron charter member names as listed in the undated and unaccredited article "Kosciusko Post Defenders of Warsaw," in *American Legion Weekly;* Cooper scrapbook, vol. 1; box 49, Cooper Papers, BYU.
20. George Palmer Putnam, "The Legion Comes to Poland: American Airmen Organize the Kosciusko Post," probably from *American Legion Weekly,* n.d.; from Cooper scrapbook, vol. 1; box 49, Cooper Papers, BYU.
21. Merian Cooper, outline of war record to Chief of Staff, U.S. Air Force, October 12, 1953, p. 7; Hoover Institution Archives.
22. Olson and Cloud, *A Question of Honor,* pp. 30–31.
23. Merian Cooper, "The Jolly Old Bolsheviks," unpublished manuscript, p. 3; box 28, folder 10, Cooper Papers, BYU.
24. Merian Cooper, letter to his father marked "At the front," n.d.; box 30, Cooper Papers, BYU.
25. "Yankee Flyers Fight Off Reds; Make Escape." No credit or publication, but dateline "Warsaw, June 14." Clipping from Cooper scrapbook, vol. 1; box 49, Cooper Papers, BYU.
26. Cedric Fauntleroy, letter to John C. Cooper from Lemberg, Poland, June 20, 1920; box 3, folder 2, Cooper Papers, BYU.
27. George Palmer Putnam, "American Air Fighters Against the Bolsheviki," unaccredited publication; article from Cooper scrapbook, vol. 1; box 49, Cooper Papers, BYU.
28. "Kosciusko Post Defenders of Warsaw," *American Legion Weekly.*
29. Translation of *Wiek Nowy* article, Sept. 16, 1920.
30. Cooper, "Jolly Old Bolsheviks," p. 3. The accounts of Cooper's capture by the Cossacks and the early ordeal that follows is drawn from this manuscript material.
31. Schoedsack, "Making of an Epic," *American Cinematographer,* p. 42.

Chapter Six: Prisoner of War

1. Mrs. Marguerite Harrison, letter to John Cooper; "Moscow, September 20," Cooper scrapbook, vol. 1; box 49, Cooper Papers, BYU.
2. The previous and following account from Merian Cooper, "Jolly Old Bolsheviks."
3. Merian Cooper, "Russian Work," unpublished manuscript, chapter 2; box 28, folder 11, Cooper Papers, BYU.
4. Merian Cooper, "Copy of Incoming Cable" from Riga to Paris, April 28, 1921; Hoover Institution Archives.
5. Merian Cooper, "Russian Work," chapter 2.
6. George Witte, "Miss U.S. Aviator on Polish Front," cable to the *Bulletin* and *Chicago News;* clipping in Cooper scrapbook, vol. 1; box 49, Cooper Papers, BYU.

7. Cedric Fauntleroy, letter to John Cooper, August 4, 1920; box 3, folder 2, Cooper Papers, BYU.

8. Bainbridge Colley, secretary of state's office, to Senator Duncan Fletcher, Aug. 16, 1920; box 30, folder 10, Cooper Papers, BYU.

9. Merian would recall being transferred to a total of three different camps during his ordeal. Merian Cooper, letter to Major Merik Magynski, May 26, 1972; box 30, folder 1, Cooper Papers, BYU.

10. Cooper, *Things Men Die For,* pp. 21–35.

11. Mrs. Harrison, letter to John Cooper, "Moscow, September 20," Cooper scrapbook, vol. 1; box 49, Cooper Papers, BYU.

12. I measured the actual strip of smuggled paper, which is filed in Merian Cooper's scrapbook, volume 1; the scrapbook's black cover is embossed in gold with the title "Captain Merian C. Cooper 20th Aero Squadron, A.E.F. Kosciusko Squadron, Poland"; box 49, Cooper Papers, BYU.

13. Marguerite Harrison, *There's Always Tomorrow: The Story of a Checkered Life* (New York: Farrar & Rinehart, 1935), pp. 347–48; provided to author by Dennis Doros.

14. Ibid., p. 349.

15. Brownlow, Cooper interview.

16. Mark Vaz, interview with Patrick Montgomery, New York City, May 13, 2004.

17. Biographical details from Harrison's obituary; various clippings, box 32, folder 5, Cooper Papers, BYU; Harrison "recall" from undated letter, Freedom of Information Act material provided to author by Patrick Montgomery.

18. Navy Department, Office of Naval Intelligence report, Sept. 15, 1918; Freedom of Information Act document provided to author by Patrick Montgomery.

19. Memorandum for Chief, War Department Office of the Chief of Staff, Sept. 29, 1918; Freedom of Information Act document provided to author by Patrick Montgomery.

20. Vaz, Montgomery interview.

21. Telegram to the War Department, Office of the Chief of Staff, Military Intelligence Division, April 14, 1920; Freedom of Information Act document provided to author by Patrick Montgomery.

22. Baltimore newspaper clipping datelined Riga, April 17, and letter from H. N. Brailsford to unidentified "Dear Sir," copy furnished by Dr. Ames; Freedom of Information Act materials provided to author by Patrick Montgomery.

23. Harrison, *There's Always Tomorrow,* pp. 349–50.

24. Secret Service report on Mrs. Margarete [*sic*] Harrison, Jan. 11, 1921; Freedom of Information Act material provided to author by Patrick Montgomery.

25. Marguerite Harrison six-page typed statement dated "New York, April 14"; Freedom of Information Act document provided to author by Patrick Montgomery.

26. Harrison, *There's Always Tomorrow,* p. 573.

27. Ibid., p. 350.

28. "Cooper remained in prison because the Russians considered him an American criminal rather than a Polish war prisoner," Orville Goldner and George E. Turner have concluded in *The Making of* King Kong (New York: Ballantine Books, 1976), p. 25.

29. "Capt. Cooper Notified Three Different Times He Was to Be Shot," one-paragraph news clipping, no location or date or byline, Cooper scrapbook, vol. 1; box 49, Cooper Papers, BYU.

30. Mark Vaz, telephone interview with Colonel Richard Cooper, June 19, 2004.

31. A *New York Times* article dated June 26, 1921, and other sources identified this final camp as Wladykino prison. Box 49, Cooper Papers, BYU. This article identifies Cooper's comrades as "Lieut. Zalewski" and "Lieut. Sokolowski."

32. Details of escape from Dorothy Jordan Cooper letter to Douglas Burden, Nov. 12, 1977; box 32, folder 12, Cooper Papers, BYU. One period newspaper account of Cooper's ordeal noted that he bribed a guard and that very night escaped through barbed-wire entanglements on a desperate run for the refuge of the Latvian border: "World War's Greatest Hero gets Safely Away from Bolsheviki," May 7, unaccredited and undated clipping in Cooper scrapbook, vol. 1; box 49, Cooper Papers, BYU.

33. "Merian Cooper Escapes," *Florida Metropolis,* April 26, 1921, Jacksonville, Florida, clipping from Cooper scrapbook, vol. 1; box 49, Cooper Papers, BYU.

34. Merian Cooper, cable from Riga to Paris, April 28, 1921; Hoover Institution.

35. Merian Cooper quote excerpted from Dorothy Jordan Cooper letter to W. Douglas Burden, Oct. 25, 1977; box 32, folder 12, Cooper Papers, BYU.

36. Michael Farbman, "American, Months in Russian Prison, Tells of Escape," *New York World,* dateline "Riga, April 26" [1921], clipping from Cooper scrapbook, vol. 1; box 49, Cooper Papers, BYU.

37. Dorothy Jordan Cooper, letter to Douglas Burden, October 25, 1977. In another account it was Zalewski, in his perfect Russian, who told the smuggler he'd be killed if he didn't carry them to freedom. Regardless, the smuggler fulfilled the bargain and led them to the frontier.

38. Ibid.

39. Merian Cooper, letter to Lowell Thomas, June 29, 1972, p. 3; box 36, folder 18, Cooper Papers, BYU.

40. "Escaping from Russia," *New York Times,* no byline, June 26, 1921, clipping, Cooper scrapbook, vol. 1; box 49, Cooper Papers, BYU. Article mentions that the great escape began the night of April 12 from Wladykino prison.

41. Merian Cooper, cable from Riga to Paris, April 28, 1921; Hoover Institution.

42. "Russia Report, May 7/21," A.R.C. report on Merian Cooper; Hoover Institution Archives.

43. "Merian C. Cooper Enjoyed Shave . . ." No byline or date but probably from a hometown paper in Jacksonville. Cooper scrapbook, vol. 1; box 49, Cooper Papers, BYU.

44. "Lieut. Col. Cooper Goes to Berlin to Greet Mrs. Marguerite Harrison Who Saved Him from Starvation," no byline, dated "August 5" [1921], *Florida Times Union;* includes August 4 Associated Press notice datelined Berlin, clipping from Cooper scrapbook, vol. 1; box 49, Cooper Papers, BYU.

45. "Poland Honors Aviators," unaccredited Associated Press item dated "Warsaw, May 10" [1921], Cooper scrapbook, vol. 1, box 49, Cooper Papers, BYU.

46. Herbert Hoover, letter to Merian Cooper, July 14, 1921; box 3, folder 2, Cooper Papers, BYU.

47. Charles E. Hughes, letter to Merian Cooper, n.d.; box 3, folder 2, Cooper Papers, BYU.

48. Hugh Gibson, letter to Merian Cooper, Sept. 1, 1921; box 30, Cooper Papers, BYU.

49. Background on Marjorie provided the author by her granddaughter, Mal-

gorzata "Daisy" Słomczyńska-Pierzchalska. Some on Maciej's side of the family have estimated that Marjorie and Merian probably met and became lovers between April and May of 1921.

50. Orville Goldner and George E. Turner, *The Making of* King Kong, p. 26.

51. Merian Cooper, letter to Miss Margaret J. Corcoran; n.d.; p. 3; box 33, folder 5, Cooper Papers, BYU.

SEA GYPSIES

Chapter Seven: Mysterious Islands

1. Edward A. Salisbury and Merian C. Cooper, *The Sea Gypsy* (New York: G. P. Putnam's Sons, 1924), p. 3.

2. The New York arrival references and quotes taken from "Back Home," six-page typewritten essay (written in upper-right corner of title page: "M. C. Cooper, 170 Sullivan Street, New York City"), n.d.; box 28, folder 11, Cooper Papers, BYU.

3. Ric Burns and James Sanders, *New York: An Illustrated History* (New York: Alfred A. Knopf, 1999), p. 312.

4. Cooper, "Untitled Piece," box 28, folder 11, Cooper Papers, BYU.

5. Cooper would buy up the initial print run for fear that his accounts of Russian prison camps would betray another female spy he met in prison, someone other than Marguerite Harrison.

6. Cooper, *Things Men Die For,* pp. 63–67.

7. Behlmer, "Adventures of Cooper," *Register to Cooper Papers,* p. 3.

8. Miklos Pinther, "The History of Cartography at the American Geographical Society," *Ubique: Notes from the American Geographical Society* (Nov. 2001): 1; provided by American Geographical Society, New York.

9. Miklos Pinther, "The History of Cartography at the American Geographical Society," *Ubique: Notes from the American Geographical Society* (March 2002): 6; provided by American Geographical Society, New York.

10. Cooper, *Things Men Die For,* p. 147.

11. An editorial note in *Asia,* the magazine to which he'd become a valued contributor, summed up the spirit of Cooper and his partner in adventure, Ernest Schoedsack: "Both have a capacity for friendship with other races. They have won the admiration and cordial good-will of every native people they have photographed and written about." *Asia,* June 1927: 719.

12. Louis D. Froelick, letter to Captain Salisbury and Merian Cooper, Aug. 30, 1922; box 30, Cooper Papers, BYU.

13. Salisbury and Cooper, *Sea Gypsy,* pp. 11–13.

14. "Scientist to Seek 'Missing Link' in Malay Archipelago," no byline, Sept. 11, 1922, *San Francisco Chronicle,* clipping from Cooper scrapbook, vol. 1; box 49, Cooper Papers, BYU.

15. Salisbury and Cooper, *Sea Gypsy,* pp. 35–38.

16. Merian Cooper, letter to W. Douglas Burden, June 22, 1964, p. 1; box 8, folder 6, Cooper Papers, BYU.

17. Salisbury and Cooper, *Sea Gypsy,* p. 117.

18. Brownlow, Cooper interview.

19. Goldner and Turner, *Making of* King Kong, p. 26.

20. Schoedsack, "Making of an Epic," *American Cinematographer,* p. 42.

21. Behlmer, "Adventures of Cooper," *Register to Cooper Papers,* p. 3.
22. Translation of official message included in Cooper article "From King Solomon to Ras Tafari," *Asia,* Oct. 1923, p. 707; box 7, folder 1, Cooper Papers, BYU.

Chapter Eight: The Golden Prince

1. Cooper, "From King Solomon to Ras Tafari," *Asia,* 707–08.
2. Timothy White, *Catch a Fire: The Life of Bob Marley* (New York: Holt, Rinehart and Winston, 1983), p. 41.
3. Ibid., pp. 36, 44.
4. Ibid., pp. 30, 35, 39.
5. Ibid., p. 36.
6. This quote and the account that follows are from Cooper's "From King Solomon to Ras Tafari," *Asia,* 707–08.
7. Merian C. Cooper, "Guardians of the Lion of Judah," *Asia,* Nov. 1923: 834; box 7, folder 1, Cooper Papers, BYU.
8. Ibid.
9. Cooper, "King Solomon to Ras Tafari," *Asia,* p. 775.
10. Ibid., p. 710.
11. The account of this gathering of the army is from Cooper's "Guardians of the Lion of Judah," *Asia,* pp. 836–37, 866.
12. Merian Cooper provides details of the warriors' feast in the last installment of his Abyssinia series for *Asia,* "As in Solomon's Day," Dec. 1923: 953–55; box 7, folder 1, Cooper Papers, BYU.
13. White, *Catch a Fire,* pp. 36, 43–44. Timothy White notes that when dignitaries and world leaders arrived for the coronation, a special envoy sent by President Herbert Hoover brought gifts ranging from an electric refrigerator to five hundred rosebushes and prints of three motion pictures: *Ben-Hur, The King of Kings,* and *With Byrd at the South Pole.*

Chapter Nine: The Last Landfall

1. Salisbury and Cooper, *Sea Gypsy,* p. 232.
2. Ibid., p. 236.
3. Ibid., p. 232.
4. Ibid., pp. 234–35.
5. Schoedsack, "Making of an Epic," *American Cinematographer,* p. 43.
6. Ibid.
7. Salisbury and Cooper, *Sea Gypsy,* pp. 236, 239. Again, note that Cooper would later claim he wrote this, so it's possible he's just placing the context from Salisbury's perspective.
8. Ibid., p. 241.
9. Ibid., pp. 262–63.
10. Ibid., p. 286.
11. Ibid., pp. 286, 289.
12. Brownlow, Cooper interview.
13. Office of the Assistant Secretary, U.S. State Department, letter to Merian Cooper, June 9, 1923; box 7, folder 1, Cooper Papers, BYU. Merian Cooper [unaccredited] "Outline of Plan for the Development of Concessions in Abyssinia," box 7, folder 1, Cooper Papers, BYU. In an undated Cooper letter from Aden, Arabia, to Kenneth Shrewsbury, Coop's former war comrade and

now legal representative, Coop noted that he'd done the work on the Abyssinian dam project and that the J. G. White & Co. had "just dropped me out of the soup quietly . . . if the blighter did steal my dope, and it looks very much like it to me, we will give 'em Hell." Box 7, folder 1, Cooper Papers, BYU.

14. "Contents and Contributors," *Asia*, Nov. 1923.
15. "Contents and Contributors," *Asia*, Oct. 1923.

NATURAL DRAMA

Chapter Ten: Journey to the Land of Grass and Life

1. Cooper, *Grass*, p. 3.
2. Harrison, *There's Always Tomorrow*, pp. 571–72.
3. Ibid., p. 572.
4. Ibid., pp. 572–73.
5. Ibid., p. 573. Decades later, Schoedsack would also grumble that the account of their adventures in Harrison's autobiography got things wrong. Harrison had the three of them beginning the adventure with an uneventful boat trip across the Atlantic even though, Shorty maintained, he'd been in Paris all the time, awaiting Coop's arrival.
6. Ibid., p. 572.
7. Merian Cooper, letter to Miss Mabel Ward, Feb. 17, 1962; Explorers Club Archives, New York City.
8. Coop's movie knowledge as estimated in letter from Mrs. Dorothy Cooper to Mr. Naficy, Aug. 27 (no year listed, but the correspondence came after Merian Cooper's death); box 7, folder 3, Cooper Papers, BYU.
9. Schoedsack, "Making of an Epic," *American Cinematographer*, p. 44.
10. Ibid.
11. Ibid.
12. Harrison, *There's Always Tomorrow*, pp. 578–79.
13. Ibid., p. 580.
14. Ibid., pp. 581–82.
15. Cooper, *Things Men Die For*, pp. 71–75.
16. Harrison, *There's Always Tomorrow*, p. 582.
17. Kevin Brownlow, *The War, the West, and the Wilderness* (New York: Alfred A. Knopf, 1979), pp. 519, 522.
18. On the trip the filmmakers also had an audience with Prince Faisal and Gertrude Bell. Cooper, in a February 22, 1969, letter to Schoedsack, would recall "the thrill" they had at Sir Wilson's descriptions and how the river and mountain were "even better than we thought, even better than the descriptions." Box 36, folder 2, Cooper Papers, BYU.
19. Cooper, *Grass*, p. 10; unless otherwise noted, the summation of the journey is gleaned from the narrative of Cooper's book. Direct quotes and corresponding page numbers are noted throughout.
20. Ibid., p. 53.
21. Ibid., p. 59.
22. Harrison, *There's Always Tomorrow*, pp. 605–06.
23. Though this passage opened his handwritten manuscript, it was probably not from Cooper's original diary but a draft for the Asia article. On the back of page 26 is scrawled the notation "Mr. C. Cooper, Manuscript, *Asia* Story." Box 7, folder 4, Cooper Papers, BYU. The passage appeared in the Putnam edition

of *Grass,* p. 101, under the diary entry "Camp of the Baba Ahmedi, April 12th [1924]."

24. Ibid.
25. Cooper, *Grass,* p. 181.
26. Brownlow, Cooper interview.
27. Cooper, *Grass,* p. 125.
28. Harrison, *There's Always Tomorrow,* pp. 615–17.
29. Brownlow, Cooper interview. "I always rode a horse," Cooper told Kevin Brownlow. "I loved those sure-footed horses of the Bakhtiari; I thought they were safer than mules. I was scared to ride a mule."
30. Schoedsack, "Making of an Epic," *American Cinematographer,* p. 110.
31. Harrison, *There's Always Tomorrow,* p. 627.
32. Schoedsack, "Making of an Epic," *American Cinematographer,* pp. 110–11.
33. Ibid., p. 111.
34. Brownlow, *War, West, and Wilderness,* p. 523.
35. Cooper, *Grass,* p. 224.
36. Merian Cooper, original *Grass* notes; box 7, folder 4, Cooper Papers, BYU.
37. Cooper, *Grass,* p. 239.
38. Harrison, *There's Always Tomorrow,* p. 622.
39. Cooper, *Grass,* pp. 233–34.
40. Ibid., pp. 284–85.
41. Ibid., p. 295.
42. Ibid., p. 317.
43. Ibid., p. 329.
44. Ernest Schoedsack, letter to Merian Cooper, Feb. 11, 1969; box 36, folder 2, Cooper Papers, BYU.
45. Cooper, *Grass,* pp. 342–43.
46. Ibid., pp. 350–51.
47. Ibid., pp. 351–52, 358–59.
48. Ibid., p. 362.

Chapter Eleven: The Jungle Story

1. "Along the Trail with the Editor," *Asia,* Sept. 1925.
2. Kevin Brownlow, Cooper interview.
3. Ibid.
4. Harrison, *There's Always Tomorrow,* pp. 617, 635.
5. Ibid., p. 643.
6. Brownlow, Ernest Schoedsack interview.
7. Brownlow, Cooper interview.
8. Ibid.
9. Schoedsack, "Making of an Epic," *American Cinematographer,* p. 113.
10. James Pond, letter to Secretary, the Explorers Club, Dec. 9, 1924; Explorers Club Archives. Cooper membership information provided to author by Ryan Haley, Explorers Club Archives, letter of November 11, 2004.
11. Explorers Club annual dinner invitation in Cooper scrapbook, vol. 1; box 49, Cooper Papers, BYU.
12. *Explorers Journal,* vol. 4, Jan.–March 1925, unaccredited article; box 49, Cooper Papers, BYU.
13. Harrison, *There's Always Tomorrow,* p. 648.
14. Brownlow, Cooper interview.

15. Brownlow, *War, West, and Wilderness,* p. 528.

16. Kevin Brownlow, Ruth Schoedsack interview from Cooper interview tapes. In letters, "Monty" was sometimes spelled "Monte."

17. Merian Cooper, letter to Kevin Brownlow, May 11, 1971; box 36, folder 2, Cooper Papers, BYU.

18. Harrison, *There's Always Tomorrow,* p. 648.

19. Blair Niles and Marguerite Harrison anniversary comments from Marguerite Harrison's résumé in the *SWG Bulletins;* provided to author by Patrick Montgomery.

20. Rudy Behlmer, May 1965 Merian Cooper interview; tape made available to author.

21. William A. Johnston, "Artistic Film Wins Defense," Oct. 10, 1926, *Detroit News;* box 49, Cooper Papers, BYU.

22. "Geographical Comment on the Motion Picture of the [Bakhtiari] Migration," from Cooper, *Grass,* p. viii.

23. Brownlow, *War, West, and Wilderness,* p. 529.

24. Harrison, *There's Always Tomorrow,* pp. 626–27.

25. Behlmer, Cooper interview.

26. Brownlow, *War, West, and Wilderness,* p. 529.

27. Brownlow, Cooper interview.

28. Brownlow, *War, West, and Wilderness,* p. 529.

29. Behlmer, Cooper interview.

30. Brownlow, *War, West, and Wilderness,* p. 529.

31. Brownlow, Cooper interview.

32. Merian Cooper, letter to Lowell Thomas, May 29, 1954, pp. 5–6; box 36, folder 18, Cooper Papers, BYU.

33. Brownlow, Cooper interview.

34. " 'Natural Drama' Found in Jungle Melodrama!" Paramount Famous Lasky Corp., *Chang* press sheet, 1927, p. 3; Margaret Herrick Library, Academy of Motion Picture Arts and Sciences, Beverly Hills, California.

35. Merian Cooper, letter to Isaiah Bowman posted from S.S. *Insuline,* Aug. 28, 1925; American Geographical Society Archives.

36. Isaiah Bowman, letter to Merian Cooper, addressed "My dear Cooper," Sept. 17, 1925; American Geographical Society Archives.

Chapter Twelve: Mr. Crooked and the Chang

1. Merian Cooper, letter to Isaiah Bowman, April 24, 1926; American Geographical Society Archives.

2. Merian C. Cooper, with photographs by Ernest Schoedsack, "Mr. Crooked: Some Pages from a Siamese Jungle Diary," *Asia,* June 1927: 475; box 7, folder 10, Cooper Papers, BYU. The account of Cooper's meeting with the Nan village chief and elders is taken from this "jungle diary," pp. 475–76.

3. Such tigers seemed akin to the fearsome gorillas described in Paul Du Chaillu's *Explorations and Adventures in Equatorial Africa* and the native belief that gorillas of extraordinary size were possessed by the spirits of departed natives, making such gorillas impossible to capture or kill.

4. Cooper wrote in his jungle diary that he sympathized with the villagers' superstitions; even though he was a product of civilization he knew what it meant to avoid the number 13 and how unlucky it was to walk under ladders. The number 13 for Cooper also represented the dates on which he'd been

shot down in World War I on September 26, 1918—double 13s—and in Poland on July 13, 1920.

5. Merian C. Cooper, with photographs by Ernest B. Schoedsack, "The Warfare of the Jungle Folk," *National Geographic Magazine*, Feb. 1928: 234, 236.

6. Merian Cooper, letter to his father in care of the American consul, n.d.; box 30, Cooper Papers, BYU.

7. Cooper, "Warfare of Jungle Folk," *National Geographic*, p. 236.

8. Brownlow, Cooper interview.

9. Cooper, "Mr. Crooked," *Asia*, pp. 481, 504.

10. Ibid., p. 508.

11. Ibid., pp. 510, 513. Cooper, in his jungle diary, would reveal that Mr. Crooked was really a female tiger. After Mr. Crooked's demise it was discovered that her right leg had been shot with a lead ball at the hip joint, a native gun causing the injury that changed the tiger from "a speedy game-catcher to a man-eater."

12. Merian Cooper, letter from Nan, Siam, to Isaiah Bowman, Jan. 6, 1926 (stamped Feb. 25, 1926); American Geographical Society Archive. The "head office" doubtless refers to Jesse Lasky at Paramount. What's interesting is the allusion that the studio urged the "slight dramatic theme." Certainly, Cooper and Schoedsack always planned a narrative structure profiling a single family. Cooper's letter also noted that the animal trapping, up to that point, had caught and brought in, unhurt, one tiger and four leopards for use in their picture.

13. As Cooper added to Kevin Brownlow: "I was very thankful the two kids weren't hurt. I don't think I ever told anyone about this. I was too ashamed." Brownlow, *War, West, and Wilderness*, p. 534.

14. Ibid., p. 532.

15. Ibid.

16. Lowell Thomas, "The Adventurous Road to 'The Most Dangerous Game,' " circa 1932 clipping; box 7, folder 14, Cooper Papers, BYU.

17. "Biography of Ernest Schoedsack," Feb. 1940, Paramount promotional material for release of *Dr. Cyclops* (directed by Schoedsack), p. 4; New York Museum of Modern Art Film Archive.

18. Merian Cooper, letter to Douglas [Burden] and Kevin [Brownlow], April 29, 1972; box 32, Cooper Papers, BYU.

19. Ibid.

20. Brownlow, *War, West, and Wilderness*, p. 534.

21. Merian Cooper, letter to Isaiah Bowman, stamped April 24, 1926; American Geographical Society Archives.

22. *Chang: A Drama of the Wilderness* production notes for Milestone Film & Video Release, 1991, p. 5; provided to author by Dennis Doros.

23. Cooper, "Warfare of Jungle Folk," *National Geographic*, p. 267.

24. Brownlow, Cooper interview.

25. Brownlow, *War, West, and Wilderness*, p. 537.

26. In a conversation with Kevin Brownlow, Cooper noted that he'd survived a cholera epidemic in Russia and knew that cholera was transmitted mostly by drinking water. During the epidemic, which hit while they were in southern Siam, Cooper personally boiled water for a full hour and also boiled his tin drinking cup to kill germs. Brownlow interview. The letter referred to is Mer-

ian Cooper's letter to Rear Admiral W. F. Fitzgerald, U.S.N. (Ret.); box 2, folder 3, Cooper Papers, BYU.

27. Merian Cooper, handwritten letter to his father marked "Chumplam, Siam," n.d.; box 7, folder 7, Cooper Papers, BYU. Cooper notes, "With luck we should be in New York in early January." They arrived home a few days before Christmas. Cooper would ruefully recall to Kevin Brownlow that while in Siam he'd handwritten "every damn fraction" of money spent on yellow sheets. "I kept every page of it. I was too god-damn honest, it took too much time—nobody [at the studio] read it. People looked at it and laughed themselves sick. Lasky didn't care what we spent. All we went over was ten thousand dollars." Brownlow, Cooper interview.

28. Brownlow, Ernest Schoedsack interview.

29. Brownlow, *War, West, and Wilderness,* p. 538. In his interview with Brownlow, Schoedsack added that the work that saved the footage was conducted at Paramount.

30. Affidavit from Douglas R. Collier, M.D., Nan, Siam, Oct. 26, 1926; box 7, folder 7, Cooper Papers, BYU.

31. Brownlow, Ruth Rose interview.

32. Merian Cooper, letter from New York to his father, undated but circa 1927; box 30, Cooper Papers, BYU.

33. Merian Cooper, letter from New York to his father, n.d.; box 30, Cooper Papers, BYU.

34. Brownlow, *War, West, and Wilderness,* pp. 538–39.

35. Gilbert Seldes, "Profiles: Man with Camera," *New Yorker,* May 30, 1931: 21.

36. Ibid., p. 23.

37. "The Talk of the Town," *New Yorker,* May 28, 1927; box 1, folder 9, Cooper Papers, BYU.

38. "Along the Trail with the Editor," *Asia,* May 1927: 359; box 7, folder 10, Cooper Papers, BYU.

Chapter Thirteen: Wandering Souls

1. Merian Cooper, letter to W. Douglas Burden, June 22, 1964; box 8, folder 6, Cooper Papers, BYU.

2. Brownlow, Cooper interview.

3. Isaiah Bowman, letter to Dr. Walter B. James, March 6, 1927, Explorers Club Archives.

4. Merian Cooper, letter to Isaiah Bowman, Jan. 6, 1926; American Geographical Society Archives.

5. Isaiah Bowman, letter to Merian Cooper, April 30, 1926; American Geographical Society Archives.

6. Merian Cooper, letter to Isaiah Bowman, April 23, 1926 (stamped, June 1, 1926); American Geographical Society Archives.

7. Behlmer, Cooper interview.

8. Merian Cooper, letter typed on letterhead marked "Merian C. Cooper c/o Osborne & Shrewsbury," to Isaiah Bowman, March 8, 1927; American Geographical Society Archives.

9. "Approximate Cost of Exploration of the Arabian Empty Quarter by Airplane," one-page document, no letterhead, credit, or date; American Geographical Society Archives.

10. Merian Cooper, letter to Isaiah Bowman, March 25, 1927; American Geographical Society Archives.

11. Merian Cooper, letter to Miss Mabel Ward at the Explorers Club, Feb. 17, 1962, p. 1; Explorers Club Archives.

12. Circa 1971 outline of Cooper's contributions to the film industry, p. 2; box 23, folder 11, Cooper Papers, BYU.

13. Merian Cooper, letter to Isaiah Bowman, n.d., written from camp in Portuguese East Africa, noted as "3:00 in the morning"; American Geographical Society Archives.

14. Isaiah Bowman, letter to Merian Cooper, January 23, 1928; American Geographical Society Archives.

15. Goldner and Turner, *Making of* King Kong, p. 34.

16. Behlmer, Cooper interview.

17. Merian Cooper, letter to W. Douglas Burden, June 22, 1964, p. 2; box 8, folder 6, Cooper Papers, BYU.

18. Goldner and Turner, *Making of* King Kong, p. 34.

19. Ibid.

20. Brownlow, Cooper interview.

21. Goldner and Turner, *Making of* King Kong, p. 34.

22. Brownlow, Cooper interview.

23. Ibid., p. 165. The permissions for the baboons had officially come to them in an August 1928 letter from the game warden at Khartoum. The permission read in its entirety: "E. B. Schoedsack Esq. & Captain M. C. Cooper are granted Special permission under Section 7 of the Preservation of Wild Animals ordinance to capture baboons." Game Preservation Department, Khartoum, Aug. 2, 1928; box 7, folder 11, Cooper Papers, BYU.

24. Merian C. Cooper, with photographs by Ernest B. Schoedsack, "Two Fighting Tribes of the Sudan," *National Geographic Magazine,* Oct. 1929: 467.

25. Ibid., p. 473.

26. Ibid., p. 476.

27. Ibid., p. 477.

28. Ibid., pp. 481, 484.

29. The British authorities in the Sudan had initially refused Cooper and Schoedsack's request to live with and film the Amarar. But after six months in the Sudan while enjoying every courtesy from the authorities, the filmmakers were finally granted permission. (Considering that the movie expedition had embarked for the Sudan in August 1927, one can surmise that the filmmakers were heading into Fuzzy-Wuzzy territory in the early months of 1928.)

30. Cooper, "Fighting Tribes," *National Geographic,* p. 485.

31. Ibid., p. 486.

32. Brownlow, Cooper interview.

33. Brownlow, Ernest Schoedsack interview.

34. Cooper, "Fighting Tribes," *National Geographic,* p. 486.

35. Behlmer, Cooper interview. Cooper estimated the *Four Feathers* budget as between $400,000 and $500,000. Cooper also remarked to Behlmer, "We spent very little shooting the African stuff, around $50,000, and the rest of it we ran into studio overhead for the first time. The real expense was the big fort and the big camp we built."

36. Ronald Haver, *David O. Selznick's Hollywood* (New York: Alfred A. Knopf, 1980), p. 57.

37. Behlmer, Cooper interview, and Goldner and Turner, *Making of* King Kong, pp. 35, 244.
38. Rudy Behlmer, ed., *Memo from David O. Selznick* (New York: Viking Press, 1972), pp. 21–22.
39. Haver, *Selznick's Hollywood,* p. 57.
40. "Random Memos," unaccredited but by Cooper; Jan. 13, 1972, "A.M."; box 32, Cooper Papers, BYU.
41. Outline of Merian Cooper's contributions to film, no date but circa 1971, p. 2; box 23, folder 11, Cooper Papers, BYU.
42. Haver, *Selznick's Hollywood,* p. 57.

MERIAN COOPER'S NEW YORK ADVENTURE

Chapter Fourteen: Flying High

1. Merian Cooper, letter to Wolfgang Langewiesche, May 31, 1961, p. 2; provided to author by George Hambleton.
2. Behlmer, "Adventures of Cooper," *Register to Cooper Papers,* p. 10.
3. "Pan American Airways," *Fortune,* April 1936: 90; San Francisco International Airport Aviation Library.
4. David Bruce, letter to Wolfgang Langewiesche, July 3, 1961; box 34, Cooper Papers, BYU.
5. Merian Cooper, "Notes re Mr. Loening . . ."; box 34, Cooper Papers, BYU.
6. Merian Cooper, letter to Wolfgang Langewiesche, May 31, 1961, p. 2. Comments on Hambleton as "a rare visionary genius, though an eminently practical one" from Cooper letter to Wolfgang Langewiesche, June 12, 1961, p. 3; letters provided to author by George Hambleton.
7. Merian Cooper, letter to Wolfgang Langewiesche, June 12, 1961, p. 4.
8. Cooper letter to Langewiesche, May 31, 1961.
9. Cooper letter to Langewiesche, June 12, 1961, pp. 3–4; "Notes re: Mr. Loening Mr. Langewiesche Meeting," by Cooper, no date but circa 1961; box 34, Cooper Papers, BYU.
10. Cooper letter to Langewiesche, May 31, 1961, p. 3. Cooper estimated the Hambleton and Lindbergh flights as taking place in late 1927 or early 1928.
11. Mark Vaz, interview with George Hambleton, New Jersey, May 16, 2004.
12. Merian Cooper, letter to W. Douglas Burden, June 22, 1964, p. 4; box 8, folder 6, Cooper Papers, BYU.
13. "Federal Aviation Corporation Capital Stock" statement (April 4, 1929); box 28, Cooper Papers, BYU. Cooper was notified of his election to the board on April 11, 1929. Notification letter to Cooper, April 18, 1929; box 28, folder 14, Cooper Papers, BYU.
14. H. M. Wright, secretary of Western Air Express Corporation, letter to Mr. M. C. Cooper, vice president, Federal Aviation Corporation, March 16, 1931; box 28, folder 17, Cooper Papers, BYU. Announcement letter for Pan Am appointment signed by Juan Trippe for notification of decision of January 27, 1931, board meeting; box 28, folder 17, Cooper Papers, BYU.
15. Jim Massey, "Jaxon's Son Makes World Trip on Zep," *Jacksonville Journal,* Aug. 8, 1929; box 1, folder 9, Cooper Papers, BYU.
16. "Col. J. A. Hambleton and Couple Killed in Airplane Crash," *Sun,* Baltimore, June 8, 1929; clipping provided to author by George Hambleton.

17. "John A. Hambleton," editorial by Cornelius V. Whitney, *Sun,* Baltimore, June 10, 1929; clippings provided to author by George Hambleton.

18. Vaz, Hambleton interview.

19. Merian Cooper, letter to W. Douglas Burden, June 22, 1964, p. 4. In his letter, Cooper noted that he brought in his old combat aviation partner Fauntleroy to run his company "Federal Aviation."

20. Goldner and Turner, *Making of* King Kong, p. 39.

21. Ibid., pp. 39–40.

22. Merian Cooper, letter to David O. Selznick, June 19, 1931; box 9, folder 8, Cooper Papers, BYU.

23. Haver, *Selznick's Hollywood,* p. 76.

24. Ibid., p. 77.

25. Ibid.

26. Behlmer, "Adventures of Cooper," *Register to Cooper Papers,* p. 11.

Chapter Fifteen: Sigh for the Wilderness

1. W. Douglas Burden, *Dragon Lizards of Komodo: An Expedition to the Lost World of the Dutch East Indies* (New York: G. P. Putnam's Sons, 1927), pp. 100–101.

2. W. Douglas Burden, letter to Merian Cooper, June 15, 1964, p. 1; box 8, folder 6, Cooper Papers, BYU.

3. Merian Cooper, letter to W. Douglas Burden, June 22, 1964, p. 2.

4. William Douglas Burden biographical material, American Museum of Natural History, research library, New York.

5. Brownlow, *War, West, and Wilderness,* pp. 548, 550.

6. Ibid., pp. 550–51.

7. Ibid., p. 558.

8. Douglas J. Preston, *Dinosaurs in the Attic: An Excursion into the American Museum of Natural History* (New York: St. Martin's Press, 1986), p. 163.

9. Ibid.

10. W. Douglas Burden, "Stalking the Dragon Lizard on the Island of Komodo," *National Geographic,* Aug. 1927: 216.

11. Burden biographical material, American Museum of Natural History library.

12. Preston, *Dinosaurs in the Attic,* pp. 165–66.

13. Burden, *Dragon Lizards of Komodo,* p. 103.

14. Ibid., p. 131.

15. Ibid.

16. Burden, *Dragon Lizards of Komodo,* p. 156.

17. Preston, *Dinosaurs in the Attic,* p. 166. Burden, *Dragon Lizards of Komodo,* pp. 181–82.

18. Burden letter to Cooper, June 15, 1964, pp. 1–2.

19. Ibid., p. 2.

20. Cooper letter to Burden, June 22, 1964, p. 1. It's interesting to note that in his mention of the date of Burden's letter, Coop was careful to include the year. This letter was written when Cooper was struggling to win the exclusive rights to *King Kong.* In the course of his battle for the rights, Cooper was typically exacting in documenting *everything.*

21. Ibid., p. 2.

22. Ibid., p. 3.

23. Ibid.

24. Brownlow, *War, West, and Wilderness,* p. 545.

25. Ibid.
26. Brownlow, *War, West, and Wilderness*, p. 545.
27. Ibid.
28. Lewis Fox Frissell, M.D., letter to Merian Cooper, July 31, 1931; box 7, folder 2, Cooper Papers, BYU.
29. Brownlow, Ernest Schoedsack interview.
30. Behlmer, Cooper interview.
31. Seldes, "Profiles: Man with Camera," *New Yorker*, p. 25.

THE EIGHTH WONDER OF THE WORLD

Chapter Sixteen: Creation

1. Fay Wray, "How Fay Met Kong, Or The Scream That Shook the World," *The Girl in the Hairy Paw: King Kong as Myth, Movie, and Monster* (New York: Avon Books/Flare, 1976), p. 223.
2. "King Kong I. Literary Property Rights," unaccredited and undated, but circa 1960s (during the *King Kong* rights battle); box 8, folder 20, Cooper Papers, BYU. Also, date of August 1931 and Beauty and the Beast reference from *Selznick's Hollywood*, p. 77. Ernest Schoedsack would later tell Kevin Brownlow that the proverb, which appears on an opening title card in the final film, should have been read by "a very dramatic voice." Brownlow, Ernest Schoedsack interview.
3. Thomas Schatz, *The Genius of the System: Hollywood Filmmaking in the Studio Era* (New York: Pantheon Books, 1990), p. 127.
4. Merian Cooper, letter to Mr. L. E. Pierson, April 21, 1931; box 35, Cooper Papers, BYU.
5. George Turner, "Rediscovering *The Lost Squadron*," *American Cinematographer*, Feb. 1996: 87.
6. Haver, *Selznick's Hollywood*, pp. 68, 70.
7. Schatz, *Genius of the System*, pp. 127–28.
8. Merian Cooper, letter to W. Douglas Burden, June 22, 1964, p. 4.
9. Behlmer, "Adventures of Cooper," *Register to Cooper Papers*, p. 11.
10. Vaz, Richard Cooper interview, June 19, 2004.
11. Merian Cooper, letter to W. Douglas Burden, June 22, 1964, p. 5.
12. "King Kong I. Literary Property Rights," unaccredited and undated, but circa 1960s (during the *King Kong* rights battle); box 8, folder 20, Cooper Papers, BYU.
13. Haver, *Selznick's Hollywood*, p. 77.
14. George Turner, "Death of an Epic: *Creation*," *American Cinematographer*, March 1987: 35.
15. Ibid., p. 34.
16. Don Shay, "Willis O'Brien: Creator of the Impossible," *Cinefex*, vol. 7, Jan. 1982: 5.
17. Ibid., p. 6.
18. Richard Rickitt, *Special Effects: The History and Technique* (London: Billboard Books, 2000), p. 151.
19. Ibid., pp. 151–53. The term "spiritist" refers to Doyle's belief in Spiritualism.
20. Turner, "Death of an Epic," *American Cinematographer*, pp. 35, 38.
21. Estimates as to how much *Creation* had spent during the preproduction period vary from $120,000 to $200,000.

22. Merian Cooper, letter to W. Douglas Burden, June 22, 1964, p. 4.
23. Shay, "Willis O'Brien," *Cinefex*, p. 33. Shay notes that Obie painted the ape, but since his women always ended up "looking like wrestlers," Crabbe got the honor of painting the exotic jungle woman.
24. Merian Cooper, one-page memo to David Selznick, December 18, 1931; box 9, Cooper Papers, BYU.
25. Shay, "Willis O'Brien," *Cinefex*, p. 34.
26. Both exchanges of Western Union telegrams, Dec. 21–22, 1931; box 9, folder 16, Cooper Papers, BYU.
27. Brownlow, Cooper interview.
28. David Thomson, *The New Biographical Dictionary of Film* (New York: Alfred A. Knopf, 2003), "Willis O'Brien," p. 645.
29. Wray, "How Fay Met Kong," *Girl in Hairy Paw*, p. 223.
30. Edgar Wallace, *My Hollywood Diary: The Last Work of Edgar Wallace* (London: Hutchinson & Co., n.d.), p. 198; excerpts from book provided to author by Rudy Behlmer.
31. Zoe Porter, "Recollections of my early days with Merian C. Cooper," four typed pages, July 14, 1971; box 1, folder 9, Cooper Papers, BYU.
32. Mark Vaz, interview with Ray Harryhausen, San Rafael, California, June 17, 2003.

Chapter Seventeen: The Dangerous Game

1. Merian Cooper, letter to Mr. Bosley Crowther, July 7, 1965; box 8, folder 7, Cooper Papers, BYU.
2. *The Marines Have Landed*, treatment dated December 7, 1932, is noted as a "temporary title." *The Roar of the Dragon* treatment and added scenes; Box S-191 RKO Collection, University of California at Los Angeles (UCLA), Arts Library Special Collections.
3. George Turner, "Hunting *The Most Dangerous Game*," *American Cinematographer*, Sept. 1987: 40.
4. *King Kong* "Daily Talent Report," Box 18, RKO Collection, UCLA.
5. Goldner and Turner, *Making of* King Kong, p. 73.
6. Archie Marshek, "King Kong: With Kong in Telluride—Memories of Kong," *American Cinemeditor*, Winter 1976–77, p. 10; Museum of Modern Art Film Archive.
7. Behlmer, Cooper interview. Cooper told Behlmer that the particular scene of Denham and his crew rushing to the jungle chasm was shot at night, after *Dangerous Game* work had wrapped for the day.
8. Goldner and Turner, *Making of* King Kong, p. 71.
9. Fay Wray, "The Gorilla I Left Behind," in "New York and the Movies," special issue of *Premiere*, 1994: 30.
10. Marshek, "King Kong," *American Cinemeditor*, p. 10.
11. Behlmer, "Adventures of Cooper," *Register to Cooper Papers*, p. 13.
12. Behlmer, *Memo from Selznick*, p. 47.
13. Goldner and Turner, *Making of* King Kong, pp. 57–58.
14. All references and quotes to the Wallace script taken from the copy among the extant scripts in the Special Collections at Brigham Young University; MSS 2114 Stephan Pickering Collection, 11/5/c/7, box 1. The script is in a manila envelope that notes: "1–5 January 1932 (dictated to, and transcribed

by his secretary Bob Curtis; given to M. C. Cooper Wednesday 6 January) 110 pages—notations in Wallace's own handwriting on some pages."

15. Script, Stephan Pickering Collection, BYU. On page 19 of his script, Wallace described a prehistoric creature attacking the lifeboat; he crossed out "two prehistoric beasts" and replaced it with "the brontosaurus."

16. Merian Cooper, RKO Studios Inter-department Correspondence to Edgar Wallace, n.d.; box 8, folder 20, Cooper Papers, BYU.

17. Selznick's appraisal of Wallace's contribution was expressed in a telegram on February 19, 1932, which concluded that "much of Edgar Wallace material is either unusable or undeveloped." Western Union telegram from DOS [David O. Selznick] to Mr. J. I. Schnitzer; box 8, folder 20, Cooper Papers, BYU. In Wallace's posthumously published *My Hollywood Diary*, he himself noted: "An announcement has been made in the local press that I am doing a super-horror story with Cooper, but the truth is it is much more his story than mine." *My Hollywood Diary*, pp. 141–42.

18. Merian Cooper, memo to "DOS," July 20, 1932; box 8, Cooper Papers, BYU.

19. Merian Cooper, RKO Inter-department Correspondence to Mr. Selznick, Jan. 23, 1932; box 9, Cooper Papers, BYU.

20. David Selznick, RKO "inter-department correspondence memo" regarding "Jungle Beast" to Merian Cooper, Jan. 22, 1932, and Mr. Tamarlane "inter-depart." memo to Merian Cooper, Feb. 22, 1932; box 9, folder 18, Cooper Papers, BYU.

21. *King Kong* Property Rights, undated and unaccredited, but circa mid-1960s outline of the evolution of the property as prepared during Cooper's legal battles for control of *King Kong*; box 8, folder 20, Cooper Papers, BYU.

22. Merian Cooper, one-page memo to James Creelman, March 12, 1932; box 9, Cooper Papers, BYU.

23. Brownlow, Cooper interview. The advantage of a theater for the display of Kong, Cooper noted, was that the straight lines would provide easy demarcation lines for the matte composite of the animation of Kong and the live action.

24. Haver, *Selznick's Hollywood*, p. 101.

25. Jim [Creelman], "Dear Coop" letter, June 1932, pp. 1, 3; box 9, folder 18, Cooper Papers, BYU. Cooper would recall this memo as Creelman's "letter of resignation" to Kevin Brownlow.

26. "The chief criticism on *Kong* seem to be that the dialogue is not consistent enough," Cooper wrote Creelman in a March 12, 1932, letter; box 9, Cooper Papers, BYU.

27. Goldner and Turner, *Making of* King Kong, p. 78.

28. Ibid., p. 80.

29. Ibid.

30. Script in BYU collection in manila envelope with typed identification: "*Kong* script by James A. Creelman + Ruth Rose, RKO Continuity script, 6 September 1932, 102 pages." MSS 2114 Stephan Pickering Collection, box 1, BYU.

31. Merian Cooper, letter to Mr. Polito, Feb. 10, 1966; provided to author by John Michlig. In a conversation with Kevin Brownlow, Cooper also added that Schoedsack directed the long shots of the airplanes taking off to attack Kong atop the Empire State Building. Brownlow, Cooper interview.

32. Steven M. L. Aronson, "Fay Wray: King Kong's Favorite Costar at Home in Los Angeles," *Architectural Digest*, April 1994: 163.

33. Merian Cooper, report to Mr. B. B. Kahane, Aug. 15, 1932; box 9, folder 15, Cooper Papers, BYU. Years later, when Cooper was at MGM Studios, he received correspondence from Selznick International Pictures with the final studio costs of *King Kong*, which Cooper had evidently requested. The final "physical cost" was computed to the penny: $427,749.37. Other costs, including the inevitable studio overhead, increased the final total, with the breakdown also listing: story and production cost, $34,916; supervision and direction, $14,621; cast cost, $35,956; physical cost, $427,749, and overhead cost, $158,913, for a grand total of $672,155. As detailed in September 14, 1938, letter from E. L. Scanlon at Selznick International Pictures to Mr. M. C. Cooper at MGM; box 9, Cooper Papers, BYU. The "overhead" included the production expenses that had been run up on *Creation*, an amount that has been estimated as up to $200,000, as well as the normal studio overhead.
34. Ibid. Cooper prophetically added in his report to Kahane: "I believe the picture will be one of the real sensations of recent years, as well as one of the biggest money makers."

Chapter Eighteen: The Homunculus

1. Vaz, Harryhausen interview.
2. Steve Archer, *Willis O'Brien: Special Effects Genius* (Jefferson, N.C.: McFarland & Company, 1993), p. 25.
3. Shay, "Willis O'Brien," *Cinefex*, p. 42.
4. Ibid., p. 36. As regards the number of Kong armatures, Marcel Delgado has written: "I made the two full body models used in *King Kong*. Both models were eighteen inches high, which is three quarter inch to the foot," from "*King Kong* and Me," a Delgado essay published in the *Kong* anthology, "The Girl in the Hairy Paw" (New York: Avon Books/Flare edition, 1976, p. 182).
5. Ibid.
6. Haver, *Selznick's Hollywood*, p. 84.
7. Mark Cotta Vaz and Craig Barron, *The Invisible Art: The Legends of Movie Matte Painting* (San Francisco: Chronicle Books, 2002), pp. 64, 67.
8. Ibid., p. 66.
9. Ibid., p. 65.
10. Marshek, "King Kong," *American Cinemeditor*, p. 11.
11. Brownlow, Cooper interview.
12. The scene of the elevated train and track being torn down by Kong was inspired by Cooper's own frustration with the noisy rail line. "I used to think I'd love to rip the damn thing down," Cooper reportedly said, "so when I decided I needed another sequence of Kong in Manhattan, I thought wouldn't that be a helluva scene to tear up one of those things." James Sanders, *Celluloid Skyline: New York and the Movies* (New York: Alfred A. Knopf, 2001), p. 97.
13. Marshek, "King Kong," *American Cinemeditor*, p. 12. The final cut, Marshek added, was a tight eleven reels.
14. Goldner and Turner, *Making of* King Kong, p. 190.
15. Merian Cooper, letter to Alan Barnard, executive editor at Bantam Books, New York, June 16, 1965; box 8, folder 2, Cooper Papers, BYU.
16. Cooper requested an immediate answer, as without the New York sequence the story would have to be rewritten. Merian C. Cooper, one-page letter to Mr. David Selznick, March 1, 1932; box 9, Cooper Papers, BYU.
17. Merian Cooper, in a letter to James Creelman on March 12, 1932, argued for

"a closer relationship between the end of the jungle sequence and the beginning of the New York sequence." Box 9, Cooper Papers, BYU.

18. James Sanders, *Celluloid Skyline*, pp. 99–100.
19. Ibid., p. 98.
20. Burns and Sanders, *New York*, p. 379.
21. Ibid., p. 382.
22. Fay Wray, "Gorilla I Left Behind," *Premiere*, p. 29.
23. Goldner and Turner, *Making of King Kong*, p. 173. The RKO call sheet for "Air Shots . . . Metropolitan Airport" on Dec. 29, 1932, was preceded by the "Airplane Process Shots" at Stage 3 on Nov. 19, 1932. The process call sheet lists "2 Bit Men," with a line crossed through it and two names added: "Merian Cooper; Schoedsack." The process work was under the direction of "Mr. Schoedsack." Call sheets from RKO Collection, UCLA.

Chapter Nineteen: Kong, Kong, Kong!

1. Marshek, "King Kong," *American Cinemeditor*, p. 13.
2. *Radio Flash*, Jan. 28, 1933, p. 5, as reproduced in Haver, *Selznick's Hollywood*, p. 119.
3. Behlmer, *Memo from Selznick*, p. 47.
4. Louella O. Parsons, Motion Picture Editor, Universal Service, "Merian Cooper Succeeds Selznick at Radio," Los Angeles, Feb. 5 [1933]; clipping from American Geographical Society Archives.
5. Betty Lasky, *RKO: The Biggest Little Major of Them All* (Englewood Cliffs, N.J.: Prentice-Hall, 1984), p. 94.
6. Behlmer, "Adventures of Cooper," *Register to Cooper Papers*, p. 14. The proposed "Lawrence of Arabia" picture was to be called *The Uncrowned King*. Photographs of Schoedsack's Arabia trip provided by Don Shay, complete with undated RKO publicity copy, also refer to the production as *A Fugitive from Glory*. Although Schoedsack shot his second-unit footage, the film was never made.
7. Brownlow, Cooper interview.
8. Merian Cooper, memo to Mr. Sol Siegel, June 14, 1960; box 23, folder 5, Cooper Papers, BYU. This letter was written to discuss the revolutionary wide-screen technology of Cinerama.
9. Lasky, *RKO*, p. 94.
10. Haver, *Selznick's Hollywood*, pp. 113, 116.
11. Vaz, Harryhausen interview.
12. Ibid.
13. Ian Kershaw, *Hitler, 1889–1936: Hubris* (New York: W. W. Norton & Company, 1999), p. 485.
14. Brownlow, *War, West, and Wilderness*, p. 450.
15. Marshek, "King Kong," *American Cinemeditor*, p. 12.
16. Shay, "Willis O'Brien," *Cinefex*, pp. 42, 45.
17. Ibid., pp. 40–41.

THE PICTUREMAKER

Chapter Twenty: The Executive

1. Lasky, *RKO*, p. 93.
2. Ibid.

3. Juan Trippe, letter to Merian Cooper, Aug. 9, 1932; box 28, Cooper Papers, BYU.

4. Merian Cooper, letter to Trippe addressed to "Dear Juan," Aug. 25, 1932; box 28, Cooper Papers, BYU.

5. Haver, *Selznick's Hollywood,* p. 122.

6. Merian Cooper, letter from Merian C. Cooper to his parents, "Dear Dad and Elizabeth," written on RKO office stationery, March 16, 1933; box 30, Cooper Papers, BYU.

7. Lasky, *RKO,* p. 96; Haver, *Selznick's Hollywood,* p. 122.

8. Cooper letter, March 16, 1933.

9. Rudy Behlmer, "King Kong: The Eighth Wonder of the World," liner notes for *King Kong: Original Motion Picture Soundtrack* (Rhino Movie Music, 1999), p. 26.

10. T. H. Watkins, *The Hungry Years: A Narrative History of the Great Depression in America* (New York: Henry Holt/Owl Books, 2000), p. 204.

11. Ibid.

12. Jerry Hoffman, "Merian Cooper, New Radio Head, Gives His Ideas," Universal Services, dateline Los Angeles, March 25, [1933]; box 32, Cooper Papers, BYU.

13. Lasky, *RKO,* p. 98.

14. Merian Cooper, Interoffice RKO memo/Night Wire to Mr. David Selznick; box 28, folder 13, Cooper Papers, BYU.

15. Lin Bonner, "Cooper Staking Job on Feminine Stars: Is He Moses or Doc Cook?" *Hollywood Herald,* Aug. 24, 1933; box 23, folder 1, Cooper Papers, BYU.

16. Behlmer, Cooper interview.

17. Ruth Rose, *Jamboree,* two-page treatment, copy dated Nov. 1, 1933; MSS 2114, Pickering Collection, folder 3, BYU.

18. Ibid.

19. Thomson, *New Biographical Dictionary of Film,* p. 785. Years later, Cooper confessed to Rudy Behlmer that the sequel wasn't a "very good picture" and that he'd never even seen it until decades later, when he'd caught it on television a year or so before talking to Behlmer. Behlmer, Cooper interview.

20. Richard B. Jewell with Vernon Harbin, *The RKO Story* (New York: Arlington House, 1982), p. 56. Of the studio's output of forty-nine films, the authors of *RKO Story* tally forty-one as studio productions, with eight independent productions released under the studio banner.

21. Behlmer, "Adventures of Cooper," *Register to Cooper Papers,* p. 14.

22. Merian Cooper, letter to Lindsay Anderson, Aug. 25, 1963; box 20, file 7, Cooper Papers, BYU. Cooper added that although he worked with Ford on the casting and with the director and Dudley Nichols on the scripts, he wasn't present at the actual shooting. "I felt I could leave these two pictures safely in John Ford's hand," he concluded.

23. Joseph McBride, *Searching for John Ford* (New York: St. Martin's Press, 2001), pp. 216–17.

24. Lasky, *RKO,* p. 98.

25. "Sh! Don't Tell a Soul!" *Los Angeles Examiner,* July 8, 1933; box 1, folder 8, Cooper Papers, BYU.

26. Alma Whitaker, "When Star Weds Executive She Puts Herself on Spot: Dorothy Jordan Well Aware of Pitfalls That Await Her as Mrs. Merian C. Cooper," *Los Angeles Times,* Sept. 17, 1933; Margaret Herrick Library, Academy of Motion Picture Arts and Sciences, Beverly Hills, California.

27. *Jordan Journal,* March 1934; box 23, folder 18, Cooper Papers, BYU.

28. Behlmer, "Adventures of Cooper," *Register to Cooper Papers,* pp. 14–15. The team of Astaire and Rogers would be taken to heights of renown by producer Pandro Berman.

29. Lasky, *RKO,* p. 105.

30. Behlmer, "Adventures of Cooper," *Register to Cooper Papers,* pp. 15–16.

Chapter Twenty-one: The Producer

1. Merian Cooper, letter to Miss Margaret J. Corcoran, n.d., p. 9; box 33, folder 5, Cooper Papers, BYU. In the letter Cooper also claimed to have turned RKO around from "an $18,000,000 loss to an $8,000,000 profit."

2. Ibid.

3. Jewell with Harbin, *RKO Story,* pp. 56, 70. Indeed, during September 1933, when Cooper's illness reportedly hit, Berman was clearly making decisions in Cooper's stead. A "Retake Request" for *Flying Down to Rio* dated September 2, 1933, was approved with the signature "Pandro Berman for M.C.C." By September 23 another retake request for *Rio* was simply signed in pencil, "Pandro S. Berman." RKO Papers, UCLA. Item on "nervous breakdown" from "What? Color in the Movies Again?" *Fortune,* October 1934: 161.

4. Merian Cooper, letter to Edmund Leonard, Nov. 22, 1934; box 34, Cooper Papers, BYU.

5. Merian Cooper, letter to Mr. Frank A. Vanderlip, Jan. 7, 1934; box 9, Cooper Papers, BYU.

6. Merian Cooper, letter of resignation to Pan American board of directors, July 8, 1935; box 28, folder 17, Cooper Papers, BYU.

7. Merian Cooper, letter to Juan Trippe, July 8, 1935; box 28, Cooper Papers, BYU.

8. Juan Trippe, letter to Merian Cooper, July 23, 1935; box 28, folder 17, Cooper Papers, BYU.

9. Date from C. V. Whitney note written on May 22, 1936; box 28, folder 17, Cooper Papers, BYU.

10. "Pan American Airways," *Fortune,* April 1936: 91.

11. Merian Cooper, letter to Edmund Leonard, Nov. 22, 1934; box 34, Cooper Papers, BYU.

12. Lasky, *RKO,* p. 106.

13. George Turner, "*She:* Empire of the Imagination," *American Cinematographer,* June 1995: 105. The tightfisted attitude was a little inexplicable; James V. D'Arc, film curator at Brigham Young University, observes that RKO Radio Pictures "was in a rare period of prosperity in 1935 with its Culver City studio running at capacity production." James V. D'Arc, "Max Steiner's Score to *She:* 'An Opera Without Arias,' " p. 2 liner notes, *She* soundtrack, Brigham Young University, Film Music Archives Production.

14. Brownlow, Cooper interview.

15. Turner, "*She:* Empire of the Imagination," *American Cinematographer,* p. 104.

16. Ibid., p. 106.

17. Lasky, *RKO,* p. 106.

18. Archer, *Willis O'Brien,* p. 25.

19. Shay, "Willis O'Brien," *Cinefex,* p. 46.

20. Brownlow, Cooper interview.

21. Behlmer, Cooper interview.

22. During 1934 Cooper seemed interested in ascertaining the up-to-the-date gross for his and Schoedsack's original adventure trilogy. In a May 23, 1934, telegram from Cooper's old war comrade and attorney Kenneth Shrewsbury to John Speaks he'd estimated gross and negative costs. The *Chang* gross was at $1,641,796; the *Grass* gross at $121,792; and the *Four Feathers* gross at $1,725,183. Box 7, folder 8, Cooper Papers, BYU.

Chapter Twenty-two: The Pioneer

1. "Color Safeguards Hollywood Supremacy: Interview with Merian C. Cooper," *Commentator* April 4, 1936, one-page article; box 23, folder 1, Cooper Papers, BYU.
2. Harrison, *There's Always Tomorrow*, p. 573.
3. Behlmer, *Memo from Selznick*, p. 48. Behlmer, in a 2004 interview with this author, noted that the effects-filled complexity of *King Kong* would have made it virtually impossible to successfully film in three-color Technicolor when that production was under way in 1932.
4. Behlmer, "Adventures of Cooper," *Register to Cooper Papers*, p. 15.
5. Haver, *Selznick's Hollywood*, p. 96.
6. H. T. Kalmus, "Adventures in Cinemaland," December 1938 essay from *A Technological History of Motion Pictures and Television*, ed. Raymond Fielding (Berkeley: University of California Press, 1967), pp. 52–53.
7. Haver, *Selznick's Hollywood*, p. 178.
8. Vaz and Barron, *Invisible Art*, pp. 71–73.
9. Kalmus, "Adventures in Cinemaland," *Technological History*, p. 57.
10. Merian Cooper, letter to Mr. E. Curtis at Eastman Kodak Company, addressed to "Dear Ted," Nov. 12, 1934; box 9, folder 8, Cooper Papers, BYU.
11. Lasky, *RKO*, p. 115.
12. "Color Safeguards Hollywood Supremacy," *Commentator*; Cooper Papers, BYU.
13. Haver, *Selznick's Hollywood*, p. 175.
14. Behlmer, *Memo from Selznick*, pp. 97–98. In *Selznick's Hollywood*, p. 172, Haver totals the financial backing for the new Selznick International as including $2.4 million from John Hay "Jock" Whitney; Mrs. Charles Payson, his sister; and his cousin Cornelius Whitney.
15. "Color Safeguards Hollywood Supremacy," *Commentator*; Cooper Papers, BYU.

WARTIME

Chapter Twenty-three: War Eagles

1. *War Eagles* production notes attributed to Cyril Hume, date noted as "11-2-39"; partial draft made available to author by Dave Conover.
2. Vaz and Barron, *The Invisible Art*, p. 87.
3. Haver, *Selznick's Hollywood*, pp. 188–89.
4. Vaz and Barron, *The Invisible Art*, pp. 87–88.
5. Behlmer, *Memo from Selznick*, pp. 119–20.
6. Haver, *Selznick's Hollywood*, p. 224.
7. Vaz and Barron, *The Invisible Art*, p. 90.
8. Behlmer, Cooper interview.
9. Shay, "Willis O'Brien," *Cinefex*, p. 42.

10. A. R. Jededian Garrison, from Lula, Georgia, letter to "Gentlemen," Radio Pictures, Inc., Hollywood, Feb. 17, 1940; box 8, folder 12, Cooper Papers, BYU.
11. Behlmer, "Adventures of Cooper," *Register to Cooper Papers,* p. 17.
12. Merian Cooper, outline for *"White Eagle* or *War Eagles,"* Sept. 20, 1938, p. 1; provided to author by Dave Conover.
13. Ibid., p. 1.
14. Archer, *Willis O'Brien,* p. 43.
15. Shay, "Willis O'Brien," *Cinefex,* p. 52.
· 16. Mark Vaz, telephone interview with Dave Conover, Sept. 3, 2004. All Conover quotes in this chapter are from this interview.
17. Behlmer, Cooper interview.
18. Cooper described the project to David Lean, who'd direct the eventual *Lawrence of Arabia;* Jan. 22, 1963, letter; box 21, folder 12, Cooper Papers, BYU.
19. Merian Cooper, letter "through channels" to the President of the United States and the Chief of Staff of the United States Air Force, Sept. 29, 1958, p. 2; box 33, folder 4, Cooper Papers, BYU.
20. Merian Cooper, Western Union Telegram to Edmund Leonard, Sept. 26, 1932; box 34, folder 26, Cooper Papers, BYU. The ensuing excerpts are from box 34, folder 26, Cooper Papers, BYU.
21. Denny Holden memorial resolution, reprinted from *Princeton Alumni Weekly,* Dec. 9, 1938; box 34, folder 10, Cooper Papers, BYU.
22. Lansing C. Holden, letter to Merian Cooper, Sept. 9, 1938; box 34, folder 10, Cooper Papers, BYU.
23. Denny Holden memorial resolution.
24. Behlmer, Cooper interview.
25. Merian Cooper, report on personal military history to Chief of Staff, U.S. Air Force, October 12, 1953.
26. Event detailed by Cooper in letter to General Robert L. Scott Jr., Aug. 15, 1958; box 13, folder 28, Cooper Papers, BYU.
27. McBride, *Searching for John Ford,* p. 347.

Chapter Twenty-four: Strike Force

1. Merian Cooper report on Doolittle Raid, written from "Headquarters American Army Forces, China, Burma, and India," Chungking, China, June 12, 1942, p. 3; box 5, Cooper Papers, BYU.
2. Robert Lee Scott Jr., *Flying Tiger: Chennault of China* (Garden City, N.Y.: Doubleday & Company, 1959), p. 114, San Francisco International Airport Aviation Library.
3. Headquarters Assam-Burma-China Ferrying Command memo signed by Colonel C. V. Haynes, April 27, 1942; box 5, Cooper Papers, BYU. Also Charles F. Romanus and Riley Sunderland, *China-Burma-India Theater: Stilwell's Mission to China* (Washington, D.C.: Office of the Chief of Military History, Department of the Army, 1953), pp. 78–79.
4. Merian Cooper, letter to Lt. General James Doolittle, USAF Ret., addressed to "Dear Jimmy," April 7, 1971, p. 2; box 5, Cooper Papers, BYU. In this letter, Cooper adds that he personally wrote out the orders, which General Arnold then signed.
5. Ibid.
6. Claire Lee Chennault, *Way of a Fighter: The Memoirs of Claire Lee Chennault* (New York: G. P. Putnam's Sons, 1949), p. 182.

7. Merian Cooper, letter to Lieutenant General James Doolittle, April 7, 1971, p. 1. The further details and direct quotes from this letter are excerpted in the ensuing text.

8. Scott, *Flying Tiger,* pp. 93, 97–98, 103.

9. Ibid., pp. 112–13.

10. Merian Cooper, letter to Lieutenant General James Doolittle, p. 1.

11. Ibid., pp. 1–2.

12. The following quotes and references are from Cooper's report, written from "Headquarters American Army Forces, China, Burma, and India," Chungking, China, June 12, 1942; box 5, Cooper Papers, BYU.

13. Merian Cooper, letter to Lieutenant General James Doolittle, p. 3.

14. Brigadier General J. H. Doolittle, letter to Mrs. Merian C. Cooper, May 21, 1942; box 5, Cooper Papers, BYU.

15. Merian Cooper, letter to Lieutenant General James Doolittle, p. 3.

16. Ibid.

17. Ibid., p. 4.

18. Chennault, *Way of a Fighter,* p. 169.

19. Headquarters Assam-Burma-China Ferrying Command memo signed by Colonel C. V. Haynes, April 27, 1942.

20. C. V. Haynes, memo to Lieutenant General Arnold Barrackpone, Feb. 1942; box 5, folder 3, Cooper Papers, BYU.

21. Ibid.

22. Scott, *Flying Tiger,* pp. 115–16.

23. Robert Scott, Kunming, China, letter to Commanding General, U.S. 10th Air Force, New Delhi, India, Aug. 27, 1942, regarding loss of recommendation for citation for Merian Cooper, p. 1; box 5, folder 6, Cooper Papers, BYU.

24. Footnote for the April 27 incident gleaned from: First Lieutenant Robert L. Hartzell, Air Corps, "Subject: Report of Judgment and Coolness Displayed by Officer in Time of Emergency," to Commanding General CATF, Peishiyi, China, Nov. 9, 1942, true copy certified by E. C. Ackerman; Report of Action on April 27, 1942, Flight of Officer in Charge, (Colonel Cooper) to Commanding General, CATF, Peishiyi, China; Nov. 10, 1942, from Captain Bert M. Carleton; Colonel Robert L. Scott in Kunming, China, Recommendation for Citation to the Chief of Army Air Forces, Washington, D.C., Nov. 20, 1942, true copy certified by E. C. Ackerman. All documents box 5, folder 6, Cooper Papers, BYU.

25. Merian Cooper, "My Life in War and Peace," pp. 25–26. Cooper was awarded a Bronze Star for helping evacuate women and children from Loiwing, which was under imminent attack from the Japanese.

26. General Chennault, letter to Dorothy Jordan, Jan. 12, 1948; box 32, Cooper Papers, BYU.

Chapter Twenty-five: The Flying Tiger

1. Scott, *Flying Tiger,* pp. 166–67.

2. Eddie Lockett, interview with Claire Chennault; Chennault was also addressing Tommy Corcoran, who was sitting in on the session. Tape 5, February 4–5, 1958; box 14, folder 2, Cooper Papers, BYU.

3. Chennault, *Way of a Fighter,* p. 135.

4. Ibid., pp. 3–4.

5. Ibid., p. 29.

6. Ibid., pp. 30–31, 72–73.
7. Cooper wrote up the order creating the China Air Task Force for Claire Chennault's signature; "the undersigned," the document ends, "assumed command of the China Air Task Force, with station at Peishiyi, China, as of July 8, 1942." Box 5, Cooper Papers, BYU.
8. Chennault, *Way of a Fighter,* pp. 181–82.
9. Merian Cooper, letter to Claire Chennault, March 25, 1949; box 32, folder 14, Cooper Papers, BYU.
10. Barbara W. Tuchman, *Stilwell and the American Experience in China, 1911–45* (New York: Bantam Books, 1972), pp. 318, 397. Also Chennault, *Way of a Fighter,* pp. 20, 168.
11. "When a Hawk Smiles," *Time,* Dec. 6, 1943, p. 29.
12. Merian Cooper, letter to Robert Scott, Aug. 15, 1958, p. 4; box 13, folder 28, Cooper Papers, BYU.
13. Chennault, *Way of a Fighter,* pp. 176, 178–79, 186.
14. Scott, *Flying Tiger,* pp. 147–48.
15. Chennault, *Way of a Fighter,* p. 182.
16. Ibid., pp. 183–85.
17. Eddie Lockett, interview with General Chennault, Tape 1 transcript; box 14, folder 2, Cooper Papers, BYU.
18. Chennault, *Way of a Fighter,* pp. 185–86.
19. In an interview with Eddie Lockett, Chennault didn't deny his combat experience with the Flying Tigers but refused to discuss it, because as a retired officer he wasn't supposed to fight and because he and Chiang Kai-shek had made a solemn promise not to discuss it. "I didn't teach anything that I didn't know," Chennault added. Lockett interview with Chennault, transcript of Reel 3, taped May 1958; box 14, folder 2, Cooper Papers, BYU.
20. Chennault, *Way of a Fighter,* pp. 188–90.
21. C. V. Haynes, letter, Headquarters Bomber Unit China Air Task Force, Kunming, China, to Colonel M. C. Cooper, Chief of Staff, CATF, September 29, 1942; box 5, folder 1, Cooper Papers, BYU.
22. Chennault summed up Cooper's role in this regard in a letter he wrote on November 30, 1942, thanking him for his service upon Cooper's transfer. Box 5, folder 1, Cooper Papers, BYU.
23. Tuchman, *Stilwell and the American Experience in China,* pp. 409–10.
24. Eddie Lockett, interview with General John Alison, March 29, 1958, interview transcript; box 14, folder 11, Cooper Papers, BYU.
25. Transcript of remarks dictated by Brigadier General John R. Alison to Edward B. Lockett of Washington, D.C., on March 29, 1958; presented as "Annex II" attachment in report by Merian Cooper addressed to the President of the United States through the Chief of Staff of the United States Air Force, dated Sept. 22, 1958, pp. 3–4; box 33, folder 4, Cooper Papers, BYU.
26. Scott, *Flying Tiger,* p. 212.
27. Chennault, *Way of a Fighter,* p. 182.
28. Tuchman, *Stilwell and the American Experience in China,* pp. 431–32.
29. Chennault, *Way of a Fighter,* pp. 212–16.
30. Scott, *Flying Tiger,* p. 212.
31. Chennault, *Way of a Fighter,* p. 216.
32. "Cooper, '15," *Shipmate,* March 1943, p. 62; box 2, folder 3, Cooper Papers, BYU.

33. Robert L. Scott, Colonel, Air Corps, China Air Task Force in Kunming, China, letter to the Chief of Army Air Force, Washington, D.C., Nov. 20, 1942. Scott was making yet another recommendation for Cooper for the Distinguished Service Medal, adding that Cooper had been transferred back to the States and, as they were no longer serving together, Scott would not benefit from his recommendation.
34. Chennault, *Way of a Fighter,* pp. 196–97.
35. Everett W. Holstrom, Captain Air Corps, testimonial, November 5, 1942; box 5, folder 3, Cooper Papers, BYU. Holstrom's testimonial added that photographs and intelligence verified destruction of the Kowloon docks, the only place for oceangoing transports in the Hong Kong docking area.
36. "Perfect mission" comment from Robert L. Scott, Colonel, Air Corps, China Air Task Force in Kunming, China, to the Chief of Army Air Force, Washington, D.C., Nov. 20, 1942; box 5, folder 6, Cooper Papers, BYU; details of Hong Kong attack and Major Hill's response from Recommendation for the Distinguished Service Cross written by Robert L. Scott Jr., Oct. 29, 1942; a true copy was also signed by Merian C. Cooper; box 5, folder 6, Cooper Papers, BYU.
37. Chennault, *Way of a Fighter,* p. 206.

Chapter Twenty-six: The Way of a Fighter

1. Ennis C. Whitehead, Major General, Deputy Commander, Headquarters Advance Echelon Fifth Air Force, APO 713, Unit 1 to Commanding General, Fifth Air Force, APO 925, April 5, 1944; box 5, folder 1, Cooper Papers, BYU.
2. Headquarters, China Air Task Force in New York, Dec. 1, 1942, signed by Lieutenant Colonel H. E. Strickland; box 5, folder 13, Cooper Papers, BYU.
3. William McGaffin, "Hollywood Colonel Spurs American Flyers in China," *Los Angeles Times,* Dec. 14, 1942; Margaret Herrick Library, Academy of Motion Picture Arts and Sciences, Beverly Hills, California.
4. "Cooper, '15," *Shipmate,* March 1943, p. 29.
5. Merian Cooper, letter to Richard M. Cooper at the United States Air Force Academy, Colorado Springs, Colorado, Oct. 5, 1958; box 33, folder 4, Cooper Papers, BYU.
6. Merian Cooper, taped statement for Kevin Brownlow; made available to author by Kevin Brownlow. Cooper added that General Douglas MacArthur had been a close personal friend since 1931 and "was able to give me every single decoration that a theater commander could give. He also wanted to go over General Marshall's head directly to President Roosevelt to make me a general." Merian's widow, while corresponding with W. Douglas Burden, later downplayed the purported private confrontation with Marshall, implying that her husband might have overdramatized the encounter. But whether it was one-on-one or through channels, Cooper clearly was a vocal supporter of Chennault and their mutual vision for China.
7. Robert L. Scott, letter to Merian Cooper, Nov. 30, 1942; box 36, folder 3; Cooper Papers, BYU.
8. Colonel Wlodzimierz Onacewicz, Military and Air Attaché, letter on Polish embassy stationery to Colonel Merian Cooper, at the Bayshore Road Hotel in Tampa, Florida, March 19, 1942. The letter ends with "best wishes for a quick recovery of your health." Box 3, folder 2, Cooper Papers, BYU.
9. McBride, *Searching for John Ford,* p. 382.
10. Behlmer, Cooper interview. In a September 3, 2004, telephone interview with

the author, Richard Cooper added that this flight took place in the continental United States, with Schoedsack flying from a test facility in Florida. The details of the accident are vague, other than that Schoedsack was on a flight to test cameras and that his goggles had come off. In those days, he added, it wasn't uncommon to push one's physiological boundaries: "I put Schoedsack in that category."

11. The Air Medal would be awarded to Cooper for the Fifth Air Force Offensive in a certificate that noted that the president had signed it "for meritorious achievement while participating in Aerial Flight Pacific Theater of Operations, on September 3, 1943." On July 23, 1947, it was signed by the major general, adjutant general, and secretary of war; box 5, folder 15, Cooper Papers, BYU.

12. David W. Hutchison, Colonel, Air Corps, "Certificate" certifying Cooper's combat operations, from Headquarters Advance Echelon Fifth Air Force APO 929, Oct. 30, 1943; box 5, folder 5, Cooper Papers, BYU.

13. Vaz, Richard Cooper interview.

14. Major General Ennis C. Whitehead, U.S. Army Deputy Air Force Commander, to Commanding General, Fifth Air Force, regarding "Recommendation for Award of the Distinguished Service Medal" to Merian Cooper, March 8, 1944; box 28, folder 13, Cooper Papers, BYU.

15. Lee Van Atta, "Col. Merian C. Cooper . . . the Cosmopolite of the Month," *Cosmopolitan,* April 1945; box 1, folder 9, Cooper Papers, BYU.

16. *Who's Who in the AFA,* on Merian C. Cooper, published by the Air Force Association in January 1948; box 1, folder 10, Cooper Papers, BYU.

17. General Chennault, letter to Dorothy Cooper, May 10, 1943; box 32, folder 14, Cooper Papers, BYU.

18. Major General Chennault, headquarters, Fourteenth Air Force, letter to Dorothy Cooper, Feb. 22, 1944; box 32, Cooper Papers, BYU.

19. Vaz, Richard Cooper interview.

20. Major General Ennis Whitehead, Headquarters Advance Echelon Fifth Air Force, Deputy Commander, letter to Lieutenant General George C. Kenney, June 13, 1944; box 5, Cooper Papers, BYU.

21. Headquarters Far East Air Forces Recommendation for Award of the Distinguished Service Medal for Merian Cooper, June 26, 1945; box 5, BYU. The recommendation added that the control of the north coast of New Guinea did not include the bypassed Japanese garrisons at Wewak and Sarmir.

22. "Duke" [John Wayne], Western Union telegram to General Merian C. Cooper at the Beverly Hilton Hotel, June 14, 1966; box 28, folder 13, Cooper Papers, BYU.

23. Brigadier General Merian Cooper, letter to Chief of Staff, U.S. Air Force, Oct. 12, 1953.

24. Tuchman, *Stilwell and the American Experience in China,* p. 664.

25. Scott, *Flying Tiger,* pp. 272–73.

26. The editors of *Look, Movie Lot to Beachhead* (Garden City, N.Y.: Doubleday, Doran and Company, 1945), pp. 126–47, and Joe Morella, Edward Z. Epstein, and John Griggs, *The Films of World War II* (Secaucus, N.J.: Citadel Press, 1973), p. 220.

27. A souvenir card decorated with the rising sun from the historic event of September 2, 1945, noted: "Certifying the presence of: Merian C. Cooper, Colonel, A.C. at the formal surrender of the Japanese Forces to the Allied Powers." Card in the Cooper Papers at BYU; box 5, folder 12.

28. Rupert Hendricks, International News Service report, dateline Hollywood, Oct. 28, 1945; box 5, folder 7, Cooper Papers, BYU.

29. Claire Chennault, letter to Dorothy Cooper, Jan. 12, 1948; box 32, Cooper Papers, BYU.

30. Chennault, *Way of a Fighter*, pp. xxi–xxii.

Chapter Twenty-seven: Cold Warrior

1. Merian Cooper, letter to the Honorable Charles Edison, Waldorf Towers, Waldorf-Astoria Hotel, New York, Nov. 11, 1958; box 13, folder 17, Cooper Papers, BYU.

2. Cooper, "My Life in War and Peace," p. 37; Cooper Papers, BYU.

3. Ibid., pp. 33–35.

4. Merian Cooper, letter to George M. Crawford of New York, addressed to "Dear Buck," Oct. 31, 1953; box 33, folder 7, Cooper Papers, BYU.

5. Merian Cooper, letter to staff, U.S. Air Force, Oct. 12, 1953; Cooper Papers, BYU.

6. Merian Cooper, letter on Merian C. Cooper Enterprises, Inc., stationery to Colonel David C. Hill of Birmingham, Alabama, Oct. 16, 1958, p. 2; box 33, folder 4, Cooper Papers, BYU. Cooper, speaking to Hill as an investor, added that if he succeeded he'd be able to "make a great deal of money for investors, and do great good for the United States."

7. The Special Committee of the Screen Directors Guild, telegram to the Honorable Martin and Thomas, Oct. 20, 1947; box 9, folder 1, Cooper Papers, BYU.

8. Merian and Dorothy Cooper, telegram to Senator Joseph McCarthy, Nov. 7, 1954; box 35, folder 7, Cooper Papers, BYU.

9. Mark Vaz, interview with Malgorzata Słomczyńska-Pierzchalska, Sacile, Italy, Oct. 12, 2003.

10. Anna Chennault, letter to Merian Cooper, addressed to "Dear Coop," Sept. 25, 1958; box 32, folder 13, Cooper Papers, BYU.

11. Merian Cooper, letter to Colonel David L. Hill, Sept. 29, 1958; box 13, folder 18, Cooper Papers, BYU.

12. Anna Chennault and Thomas G. Corcoran, Western Union telegram to Merian Cooper, Aug. 22, 1958; box 13, folder 19, Cooper Papers, BYU.

13. Merian Cooper, "Chennault of China," treatment for Merian C. Cooper Enterprises, Inc., March 19, 1959, pp. 3–4; box 13, folder 21, Cooper Papers, BYU.

14. Merian Cooper, letter to Mr. Richard K. Mellon, Pittsburgh, Pennsylvania, Nov. 5, 1958; box 13, folder 18, Cooper Papers, BYU.

15. Merian Cooper, letter to Mr. Donald E. Baruch, May 6, 1959; box 13, folder 3, Cooper Papers, BYU. In a September 8, 1960, letter and contract to Farrow, Cooper got the director to sign a letter confirming certain agreements and Cooper's ultimate rights to the property and laying the groundwork for Farrow to write the final screenplay; box 13, folder 26, Cooper Papers, BYU.

16. Merian Cooper letters to John Farrow, Aug. 12, 1958; April 3, 1959; and Sept. 15, 1960; box 13, folder 26, Cooper Papers, BYU.

17. Merian Cooper, letter to W. C. McDonald Jr. of Birmingham, Alabama, Feb. 2, 1961; box 13, folder 10, Cooper Papers, BYU. There was also a belief in some quarters—as was noted in confidence to this author—that there may have been some resistance in Hollywood in the 1960s to a film that would glorify the army.

18. Merian Cooper taped dictation for Kevin Brownlow; made available to author by Kevin Brownlow.
19. O. C. Doering, letter to W. Douglas Burden, Nov. 4, 1977, p. 2; box 32, Cooper Papers, BYU.
20. Vaz, Richard Cooper interview.
21. Merian Cooper, letter to Air Cadet Richard M. Cooper, United States Air Force Academy, Oct. 5, 1958, pp. 3–5.
22. Vaz, Richard Cooper interview.
23. Cooper, taped monologue for Kevin Brownlow.

EMPIRE OF THE IMAGINATION

Chapter Twenty-eight: Argosy

1. Argosy Pictures Corp. News Bureau copy, circa 1949; box 1, folder 10, Cooper Papers, BYU.
2. James D'Arc, interview with Donald Dewar at 211 South Spalding Street, Beverly Hills, California, March 25, 1996; MSS OH 1895, BYU Special Collections. Dewar was with Argosy from 1947 to around 1951.
3. O. C. Doering Jr. letter to W. Douglas Burden, Nov. 4, 1977, p. 2; box 32, Cooper Papers, BYU.
4. McBride, *Searching for John Ford,* pp. 421–22.
5. Ibid., p. 423.
6. D'Arc, Dewar interview.
7. McBride, *Searching for John Ford,* p. 441.
8. Vaz, Richard Cooper interview.
9. News release, Argosy Pictures Corp. News Bureau, circa 1949; box 1, folder 10, Cooper Papers, BYU.
10. "Memorandum Exploitation," "rough draft," seven-page internal document, March 31, 1948, pp. 1, 6; MSS 1849, box 13, folder 8, Argosy Pictures Corporation Papers, BYU.
11. Ibid., p. 7.
12. "Grass" outline, Dec. 17, 1947, p. 1; MSS 1849, box 13, folder 8, Cooper Papers, BYU.
13. Brownlow, Ernest Schoedsack interview.
14. Behlmer, Cooper interview. Cooper later admitted to Rudy Behlmer that he'd "put up the dough" for not only the failed Persian trip but a total of seven various far-flung movie expeditions. "I picked the best people I could but they brought me back nothing! All failures!"
15. Merian C. Cooper and Laurence Stallings, "Imaginative Films," n.d., pp. 1–2; MSS 1849, box 13, folder 8, Argosy Papers, BYU.
16. Although the Argosy-RKO deal allowed Argosy creative control and ownership, *Mighty Joe Young* would be jointly owned.
17. Vaz, Harryhausen interview.
18. Merian Cooper, telegram to Donald Dewar at Argosy, "Mexico City April 28"; MSS 1849, box 26, folder 7, Argosy Papers, BYU.
19. Barbara Hall, oral-history interview with Adele Balkan, pp. 104–05; 1999 Academy Foundation, Oral History Program, Margaret Herrick Library, Academy of Motion Picture Arts and Sciences.
20. Behlmer, "Adventures of Cooper," *Register to Cooper Papers,* p. 19.

21. Ernest Schoedsack, "Grow Young with Joe Young," n.d.; MSS 1849, box 26, folder 12, Argosy Papers, BYU.

22. Merian Cooper, letter to Lindsay Anderson, Aug. 21, 1963; Cooper Papers, BYU.

23. McBride, *Searching for John Ford,* p. 528.

24. D'Arc, Dewar interview.

25. Ibid.

Chapter Twenty-nine: This Is Cinerama!

1. Merian Cooper, "Night Letter (Paraphrase)" telegram to Lowell Thomas, Aug. 13, 1953; Academy of Motion Picture Arts and Sciences Library.

2. "Fred Waller had done one or two of the special effects shots on *Four Feathers* when he was at Paramount, and I knew him as far back as *Grass* and *Chang,*" Cooper would recall. Behlmer, Cooper interview.

3. "Fred Waller, Cinerama Inventor...," *Cinerama* World Premiere program, Cinerama, Inc., and Cinerama Productions Corp., 1952, p. 7; program provided to author by Craig Barron.

4. Ibid., p. 6.

5. The "publicity" mentioned refers to the *Cinerama* program.

6. Merian Cooper, letter to Lowell Thomas, July 3, 1951; box 36, folder 18, Cooper Papers, BYU.

7. "A New Kind of Hero," essay, *Cinerama* program, p. 4.

8. Ibid., p. 5.

9. Merian Cooper, letter to the Board of Directors, Cinerama Productions Corp., Nov. 10, 1953; box 23, folder 8, Cooper Papers, BYU.

10. Merian Cooper, thirty-nine-page letter to Lowell Thomas, Dec. 5, 1953, p. 12; box 36, folder 18, Cooper Papers, BYU.

11. Behlmer, Cooper interview.

12. Merian Cooper, letter to Lowell Thomas regarding *Cinerama* release, May 29, 1952; box 23, folder 8, Cooper Papers, BYU.

13. Behlmer, Cooper interview.

14. Ibid. Cooper would also recall for Brownlow that *Cinerama* had cost an estimated $512,000 and grossed over $35 million. "The Cypress Gardens I spent about $18,000, flying across the continent I spent about $40,000, and the European [material] cost around $250,000. The rest was negative, cutting, printing."

15. Bruce Handy, "This Is Cinerama," *Vanity Fair,* April 2001: 264.

16. Bob Murphy, "Where Adventure Calls: Ex-City Reporter Reviews Course of Many Fabulous Careers," *Minneapolis Sunday Tribune,* Dec. 6, 1953; box 23, Cooper Papers, BYU.

17. Merian Cooper, letter to Edmund Leonard, March 16, 1949; box 34. In 1954 Cinerama innovator Fred Waller also passed away.

18. Merian Cooper, letter to Edmund Leonard, Sept. 24, 1953; box 34, folder 26, Cooper Papers, BYU.

19. Merian Cooper, letter to Edmund Leonard, Nov. 9, 1953; box 28, Cooper Papers, BYU.

20. Elmer S. Eggan, letter to Merian Cooper, March 25, 1954; box 34, folder 26, Cooper Papers, BYU.

21. Merian Cooper, "Ideas for Possible New Series," typed letter to Robert L. Bendick, March 7, 1958; box 28, folder 4, Cooper Papers, BYU.

22. Handy, "This Is Cinerama," *Vanity Fair,* p. 264.
23. Rickitt, *Special Effects,* pp. 24–25.
24. Merian Cooper, letter to the Board of Directors, Cinerama Productions Corp., Nov. 10, 1953, pp. 4–5.
25. Telegram from "Coop" to Lowell Thomas at Rockefeller Plaza in New York, Aug. 13, 1953. This was the telegram in which Cooper hailed Cinerama as the stuff of "spirit and soul."
26. Merian Cooper, letter to the Board of Directors, Cinerama Productions Corp., Nov. 10, 1953, pp. 7–8.
27. McBride, *Searching for John Ford,* p. 530.
28. Merian Cooper, "Story Ideas, 1962" and various one-page typed subject notes, Oct. 10 and Oct. 11, 1962; box 23, folder 9, Cooper Papers, BYU.
29. *Citizen News* clipping, April 16, 1953; box 28, folder 18, Cooper Papers, BYU. The event was sponsored by the Beverly Hills Junior Chamber of Commerce.
30. Merian Cooper, unaccredited, "Rocketry (Astronauts)," Oct. 10, 1962; box 23, folder 9, Cooper Papers, BYU.
31. Merian Cooper, five-page proposal to Nicolas Reisini, President, Cinerama Inc., in care of Beverly Hills Hotel, July 21, 1961; box 23, folder 6, Cooper Papers, BYU.
32. Ibid., p. 3.
33. Merian Cooper, letter to Lowell Thomas, June 29, 1972; box 36, folder 18, Cooper Papers, BYU.
34. Merian Cooper, letter from Dublin, Ireland, to Charles B. FitzSimons, Jan. 23, 1970; box 7, folder 7, Cooper Papers, BYU.

Chapter Thirty: The Return of King Kong

1. Haver, *David Selznick's Hollywood,* p. 118.
2. Dianne Tittle De Laet, *Giants and Heroes: A Daughter's Memories of Y. A. Tittle* (South Royalton, Vt.: Steerforth Press, 1995), pp. 155–56.
3. Merian Cooper, letter to Mr. Polito, Feb. 10, 1966, p. 3; copy made available to author by John Michlig.
4. Willis O'Brien, letter to Merian Cooper, Jan. 25, 1962; box 23, folder 16, Cooper Papers, BYU.
5. John Beck, (copy of) letter to Mr. Daniel T. O'Shea, April 2, 1960; letter to "Obie" from Dan O'Shea, June 14, 1960; box 23, folder 15, Cooper Papers, BYU.
6. Draft letter signed by Richard M. Goldwater, n.d.; box 8, folder 20, Cooper Papers, BYU.
7. Merian Cooper, letter to Mr. Robert Bendick, Sept. 4, 1964; box 8, folder 20, Cooper Papers, BYU.
8. David O. Selznick, letter to Merian C. Cooper, July 23, 1963; box 9, Cooper Papers, BYU.
9. David O. Selznick, letter to Mr. A. Loewenthal, Aug. 16, 1932; box 8, folder 11, Cooper Papers, BYU.
10. Charles FitzSimons, letter to Mr. Fulton Brylawski, Jan. 14, 1965, p. 2; box 8, folder 5, Cooper Papers, BYU.
11. Merian Cooper, letter to John Cobb Cooper, June 17, 1965; Cooper Papers, BYU.
12. David Bruce, letter to Merian Cooper, Oct. 7, 1964; box 8, folder 20, Cooper Papers, BYU.

13. Gordon E. Youngman of Youngman, Hungate & Leopold, letter to Mr. Charles B. FitzSimons, Aug. 26, 1964; box 8, folder 20, Cooper Papers, BYU.

14. Draft letter from Charles FitzSimons to Mr. Gordon Youngman, Aug. 31, 1964; box 8, folder 20, Cooper Papers, BYU.

15. Merian Cooper, letter to W. Douglas Burden, Aug. 27, 1964; box 32, folder 10, Cooper Papers, BYU.

16. Rudy Behlmer, "Merian C. Cooper Is the Kind of Creative Showman Today's Movies Badly Need," *Films in Review*, Jan. 1966: 35.

17. Tribute to Willis O'Brien by Merian Cooper, *Hollywood Reporter*, Nov. 27, 1962, p. 9; box 23, folder 15, Cooper Papers, BYU. Cooper's comment on Selznick shared with author by Rudy Behlmer.

18. "Monte" Schoedsack, letter to "Coop," March 12, 1969, p. 2; box 36, folder 2, Cooper Papers, BYU.

19. Charles R. D'Olive, letter to Merian Cooper, July 2, 1961; box 2, folder 8, Cooper Papers, BYU.

20. Merian C. Cooper, letter to Mr. Dewey O. Tharp, June 7, 1961; box 2, folder 7, Cooper Papers, BYU.

21. Charles FitzSimons, letter to Merian Cooper, addressed to "Dear Coop," Feb. 6, 1969; box 8, folder 14, Cooper Papers, BYU.

22. Merian Cooper, letter to Charles FitzSimons, Jan. 30, 1969; box 8, folder 14, Cooper Papers, BYU.

Chapter Thirty-one: Journey to the Undiscovered Country

1. Merian Cooper, letter to Miss Ward, Feb. 17, 1962, p. 3; Explorers Club Archives.

2. Merian Cooper, letter to W. Douglas Burden, Jan. 22, 1972, p. 2; box 32, Cooper Papers, BYU.

3. Brownlow, interview with Cooper and company, circa late 1960s.

4. This and the following from Vaz, Patrick Montgomery interview.

5. Merian Cooper, letter to Ray Bradbury, June 1, 1972; box 32, folder 6, Cooper Papers, BYU.

6. Merian Cooper, letter to W. Douglas Burden, Jan. 22, 1972, p. 3.

7. Merian Cooper, letter to Mrs. Richard Baker, June 20, 1961, pp. 2–3; box 32, Cooper Papers, BYU.

8. Merian Cooper, letter to Bosley Crowther at *New York Times*, July 7, 1965; Explorers Club Archives.

9. Merian Cooper, "Personal and Confidential" letter to "Puck" [Frederick W. Pennoyer Jr.], June 17, 1961; box 35, Cooper Papers, BYU.

10. Merian Cooper, letter to Captain F. W. Pennoyer III; June 28, 1961, p. 2; box 35, Cooper Papers, BYU.

11. Merian Cooper, letter to W. Douglas Burden, May 9, 1972; box 32, Cooper Papers, BYU.

12. Merian Cooper, letter to "Monte" Schoedsack, Feb. 17, 1970; box 36, folder 2, Cooper Papers, BYU.

13. Merian Cooper, letter to John Wayne, addressed to "Dear Duke," April 29, 1971; box 33, folder 4, Cooper Papers, BYU.

14. Coop also replied on whether *The Lost World* had influenced *King Kong*, one of the enduring controversies: "I never saw 'The Lost World' until that genius, Willis O'Brien, got me a print in Hollywood after I had finished shooting the

so-called 1200 feet test reel [for *Kong*], which is still in the picture." Cooper letter to Kevin Brownlow, Feb. 2, 1972; box 32, folder 7, Cooper Papers, BYU.

15. Merian Cooper, letter to Gilbert M. Grosvenor at the National Geographic Society, Aug. 14, 1971; Feb. 14, 1972; box 35, Cooper Papers, BYU.

16. "Waddy" Pohl, letter to "Coop," May 16, 1971; box 35, Cooper Papers, BYU.

17. Merian Cooper, letter to Kevin Brownlow, May 2, 1972; box 30, folder 1, Cooper Papers, BYU.

18. Merian Cooper, letter to Advanced Projects investors, May 5, 1972, p. 2; box 30, folder 1, Cooper Papers, BYU.

19. Merian Cooper, letter to W. Douglas Burden, May 9, 1972.

20. Merian Cooper, letter to David Bruce, May 9, 1972; box 32, folder 8, Cooper Papers, BYU.

21. Merian Cooper, letter to Lowell Thomas, Feb. 2, 1972, p. 1; box 36, folder 18, Cooper Papers, BYU.

22. The Explorers Club, program for sixty-eighth annual dinner; box 33, folder 2, Cooper Papers, BYU.

23. Eulogies for Steiner were also delivered by David Raksin and Elmer Bernstein.

24. Merian Cooper, letter to O. C. Doering, July 6, 1972; box 30, folder 1, Cooper Papers, BYU.

25. "Monte" Schoedsack, letter to "Dear ol' partner Coop," Sept. 24, 1972; box 36, folder 2, Cooper Papers, BYU.

26. One typed page, written in pencil, "July . . . 1977 letter"; box 32, Cooper Papers, BYU.

27. Fourteenth Air Force Association "In Memoriam" card; excerpt from Lowell Thomas radio broadcast; both box 1, folder 12, Cooper Papers, BYU.

28. Maciej Słomczyński, letter to Zoe Porter, 1973; provided to author by Malgorzata Słomczyńska-Pierzchalska.

29. Maciej Słomczyński letter excerpted in Distant, Difficult, and Dangerous exhibition program, p. 4, Le Giornate del Cinema Muto 2003.

30. "In Memoriam, 20th Aero Squadron Bulletin #3, 1972–1973"; box 2, folder 7, Cooper Papers, BYU.

31. One-page note on Polish commemorative services, n.d.; box 1, folder 13, Cooper Papers, BYU.

32. Ector LeDuc, M.D., letter to Mrs. Dorothy Cooper, June 6, 1973; box 1, folder 11, Cooper Papers, BYU.

33. Dorothy Jordan Cooper, letter to "Tommy" [Corcoran], Feb. 11, 1974; box 33, folder 5, Cooper Papers, BYU.

34. Mark Vaz, interview with Randy R. Merritt, Los Angeles, April 15, 2004. Colonel Richard Cooper, in a telephone conversation with the author on September 3, 2004, added that FitzSimons had heard the sonic boom in Los Angeles, which was "a little odd, it's rare," since jets breaking the sound barrier were relegated to places where there wouldn't be a lot of people, such as the "supersonic corridor" in the Mojave Desert at Edwards Air Force Base.

THE LEGEND

Chapter Thirty-two: "Distant, Difficult, and Dangerous"

1. Mark Vaz, interview with James D'Arc, Sacile, Italy, 2003.

2. Marshek, "King Kong," *American Cinemeditor,* pp. 8–9, 13.

3. Paul Mandell, "An Open Letter to Dino De Laurentiis," *Cinefantastique,* 1976, pp. 42–43; New York Library for the Performing Arts.

4. Don Shay and Jody Duncan, *The Making of Jurassic Park* (New York: Ballantine Books, 1993), p. 22.

5. The narrative of *King Kong* litigation in the 1970s is based on information set forth in the factual summaries contained in two court opinions from federal court in New York, *Universal City Studios, Inc. v. Nintendo Co., Ltd.,* 578 F. Supp. 911 (S.D.N.Y. 1984) and *Universal City Studios, Inc. v. Nintendo Co., Ltd.,* 615 F. Supp. 838 (S.D.N.Y. 1985). Additional facts and background obtained through an interview and subsequent talks with Randy Merritt, an attorney representing Colonel Richard Cooper, who has engaged in an extensive survey and analysis of copyright and trademark rights related to Merian Cooper's great ape creations, King Kong and Mighty Joe Young.

   The copyright action could not have been brought in the state court because the federal court has jurisdiction over claims brought under the federal Copyright Act.

6. Charles B. FitzSimons, letter to Earl S. Wright, June 18, 1975; box 8, Cooper Papers, BYU.

7. The narrative that follows is drawn from the factual description set forth in the legal opinions in both the district court in New York and the Second Circuit Court of Appeals: *Universal City Studios, Inc. v. Nintendo Co., Ltd.,* 578 F. Supp. 911 (S.D.N.Y. 1983); *Universal City Studios, Inc. v. Nintendo Co., Ltd.,* 615 F. Supp. 838 (S.D.N.Y. 1985); *Universal City Studios, Inc. v. Nintendo Co., Ltd.,* 746 F.2d 112 (2d Cir. 1984); *Universal City Studios, Inc. v. Nintendo Co., Ltd.,* 797 F.2d 70 (2d Cir. 1986).

8. *Universal,* 578 F. Supp. at 923.

9. *Universal,* 578 F. Supp. at 924.

10. "People" item, *Time* magazine, April 25, 1983, p. 107; box 9, Cooper Papers, BYU.

11. Ray Bradbury, "The Thirties," from *Graven Images: The Best of Horror, Fantasy, and Science-Fiction Film Art* (New York: Grove Press, 1992), pp. 41–42.

12. Kevin Brownlow, letter to Dorothy Jordan Cooper, addressed to "Dear Dorothy," Jan. 9, 1980; box 32, folder 7, Cooper Papers, BYU.

13. Kevin Brownlow, letter to Dorothy Cooper, April 7, 1979; box 32, Cooper Papers, BYU.

14. This and the following Behlmer comments from Mark Vaz telephone interview with Rudy Behlmer, May 1, 2004.

15. Kevin Brownlow, letter to Dorothy Jordan Cooper, Nov. 16, 1981; box 32, Cooper Papers, BYU.

16. "A Historic Occasion: British Museum Receives 'Chang,' " *Kinetograph Weekly,* Sept. 18, 1927; article made available at Le Giornate del Cinema Muto 2003.

17. Kevin Brownlow, letter to Dorothy Jordan, Nov. 16, 1981.

18. Mark Vaz, interview with Dennis Doros, Oct. 13, 2003.

19. Merian Cooper, Directorial Career List, March 20, 1968; box 35, Cooper Papers, BYU.

20. Vaz, Doros interview.

21. Vaz, D'Arc interview.

22. Mark Vaz, Malgorzata "Daisy" Słomcyzński-Pierzchalska interview. In a September 3, 2004, telephone interview ith the author, Richard Cooper recalled that he was a young boy when he learned the family secret about his out-of-

wedlock half brother. "I think I came across a letter being posted to Poland and I asked about it. My mom or my dad let me know there was a woman he had known during his stay in Poland and there was a son. I knew what that meant. I never questioned it and he never talked about it. My dad kept this very private. I just knew she was being taken care of."

23. David Ansen and Jeff Giles, "The New Visionaries," *Time,* Feb. 9, 2004: 61.

Chapter Thirty-three: Mythic Vision

1. Tad Friend, "The Pictures: Wrecked Again," *New Yorker,* May 24, 2004: 35.
2. Mark Vaz, interview with Ray Harryhausen, Ray Bradbury, and Forrest Ackerman at Clifton's restaurant, Los Angeles, April 16, 2004.
3. In 1995 the American Museum of Natural History celebrated its 125th year with a program highlighting fifty "treasures," among them "Komodo Dragons" (number forty-three on the list). *Expedition: Treasures from 125 Years of Discovery* (New York: American Museum of Natural History, 1995), p. 30.
4. Thomson, *New Biographical Dictionary of Film,* "Fay Wray," p. 948.
5. "Fay Wray, Star Who Stole Kong's Heart, Dies at 96," *New York Times,* Aug. 10, 2004.
6. Mark Vaz, telephone interview with Justin "Bud" Clayton, Aug. 8, 2004.
7. Caryn James, "The Inseparable Trio: Girl, Ape, Skyscraper," Internet article: NYTimes.com, Aug. 15, 2004.
8. Mark Vaz, interview with Fay Wray, New York City, May 8, 2004.

AUTHOR'S NOTE

The legend of Merian Cooper captured my imagination in the early 1990s when I saw the reissue of his classic *Chang* at the Castro Theatre in San Francisco. As a writer on film and a contributor to *Cinefex,* "the journal of cinematic illusions," I was already a fan of *King Kong* and vaguely familiar with the name of Cooper, if not the details of his life. What truly drew me to Cooper was his inherent code of honor and idealistic vision of life, while his treks to far-flung lands and encounters with different cultures struck a personal chord. I've studied traditional Chinese martial arts and was given a Tibetan Buddhist name in the course of an overland journey from London through the deserts of Iran and Pakistan, into India, the Ladakh region north of Kashmir, and Nepal. I also met the Dalai Lama in India while covering the Tibetan refugee communities there for *Yoga Journal* magazine, interviewed the leader of the Maroons in the Blue Mountains of Jamaica during a trip under the auspices of *Sierra* magazine, and met Navajo and Hopi medicine men in the Southwest for my first book, *Spirit in the Land.* Such adventures gave me insight into the heart and spirit of that man who once sat in a tent in Persia, writing in his diary one moonlit night by the unwavering light of a candle on the eve of the nomadic migration of the Bakhtiari. I felt a kinship with him, there on the eve of adventure, and understood that pure adrenaline joy when Merian Cooper wrote: "Lord! But this is good!"

—*Mark Cotta Vaz*

INDEX

Gone With the Wind (Mitchell), 273
G. P. Putnam's Sons, 80, 83, 133, 135, 189
Grace, Dick, 251
Graf Zeppelin, 183
Graham, J. C., 392
Grass (Cooper), 109, 129–30
Grass (film), 7, 106, 109–38, 161, 209–10,
    231, 264, 367–68, 378
  absence of love interests in, 185
  advertising for, 133
  assault on Zardeh Kuh in, 128–29, 137
  attempted remake of, 339–40
  comparisons between *Chang* and,
    137–38, 149, 153, 158
  comparisons between *King Kong* and,
    237–38
  Cooper's lecture on, 134
  criticisms of, 136–37
  discarded footage from, 132
  dust storm in, 115
  editing of, 132–33, 135–36
  finances of, 111, 123, 132–33, 135–37
  first showing of, 134
  Karun River crossing in, 123–25, 137
  legal disputes over, 358
  Persia and, 111–12, 114, 117–32,
    136–37, 339
  resurrection of interest in, 391, 393–95
  Salt Desert crossing in, 113, 115
  theatrical release of, 134–37
  transporting exposed film of, 131–32
Grauman's Chinese Theatre, 236–37,
    389–90, 401
Great Britain, 73–74, 84–85, 116–17, 131,
    324–25, 328–29, 398, 401
  The Four Feathers and, 163, 172
  Harrison's espionage work and, 66–68
  Revolutionary War and, 12
  Sudanese warrior tribes and, 167–68,
    171–72
  in World War I, 21, 23, 27, 35
  in World War II, 284, 293, 324, 404
Great Depression, 4, 201–3, 236, 246,
    260, 374, 404
Great Train Robbery, The, 18
Grosvenor, Gilbert M., 136, 373
Grove, William R., 51

H
Haggard, H. Rider, 259, 261, 353
Haidar Khan, 119–21, 123, 125–27, 129,
    137

Haile Selassie, Emperor of Ethiopia,
    88–95, 97–100, 281, 373, 394
  Cooper's meetings with, 93–95, 98–99,
    105
  Cooper's proposed film on, 105–6
  coronation of, 100
  feast of warriors hosted by, 98–99
  Lyg Yasu deposed by, 92–93
  palace of, 92–95, 97–98
  physical appearance of, 89, 94–95, 97,
    99
Hambleton, George, 181–82, 184–85
Hambleton, John, 259, 370
  Arabian Empty Quarter expedition
    and, 162–63, 180, 184
  commercial aviation ideas of, 104, 162,
    175, 180
  commercial aviation ventures of,
    179–82, 184–85
  death of, 184–85
  in World War I, 34, 180
Hambleton, Margaret Elliott, 184–85
Handy, Bruce, 351, 353
Harbin, Vernon, 204
Harris, Walter, 25
Harrison, Marguerite E., 6–7, 367–69
  Cooper described by, 109, 111
  Cooper's imprisonment and, 56,
    63–68, 72, 111, 367–68
  death of, 367–68
  espionage work of, 7, 64–68, 368
  finances of, 111, 123, 133, 135–37,
    367
  Grass and, 106, 109–23, 125–32,
    134–36, 138, 209, 264, 367–68
  imprisonment of, 66–68, 72
  journalism career of, 63–66, 367
  in Poland, 49, 64, 66
  released from prison, 72
  speeches of, 133
Harrison, Thomas B., 65
Harryhausen, Ray:
  Empire State Building visited by, 402,
    409–10, 412–13
  honors of, 400–401
  King Kong and, 210, 225, 237, 341,
    389–90, 400–402, 404, 406–7,
    412–13
  Mighty Joe Young and, 210, 341–42,
    406–7
  War Eagles and, 279–80
Haver, Ronald, 186, 267, 275, 360, 391

ABOUT THE AUTHOR

MARK COTTA VAZ has authored such *New York Times* bestsellers as *The Art of Star Wars: Attack of the Clones* and *Behind the Mask of Spider-Man*. *Living Dangerously* is his nineteenth published book. His works include the critically acclaimed *The Invisible Art: The Legends of Movie Matte Painting* (co-authored with filmmaker Craig Barron), which won the Theatre Library Association of New York award for outstanding book on film in 2002 and the United States Institute for Theatre Technology's "Golden Pen" book award. He has recently completed a first novel and is currently at work on a history of the segregated units of World War II.

ABOUT THE TYPE

The text of this book was set in Legacy, a typeface family designed by Ronald Arnholm and issued in digital form by ITC in 1992. Both its serifed and un-serifed versions are based on an original type created by the French punch-cutter Nicholas Jenson in the late fifteenth century. While Legacy tends to differ from Jenson's original in its proportions, it maintains much of the latter's characteristic modulations in stroke.